An Economic History
of West Africa

The Columbia Economic History
of the Modern World

The publication of the present book launches *The Columbia Economic History of the Modern World*. The principal object of this series, which will include more than a dozen volumes when complete, is to clarify the processes by which leading countries and areas have modernized their economies and social structures. Dr. Hopkins' book sets a high standard not only for the remaining volumes in the series, but also for scholars everywhere who bring to the study of history the outlook and methods of the social sciences.

Dr. Hopkins draws upon the work of economists, anthropologists and geographers as well as historians for the concepts which frame his analysis. His organizing principle is that of "the market," which he conceives in quantitative, spatial, and social structural terms. Arguing persuasively that the distinction between "traditional" and "modern" societies illuminates historical reality less well than does economic theory, he emphasizes the economic barriers to market growth, shows how strong linkages were established between the expansion of "legitimate" trade in the nineteenth century and the development of the domestic economy, and examines changes therein and in the export sector that marked the beginnings of industrialization. Rich in its insights into factors making for partition in one century and nationalism in the next, Dr. Hopkins' book is a significant contribution not only to the field of African studies but also to the economic history of the developing world.

COLUMBIA UNIVERSITY   STUART BRUCHEY

An Economic History of West Africa

A. G. Hopkins

Columbia University Press

New York   1973

Published in 1973 by Longman Group Ltd, London, and Columbia University Press, New York.

© 1973 Longman Group Ltd
Printed in Great Britain

Library of Congress Cataloging in Publication Data
Hopkins, Anthony G
  An economic history of West Africa.
    (Columbia economic history of the modern world)
    Includes bibliographies.
    1. Africa, West—Economic conditions. I. Title.
HC517.W5H66   330.9'66   72-11798
ISBN 0-231-03739-2

Contents

List of Maps

List of Figures

Acknowledgements

The publishers are grateful to the following for permission to base maps and graphs used in this book on those appearing in the publications mentioned:

Methuen & Co. Ltd. for maps 1, 2, 3, 4, 13, 15, 16 and 17, based on pages 209, 16, 101, 135, 473, 94, 578 and 672 of *West Africa* by W. B. Morgan and J. C. Pugh (1969); the Controller of Her Majesty's Stationery Office for map 7, based on page 151 of the *Journal of Local Administration Overseas*, Vol. I. No. 3, July 1962; Cambridge University Press for maps 6 and 10, based on pages 69 and 131 of *Colonialism in Africa, 1870–1960*, Vol. I *The History and Politics of Colonialism, 1870–1914*, ed. L. H. Gann and Peter Duignan (1969), and for map 7, based on page 15 of *A History of West Africa* by J. D. Fage (1969); Yale University Press for figure 4, based on pages 136–7 of *Government and Economic Development*, ed. Gustav Ranis (1971); Richard D. Irwin, Inc. for figures 1 and 3, based on material compiled by G. K. Helleiner in *Peasant Agriculture, Government, and Economic Growth in Nigeria* (Homewood, Illinois, 1966), pages 494–5 and 500; École Pratique des Hautes Études, VIe Section, *Études et mémoires*, 37, for figures 2 and 5, based on pages 24, 27 and 135 of *Les relations économiques extérieures des pays d'Afrique noire de l'union française, 1925–1955* by J. J. Poquin (1957); and Jurisprudence Générale Dalloz for figure 6, based on page 119 of *Essai sur la conjoncture de l'Afrique noire* by H. Durand (1957).

Preface

In writing this book I have developed a close affinity with one of the more popular figures of modern Scottish folklore, the man who, so the story goes, spends all his life painting the bridge spanning the Firth of Forth. His job is never finished because by the time he reaches one end the other (by then barely visible) needs painting again. My own task has also seemed an endless one: every time I put the finishing touches to Chapter 7 I had to double back and start, once more, to cover the cracks which were beginning to show in Chapter 2. Unlike my mythical Scots friend, however, I have now decided to down tools, not because perfection has been reached—far from it—but because there comes a time when the pursuit of unattainable goals threatens to undermine the sanity of the pursuer. My diary tells me that I began work on the manuscript about six years ago, though there have been periods when the job has seemed to me, and doubtless to my patient publishers too, to have occupied a lifetime. The Forth Bridge painter, being a self-sufficient man as well as a persistent one, always works alone. I, too, have wielded the brush, but my efforts have been supported by skilled helpers, who have mixed the paint, assisted me in reaching into awkward corners, and, occasionally, used a blowlamp on my work.

I am indebted to John Fage, the Director of the Centre of West African Studies, for encouraging the study of West African economic history at Birmingham, for sharing with me his unrivalled knowledge of West African history, and for creating in the Centre an atmosphere which has benefited the work of staff and students alike. Two colleagues in the Centre, Marion Johnson and Douglas Rimmer, answered a variety of questions during the writing stage, read substantial sections of the manuscript, and suggested improvements covering matters of style, fact and logic. The sudden, premature death of another colleague, R. E. Bradbury, occurred when the manuscript was still in an elementary state, but at a time when we had entered on a series of stimulating discussions about the relationship between social anthropology and economic history. This book would have gained considerably from Brad's comments. I have tried to keep his high standards in mind, even if I have not been able to match them.

I have also benefited greatly from my position as an attached member of the Department of Economic and Social History. The late W. H. B. Court's gentle nature and catholic view of the study of economic history were particularly congenial to me as a young and inexperienced apprentice to the craft. The present Head of the Department, John Harris, encouraged me when I was beginning to flag, and found time, despite severe pressure of work, to read a large part of the manuscript. I am grateful, too, to Cyril Ehrlich of The Queen's University, Belfast, and to Stuart Bruchey of Columbia University, New York, both of whom made valuable comments on sizeable sections of an earlier draft of the manuscript.

All these scholars have helped to improve an imperfect work. The failings which remain are entirely my own.

Specific debts to other writers, too numerous to record here, are acknowledged in the footnotes and in the bibliography. Any clarity of argument and presentation which this work now possesses owes a great deal to questions raised by undergraduate and graduate students who have taken my courses at Birmingham since 1964. Their reward, belated though it is, is that they have helped to ease the burden of learning for their successors.

In the academic year 1969–70 I had the good fortune to hold a Research Fellowship at the University of Leicester. It was during this break from teaching and administrative duties that I had time to appreciate the full extent of the inadequacies of the first draft of the manuscript, and to begin work on what was to become the final version. I am grateful to the University of Leicester for its generosity, and to Ralph Davis and the other members of the Department of Economic History for the warmth of their welcome. Happily, friendships made in that year have survived my departure from Leicester.

The substantial task of compiling the bibliography was made easier by the thorough assistance given by Robert Irving and Jocelyn Abbey. The equally substantial task of typing the manuscript was undertaken, very willingly and between other duties, by the secretarial staff of the Centre of West African Studies, by Helen Thompson of the School of Education, and, above all, by Cathy Macartney of the Department of Economic and Social History, who, unlike the author, remained calm and efficient even in the final, hectic stages.

My parents and my wife have been called on, over a period of years, to show forbearance in the face of neglect, to believe in the hopelessly optimistic forecasts which authors habitually make, and to remind me at times of depression that the Economic History of West Africa is not the totality of life's experiences. If this book has sufficient merit, it is offered, in part compensation, to them.

Centre of West African Studies,   A. G. Hopkins
University of Birmingham.

one

Approaches to Africa's economic past

Historians do not always offer an explicit justification of their work. Those who select established subjects, such as the industrial revolution or the French Revolution, seldom feel impelled to explain why they have decided to write about events which are generally agreed to have been of fundamental significance. Those who are also nationals of the countries they study share with their readers a number of basic assumptions, which often remain unstated. In both cases reticence is understandable, though it is arguable that established priorities and common values may make it hard to achieve an entirely fresh interpretation. Historians who decide to specialise in relatively unknown subjects find it more difficult to avoid accounting for their choice. They need to demonstrate that their topic has not remained obscure because it is unimportant, and, if they write about a country other than their own, they need to explain their approach to readers whose perspective on the past may be very different. The justification for publishing the present book is contained in two, related, propositions: it is designed first to fill a gap in African studies, and second to contribute, in a small way, to the economic history of the underdeveloped world.

As yet, there is no reasonably full account of the economic history of West Africa. Existing historical studies of the region, valuable though they are, have a mainly political bias. The reader will find little discussion here of large states and great leaders, or of foreign explorers, missionaries and pro-consuls. Yet economic history is not necessarily narrow history, nor is it history without people. On the contrary, in trying to reconstruct the history of agriculture and internal trade, the economic historian is brought into close contact with the lives of the great majority of Africans —women as well as men. The geographical dimension of the title may strike non-specialists as being rather narrow. However, West Africa, though only part of the African continent, is itself almost as large as the whole of Europe, excluding Russia, and its population is now approaching the substantial total of 100 million. Admittedly, imperial history spanned the globe, but it did so only by treating the inhabitants of other continents as extras in an essentially European epic: they paraded on ceremonial occasions; they smiled inscrutably in the mysterious East; and they conducted obscure 'native wars' in darkest Africa. The limitations of the imperial perspective became apparent once it was realised that Africans and Indians occupied a central place in the history of their own continents. It is now clear that West Africa has a long and varied history. To attempt to comprehend even the economic aspects of this history in one volume is to stretch generalisations as far as safety will permit.

Although this book seeks to fill a gap in African studies, it would be misleading to suggest that it is entirely original. Without the labour of the early pioneers of West African economic history the present work could not have been conceived, and without the detailed research which has been undertaken during the past ten or fifteen years it could not have been completed.

The first sizeable landmark was undoubtedly Allan McPhee's classic study, *The Economic Revolution in British West Africa*, which appeared in 1926.[1] In the preface to his book McPhee justified his efforts by drawing attention to the fact that the economic history of the empire in general, and of British West Africa in particular, had been almost entirely ignored, just as the economic history of England had been neglected before the work of Thorold Rogers and William Cunningham. McPhee's hope that his book would immediately point the way for other scholars was unfulfilled. It was not until 1942 that some of the topics he had dealt with were taken up again, this time by W. K. Hancock, whose celebrated *Survey of British Commonwealth Affairs* included a penetrating study of the traders' frontier in West Africa. Between them, these two works established a rather isolated, and often deserted, academic outpost. That they achieved even this was mainly because they treated West Africa as part of the wider theme of imperial history.[2] The French were possibly even less concerned with the economic history of their West African territories. Georges Hardy's *La mise en valeur du Sénégal de 1817 à 1854*, published in 1921, was another lone work cast in the mould of imperial history. Only two books published before the 1950s looked at West Africa's economic past from an indigenous point of view. These were E. W. Bovill's *Caravans of the Old Sahara*, first published in 1933,[3] and George W. Brown's neglected study, *The Economic History of Liberia*, which appeared in 1941. These books, too, were very much products of their time: Bovill's scholarly, yet popular, account emphasised the more colourful and adventurous side of African history; while Brown's careful research was partly inspired, like other works by negro intellectuals at that time, by the ideal of African independence which Liberia represented.

The last fifteen years have seen a marked increase in the number of scholarly publications on Africa, though relatively few of these have focused on economic history. As will be clear from the footnotes and bibliography, a great deal of the evidence and argument of this book rests on the work of economists, anthropologists and geographers. Beginning in 1956, with the appearance of K. O. Dike's *Trade and Politics in the Niger Delta, 1830–1885*, most of the work conventionally regarded as economic history concentrated on Afro-European trade relations, chiefly because

[1] A fuller appreciation of McPhee's work can be found in the 'Introduction' to the new edition of his book published in 1971.

[2] However, these books were also exceptionally skilled in their handling of the African side of the imperial story.

[3] A new, and extensively revised, version of this book is available as *The Golden Trade o the Moors*, 1968.

this was a theme which presented relatively few research problems. During the 1960s the emphasis began to shift towards the study of indigenous economic activities, as explored, for example, in Polly Hill's *The Migrant Cocoa-Farmers of Southern Ghana*, published in 1963, and in the collection of essays edited by Claude Meillassoux entitled *The Development of Indigenous Trade and Markets in West Africa* (1971). Research into production and exchange in the domestic economy will probably become the chief preoccupation of economic historians of Africa during the 1970s.

Reliance on the work of scholars other than historians is not simply a matter of necessity, but also of choice. History needs to be related closely to the social sciences for two reasons. In the first place, both historians and social scientists are involved in studying social stability and social change, though these themes are not, of course, their sole interest. Secondly, their approach to these subjects has much more in common than is often allowed. The assertion that historians are concerned with unique events, while social scientists search for general laws, is an article of faith rather than an accurate description of what both actually do. In practice, historians of Africa have already moved some way towards achieving an inter-disciplinary approach. Statistical analysis has been used to study the development of bureaucracy in the pre-colonial period;[4] econometric techniques have been employed to analyse structural change in the more recent past;[5] the concepts and tools of social anthropology have been applied to social structures and to political systems;[6] and explicit attention has been paid to philosophical problems in historical causation.[7] Historians who still regard the study of Africa's past as an unrewarding exercise,[8] should consider whether, by refusing to put their eyes to the telescope, they have failed, as Galileo's critics failed, to see that the world extends beyond Europe. They should also consider the possibility that they might learn from, as well as contribute to, the methodology and research techniques used by historians of Africa.

The second justification for this volume is as a contribution to the study of the underdeveloped world. This aspect of the book can be seen most clearly in the treatment of themes such as the characteristics of 'traditional' societies, the nature of pre-industrial exchange, the imperialism of industrial Europe, the economics of colonialism, and the rise of nationalism, most of which will be familiar to historians specialising in underdeveloped regions other than West Africa. It is worth pointing out in this connection that hardly any comprehensive economic histories of countries in the underdeveloped world have been written. Books dealing with all sectors of the economy tend to have a chronological limitation, being confined to the period since

---

[4] Ivor Wilks, 'Aspects of Bureaucratization in Ashanti in the Nineteenth Century', *Journal of African History*, 7, 1966, pp. 215–32.

[5] R. Szereszewski, *Structural Changes in the Economy of Ghana, 1891–1911*, 1965.

[6] See, for example, *History and Social Anthropology*, ed. I. M. Lewis, 1968.

[7] R. S. Smith, 'Event and Portent: the Fall of Old Oyo, a Problem in Historical Explanation', *Africa*, 41, 1971, pp. 186–99.

[8] For recent references to 'unhistoric' Africa see H. R. Trevor Roper, 'The Past and the Present: History and Sociology', *Past & Present*, 42, 1969, pp. 3–17.

the nineteenth century,[9] while those relating to earlier periods tend to concentrate on particular sectors of the economy.[10] Africa is especially interesting for comparative purposes because the continent occupies an important place in the mythology of underdevelopment. Pre-colonial Africa is popularly regarded as forming an economic Plimsoll Line drawn to mark subsistence activities. Above this line are placed the supposedly more advanced economies of other pre-industrial regions, with the loftiest quarters being reserved for European countries. West Africa provides a good test of the accuracy of this ranking, and of the beliefs about 'traditional' societies which underlie it, because this part of the continent can be studied in some depth from an early date, and without the complicating presence of white settlers.

Assuming that a case has been made out for undertaking a survey of West African economic history, the problem now arises as to how to organise the great variety of specialised research which forms the basis of this book. The issue is a complicated one because the research in question covers several disciplines, and is also uneven in its treatment of subjects which require approximately equal emphasis in a study of West Africa's economic past. Furthermore, no chronology appropriate to economic history has yet been advanced. In these circumstances, the temptation to let the facts 'speak for themselves' is very strong. Unfortunately, the facts have no innate capacity for ordering themselves. What we do not know and what we choose to omit may be as important, or more important, than what we include, and what we include is determined partly by our assumptions about what is important. The narrative approach adopted by many historians often smothers explanation in description, and disguises the assumptions which influence the selection of material. Economists would probably favour a solution which used the concepts and techniques of national accounting to measure changes in national and personal income and expenditure. This procedure also presents difficulties. The data needed for an investigation of this kind are not available before the twentieth century, and in any case there are conceptual problems relating to the definition of 'national' units in the pre-colonial period.[11]

An organising principle is required which is broad enough to cover the totality of economic activities over many centuries, yet specific enough to provide a coherent

[9] Only a few studies can be cited here: Celso Furtado, *Economic Development of Latin America: a Survey from Colonial Times to the Cuban Revolution*, Cambridge 1970; James C. Ingram, *Economic Change in Thailand, 1850–1970*, Stanford 1971; Frank C. D. King, *A Concise Economic History of Modern China*, 1970; and W. W. Lockwood, *The Economic Development of Japan*, Princeton 1954.

[10] Again, only a few examples can be noted: I. Habib, *Agrarian System of Mughal India*, Bombay 1963; D. H. Perkins, *Agricultural Development in China, 1368–1968*, Edinburgh 1971; and Thomas C. Smith, *The Agrarian Origins of Modern Japan*, Stanford 1959. *Studies in the Economic History of the Middle East from the Rise of Islam to the Present Day*, ed. M. A. Cook, 1970, covers a longer time span and a variety of themes.

[11] Colonialism did not resolve this problem merely by establishing clearly-marked boundaries. A major weakness of Szereszewski's book, *Structural Changes in the Economy of Ghana, 1891–1911*, 1965, is that the national unit in question (the Gold Coast) was not an economic entity at that time.

theme for the book as a whole. The organising principle which best meets these criteria is that of the market. This concept, as defined here, has three dimensions: first, the volume and value of goods and services transacted, which determine the extent of the market in quantitative terms; second, geographical variations in exchange activity, which fix the extent of the market in spatial terms; and third, the number and social status of the parties engaged in exchange, which influence the composition of the goods and services traded. The market is a theme that can be followed with the help of both qualitative and quantitative evidence. The former is predominant in the pre-colonial period, and the latter becomes important in the twentieth century.

Two further observations need to be made about the way the concept of the market will be used. In the first place, it is important to guard against the assumption that there is a natural tendency towards development, and that deviations from this trend require special explanation. Otherwise, the market can easily become part of an evolutionist saga, which begins with subsistence economies and ends with industrialisation. The search for the origins of the market is as fruitless as the quest once undertaken by political philosophers for the origins of the state. Trade in Africa, as elsewhere, is as old as man himself, and the concept of the market is appropriate to early as well as to more recent times. Moreover, exchange and subsistence activities were (and still are) integrated. An explanation of the one involves a consideration of the other, for the size of the market cannot be understood without reference to non-market activities. Change occurs, but not necessarily in the direction of industrialisation. It is important to identify the factors which enable the market to expand, but it is equally important to remember that growth can be slowed, that the market can contract, and that future trends are more a matter of speculation than of accurate prediction.

The second observation relates to the interpretation of exchange activities in pre-industrial societies. When historians discuss markets and trade, they tend to assume that prices are determined by supply and demand, and that the profitability of various transactions influences the volume and type of goods placed on the market and the factor combination required to produce them. However, it is possible that these rules may not apply universally. All societies have an economic system, in that they provide material goods to satisfy biological and social wants, but the code devised for operating this system may not centre on economising and maximising principles of the kind which are thought to predominate in modern, industrial societies. In pre-industrial societies transactional rules other than price may be more important in determining the terms on which goods are exchanged. The principles governing market activity in these societies may be those of reciprocity (obligatory gift-giving among friends and kinsmen) and redistribution (the reallocation of customary receipts by a socially-determined authority).

The contrast between these two sets of behavioural rules is a prominent theme in modern sociological thought, and has formed the basis of a substantial literature on rural–urban differences. Its origin can be traced to Tönnies's distinction between *Gemeinschaft* and *Gesellschaft*, that is between a community bound by kinship and an association held together by contract, and to Weber's distinction between sub-stantive (traditional) and formal (modern) rationality. The substantivist interpreta-tion has been applied to Africa by writers such as Polanyi and Dalton, who have contended that traditional exchange was conducted according to the principles of reciprocity and redistribution.[12] The formalist view has been advanced by a larger group of scholars, headed by Firth and Jones, who have argued in favour of the selective applicability of Western economic theory.[13]

To analyse market activities in Africa without considering the possibility that the rules governing economic behaviour might be very different from those prevailing in the industrial world, is to risk adopting an ethnocentric and anachronistic approach. However, the substantivist viewpoint, stimulating though it is, has less to recom-mend it than the modified formalism of Firth and Jones. There are two main reasons for this judgement, both of which will be elaborated in Chapter 2. First, the sub-stantivists are mistaken in arguing that the values and motivation of pre-industrial societies differ in kind rather than in degree from those of industrial societies. Indeed, even differences of degree may be much smaller than is often assumed. Second, the substantivist case fails to meet the empirical test: the economy of pre-colonial West Africa simply did not function in accordance with principles which are supposed to characterise 'traditional' societies. Indeed, the concept of a 'tradi-tional' society is an ideal-type which is of questionable value in understanding reality.

The argument of the book is derived from its theme, and relates to stability and change in the market. The analysis of the pre-colonial domestic economy presented in Chapter 2 is basic to the rest of the book. This chapter attacks the mythology which has grown up about the characteristics of 'traditional'societies, demonstrates that exchange was widespread, identifies the forces trying to expand the market, and reaches conclusions about internal constraints on growth. Chapter 3 investigates West Africa's external commercial relationships in the period before the industrial revolution in Europe, and makes use of a simple model of international trade to explain why Saharan and Atlantic commerce failed to overcome existing barriers to market growth. Chapter 4 shows how, for the first time, strong linkages were established between external trade and the domestic economy as a result of the expan-sion of 'legitimate' commerce in the nineteenth century. This development, it is

---

[12] *Trade and Market in the Early Empires*, ed. K. Polanyi, C. W. Arensberg, and H. W. Pearson, Glencoe 1957. The best guide to Polanyi's thought is S. C. Humphreys, 'History, Economics, and Anthropology: the Work of Karl Polanyi', *History and Theory*, 8, 1969, pp. 165–212. References to Dalton's earlier, formative work can be found in his recent article, 'Theoretical Issues in Economic Anthropology', *Current Anthropology*, 10, 1969, pp. 63–102. Dalton has also edited a collection of readings, *Tribal and Peasant Economies*, New York 1967, which presents the substantivist viewpoint.

[13] An excellent review of this controversy can be found in *Themes in Economic Anthropology*, ed. Raymond Firth, 1967, which represents a qualified, formalist approach. A similar view is expressed in *Economic Anthropology*, ed. Edward E. LeClair and Harold K. Schneider, New York 1968. The first, detailed statement of the formalist interpretation of African economic behaviour was W. O. Jones's important article, 'Economic Man in Africa', *Food Research Institute Studies*, 1, 1960, pp. 107–34.

suggested, marks the beginning of the modern economic history of West Africa, and is also central to an understanding of why the region was partitioned by European powers. Chapter 5 provides a brief, perspective view of the colonial period. The concepts of 'open' and 'closed' economies are employed to analyse the main structural features of colonialism, and quantitative data are used to chart the performance of the colonial economies between 1900 and 1960. Chapter 6 assesses the contributions of expatriates and Africans to the completion of the open economies of West Africa during the first half of the colonial era (1900–30). It is contended that the open economy was a formalised version of the economy which was already beginning to emerge in the nineteenth century before partition, and that export growth resulted primarily from mobilising factors within the domestic economy. Chapter 7 deals with the modifications which were made to the open economies in the second half of the colonial period (1930–60), and presents an interpretation of the rise of nationalism and of the beginnings of industrialisation based on an analysis of developments in the export sector and in the domestic economy.

This prospectus is offered in the hope that it will guide the reader through the details which now follow.

two

The domestic economy: structure and function

To begin at the beginning is logical. It is also particularly desirable in the present context, given the now widespread recognition of the importance of writing the indigenous history of Africa. It is precisely at this point, however, that the historian of Africa faces the greatest difficulty with regard to source material. In the first place, there is a shortage of evidence, especially in the case of the forest zone, where indigenous written records were virtually unknown before the nineteenth century. Secondly, the sources which do exist have rarely been used to study the history of the domestic economy in the pre-colonial period, that is before about 1900.[1] Possessing only a bare patchwork of data, it is hard to avoid presenting a composite picture of the 'traditional' economy. Lacking a coherent chronology, it is harder still to escape a static, timeless account of the local economy in the centuries before the coming of European rule.

These remarks, though necessary as a guide to the limitations of the present chapter, are not intended to strike an immediate note of anti-climax, still less to set the tone for the whole of the discussion which follows. On the contrary, there is some room for optimism, even within the bounds set by the current state of knowledge. There is a certain amount of evidence, though it may not measure up to the Domesday Survey;[2] there is a variety of secondary sources, some of which have suffered an extraordinary and totally unjustified neglect;[3] and there is a great deal

[1] Raymond Mauny's, *Tableau géographique de l'ouest africain au moyen âge*, Dakar 1961, is a valuable exception, but even this work says more about trade than about agriculture, though the latter was the basis of the economy in most parts of West Africa.

[2] Briefly, it can be said that for the period down to the eighth century the historian is reliant on archaeological, linguistic and botanical research. From the eighth century onwards the flow of information begins to increase, mainly as a result of records kept by Arab travellers, though this evidence is patchy and refers chiefly to the region known as the Western Sudan. After the fifteenth century, with the arrival of Europeans, the volume of material relating to the forest zone also starts to grow, but is confined, before the nineteenth century, largely to the coastal area.

[3] One book in particular must be accorded, quite undeservedly, the title of the least used secondary work in the field of West African economic history. This is Lars Sundström's *The Trade of Guinea*, Lund 1965, which is a mine of information about the internal trade of West Africa in the eighteenth and nineteenth centuries. This study has hardly been noticed even by specialists.

which historians can learn from the pioneering work carried out by scholars in other disciplines.[4]

It is possible, simply by making use of existing knowledge, to advance some way towards achieving two aims. First, there is sufficient evidence to reconstruct at least an outline of the pre-colonial economy, and to note a few of the more important chronological developments and regional variations. At the same time, it must be emphasised that this chapter is no more than a beginning. Those who are provoked, quite rightly, by its shortcomings, are invited to undertake the research needed to eliminate them.[5] Second, this outline, though incomplete, leads to a reappraisal of the myths, ancient and modern, which have grown up about the African past, and, indeed, about underdevelopment in general. Unfortunately, neither a lack of evidence nor a failure to consult work already published has inhibited the expression of views about the economic backwardness of Africa in the period before European rule. On the contrary, opinions have been stated with a degree of conviction which sometimes appears to be inversely related to the amount of historical knowledge acquired. It is hoped that the conclusions reached here will produce a more accurate appreciation of the constraints operating on the West African economy in the pre-colonial period. They should also have a wider relevance, for generalised versions of the myths associated with Africa can be found in books which purport to explain economic backwardness in many other parts of the underdeveloped world today.

An amalgamated version of the beliefs about the economic backwardness of Africa in the pre-colonial period would include the following major points. The domestic economy was a subsistence economy, which was uniform, unchanging and therefore uninteresting. Such an economy is worthy of only cursory attention because the obstacles impeding its development can readily be identified and are familiar enough—at least to experts. The dominant agricultural sector, so it is alleged, was virtually immobilised by a combination of primitive technology, communal land tenure and the extended family. The development of key entrepreneurial groups was inhibited by the prevalence of an anti-capitalist value system. This ideology was reinforced by African political systems, which were either conservative gerontocracies based on ascribed status, or were so egalitarian that it was impossible for prospective innovators to accumulate savings. Such exchange as did occur did not follow the rules of supply and demand, as understood in the Western world, but was conducted with the aim of maximising social rather than economic values. Consequently, there was no factor market: that is to say, there was no regular, institutionalised means of selling land, hiring labour, or raising money. The result was that potentially productive factors were kept idle.

Interpretations of pre-colonial underdevelopment are basically variations on two themes, which will be familiar, in somewhat different guises, to historians of other

---

[4] Valuable contributions have been made to the study of 'traditional' agriculture and markets by geographers, anthropologists and field economists, though, understandably, their work lacks the chronological dimension which is central to the writing of history.

[5] Some possible research topics will be suggested in subsequent sections of this chapter.

parts of the world. On the one hand there is the myth of Primitive Africa, which pictures the inhabitants of the continent as living, like Alfred Marshall's savages,

> under the dominion of custom and impulse; scarcely ever striking out new lines for themselves; never forecasting the distant future; fitful in spite of their servitude to custom; governed by the fancy of the moment; ready at all times for the most arduous exertions, but incapable of keeping themselves long to steady work.[6]

This state of affairs prevented what Western observers regarded as progress, both moral and material. According to this interpretation, Africa's release from barbarism waited until the close of the nineteenth century, when the Europeans came, like cavalry over the hill, to confer the benefits of Western civilisation on Kipling's

> New caught, sullen peoples,
> Half devil and half child.

On the other hand, there is the newer, more fashionable, myth of Merrie Africa, which has come to the fore during the past ten or fifteen years. On this view the pre-colonial era was a Golden Age, in which generations of Africans enjoyed congenial lives in well-integrated, smoothly-functioning societies. The means of livelihood came easily to hand, for foodstuffs grew wild and in abundance, and this good fortune enabled the inhabitants to concentrate on leisure pursuits, which, if some sources are to be believed, consisted of interminable dancing and drumming.[7] The Europeans, so it is alleged, disrupted a state of harmony: cohesion based on shared values was replaced by artificial unity backed by force, and ruthless exploitation reduced the indigenous peoples to a degree of poverty which they had not known in the past. The Merrie Africa myth is closely associated with what might be termed, in deference to West Africa's oldest political party, the True Whig interpretation of African history.[8] This interpretation sees the present states and rulers of West Africa as direct descendants of those of the pre-colonial era. It follows from this assumption that the traditional order has to be described with an approving eye if history is to fulfil its contemporary function of legitimising the present. African slave traders become proto-nationalists, and large empires are acclaimed because their example can be used to combat the centrifugal tendencies which have been a common, and sometimes tragic, feature of the post-colonial period.

[6] Alfred Marshall, *Principles of Economics*, 8th ed., 1938, pp. 723–4.

[7] Films and travel brochures provide an important and neglected source for those interested in the history of ideas, for both reflect, and in some cases reinforce, stereotypes. For example, Horizon Travel Ltd invited those thinking of taking a foreign holiday in 1972 to visit the Gambia, where 'the drum beat of black Africa captivates and enthrals you as you watch the happy-go-lucky natives dance at the drop of a hat, as twilight descends on Bathurst'. Similarly, films designed to encourage foreign tourists to England give the impression that the population is divided roughly equally between Yeomen of the Guard and morris dancers.

[8] Herbert Butterfield in *The Whig Interpretation of History*, 1931, was the first to identify the historical school which made use of past events in order to justify and reinforce the current political regime. The True Whig Party was founded about 1870, and has been in power in Liberia more or less continuously since then.

The foregoing survey of established approaches to Africa's economic past will be used in this chapter as a point of departure for what is hoped will be a more satisfactory appraisal of the nature of underdevelopment in the pre-colonial period, and one which takes account of the interests of the ninety-nine per cent of the population who were neither proto-nationalists nor rulers. Their history is certainly not that of primitive savages, as will soon become abundantly clear, but it cannot be fitted into the congenial schema provided by the Whig interpretation either. Some of the older arguments caricatured here have already been demolished by others, and there is no point in attacking them at great length. They will be noted simply to direct non-specialists to what is now generally regarded as a more accurate point of view. Other interpretations, especially those, mostly of recent origin, that are still a matter of debate among specialists, will be dealt with more fully and accorded the critical respect they deserve. The analysis presented in this chapter is divided into four parts covering the following topics: natural and human resources; production; the internal distributive system; and conclusions about the constraints operating on the local economy.

1 Natural and human resources

Historians commonly treat the natural environment as a 'background' to the events which are their prime concern. This approach, while quite acceptable for political biography or diplomatic studies, is less satisfactory in the case of economic history. Indeed, West Africa's economic past is the record of a continuous dialogue between geography and history—from the very beginnings of agriculture to the introduction of modern industry. The sketch of natural resources provided here is to be seen merely as a preface to a story of interaction that can be followed later on in this and subsequent chapters.[9] The brevity of the present outline is intended to lend support to its main purpose, which is to deny that the physical environment is immutable, or that it has determined the course of African history.

From Dakar to Lake Chad, a distance of over two thousand miles, there extends a belt of undulating grassland studded with trees. This area, known as the Western Sudan, forms a corridor about 600 miles wide. To the north lies the Sahara desert, which reaches out about one thousand miles towards North Africa. To the south, and almost touching the sea, stretches a belt of tropical forest, again running from west to east, but covering no more than 200 miles from north to south even at its widest, and punctuated in the middle (roughly between Accra and Porto Novo) by the savanna. Winter never comes to West Africa, so low temperatures are no obstacle to plant growth, and rainfall is the chief physical determinant of the character and extent of the vegetation. The amount of rainfall decreases from the south,

[9] Readers who require more geographical information are referred to the monumental work of scholarship by W. B. Morgan and J. C. Pugh, *West Africa*, 1969, which should also be consulted with reference to subsequent sections of the present chapter and to Chapters 6 and 7.

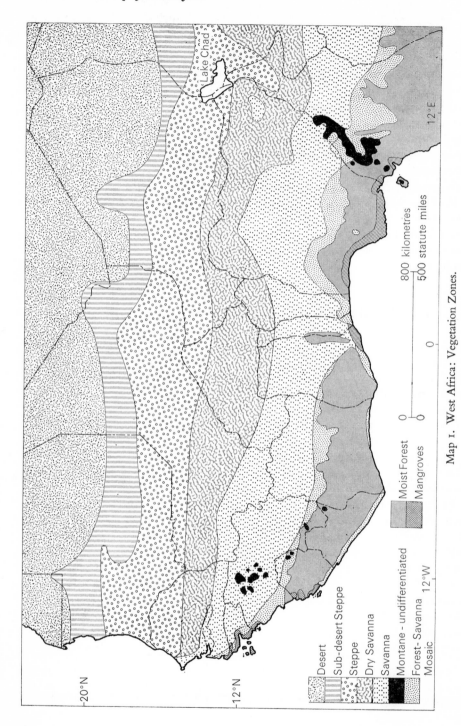

Map 1. West Africa: Vegetation Zones.

where it might exceed 100 inches a year, to the north, where it might be non-existent in some years. It is this variation which largely explains the great contrast between the humid forest and the dry, bare desert, and also the tendency for vegetation zones to run in parallel bands from west to east. This alignment is not seriously modified by changes in altitude, for only rarely does the land rise much above two thousand feet. The main vegetation zones have been present since about 3000 B.C., and are the product of a drying-out process which started ten or twelve thousand years ago. Before then, and beginning approximately seventy thousand years ago, there was an era of reduced temperatures and higher rainfall that encouraged Mediterranean vegetation and human settlement in parts of West Africa which are now desert.

It used to be thought that this environment was naturally well endowed and potentially very rich. Huntington, whose theories achieved considerable popularity in the 1920s and 1930s, incorporated this belief into his explanation of the economic backwardness of the tropics. According to him, 'low mentality, inertia, disease or the relative ease of life in a tropical climate may prevent people from having new ideas or putting them into execution.'[10] There were two main reasons why opinions of this kind came to be held about West Africa. In the first place, early European observers seem to have regarded the luxuriance of the tropical forest as an indication of the general fertility of the region. Secondly, the long association between the Western Sudan and the gold trade encouraged the view that the savanna was a rich and desirable area.[11] In the 1940s and 1950s, however, a different interpretation began to emerge, partly, it is interesting to note, as a result of the failure of a number of post-war colonial projects for improving tropical agriculture. Tropical soils, so it was said, were inherently infertile, raising agricultural productivity was a difficult task, and the development prospects of the tropics were, in consequence, rather bleak.[12] Today, geographers are agreed that the problem is much more complex than was suggested by earlier writers, and that a great deal remains to be learned about the properties of tropical soils.[13] However, there is sufficient evidence to show that the alleged natural richness of the tropical environment, and the associated idea that life on the equator is relatively easy, are both myths. It is now recognised that savanna soils tend to be low in organic and mineral content, and are easily eroded, while the rainfall of the area, besides being scanty, is also subject to marked seasonal variations. The forest zone has deeper soils, but these, too, are frequently low in nutrients, especially phosphorus. Beyond this point there is considerable uncertainty about the relationship between climate and soils in the tropics and the development potential of the area.

Comparing the natural resources and climates of different parts of the world in order to draw conclusions about whether they stimulated or retarded the economic

[10] Ellsworth Huntington, *Mainsprings of Civilisation*, New York, 1945, p. 4.

[11] The gold trade is dealt with in Chapter 3. The alleged wealth of the Western Sudan played a part in shaping European attitudes towards West Africa in the nineteenth century, as is noted in Chapter 4.

[12] Pierre Gourou, *The Tropical World*, 4th ed., 1966.

[13] B. W. Hodder, *Economic Development in the Tropics*, 1968, p. 11.

progress of particular societies is a tempting but unprofitable exercise—rather like trying to decide if life is more difficult for penguins in the Antarctic or camels in the Sahara. All that can safely be said is that the peoples of the underdeveloped countries have much more in common than divides them. Their activities, whether in temperate or tropical zones, centre on the production of the goods and services needed for survival at low levels of income. To achieve this end each society adapts to, and at the same time tries to mould, its environment. The natural endowment of a particular region may set broad limits, under a given technological, social and political regime, to the kinds of activities which are carried out at any one point in time, but there is still room within these limits for experiment and change. It is likely, to take a West African example, that the forest was once more extensive than it is today, and that part of the savanna was derived from it by the action of man.[14] A rise in population in the savanna, through natural increase or migration, encouraged the clearing of additional land by burning the forest. Once this occurred, fire-resistant grasses invaded the area, and a new type of agriculture evolved, associated, in some cases, with the keeping of livestock. Man's experiments, on occasion, have pushed back the boundaries which previously constrained his activities and achievements. Such was the case with the neolithic revolution based on the invention of agriculture and on the domestication of animals, and with the industrial revolution which began in England in the late eighteenth century.

The physical environment has not been an immutable determinant of man's activities either in West Africa or in other parts of the world. Natural resources and climate may help to identify the particular type of underdevelopment which exists in one region rather than another, but do not, by themselves, explain the phenomenon of underdevelopment itself. An enquiry into the causes of the poverty and wealth of nations should begin by rejecting the assumption that man and his environment can be treated as distinct entities having a fixed relationship, for man is an essential and dynamic element in geography no less than in history.[15]

Demography is, or, more accurately, should be, a central theme in African economic history, for the greater part of the continent's gross 'national' product was, and still is, derived from the application of human power to the land. It now seems likely that Africa, so long regarded as a borrower rather than a lender in world history, was the original home of man, and it has been established recently that peoples of negro stock were present in parts of West Africa about eleven thousand years ago.[16] Migrations and intermarriage (which still continue today) have helped

[14] Even this statement oversimplifies a complex problem, on which research is only just beginning. See the preliminary study by W. B. Morgan and R. P. Moss, 'Savanna and Forest in West Africa', *Africa*, 35, 1965, pp. 286–93.

[15] The approach adopted in the foregoing paragraphs owes a great deal to two complementary articles: June Helm, 'The Ecological Approach in Anthropology', *American Journal of Sociology*, 67, 1962, pp. 630–9, and W. B. Morgan and R. P. Moss, 'Geography and Ecology: the Concept of the Community and its Relationship to Environment', *Annals of the Association of American Geographers*, 55, 1965, pp. 339–50.

[16] J. D. Clark, *The Prehistory of Africa*, 1970, pp. 164–9.

to develop a wide variety of communities in the region.[17] In the discussion that follows, West Africa's human resources will be considered in two parts, the first dealing with the size, quality and distribution of the population, and the second with the ways in which the labour force was organised.

Serious efforts to assess the numbers of people in West Africa date only from the start of the twentieth century, when the total population was reckoned to be about thirty-six millions. Extrapolation from this figure, which is itself an informed estimate rather than a precise calculation, is risky, though it has been suggested on this basis that the population was roughly twenty-five millions in 1800. However, even if the total relating to the beginning of the colonial period is taken to apply to a much earlier date, it can still be said that the population of West Africa was small in relation to the size of the region and to the land suitable for cultivation. Terms such as 'overpopulation' and 'underpopulation' contain a number of difficulties, and imply the existence of an 'optimum' population, which is a rather elusive concept.[18] Nevertheless, the indications are that overpopulation was not, in general, one of West Africa's problems. On the contrary, it is likely that West Africa can stand as an example of underdevelopment in an underpopulated area.[19] Put at its simplest, the evidence suggests that in aggregate terms there was more land available than there was labour to cultivate it. Even today, when the population is well over twice as great as it was at the beginning of the twentieth century, land shortage has yet to become a major problem, except in certain localities.

The foregoing generalisations require amplification. To begin with, it is important to recognise that sparse population and underpopulation are not necessarily identical. The small number of people in a given area may well be accounted for by the inadequacy of its natural resources. The population of the Sahara is sparse, but the region cannot be said to be underpopulated. There is some evidence that in West Africa low population densities, especially in parts of the Western Sudan, were related to poor soils and to a lack of biological essentials, such as water and salt.[20] In areas where the land could have supported greater densities, an explanation of underpopulation is to be sought primarily in the influences affecting rates of fertility and mortality, though it is also likely that political constraints on the movement of peoples played a part in preventing the colonisation of particular localities. Little is known about the factors which governed fertility in African societies, though it does seem that child-rearing practices reduced the number of possible births in some

[17] For further details see the classification adopted by Morgan and Pugh, *West Africa*, pp. 17–32, which seems to be the most helpful one for economic historians.

[18] E. A. Wrigley, *Population and History*, 1969, p. 36.

[19] The implications of this observation are considered, from an economist's point of view, by Gerald K. Helleiner, 'Typology in Development Theory: the Land Surplus Economy (Nigeria)', *Food Research Institute Studies*, 6, 1966, pp. 181–94. For an exhaustive, geographical study of the phenomenon of underpopulation see G. Sautter, *De l'Atlantique au fleuve Congo: une géographie du sous-peuplement*, 2 vols, Paris 1968.

[20] For a general survey see Boleslaw Dumanowski, 'The Influence of Geographical Environments on the Distribution and Density of Population in Africa', *Africana Bulletin*, 9, 1968, pp. 9–33.

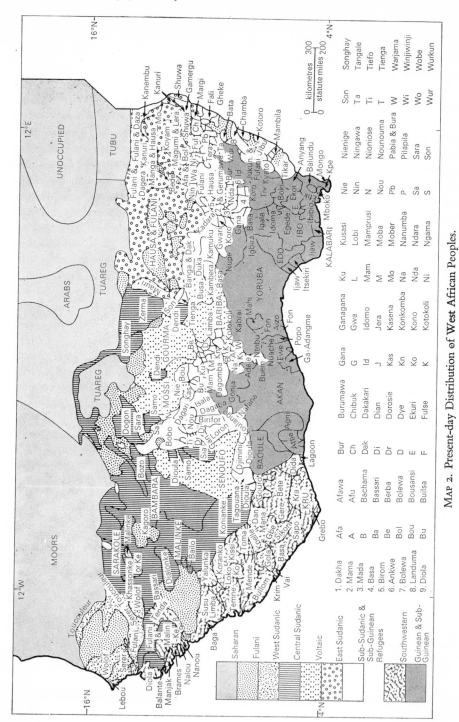

MAP 2. Present-day Distribution of West African Peoples.

communities, but there is evidence to indicate that mortality from diseases such as malaria, smallpox and trypanosomiasis (sleeping sickness) was high. It has been established that these diseases are of great antiquity in West Africa,[21] and that there were severe epidemics of smallpox, meningitis and plague. It has been suggested, for example, that epidemics and famine greatly reduced the population in the central part of the Western Sudan in the seventeenth and eighteenth centuries.[22]

Next, it is necessary to correct the impression, which is still widespread outside the ranks of demographers, that underpopulation is an exceptional condition requiring special explanation. This view derives from the assumption that there is a normal tendency for population to press against the limit of resources in accordance with the principle that 'nature abhors a vacuum'. This idea was first popularised by Malthus, and it has received support in recent years because the population in many underdeveloped countries is undoubtedly growing rapidly. However, the population 'explosion' is a comparatively modern event in world history. Pre-industrial populations were small: underpopulation was at least as common as overpopulation down to the nineteenth century, and was certainly not peculiar to West Africa or even to Africa as a whole. India and Latin America were underpopulated until at least the beginning of the twentieth century, and so, too, were countries of white settlement, such as North America and Australia. The notion that underpopulation is in some ways preferable to overpopulation is equally common, but is also without foundation. Underpopulation may be the result of especially high rates of mortality, and it presents serious obstacles to the development of a market economy, as will become clear later in this chapter.

There is no reason to suppose that the quality of the labour force differed materially from that of other pre-industrial societies.[23] The average expectation of life at birth was probably around thirty-five years, much as it was in medieval Europe, and as it remains in parts of West Africa today. The number of hours worked in farming and associated activities was low, perhaps averaging about half the day throughout the year, and sometimes rather less.[24] However, it would be wrong to conclude either that there was massive underemployment in traditional African societies, or that Africans suffered from a special disability, chronic lethargy. In the first place, the average number of hours spent in farming was substantially less than the average spent in productive employment as a whole, because farmers also engaged in other activities, such as craft production and trading, on a part-time or seasonal basis. Secondly, it has been shown that the energy costs of common agricultural tasks in

[21] It has been argued that the tsetse fly, which transmits trypanosomiasis, is as old as man himself. See Frank L. Lambrecht, 'Aspects of the Evolution and Ecology of Tsetse Flies and Trypanosomiasis in Prehistoric African Environment', *Journal of African History*, 5, 1964, pp. 1–24.

[22] Sèkéné-Mody Cissoko, 'Famines et épidémies à Tombouctou et dans la boucle du Niger du XVIe au XVIIIe siècles', *Bulletin de l'IFAN*, B, 30, 1968, pp. 806–21.

[23] See, for example, D. C. Coleman, 'Labour in the English Economy of the Seventeenth Century', *Economic History Review*, 8, 1956, pp. 280–95.

[24] Rowena M. Lawson, 'The Traditional Utilisation of Labour in Agriculture in the Lower Volta, Ghana', *Economic Bulletin of Ghana*, 12, 1968, pp. 54–61.

West Africa are severe, and that about half the day is needed for recuperation, especially in communities where malnutrition and disease are common.[25] Hunter's remarkable study of Nangodi demonstrates that the majority of the population suffers a serious loss in body-weight in the critical period before the harvest, when food is short, yet when energy is needed to gather the crops.[26] Where there *was* underemployment in West Africa, in the sense that the labour force, though healthy, was working below capacity in all occupations, it was due to lack of opportunities rather than to a culture-bound leisure preference, for preference implies choice, and choice was often absent. The 'lazy' African is in reality usually either debilitated or without a market for his labour—or both.

The distribution of human resources provides an important clue to the ways in which natural resources were utilised. West Africa's small population was spread unevenly throughout the region. This inequality was partly a reflection of the natural endowment of the various microenvironments: fertile and healthy areas were obviously more attractive than those which contained poor soils and fatal diseases.[27] More impressive, and in sharp contrast to the old, determinist viewpoint, is the degree to which the distribution of settlements was the result of the agricultural, commercial and political activities of man.

Man's inventiveness in discovering and adopting different types of crops had a profound effect on the carrying capacity of the land. Root crops, for example, produce about ten times as much weight of food per unit of land as cereals, and are capable of supporting greater population densities. The fact that roots are grown mainly in the forest has helped to compensate for some of the less attractive features of that region. The expansion of trade was responsible for concentrations of population in some unlikely places, such as the Sahara, where complex settlements with as many as 10,000 inhabitants developed in the pre-colonial era.[28] Inter-state conflicts also had a major influence on the distribution of population. Fugitives from aggression were sometimes compelled to seek sites which could be defended easily, though in other respects they were inhospitable. Islands of settlement were found in remote

[25] P. G. Phillips, 'The Metabolic Cost of Common West African Agricultural Activities', *Journal of Tropical Medicine and Hygiene*, 57, 1954, pp. 12–20.

[26] J. M. Hunter, 'Seasonal Hunger in a Part of the West African Savanna: a Survey of Bodyweights in Nangodi, N.E. Ghana', *Institute of British Geographers Transactions*, 41, 1967, pp. 167–86. On the need for caution in discussing the so-called 'hungry gap' see the earlier article by Marvin P. Miracle, 'Seasonal Hunger: a Vague Concept and an Unexplored Problem', *Bulletin de l'IFAN*, 23, 1961, pp. 273–83. The 'hungry gap' is less serious in root-growing forest areas, where seasonal variations in the availability of foodstuffs are not so marked.

[27] A tragic variation on this principle has been studied by Hunter, who has shown how hunger drives migrants into fertile and inviting riverine areas, where they contract river blindness and are forced to leave after a few years—with their numbers greatly reduced. See J. M. Hunter, 'River Blindness in Nangodi, Northern Ghana', *Geographical Review*, 56, 1966, pp. 398–416.

[28] In contrast to the popular view of the desert oasis as consisting of a few palm trees surrounding a small pond of clear water. For a detailed study of one large Saharan settlement see J. Laufray, 'Chronique de Ghadames', *Ibla*, 32, 1945, pp. 367–85; 33, 1946, pp. 343–71.

highland fortresses, such as the Jos plateau in central Nigeria, and on smaller insel-bergs, where a limited amount of surrounding lowland was used for cultivation, as in the south-east part of what is now the Gold Coast.[29] Occasionally, an expanding power concentrated settlement as a matter of policy. This was the case with the Fulani, who conquered the Fouta Djallon highlands in the seventeenth and eighteenth centuries, and settled slaves there to cultivate the land.[30]

Concentration was frequently associated with a striking degree of urbanisation, both in the savanna and in the forest. It has been estimated that three of the largest towns in the Western Sudan, namely Gao, Timbuctu and Djenne, had populations which ranged from 15,000 to 80,000 in the fifteenth and sixteenth centuries.[31] About half the population of Hausaland (in what is now northern Nigeria) lived in towns in the period before 1900, the most prominent example being Kano, whose popula-tion in the middle of the nineteenth century was reckoned by the famous traveller, Barth, to be about 30,000, a figure that doubled at the height of the trading season. The Yoruba, further south and partly in the forest zone, were also highly urbanised. In the nineteenth century Yorubaland contained about a dozen towns with popula-tions of over 20,000, the largest being Ibadan, which had about 70,000 inhabitants and an outer wall measuring twenty-four miles in circumference.[32] Further east, the forest city of Benin was reckoned to have a population of 15,000 at the end of the eighteenth century, and was thought to have been much larger two or three centur-ies earlier. At the beginning of the seventeenth century a Dutch visitor to Benin recorded the following impressions:

> The towne seemeth to be very great, when you enter into it, you goe into a broad street, not paved, which seemeth to be seven or eight times broader than the Warmoes street in Amsterdam, which goeth right out, and never crooketh, and where I was lodged . . . it was at least a quarter of an houres going from the gate, and yet I could not see to the end of the street. . . .[33]

It is impossible here to enter into a general discussion of the origin and structure of pre-industrial towns.[34] However, it is important to point out that the view that urbanisation becomes quantitatively significant only after industrialisation needs to be stated carefully if the contrast between 'traditional' and 'modern' societies is not

[29] These settlements have been studied by M. B. Gleave, whose work is listed in the biblio-graphy for Chapter 6.

[30] J. Richard-Molard, 'Les densités de population au Fouta-Djallon', *Présence Africaine*, 15, 1952, pp. 95–106.

[31] For further information see Raymond Mauny, *Tableau géographique de l'ouest africain au moyen âge*, Dakar 1961, pp. 495–503, though the figures quoted here reflect the results of more recent research.

[32] William R. Bascom, 'Urbanism as a Traditional African Pattern', *Sociological Review*, 7, 1959, pp. 29–43.

[33] Quoted in Thomas Hodgkin, *Nigerian Perspectives*, 1960, pp. 119–20. The visitor was the anonymous 'D.R.', possibly Dierick Reuters.

[34] For further consideration of this question see Gideon Sjoberg, *The Preindustrial City*, Glencoe 1960.

to be overemphasised. Towns and large villages were a common feature of the West African landscape in the pre-colonial era. Admittedly, their occupational structure differed from that of modern cities in that they were primarily places where agriculturalists gathered for non-agricultural purposes, above all for defence and trade. Many African urban dwellers commuted daily to their farms outside the town walls, whereas in the Western world suburban man travels into the city centre to work in industry and commerce. This evidence shows what is not in dispute, namely that West African towns were not industrial towns in the modern sense, but it cannot be used to argue that they were essentially different from the towns which existed, for instance, in late medieval Europe. African towns not only sheltered farmers, they housed specialised personnel, such as craftsmen, transport contractors, hoteliers and merchants; they were focal points for the exchange of goods of all kinds; and they were important administrative and religious centres. Indeed, some towns on the Sahara-savanna border concentrated on trade to such an extent that they were almost entirely dependent on external supplies for their basic food requirements. Like their counterparts in the medieval world, West African towns were wealthy enough to support a small, leisured group, and they encouraged, indirectly, the development of a 'high' culture, as witness the now famous 'bronzes' of Ife and Benin, and the centre of Muslim scholarship in the legendary city of Timbuctu.[35]

There is one final aspect of the distribution of population which needs to be stressed, namely its mobility. The movement of the labour force, whether in long waves of several generations, or whether seasonal (or even daily), far from being a novelty introduced by colonialism, was an established feature of the traditional economy. Even the now justly-celebrated migration of the farmers who founded the Gold Coast cocoa industry at the turn of the present century should be seen, in the context of West African history as a whole, as a relatively small movement in terms of numbers and distance. Legends of the origins of West African peoples, which have been traced, in some cases, as far back as the eighth century, all emphasise the importance of mobility as a means of escaping alien control or of acquiring new wealth in the form of land, gold or salt.[36] Besides those who were forced, for political reasons, to live in cramped conditions, there were others who gained from the security which resulted from the expansion of state power, whether in the savanna kingdoms, such as Mali and Songhai, or in the forest states, such as Benin and Ashanti. During the dry season, when labour demands on the farm were light and travelling conditions were at their best, the roads came alive with traders and porters, and the towns bulged with noisy and acquisitive visitors. As will become apparent later on, migration made economic sense, for it reflected the prevailing land–labour ratio and the differential spatial distribution of market opportunities.

The organisation of the labour force is central to an understanding of the utilisation of natural resources. The work force of pre-industrial societies is usually regarded as

[35] Ife and Benin brass work is thought to date from the thirteenth century. Timbuctu, founded in the twelfth century, had become a noted seat of learning by the fourteenth century.

[36] See the studies by Dorjahn and Tholley, Guèye, Holas, Kup, Niane, Pageard, Perie and Sellier, and Riad listed in the bibliography.

being based on unspecialised and inefficient family labour, whereas industrial countries are said to organise their workers on the basis of contract instead of kinship, to allocate tasks according to skills rather than social obligations, and to be highly efficient. It will be contended here that the labour force in pre-colonial Africa was more varied, more flexible and more efficient than is customarily supposed, and that, in this respect at least, the contrast between 'primitive' and 'modern' societies has been exaggerated.

The most important economic unit in virtually all West African societies was, and still is, the household. The household was not always identical with the family, and was quite capable of adapting its size and skills to meet changing circumstances and to create new opportunities. Each household approximated to the optimum size for the conditions in which it operated. A large household could divide itself into several smaller units, though without necessarily breaking up the family too. Netting's research has demonstrated that small households predominated among the Kofyar of central Nigeria because they were best suited to the system of intensive agriculture which prevailed in the area.[37] The household was also capable of expanding. Reyburn's study of Cameroon, for example, has suggested that the demand for extra labour was a principal cause of the existence and growth of polygynous families.[38] Households of all sizes were usually in a position to mobilise additional labour at times of peak demand. Communal labour was used by the Yoruba (in Nigeria) to prepare and weed farms, and by the Adioukrou (in the Ivory Coast) to exploit groves of palm trees. Many African societies distinguished between the labour of men and women, though the line was not always drawn at the same point. In Bamenda (Cameroon) women were especially important in farming, whereas in Yorubaland they spent much more of their time trading. However, there was a considerable degree of occupational specialisation, both seasonal and permanent, which cut across divisions of sex. In any case, it is by no means clear that the division of labour between men and women represented a serious misallocation of human resources. Although the spread of Islam from the eighth century onwards encouraged a more restrictive attitude towards the activities of females, African women adjusted to this situation with characteristic ingenuity by devising a marketing system which was based on the compound rather than on the village square.[39]

There is no evidence to show that the household labour force was inefficient, and it is hard to envisage organisational changes which would have cut production costs or greatly improved the range, quality or volume of output. It is noteworthy that the household, far from dissolving under the impact of Western capitalism in the twentieth century, or for that matter surviving to obstruct economic progress,

[37] Robert McC. Netting, *Hill Farmers of Nigeria*, Seattle 1968. A similar thesis is developed by Irene B. Taeuber, 'The Family of Chinese Farmers', in *Family and Kinship in Chinese Society*, ed. Maurice Freedman, Stanford 1970, pp. 63–85.

[38] William D. Reyburn, 'Polygamy, Economy and Christianity in the Eastern Cameroun', *Practical Anthropology*, 6, 1959, pp. 1–19.

[39] Polly Hill, 'Hidden Trade in Hausaland', *Man*, 4, 1969, pp. 392–409, has studied this system as it operates today.

became a dynamic agency for the development of new export crops and for the expansion of internal trade. Households could change their size and suffer serious losses, but they rarely went out of business. It is suggested, speculatively, that the tenacity of the household as a unit of production can be explained partly by viewing its labour force as a fixed overhead rather than as a variable cost.[40] In practice overheads were kept low because all members of the household began working at a very early age and remained in employment until they became infirm or died, while those who were unemployed could be maintained relatively cheaply. The household was highly competitive because family labour was costless (in the formal sense of not receiving a wage) and could be used to the point where its marginal product was zero.[41] Traditional roles proved to be flexible. In the twentieth century, for example, men became more involved in farming than they had in the past. Furthermore, the much-maligned extended family, far from being a 'drag on development', often provided the funds which enabled enterprising individuals and groups to launch new undertakings, and it offered them a refuge if their ventures failed. The large household and the extended family undoubtedly placed obligations on successful entrepreneurs, but they usually had the skill to balance private interest against the claims of their kinsmen.[42]

Allegations about the inefficiency of the traditional labour force are the product not only of an inadequate appreciation of the historical evidence relating to Africa, but also of an exaggerated sense of the superiority and modernity of labour organisation in Europe. Yet it is not hard to show that Western reality diverged from the Western ideal, though it is the latter rather than the former which has been used to judge the performance of the underdeveloped countries. The household firm, for instance, remained an important unit of production in England long after the industrial revolution. In the late nineteenth century the vast majority of manufacturing firms continued to be family businesses, though they also used contracted labour.[43] Today, the family firm is prominent in retailing and farming, and often employs little or no additional help. The extended family also proved to be a dynamic force in Europe, as the examples of the Rothschilds (in banking) and the Cadburys and Pilkingtons (in industry) make clear.[44] Restrictive practices based on 'tradition' are

[40] As was the case with the Russian peasant farm in the late nineteenth century. See James R. Millar, 'A Reformulation of A. V. Chayanov's Theory of the Peasant Farm Economy', *Economic Development and Cultural Change*, 18, 1970, pp. 219–29.

[41] The Europeans who tried to establish plantations in West Africa in the early years of the twentieth century found themselves at a disadvantage because they had to employ paid labour, and they could operate profitably only while the marginal product of labour was greater than the wage which had to be paid.

[42] E. Wayne Nafziger, 'The Effect of the Nigerian Extended Family on Entrepreneurial Development', *Economic Development and Cultural Change*, 18, 1969, pp. 25–33.

[43] P. L. Payne, 'The Emergence of the Large-scale Company in Great Britain, 1870–1914', *Economic History Review*, 20, 1967, p. 520.

[44] Even in America, the heartland of advanced capitalism, the extended family is still an important, if neglected, institution. See R. Hill, *Family Development in Three Generations*, New York 1970.

still enforced in the 1970s by trade unions and professional organisations. Female labour may well be underused to a greater extent in England than in West Africa. It is the practice among certain social classes, Christians and agnostics alike, to 'confine' their women to the home mainly for cultural reasons, it being considered an adverse reflection on the husband if his wife has to go out to work. Those women who do try to make use of their abilities still experience discrimination. In 1971, about two hundred years after the beginning of the industrial revolution, the London Stock Exchange voted for the third time in four years not to admit women to membership.[45]

Not all labour was organised on the basis of multifunctional domestic units. Additional labour was provided mainly by slaves, though a small number of hired hands was used as well. Travellers to African states in the pre-colonial period estimated the numbers of slaves at between a quarter and one half of the total population, but little credence can be given to guesswork of this kind. Many of these figures relate to the eighteenth and nineteenth centuries, when the number of domestic slaves had been swollen by the development of the notorious Atlantic trade. The problem of numbers is complicated by the difficulty of defining terms. Many of the 'slaves' recorded by foreign visitors may well have been, like the 'slaves' of the Tsars of Russia, loyal, if subordinate, citizens of the state, while others, though formally of slave status, were in practice integrated into the household and were virtually indistinguishable from free men. At the same time, it is important to recognise that slave labour was present in West Africa long before the rise of the Atlantic trade,[46] and that some slaves were bought, sold and otherwise used like the chattel slaves of the Americas. A substantial minority of the population in certain areas occupied a position of legal subordination and practical dependence which was less advantageous than that enjoyed by free men. Not all slavery was a misnomer.

If it is accepted that slavery in West Africa was not simply a European invention, then it becomes necessary to explain the existence, longevity and variety of the institution, and to consider whether the presence of slave labour qualifies or supports the argument advanced so far regarding the efficiency of labour organisation in the pre-colonial period.[47]

The main concentrations of slaves were in areas where the development of domestic exchange activities created employment opportunities which could not be met by local, free labour. In West Africa, as in many other parts of the pre-industrial world, such as Greece and Rome, it was large states, such as Mali and Songhai in the savanna and Ashanti and Dahomey in the forest, which had the greatest need for slaves and also the means to buy or capture them. Slaves were usually fairly specialised workers, though they were found in a variety of occupations. A few privileged

---

[45] *The Times*, 26 June 1971, p. 1.

[46] Allan G. B. Fisher and Humphrey J. Fisher, *Slavery and Muslim Society in Africa*, 1970.

[47] Further research is needed before adequate answers can be given to these questions. The most detailed study yet made of domestic slavery in West Africa is E. Adeniyi Oroge, *The Institution of Slavery in Yorubaland with Particular Reference to the Nineteenth Century*, University of Birmingham Ph.D. thesis, 1971.

slaves held senior civil and military positions. These powerful 'trusties' often possessed numerous slaves of their own. Others were found in skilled jobs, such as craft manufacture. The majority, however, performed work which was usually menial, sometimes gruelling and occasionally dangerous.[48] Slaves were employed as domestic servants, they acted as carriers, they maintained oases and cut rock salt from the desert, they laboured to build towns, construct roads and clear paths, they were drafted as front line troops, and they were common in all types of agricultural work. Farm slaves were not used, as in many other parts of the world, to produce an export surplus, but rather, as in Songhai in the fifteenth century, to provide food-stuffs for leading state officials, for their immediate circle of dependants, and for the army. Agricultural slaves were essential to societies which were not themselves specialist food producers. The fertile valley of Tamourt in Mauritania, for example, has been the granary of Saharan nomads since the fourteenth century, when they first enslaved the negro cultivators of the region.[49]

The question now arises as to why the shortage of labour in certain parts of West Africa was remedied by enslavement and by an enforced redistribution of the region's human resources. Countries which have faced a labour shortage during the industrial era have often been able to employ machinery instead. Indeed, high labour costs have sometimes provided an incentive for the introduction of advanced technology.[50] However, West African entrepreneurs, living in a pre-industrial, pre-Newtonian world, were unable to adapt in this way. An alternative solution, and one which was open to them, was to attract labour by paying wages. Many goods and some services were bought and sold for money, so it is incorrect to assume, as is sometimes done, that Africans failed to devise an acceptable means of payment. It is suggested here that the use of slave rather than wage labour was a matter of deliberate choice on the part of African employers.[51] As noted earlier, the scarce factor of production in West Africa was labour rather than land. In these circumstances there was a natural tendency towards dispersed settlement and extensive agriculture, since

[48] There was no sharp division of labour between male and female slaves, but it is probably true to say that women were used principally in domestic work, craft production and agriculture. However, not all women occupied subordinate positions. Some, such as the famous Madam Tinubu of Abeokuta, struck a blow for women's equality by buying large numbers of male slaves.

[49] Charles Toupet, 'La vallée de la Tamourt en Naaj: problèmes d'aménagement', *Bulletin de l'IFAN*, B, 20, 1958, pp. 68–110.

[50] As has been suggested was the case in North America in the nineteenth century. See H. J. Habakkuk, *American and British Technology in the Nineteenth Century*, Cambridge 1962.

[51] This explanation is essentially that advanced by H. J. Nieboer, *Slavery as an Industrial System: Ethnological Researches*, The Hague 1900. There are signs now of a revival of interest in this classic. See Evsey D. Domar, 'The Causes of Slavery or Serfdom: a Hypothesis', *Journal of Economic History*, 30, 1970, pp. 18–32. A word of caution should be added here: Nieboer's theory is neither a necessary nor a sufficient condition for the existence of slavery, though it so happens to fit the African case. Slavery and serfdom can exist without there being a labour shortage. Conversely, a labour shortage does not always lead to enslavement; the decline of population in fourteenth-century England enabled labourers to increase their bargaining power, and so hastened the end of serfdom.

the optimum factor combination was that which economised on labour and made as much use of land as possible. As long as the labour force remained mobile and could engage freely in a variety of occupations, hired labour would be expensive. Production costs in common activities, such as farming and craft production, would be higher for wage labour than for independent households. Where the two did not compete directly, as in the case of salt mining and military employment, the wage paid to contracted labour would have had to be considerable to compensate for the loss of alternative earnings, and for the arduous and risky nature of the work. Slaves were preferred because the costs of acquiring and maintaining them were less than the cost of hiring labour.

Against this view it might be objected, as Montesquieu and Adam Smith objected, that the additional cost of free labour was more than justified by its greater efficiency. However, it is now recognised that many of the stock allegations regarding the inefficiency of slave labour are either misconceived or greatly exaggerated, and it seems highly unlikely that African employers would have failed, during the course of many centuries, to act in their own interests. Employers elsewhere were satisfied with the performance of their slaves. In the case of the Roman Empire, slavery collapsed not because it was inefficient, but because of the decline (for other reasons) of the staple products for which slave labour was best suited.[52] Similarly, it is generally agreed (though the exchange of equations continues) that plantation slavery in the American south was efficient and profitable during the nineteenth century.[53] From the point of view of economic development the chief disadvantage of slavery is not that it is inefficient, but that it limits the expansion of the market by holding down purchasing power and by concentrating effective demand in the hands of a few luxury consumers. This consideration was irrelevant to the aims of West African rulers. Politics in a pre-industrial society is largely the art of redistributing a relatively fixed national income with a degree of inequality which is sufficient to make life luxurious for the rulers without at the same time provoking discontent on such a scale as to endanger the existence of the state. It is not enough to be born 'more equal than others'; the problem is to stay that way. Those who achieve success need to be skilled in retaining the loyalty of their subjects, but the means at their disposal do not include the offer of cumulative economic growth based on a mass market.

With regard to the longevity of the institution of slavery, it is sufficient at this stage simply to note that the conditions underlying the existence of slave labour in West Africa survived down to the twentieth century.[54] Indeed, the colonial rulers discovered, as African employers had discovered long before them, that the supply price of unskilled labour was higher than they could afford, or at least were prepared

---

[52] Cedric A. Yeo, 'The Economics of Roman and American Slavery', *Finanzarchiv*, 13, 1951–2, pp. 445–85.

[53] Alfred H. Conrad and John R. Meyer, *Studies in Econometric History*, 1965, chs 3 and 4. Also Stanley L. Engerman, 'The Effects of Slavery upon the Southern Economy: A Review of the Recent Debate', *Explorations in Entrepreneurial History*, 4, 1967, pp. 71–97.

[54] The decline of slavery and the rise of a wage labour force are dealt with in Chapter 6, part 2.

to pay. Administrators in both British and French West Africa faced a labour short-age during the early part of the colonial period, and they resorted to the use of forced labour, even though they were committed to the abolition of slavery. The colonial mind resolved this paradox by declaring slavery to be uncivilised, and forced labour to be a necessary way of instructing primitive people about the advantages of modernity.

The diverse nature of slavery reflected prevailing conditions of supply and demand in West Africa. Since labour was relatively scarce, the cost of replacing slaves was high, and owners had a strong motive for maintaining at least a proportion of their slaves in reasonable condition and encouraging them to breed. Where supplies were abundant, as was to be the case in the Caribbean, employers had little incentive to invest in the long-term welfare of their slaves. The result was that slaves were 'run' at full capacity and treated as chattels. The demand for labour in West Africa was also much more varied than in the Caribbean, and the differential treat-ment which slaves received was related to some extent to the roles assigned to them. Moreover, slaves in West Africa, besides being inputs in the productive system, per-formed an important political function. Africans measured wealth and power in men rather than in acres; those who exercised authority were man-owners rather than landowners. In some circumstances obedience could be coerced, but in others it was judged advisable to secure support by offering slaves a modest stake in the existing political system.

Societies which made extensive use of slave labour exhibited two concurrent tendencies. On the one hand, the influx of new slaves and the presence of slaves whose ethnic origins limited their chances of integration, created a dispossessed and poten-tially disaffected group. Discontented slaves occasionally rose against their masters: one of the earliest known slave revolts in West Africa occurred in 1591, when the ruler of Songhai's slaves asserted themselves after their owner and his troops had been defeated by the Moroccan army. On the other hand, there was a trend towards assimilating slaves into society by offering them certain rights in return for loyalty. The Hausa (in northern Nigeria) distinguished between the *bayi*, who had been captured or bought, and who had few rights, and the *cucenawa*, who, as second generation slaves, occupied a position that was closer to serfdom than to chattel slavery. In attempting to strike a balance between total exploitation and an entirely free community of farmers, employers were expressing their appreciation of the need to develop a subtle form of dependent labour, one which was more profitable than hired labour, yet which was also capable of fulfilling extra-economic functions.

The foregoing assessment of slavery points to amendments to three common assumptions concerning the nature of pre-industrial societies. In the first place, and contrary to the belief of the substantivist school of anthropologists, there *was* a long-established labour market in Africa. The fact that this market took the form of slave labour rather than wage labour was the result of a deliberate choice based on an elementary, but broadly accurate, cost–benefit analysis, that is to say on principles which the substantivists regard as peripheral or non-existent in 'traditional' societies.

To interpret slave-raiding as an expression of what Balandier has called 'economo-drama', that is an economic game played for social ends, is to misunderstand, or at least to oversimplify, the motives underlying the need for an unpaid, dependent labour force. Secondly, the existence of slave labour provides evidence of the inequalities which were present in pre-colonial society. Traditional societies are said to have levelling mechanisms which 'play a crucial role in inhibiting aggrandisement by individuals or by special social groups'.[55] These mechanisms take the form of forced loans levied on those whose incomes show signs of rising above the average, feasting and free gifts, and result, so it is claimed, in a 'democracy of poverty'.[56] These ideas fit neatly with the notion of Merrie Africa, but they fail to recognise that national income, though small in aggregate terms, can still be distributed unevenly, and they are not supported in the case of West Africa by satisfactory historical evidence. From early times wealth was achieved through the labour of slaves. In the eleventh century there were merchants in Awdaghost, on the Sahara-savanna margin, who possessed more than one thousand slaves; elsewhere, and in later centuries, even larger slave owners were found. These were the men who could afford expensive items, such as meat, wheat or yams, salt and luxuries from abroad, and who, like the Fulani conquerors in the Guinea highlands, lived 'la vie de château'.[57] The poor, who are often presumed not to have existed in pre-colonial West Africa, had to content themselves with carrion, inferior grains or cassava and imperfect salt substitutes, and at times of extreme need free men had to place themselves or members of their family in pawn to wealthy creditors.[58] Thirdly, the theory that pre-industrial societies owe their cohesiveness to freely-accepted and equally-shared values ignores the possibility that the interests of dependent labourers may not be identified completely with those of their masters, and it fails to appreciate that solidarity can be the result of compulsion. Elements from both conflict and functionalist approaches are needed if change and stability in pre-industrial societies are to be understood.

2   Production

This section will begin to examine the productive activities which resulted from the interaction of natural and human resources in the pre-colonial period. The aim of the discussion is both descriptive and analytical. Description is needed because general histories of West Africa scarcely mention domestic production, and deal only with

[55] Manning Nash, *Primitive and Peasant Economic Systems*, San Francisco 1966, p. 35.

[56] Manning Nash, 'The Social Context of Economic Choice in a Small Society', *Man*, 219, 1961, p. 190.

[57] E. F. Gauthier, *L'Afrique noire occidentale*, Paris, 1943, p. 171.

[58] For a clear statement of economic and social inequalities at the beginning of the sixteenth century see Walter Rodney, *A History of the Upper Guinea Coast, 1545–1800*, Oxford 1970, pp. 34–8. The system of pawning, by which debts were repaid by providing free labour for a specified period, is one which needs further research.

trade, especially foreign trade. Analysis is required to relate the information presented here to the myths (outlined at the beginning of the chapter) of a static, inflexible, uniform, and essentially simple, subsistence economy. It will be argued that the indigenous economy experienced major historical changes; that it was capable of accepting and initiating novel types of activity; that it exhibited regional and occupational diversity; and that its organisation was complex. This analysis, it is suggested, points to the need to revise a number of standard explanations of economic backwardness in 'traditional' societies.

Throughout their history, most West Africans have won their living from the land. Agriculture was the chief activity in the greater part of the region, as it was in other pre-industrial societies, and today foodstuffs still account for the largest share of the value of the goods and services produced each year by West African countries. Moreover, agriculture remains, as in the past, the 'matrix in which all other indigenous economic activity is set.'[59] It is not, and it was not, necessary to give up farming in order to enter occupations such as craft manufacture and trade, which are frequently undertaken on a part-time or seasonal basis. On the contrary, an agricultural surplus often made it possible to finance additional types of productive enterprise.

For the past five centuries the staple foodstuffs have been grains, such as millet (mainly sorghum and pennisetum), maize, rice and fonio (hungry rice), and roots, chiefly yams, cocoyams, cassava (also known as manioc) and plantains. These crops are grown in association with a variety of legumes, bulbs and fruit. Cereals tend to predominate in the savanna, and roots in a large part of the forest, a division which reflects the physical requirements of the crops and the geographical differences between the two regions. Rainfall is particularly important in this context. In the savanna rainfall is sparse and falls in a period of three to five months, which explains why the main crops are annuals, such as cereals. In the forest rainfall is greater and spreads over about seven months of the year, which means that perenniels, such as tree crops and a number of roots, can be grown. These generalisations require qualification. In the first place, there is a considerable overlap between these regions, where combinations of cereals and roots are grown. Secondly, there are local variations within the two major regions themselves, the most important being in the forest, where there is a distinction between the predominantly rice-growing area in the west, and the predominantly yam-dominant area in the east, the dividing line being the Bandama river in what is now the Ivory Coast. The reasons for this distinction are not fully understood. It may have a physical basis, the soils and lower rainfall of the eastern region being better suited, perhaps, to yams than to rice, and it may be the result of cultural differences between the peoples of the forest.[60] If the latter interpretation is correct, then the distinction between the western and eastern parts of the forest can be said to represent a striking example of the variable nature of human reactions to broadly similar environmental conditions.

[59] Polly Hill, 'Some Characteristics of Indigenous West African Economic Enterprise', *Economic Bulletin of Ghana*, 6, 1962, pp. 3–14.
[60] This suggestion has been made by J. Miège, 'Les cultures vivrières en Afrique occidentale', *Cahiers d'Outre-Mer*, 7, 1954, pp. 25–50.

Agriculture is such a pervasive and long established activity in West Africa that it is easy for economists, and even historians, to take its existence for granted. Yet the domestication of plants and animals, the 'neolithic' revolution which Gordon Childe did so much to elucidate,[61] was one of the great events in world history, and one of the outstanding achievements of the indigenous inhabitants of Africa. Agriculture provided more assured supplies of food; it made possible the creation (and appropriation) of a surplus; it stimulated a degree of urbanisation and specialisation; and it permitted an increase in population, since the maximum size no longer depended on the numbers that could be supported at the leanest time of the year by hunting and gathering.

The origins of the food-producing revolution in West Africa have been the subject of considerable controversy among specialists.[62] The established view of the majority of archaeologists, headed by Clark, is that agriculture began in the savanna around 2000 B.C., following the diffusion of ideas and plants from Egypt. However, objections to this interpretation have been raised from several quarters during the last ten or fifteen years. Murdock, an ethnographer, has argued that agriculture began independently in West Africa about 5000 B.C. Portères, a botanist, has also suggested that West African agriculture was an independent development, but considers that it originated between 2800 and 1500 B.C. Wrigley, a historian, has advanced a case to show that certain kinds of agricultural practices originated in West Africa, and that the forest may have been an independent centre of origin. These arguments, though often speculative with regard to dates and evidence, have brought to the fore hypotheses which are beginning to receive serious attention. The diffusionist theory, once unquestioned, is no longer stated with confidence, and the latest archaeological research has tended to stress both the antiquity and the variety of prehistoric agriculture in West Africa.[63]

If, as seems likely, new archaeological discoveries are made in the near future, current views will almost certainly need radical revision. At the moment, and for present purposes, it can be said that West African agriculture, besides being of prehistoric origin, did not lag far behind primary centres of origin, such as the Near East; that at this early date the main staples were millet, rice and fonio in the savanna, and yams and the oil palm in the forest; that while external contacts were of great importance there is evidence to suggest that there was an indigenous, West African neolithic agriculture; and that the assumption that agriculture developed earlier in the savanna than in the forest must be regarded as dubious.

The development of agriculture was not a sudden event, nor did it place such demands on the allegedly limited capacities of the indigenous people as to cause

---

[61] *What Happened in History*, 1942.

[62] For a useful survey of the literature see M. A. Havinden, 'The History of Crop Cultivation in West Africa: a Bibliographical Guide', *Economic History Review*, 23, 1970, pp. 532–55. Eighteen important articles from the *Journal of African History* have been selected by J. D. Fage and R. A. Oliver and published under the title *Papers in African Prehistory*, Cambridge 1970.

[63] Clark himself has taken account of this work in his latest book. See J. Desmond Clark, *The Prehistory of Africa*, 1970, pp. 199–206.

them to drift through subsequent centuries in a state of lassitude, bereft of initiative and ripe for colonial rule. Connections with other parts of the world remained strong, and the flow of plants and seeds continued. Asian yams, cocoyams, bananas, and plantains reached West Africa by way of the Near East between the first and the eighth centuries A.D. By the time the first written records become available, it is clear that agriculture was well established throughout West Africa. In the tenth century al-Muhallabi, writing of the Kingdom of Kanem (north-east of Lake Chad) reported that 'the length of their land is a fifteen days' journey through habitations and cultivations all the way. . . . Millet chiefly is cultivated in the land, and beans, also wheat. Most of the ordinary people . . . spend their time cultivating and looking after their cattle.'[64] In the thirteenth century, if not before, the ruler of Kanem maintained an experimental farm, which grew a variety of cereals and fruits. When the Portuguese arrived on the coast of West Africa two centuries later, they found that upland and swamp rice were widely cultivated in the western part of the forest, and that yams were the main staple in the east. The English traveller, Jobson, who visited the Gambian coast in the seventeenth century, noted that 'the generall Trade from which none but the Kings and principall persons are exempted, is Husbandry, whereto . . . the people of all sizes after their abilitie are subject'.[65]

The coming of the Europeans in the late fifteenth century led to the introduction of a number of crops which are now regarded as typical of West African agriculture. The most important of these were maize, cassava, groundnuts, tobacco and, later on, cocoa, as well as a variety of fruits. The principal source of supply was South America, and the two main channels of diffusion were a direct route from Brazil, and an indirect route via Iberia, both of which were established by the Portuguese. There has been some debate over the timing of the introduction of one of these crops, namely maize. According to one school of thought, maize was present in West Africa before the Europeans made contact with America. This is a possibility which has not been proved, and the balance of the evidence favours the view expressed here that maize was imported from South America.

The effect which these crops had on the local economy, though more important than the precise timing of their arrival, has yet to attract serious historical attention. The spread of Asian and American crops was undoubtedly a lengthy process, and is still going on today, but the slow pace of change should not be taken as evidence that indigenous farmers were unreceptive to new opportunities. First, it took time for knowledge of foreign seeds and plants to spread throughout the region as a whole. Second, new crops were tried out cautiously because no community was going to place its established food supplies at risk through the hasty adoption of untested novelties. Third, the rate of diffusion was sometimes inhibited by technical problems. Cassava, for example, though introduced in the sixteenth century, did not begin to spread rapidly until the close of the eighteenth century, when it became known how

[64] Quoted in Roland Oliver and J. D. Fage, *A Short History of Africa*, Harmondsworth 1962, p. 47.
[65] Quoted in Basil Davidson, *The African Past*, Harmondsworth 1966, p. 205.

to process the crop in such a way as to remove the prussic acid which some varieties contained. Fourth, the speed of adoption was related to the growth of demand for foodstuffs. In the twentieth century, for instance, the rise of a wage labour force and the development of specialised export producers encouraged farmers in certain areas to concentrate on producing food for the internal market.

Where new plants and seeds were adopted, it was not because they caught the fancy of a primitive people, but because they were seen as useful additions to the existing range of foods, being worth more than the extra cost of producing them; or alternatively because they were regarded as good substitutes, yielding a higher return for the same input than the crops they displaced. Thus maize has spread in areas formerly dominated by yams and sorghum because it gives two crops a year, both of which have fairly good yields, while cassava has become common in yam-producing regions because it is easy to grow and produces food throughout the year. Yams are still the preferred food and they have greater nutritional value, but they make heavy demands on the soil and they need a great deal more labour. The host communities also showed themselves willing and able to adapt existing forms of agricultural organisation where necessary. Three types of alteration were called for. First, the length of time particular plots were farmed often had to be increased in order to accommodate a greater number of new crops. Second, new techniques of cultivation had to be adopted on occasion. For instance, the spread of swamp rice in Sierra Leone during the nineteenth century was associated with a new method of transplanting the seedlings from nursery beds to underwater fields.[66] Third, a certain amount of occupational change was required. The spread of cassava among the Yoruba, for example, meant that women became more involved in agricultural production, for they were allocated the task of processing the crop.

The foregoing analysis suggests the following conclusions. Agricultural history in the pre-colonial period is a story of innovation rather than stagnation. The assumption that the economy was static, having been frozen at the very dawn of African history, is untenable, and the timeless concept of the 'traditional' society needs to be used with care, or, better still, not used at all. Although contact with other continents led to the introduction of some troublesome weeds, such as spear grass, there is no doubt that on balance the import of seeds and plants was of great benefit to West Africa. The new crops offered the means of improving nutrition, they reduced the risk of famine, and they made it possible to support a larger population.[67] A study of pre-colonial history offers a new perspective on the rapid and well publicised expansion of export-crop production in the twentieth century. Export growth should be seen not as the miraculous reaction of a backward people to wholly novel external demands, but as one further development in a long history of agricultural experiment and adaptation.

[66] This technique is thought to have originated in Casamance, on the southern coast of present-day Senegal.

[67] Other continents gained in similar ways. Another South American export, the potato, became a staple food in Europe in the eighteenth and nineteenth centuries.

2*

To demonstrate that African farmers were flexible in their attitude towards the adoption of new crops is certainly a step forward. Nevertheless, it could still be argued that the indigenous system of cultivation was primitive, that technology remained crude, that the rules governing land tenure shackled enterprise, and that for these reasons agriculture was stuck virtually at subsistence level. An examination of these beliefs, which have been nourished by repetition in textbooks of economic development, will show that they rest on evidence which is either incomplete or misinterpreted.

Colonial officials formed a generally unfavourable impression of the capabilities of African farmers. They looked at unoccupied land and thought that it was unused or spare territory, which Africans, through lack of skill or initiative, were incapable of developing. They noted the absence, especially in the forest, of the neat, hedged fields which were so familiar to them at home, and concluded that the standard of farm management was poor. They pointed to the lack of the plough, and decided that local farmers were uninventive. These observations, recorded in reports over many years, influenced policies during the colonial era, and can still be found in some secondary works today. However, an account of traditional farming which is confined to shifting cultivation and to allegedly wasteful slash and burn techniques, though it accords well with Trevor Roper's notion of African history as the story of the 'unrewarding gyrations of barbarous tribes',[68] scarcely does justice to the complex reality revealed by geographical research. Indeed, according to Morgan and Pugh's authoritative work, no less than seven headings are needed to classify the leading systems of cultivation practised in West Africa.[69] These are: shifting cultivation; rotational bush fallow; rotational planted fallow; mixed farming; permanent cultivation; tree cultivation; and floodland and irrigated farming. All seven systems were in use by about the sixteenth century, and were almost certainly present long before then.

Shifting cultivation involves the periodic movement of settlement. Virgin land, or land having abundant secondary vegetation, is cleared with the aid of fire, and the resulting irregular, tree-studded plots are cropped for one or two years before being abandoned, as the community moves on to new land elsewhere. Shifting cultivation may well have been the principal system of agriculture in West Africa during prehistoric times, but today (and contrary to a common assumption) it is dominant in only a few areas. The chief method of cultivation in recent centuries has been rotational bush fallow, which is widespread in savanna and forest, and is used for growing both cereals and roots. In this system settlement is fixed, and the land under cultivation rotates over a defined area of fallow grasses or woody plants, though the woodland itself if not allowed to regenerate. Cleared land is usually cropped for between three and six years (though in the rice-growing forest lands of the west one or two years is the norm), and the period of fallow ranges from four to ten years. The relatively long cropping period entails careful farm management and

---

[68] Hugh Trevor Roper, *The Rise of Christian Europe*, 1965, p. 9.
[69] W. B. Morgan and J. C. Pugh, *West Africa*, p. 100.

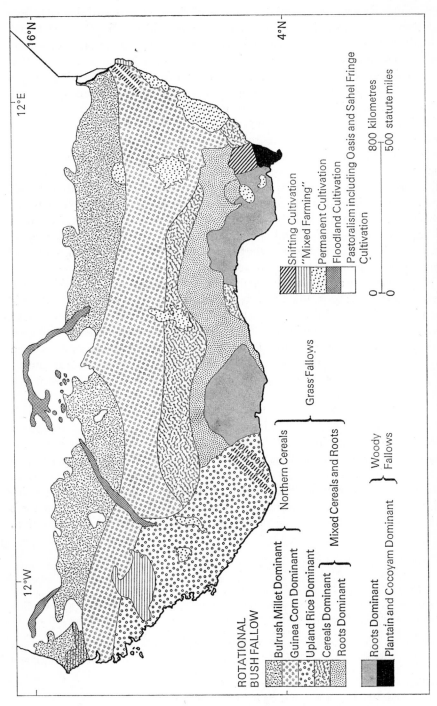

MAP 3. Present-day Agricultural Regions: Subsistence and Internal Market Crops.

ROTATIONAL BUSH FALLOW

Bulrush Millet Dominant
Guinea Corn Dominant } Northern Cereals
Upland Rice Dominant
Cereals Dominant } Mixed Cereals and Roots
Roots Dominant

Roots Dominant } Woody Fallows
Plantain and Cocoyam Dominant

Grass Fallows

Shifting Cultivation "Mixed Farming"
Permanent Cultivation
Floodland Cultivation
Pastoralism including Oasis and Sahel Fringe Cultivation

0   800 kilometres
0   500 statute miles

16°N
12°E
12°W
4°N

33

the use of annual rotations, crop mixtures and successions.[70] Rotational planted fallow is a distinct, but comparatively unimportant, system, which differs from rotational bush fallow in that the fallow cover is selected and deliberately planted. Mixed farming involves a combination of cultivation and animal husbandry. Only a few communities, such as the Serer of Senegal, employ mixed farming as their principal system of production, though other groups, such as the Fulani, may keep cattle and cultivate the land without fully integrating the two activities. Where permanent cultivation is practised, the same land is farmed annually and is rarely allowed to revert to fallow. Few communities rely on permanent cultivation for the greater part of their supplies of food, but most have some small plots near the village or compound, which are kept under crops continuously.[71] Tree cultivation, like permanent cultivation, is found in conjunction with other systems, especially rotational bush fallow. The most important tree crops in the pre-colonial period were the oil palm, the kola tree and the shea tree, all of which are indigenous to West Africa. Floodland and irrigated cultivation is found in restricted areas, such as the south-west coast, where swamp rice is grown, and on the flood-plains of the Niger and Senegal rivers, where millet, maize and rice are cultivated.

The question now arises as to whether there is any unifying principle linking these different methods of agriculture. Gourou's contention that the system of land use is determined chiefly by soils and climate is unsatisfactory because rotational bush fallow, the dominant system in West Africa, is practised over a wide range of geographical conditions, while shifting cultivation was used in parts of Europe, a temperate zone, as late as the nineteenth century.[72] Boserup's stimulating argument that systems of cultivation are determined basically by population density also needs qualification, for different systems can be found in parts of West Africa which do not show marked demographic variations.[73] It is suggested here that land use is best understood in terms of a continuum ranging from virgin land to permanent cultivation, and containing a number of subdivisions at intervening points, these being decided by the length of the fallow period. Rotational bush fallow occupies one of these intermediate spaces. The length of the fallow period represents an adjustment to some or all of the following variables: population density; the availability of fertiliser; and the range of crops. The concept of a continuum of land use is best illustrated by the two extremes of shifting cultivation and permanent cultivation.

---

[70] Rotations make certain that demands on the soil are varied from year to year; mixtures, that is growing several crops on the same plot and in the same season, ensure a high density of plants and economy of weeding; and successions, that is planting crops one after another during the same season, spread labour requirements and provide a more even flow of foodstuffs by staggering the harvests.

[71] For a study of the ways in which communities combine various systems of land use, including permanent agriculture, see W. B. Morgan, 'The Zoning of Land Use around Rural Settlements in Tropical Africa', in *Environment and Land Use in Africa*, ed. M. F. Thomas and G. W. Whittington, 1969, pp. 301–19.

[72] Pierre Gourou, *The Tropical World*, 1954.

[73] Ester Boserup, *The Conditions of Agricultural Growth*, 1965.

Shifting cultivation and other forms of extensive agriculture were found where some or all of the following conditions prevailed: a low population density; a shortage of fertiliser; and an insufficient variety of crops. Where population was sparse and land abundant, farmers realised that it was important to maximise output per man rather than output per acre. European observers, obsessed by the notion (derived from their own experience) that output per acre was a priority of universal applicability, failed to grasp the principles underlying shifting cultivation. Yet clearing the land by burning the undergrowth was the quickest and cheapest method in terms of labour costs, and had the added advantage of returning mineral matter to the soil rapidly. Output per man hour under this system was extremely high, which partly explains its tenacity in the face of alternative methods which, though technically superior, increased overall costs and reduced net returns to the farmer. Where there was a shortage of manure, a long period of fallow was needed to restore nutrients to the soil. This deficiency was common in various parts of West Africa, but was particularly marked in the forest, where disease and the difficulty of maintaining pasture severely restricted animal husbandry. Where there was a lack of variety in the crops available, the number of rotations was limited, the soil soon became exhausted, and farmers were forced to move on to new land. European commentators were scandalised by this 'wasteful' means of cultivation because they failed to appreciate that unused land was an integral part of a method of cultivation which involved the maintenance of long fallows, and that to use it for another purpose (such as European plantations) was to risk dislocating the indigenous system of production.

Permanent cultivation, at the other end of the continuum, was found chiefly in areas where population was relatively dense, where there was a regular supply of fertiliser, and where a considerable variety of crops was available. This system was geared to achieving high returns per acre rather than (or as well as) per man hour, and it demonstrates the ability of African farmers to adjust factor proportions in order to achieve optimum results with the resources at their disposal. Animal manure and household refuse were used as fertilisers, and crop mixtures, rotations and successions were employed to ensure that as much use as possible was made of cleared land. Intensive agriculture was not an important mode of production in what, in terms of economic and political development, are usually regarded as the most advanced areas of West Africa. On the contrary, it was dominant among some of the most underprivileged and least powerful of West African peoples. For example, the inhabitants of the Mandara uplands (on the border between Nigeria and the Cameroons) developed a system of intensive agriculture which included soil conservation, the use of fertilisers, crop rotations, the planting and protection of trees and animal husbandry. A British official, who was sent to inspect the area in 1939 with a view to improving its agriculture, reported that the methods in use already included 'practically every principle that Agricultural Departments throughout Africa are trying to instil into the "backward" peoples.'[74] What is particularly interesting about this case

[74] Stanhope White, 'The Agricultural Economy of the Hill Pagans of Dikwa Emirate, Cameroons (British Mandate)', *Empire Journal of Experimental Agriculture*, 9, 1941, pp. 66–7.

is that permanent agriculture was not a result of favourable soils or climate in the micro-environment, but was the outcome of political pressures, for the dense settlement and the relative immobility of the inhabitants were brought about originally by a desire to escape the predatory attentions of more powerful slave-raiding neighbours.

Historians and economists are inclined to rank agricultural systems in linear progression from 'backward' to 'advanced'. However, the idea of an agricultural league table can be very misleading. Different systems of cultivation, including those commonly regarded as advanced, co-existed in pre-colonial West Africa, as they did in pre-industrial Europe. None was anachronistic, for each was subtly adapted to particular circumstances. Furthermore, to equate permanent agriculture with market activity, and shifting cultivation with subsistence farming, is tempting, but mistaken. The methods varied, but the economic goals of both systems were often the same.

It is hoped that enough has been said to indicate that Africans were expert farm managers. Nevertheless, it could still be argued that agriculture remained stuck in a subsistence groove because indigenous farmers failed to invent or adopt the technology needed to raise productivity. This contention is usually based on assumptions about the role of the plough. White has shown that the plough played a crucial role in the development of European agriculture from the sixth century onwards,[75] and Goody has argued that its absence from Africa south of the Sahara helps to explain some major economic and political contrasts between the two continents.[76] To cite the plough as an example of the technological disparity between Europe and Africa is to draw attention to an important, if undisputed, fact. To imply that the presence of the plough would have transformed the development potential of West Africa is to advance a very different case, and one that is open to question.

African farmers relied on simple tools, such as the digging stick, the hoe and the matchet, though a hand plough, which, technically, was half-way between a hoe and a simple mouldboard plough, was used in the Gambia at an early date. It is possible that West Africans did not employ the heavy, European plough because they did not know of its existence. This explanation is unsatisfactory because West Africa had long-standing and close connections with North Africa, where ploughs other than the simple, scratch plough, were common. Perhaps West Africans were aware of the existence of the plough, but, being stuck in a 'traditional' society, were unwilling or unable to adopt progressive techniques. This, too, must be regarded as an unlikely explanation in view of the arguments developed so far in connection with the organisation of the labour force, the history of agriculture and the variety of systems of cultivation.

It is suggested here that the plough was not used in West Africa because it was unsuitable, or too costly, or both. The plough is of greatest use in areas where soils are heavy and land cannot be cleared by fire. These conditions are more typical of

[75] Lynn White, *Medieval Technology and Social Change*, Oxford 1962, pp. 39–57.
[76] Jack Goody, *Technology, Tradition, and the State in Africa*, 1971, pp. 25 and 76.

Europe than of Africa. Moreover, draught animals are needed to work a plough effectively. Draught animals could not survive in the forest, where, in any case, the plough was ill-suited to the dominant pattern of irregular, tree-studded plots. Ploughing in the savanna could easily lead to soil erosion, as experiments undertaken in French West Africa during the 1920s amply demonstrated. All the same, the plough could have been used in some parts of West Africa, where the soils were not likely to erode easily, where draught animals were available, and where cereal culti-vation favoured the creation of a field-type landscape. The plough was not adopted in these areas because its greater cost did not guarantee a more than proportionate increase in returns. Ploughs and draught animals were expensive to buy, and the latter were also expensive to maintain. The plough can prepare more land in a shorter time than can manual labour, but this achievement often involves a fall in output per man hour,[77] and, in some cases, in output per acre as well.[78]

Farmers' incomes need to rise some way above the level needed for subsistence before they can afford to adopt new techniques, such as the plough. Even so, a more advanced technology will be used only if it is more profitable than existing methods of production, or if it is essential to ensure survival. Neither of these conditions appears to have applied to pre-colonial West Africa, which, like India, developed a relatively simple technology, but one that was well suited to its requirements.[79] If ploughs had been available in West Africa in the pre-colonial era, they would have been treated as conversation pieces rather than as agricultural implements. Indeed, that is just what many of them became during the colonial era, when officials tried to convert Africans to the use of technically superior, but economically unrewarding, farm implements. It is as well to remember that virtually the whole of the massive expansion of domestic foodstuffs and export crops which occurred during the twentieth century was produced with the aid of traditional tools. To suppose that the failure to adopt a more complex agricultural technology was a cause of under-development in Africa is to put plough before ox, and invention before need.

It remains to see whether or not the system of land tenure which prevailed in the pre-colonial period inhibited the development of natural resources. According to Pedler, 'land, an essential factor of production, has been prevented by custom and law from coming under the influence of economic forces';[80] and it is still common,

---

[77] Boserup, *The Conditions of Agricultural Growth*, pp. 32–4.

[78] Peter M. Weil, 'The Introduction of the Ox Plow in Central Gambia', in *African Food Production Systems*, ed. Peter F. M. McLoughlin, Baltimore 1970, pp. 251–2.

[79] For a comparative analysis on similar lines see Irfan Habib, 'Potentialities of Capitalistic Development in the Economy of Mughal India', *Journal of Economic History*, 29, 1969, pp. 62–4. Lack of space has confined this discussion to the case of the plough. However, the argument developed here could also be used to explain the relative unimportance of irrigated agriculture in West Africa. Geographical considerations aside, irrigated agriculture will not be widespread in areas where extensive agriculture is possible because of its high capital and maintenance costs. The wells and irrigated works found in parts of the Sahara and savanna were operated by slave labour. When slavery declined in the twentieth century, so, too, did the wells and oases because of the high cost of employing wage labour.

[80] F. J. Pedler, *Economic Geography of West Africa*, 1955, p. 215.

especially in non-specialist works, to find indigenous land law summarised simply as 'communal' ownership, measured against the presumed advantages of individual tenure, and finally condemned as a primitive obstruction to economic development. A full review of African land laws is impossible here, but some general observations, based on recent research, need to be made in order to correct a few of the more widespread and mistaken assumptions.[81]

In the first place, the conventional dichotomy between backward, communal ownership and advanced, individual tenure is very misleading. African land laws, no less than indigenous systems of cultivation, varied greatly even within restricted areas, and ranged from land that was indeed communally owned and worked, to land that was held virtually as freehold.[82] Households frequently made use of common land and individual holdings simultaneously, as they did in medieval Europe. If individual tenure is to be the criterion of a progressive system of land law, then there was undoubtedly an element of modernity in the rules governing the use and disposal of land in West Africa. Secondly, even if it is acknowledged that the greater part of the land was, in some sense, owned communally, it would be wrong to conclude that this arrangement was a barrier to progress. Under systems of extensive agriculture, such as shifting cultivation and rotational bush fallow, it was important for the farmer to secure the general right to cultivate land within a given area, but the actual ownership of a specific plot, which was destined to lie fallow for a number of years, was not a matter of great significance. Usufructuary rights were more crucial, and these were clearly delineated and could often be inherited. Furthermore, the household or individual concerned usually had a clear title to the crops produced on communally-owned soil, and received guarantees regarding tenure. In other words, it was the product of the scarce factor, labour, which was closely defined, whereas rights over land, which was in general an abundant resource, were less specific. Where population was dense and the period of fallow short or non-existent, as was the case with permanent cultivation, then claims on individual plots became stronger, and in these circumstances freehold tenure, pledging, and even the sale of land were recognised in customary law.

It is important to note that methods of acquiring, holding and disposing of land differed not only spatially, but also through time. As yet, however, little attention has been paid to the historical development of African law in the pre-colonial period, and most research in this field has focused on the effect of the introduction of European law in the twentieth century on indigenous legal systems. An interesting exception, and one which is mentioned here in the hope that it will prompt further research, is Guèye's study of the legal consequences of the establishment of Muslim

---

[81] Readers who wish to consider this subject further should begin by looking at the excellent collection of papers in *African Agrarian Systems*, ed. Daniel Biebuyck, 1963.

[82] For two of many cases where individual tenure was common see Ronald Cohen, 'From Empire to Colony: Bornu in the Nineteenth and Twentieth Centuries', in *Colonialism in Africa, 1870–1960*, 3, ed. Victor Turner, Cambridge 1971, p. 100, and Olga Linares de Sapir, 'Agriculture and Diola Society', in *African Food Production Systems*, ed. Peter F. M. McLoughlin, Baltimore 1970, pp. 207–8.

rule in Fouta Toro (now part of northern Senegal) at the close of the eighteenth century.[83] Guèye shows how Muslim law, by establishing the equality of all male heirs, contributed to the fragmentation of holdings, encouraged a greater degree of individual exploitation of land, and led to the migration of heirs whose inheritance was too small to provide them with a living.[84] This study provides a glimpse of the movement and dynamism of pre-colonial legal history, and it serves as a reminder that the concept of traditional law, like the concept of the traditional society, is a convenient fiction which achieves order at the expense of reality.

In summary, indigenous land laws were neither irrational nor antediluvian, but were a reflection of the conditions governing agricultural production in West Africa. There was a factor market in land, though it was very limited. The explanation of this limitation is not that Africans were busy maximising social rather than economic values, but that land was not scarce enough to acquire a market value. Households (and individuals within households) had scope for enterprise in securing and exploiting land within the dominant, so-called communal system of property ownership. Those who claim that indigenous land laws were a constraint on development must explain how it was that these laws were consistent with a widespread and rapid expansion in the production of export crops during the early part of the colonial period. African systems of land tenure undoubtedly underwent important changes in the twentieth century, but these were a consequence and not a prerequisite of export growth.

Animal husbandry, the other feature of Childe's neolithic revolution, is at least as old in West Africa as agriculture. Pastoralists first appeared in the Sahara about 5000 B.C., and are known to have kept both long- and short-horned cattle, as well as sheep and goats. Animal husbandry was not indigenous to West Africa, and is thought to have been introduced from Asia via Egypt, though there may also have been a North African centre of domestication. Cattle, goats and sheep remained the most important livestock, though different breeds and different animals were introduced in subsequent centuries.[85] A survey of sources relating to the period between the tenth and the sixteenth centuries shows that animal husbandry was already well developed in those parts of West Africa which are major centres today.[86] In contrast to agriculture, which was practised throughout West Africa, animal husbandry was significant only in the northern part of the Western Sudan and the southern part of

[83] Youssouf Guèye, 'Essai sur les causes et les conséquences de la micropropriété au Fouta-Toro', *Bulletin de l'IFAN*, B, 19, 1957, pp. 28–42.

[84] It would be interesting to know whether there was a connection between these migrants and the development of groundnut farming in the nineteenth and twentieth centuries. For a comparative study of the relationship between dispossessed heirs, migration and innovation (among the Basques) see Leonard Kasdan, 'Family Structure, Migration and the Entrepreneur', *Comparative Studies in Society and History*, 7, 1965, pp. 345–57.

[85] The role of camels, horses, oxen and donkeys will be considered in section 3 of this chapter.

[86] Tadeusz Lewicki, 'Animal Husbandry among Medieval Agricultural People of Western and Middle Sudan', *Acta Ethnographica*, 14, 1965, pp. 165–78.

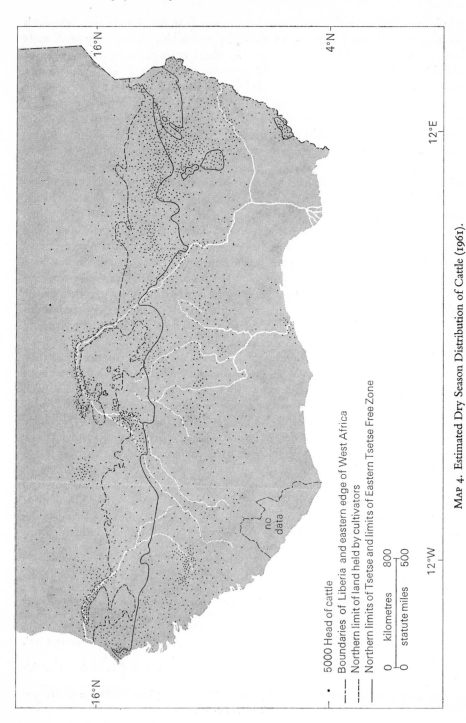

5000 Head of cattle

Boundaries of Liberia and eastern edge of West Africa

Northern limit of land held by cultivators

Northern limits of Tsetse and limits of Eastern Tsetse Free Zone

kilometres 0 — 800

statute miles 0 — 500

MAP 4. Estimated Dry Season Distribution of Cattle (1961).

the Sahara, where there was comparative freedom from fatal diseases, such as trypano-somiasis, and where pasture was available. The principal specialists in this region were the Moors, the Tuareg and the Fulani. Certain breeds of cattle, such as the small Ndama variety, had a high resistance to trypanosomiasis, and so could be kept in the south, providing pasture could be found, but these hardy survivors were poor in quality and few in number.

The activities of specialists in animal husbandry, no less than the behaviour of African farmers, have been cited as typifying many of the presumed characteristics of the 'traditional' society. Their mobility, the pastoral counterpart of shifting cultivation, has been seen as an expression of endemic wanderlust. Their pride in their cattle has been interpreted (and not only in the case of Africa) as proof of pre-industrial man's pre-occupation with social rather than economic values. These beliefs, which themselves rank high among the 'sacred cows' of development theory, need revision.

Migration was a well ordered and necessary feature of animal husbandry in West Africa. The movements of pastoralists, far from being aimless, are divisible into three analytically distinct categories: transhumance, which involved a regular, annual trek from the Saharan margins down to the savanna and back again; migratory drift, which involved a shift in the orbit of transhumance; and full migration, which entailed a transfer to a completely new area and the creation of a fresh orbit of trans-humance.[87] The nature and extent of pastoral migration are explicable in terms of a combination of three factors. First, the size of the herd owned by a particular community had an important influence on the amount of land required. An increase in numbers, through breeding or purchase, meant that more land was needed. A decrease, through disease or sale, had the opposite effect. Loss of cattle was a disaster for the herdsman, as loss of crops was for the farmer. The threat of disaster explains why the annual trek into the savanna was reversed when the onset of the rainy season spread fly-borne diseases. Second, the extensive character of animal husbandry was partly a reflection of the natural distribution of essential foodstuffs. Water and salt were scarce, and pasture tended to be poor and sparse. Hence the herdsmen moved down into the savanna during the dry season in search of better grazing land. Third, migration was undertaken for purposes of trade. Pastoralists and cultivators in West Africa, as in other parts of the world, developed a symbiotic relationship. Each needed the products of the other, and one of the main purposes of transhumance was to exchange animal products for grain. Yet farmers feared the destructive effects of livestock on their crops, and conflicts between the two parties sometimes led to a shift in the orbit of transhumance, or to migration to an entirely new area. In this way pastoralists became colonists too. Successive changes in the pattern of their migratory movements created new economic and sometimes political frontiers, as in the case of the Fulani, who spread across the Western Sudan between the eleventh and seventeenth centuries.

[87] D. J. Stenning, *Savannah Nomads*, 1959. On the movement of pastoralists in Mauritania see J. Cauneille and J. Dubief, 'Les Reguibat Legouacem: chronologie et nomadisme', *Bulletin de l'IFAN*, B, 17, 1955, pp. 528–50.

Livestock were kept for their meat, milk, manure, hides and, in the case of sheep, for their wool. The belief that Africans refused to sell their cattle rests on a misunderstanding of the way in which the pastoral economy operated. It is clear from numerous sources that the cattle trade long antedates the coming of the Europeans in the fifteenth century, and was certainly not a result of the presumed disintegration of 'tribal' values in the twentieth century. Admittedly, only a small proportion of the herd was sold, but this was not because of limitations imposed by a pre-capitalist value system. Cattle in pastoral societies were not simply a consumption good, but were also its main stock of capital. Returns on capital took the form of sales of milk and manure to farming communities. It is not surprising that the herdsman took care to conserve his capital, for cattle were a long term investment, and one which could easily be lost through disease, as happened for instance in the late nineteenth century, when rinderpest decimated herds in many parts of the continent. Cattle were indeed highly prized, but their function as a status symbol derived from society's appreciation of their economic worth. The man who possessed a large number of cattle was respected not for his unthinking devotion to ascribed values, but for his skill in controlling a major resource.[88]

The concept of a neolithic revolution is useful for focusing attention on developments which are of fundamental importance in world history, but the term 'revolution' can be misleading if it is interpreted to mean that previous ways of securing a livelihood, notably by gathering, hunting and fishing, speedily became redundant. All three means of subsistence survived and were adapted to the new, agricultural economy. Gathering was the least specialised and most widespread of these activities. However, it would be wrong to envisage a situation where, as one nineteenth-century explorer put it, the 'fruits of the earth grow spontaneously, or with little cultivation; so that wherever rivers run, the land may be truly said to overflow with milk and honey'.[89] Equally, it might truly be said that wherever rivers ran there was a danger of water-borne diseases and of serious flooding during the rainy season. The stereotype of the contented tropical dweller gathering his daily breadfruit and then relapsing into a state of chronic lethargy until roused by a passing foreign explorer (or nowadays by a television crew) has no basis in fact and should be banished from book and screen alike. Collecting wild grains, roots and fruit was usually no more than an occasional supplement to agriculture. Where gathering was important to the local economy, as in parts of the savanna during the dry season, it was an indication not of luxury but of hardship—the inhabitants being driven by necessity to seek additional food supplies.[90]

---

[88] For a similar viewpoint on East Africa see the valuable essay by Harold K. Schneider, 'Economics in East African Aboriginal Societies', in *Economic Transition in Africa*, ed. Melville J. Herskovits and Mitchell Harwitz, 1964, pp. 53–75. It is hoped that these comments will lead to further study of the economic history of animal husbandry (including goats and sheep, as well as cattle) in the pre-colonial period.

[89] John Whitford, *Trading Life in Western and Central Africa*, Liverpool 1877, p. 334.

[90] This is still true today. See Edmond Bernus, 'Cueillette et exploitation des resources spontanées du Sahel nigérien par les Kel Tamasheq', *Cahiers ORSTOM*, 4, 1967, pp. 31–52.

Hunting and fishing were more specialised activities than gathering because they required a greater degree of skill. Hunting was especially important in the forest, where there was a shortage of meat, and it reached a seasonal peak during the dry season, when the demand for farm labour was at its lowest, and when restricted water supplies made it easier to locate game. Little is known about the historical development of hunting in West Africa. There are examples of hunting communities colonising an area, settling down and becoming cultivators. This almost classical evolution appears to have happened in the case of the Adioukrou after they arrived in the southern part of the Ivory Coast at the close of the eighteenth century. On the whole, however, it seems more realistic to treat hunters as semi-specialists who were integrated with the farming community, rather than as antiquated survivors from a pre-historic, pre-agricultural age. Traditionally, professional hunters used traps, spears, clubs and bows and arrows, but with the expansion of trade with Europe after the fifteenth century they began to use guns as well.[91] Provided they worked properly (and some of the imports were of poor quality), firearms must have increased the efficiency of the hunters, and so may have helped to improve the diet of communities living in the forest. Firearms also enabled hunters to play a part in some of the major state building (and destroying) movements of the pre-colonial era.

Fishing was practised along the coast, particularly in the region of Senegambia and the Gulf of Guinea, and also in many inland waters, two of the largest centres being Lake Chad and the great bend of the Niger in the Western Sudan. Specialised communities of highly skilled fishermen are known to have developed in these areas at an early date. In the sixteenth century, for example, the Sorkawa and Bozo, who fished the middle Niger, paid their taxes to the rulers of the Songhai empire exclusively in dried fish. There was no technical innovation in fishing comparable to that brought about in hunting by the introduction of firearms: canoes were the main craft in use, and harpoons, nets, lines and traps remained the principal means of catching fish. In other respects the history of fishing was far from static. The availability of fish fluctuated with the tidal movements of the sea and with the different flood periods of the rivers, so fishermen tended to migrate in search of their catch. On the coast the Fante moved periodically from the Gold Coast west to the Ivory Coast and east to Nigeria, while in the interior the Sorkawa and Bozo travelled hundreds of miles each year along the Niger. Once again a connection can be perceived between migration and innovation in West Africa: migration led to the development of new fishing grounds and also to the foundation of new settlements. Lagos, now the capital of Nigeria, was itself first colonised by fishermen in the sixteenth century.

The discussion of production will be completed by a survey of mining and manufacturing activities. These subjects are often treated in a cursory manner in surveys of underdeveloped economies, principally, it seems, because it is assumed either that they were unimportant in the 'traditional' economy, or that they are of little relevance to modern industrialisation programmes. In reality, a consideration of pre-colonial mining and manufacturing raises a number of significant questions regarding

[91] And to produce ivory for export as well as meat for domestic consumption.

the acquisition of technical skills, the type and degree of specialisation, the supply of capital to non-agricultural, non-mercantile occupations, and the volume and character of demand for manufactured goods. Furthermore, indigenous manufactures are worth considering in the context of current industrialisation policies. Modern manufacturing in West Africa began not with heavy industries, but with relatively simple import-substituting activities, some of which can be based (with suitable modifications) on established crafts.[92]

Iron, gold and salt were the most important minerals produced in pre-colonial West Africa, though copper, tin, and silver were also mined in small quantities.[93] The region has few deposits of coal, and the principal domestic and industrial fuels were wood and charcoal.

Knowledge of iron working reached West Africa during the first millennium. Iron was being smelted at Nok, in what is now northern Nigeria, around 500 B.C., and iron-producing techniques had spread throughout the region by about the fourth century A.D. Iron implements, chiefly hoes, knives, spearheads and swords, marked a great advance on stone and wooden tools: they improved the efficiency of hunters; they made it easier to clear the forest; and they placed more power in the hands of the builders (and destroyers) of towns and states. Relatively accessible deposits of iron ore were distributed fairly widely in West Africa, though mostly on a small scale. However, there were a few large centres, such as Oume in the southern Ivory Coast, where the remains of 100 furnaces and about 10,000 tons of slag were discovered in the 1920s, and also around Oyo in south-west Nigeria, where a complex of highly specialised mining villages flourished during the pre-colonial period. In 1904 one of these settlements had a population of between 100 and 120, all of whom (including women and children) were engaged in the various stages of iron mining and manufacturing. The output of this settlement supplied an area which covered several hundred square miles. It is no coincidence that these large centres were located in well-wooded regions, for the greater part of total production costs was accounted for by timber, which was needed to make charcoal.

Pig iron was produced by digging lumps of ironstone out of shallow pits and quarries, and heating them with a flux in a clay furnace fired by charcoal. However, the methods in use were neither simple nor uniform. In the eighteenth century the Mandingo used a circular kiln about ten feet high and three feet in diameter with seven vents at the base.[94] The kiln was filled with alternate layers of ironstone and charcoal and heated for three days. The contents were allowed to cool and then reheated again until pig iron of an acceptable quality was produced. The miners near Oyo used a rather different method in the nineteenth century.[95] To begin with, they

[92] Archibald Callaway, 'From Traditional Crafts to Modern Industries', *Odu*, 2, 1965, pp. 28–51.

[93] For copper see Lars Sundström, *The Trade of Guinea*, Lund 1965, pp. 217–51; on tin see A. O. Anjorin, 'Tin Mining in Northern Nigeria during the Nineteenth and Early Part of the Twentieth Centuries', *Odu*, 5, 1971, pp. 54–67.

[94] Naval Intelligence Division, *French West Africa*, 1, 1943, pp. 236–7.

[95] C. V. Bellamy, 'A West African Smelting House', *Journal of the Iron and Steel Institute*, 11, 1904, pp. 99–126.

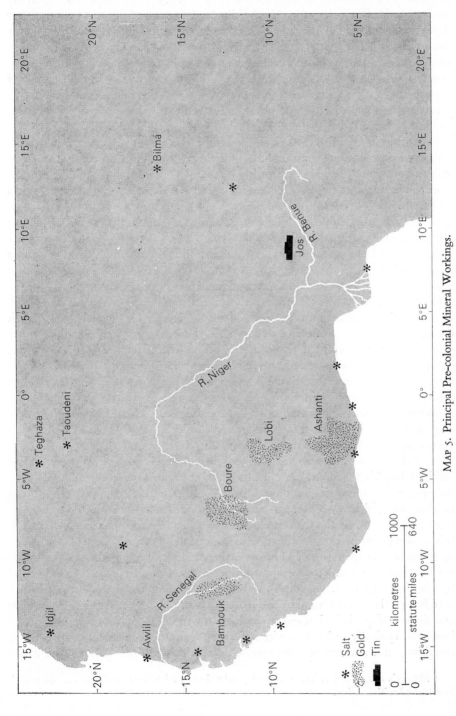

MAP 5. Principal Pre-colonial Mineral Workings.

prepared the ironstone by heating it over an open fire. It was then pounded, washed and screened before being placed in the kiln. In this case the kiln was about four feet high and seven feet in diameter, and had six vertical vents. The kiln was charged for about thirty-six hours, and fed with ore ten times during this period. At least a dozen tools were used in the course of filling, regulating and emptying the kiln. The pig iron was allowed to cool, and then sold to smiths, who puddled it and fashioned implements of various kinds. An analysis of samples carried out in 1904 showed that producers had selected the best possible flux, and that the finished product was puddled or forged steel, and not simply wrought iron.

The smiths in Oyo had crude iron brought to them. Similarly, Bambara smiths, who were settled among communities along the middle Niger, purchased iron from traders. Sometimes, however, the smiths themselves travelled to the mining centres, worked pig iron with portable tools, and then returned home to peddle their wares. The Awka and Nkwerri, for example, were itinerant smiths who served between them virtually the whole of Ibo country. Future research on pre-colonial mining operations will clarify the reasons underlying these variations in production and distribution. Meanwhile, it seems clear that 'primitive' mineral production, no less than 'primitive' agriculture, was a more complex and a more efficient undertaking than a superficial assessment of the techniques employed would suggest.

Gold was mined in West Africa as early as the first millennium, but it was not until about the eighth century A.D., with the development of commercial contacts with the Arab world, that production underwent a marked expansion. The greater part of total output was exported, though a proportion entered the domestic economy in the shape of ornaments and as currency. Output is commonly assumed to have reached a peak in the late Middle Ages, when West Africa became the principal source of supply for Western Europe. However, the quantitative basis for this judgement is virtually non-existent,[96] and it is interesting to note that as late as 1937 there were still many thousands of independent African producers, whose total output in French West Africa was estimated in that year to be three and a half tons. Gold was found in four main areas: around Bambouk, Boure and Lobi in the Western Sudan, and in Ashanti in the forest. The chief methods of production were panning alluvial streams, which was a simple, though time-consuming, task, and quarrying gold-bearing ore, which was a more complex operation. Akan miners in the eighteenth century dug slanting pits with broad steps to a depth of as much as 150 feet. The miners at the bottom dug out the ore and loaded it on trays, which were then passed up to the surface by means of a human chain. At Boure, on the other hand, parallel vertical shafts were sunk to a depth of about forty feet and then joined underground by a horizontal tunnel. The miners at the face used picks to dislodge the ore, which was then put in a calabash and hauled to the surface. This system required a considerable degree of specialisation and co-ordination within each unit of production, and involved, typically, miners, carriers, washers, a smith to maintain tools in good condition, and a foreman, who directed operations, sold the gold to smiths and

[96] Mauny's oft-quoted estimate of total production (*Tableau géographique* . . . , p. 301) is best treated with caution.

traders, and bought necessary supplies of foodstuffs. The ore extracted by these means was either pounded, washed, screened and packaged in the form of gold dust, or placed in a furnace and heated with a flux in order to purify it, in which case the final product was made up into bars or wires.

Rulers who were fortunate enough to have gold deposits in their territories sought either to control production or to tax the sales of independent producers. The extent of the wealth which a privileged minority was able to acquire by these means is illustrated by the famous pilgrimage of Mansa Musa, the ruler of the Mali empire, who left West Africa for Mecca in 1324. His splendid passage through Cairo had an unsettling effect on exchange rates, as al-Omari noted: 'the people of Cairo earned incalculable sums from him whether by buying and selling or by gifts. So much gold was current in Cairo that it ruined the value of money. . . .'[97] Such profligacy also nearly ruined Mansa Musa, who experienced serious political troubles on his return to West Africa.

Salt was in many ways the most interesting and important of the minerals produced in West Africa. Salt, like water, is a biological requirement of both humans and livestock, a regular intake being necessary for survival. Salt deprivation is a particularly acute problem in hot areas, where salt resources are limited or far from the centres of demand, where the consumption of meat or fish is generally low, and where the diet is based largely on cereals. Much of West Africa, and especially parts of the Western Sudan, fell into this category.[98] In Gao, the capital of the Songhai, salt was so rare that it was kept in the stores of the royal treasury in the tenth century. Security arrangements are understandable because salt sometimes exchanged at par with gold on a weight for weight basis. No wonder Arab travellers of the period remarked that to avoid waste rock salt was always licked, and never ground and sprinkled!

Along the coast of West Africa salt was obtained by boiling sea water and occasionally by natural evaporation. In the interior, however, salt was harder to come by because the main sources lay far from the centres of demand. The Western Sudan drew its supplies from five major deposits situated in, or close to, the Sahara. At Awlil in the west and Bilma in the east salt was obtained by leaching saline soils. Production at Awlil, which was close to the sea, was a seasonal and ancillary occupation of local fishermen. The resources at Bilma were in the hands of the Tuareg, who controlled the oases of the area. In the second half of the nineteenth century Bilma exported over 50,000 camel loads of salt annually, and the trade continues today, though on a reduced scale. Rock salt was obtained from Idjil, Teghaza and Taoudeni. The resources at Idjil, seven layers deep, were developed between the eleventh and fifteenth centuries. Teghaza, east of Idjil, was probably the leading source of supply from the eighth century until its capture by the Moroccans in 1585. Taoudeni, about one hundred miles to the south, began to expand after the decline of Teghaza, but

---

[97] Quoted in Basil Davidson, *The African Past*, Harmondsworth 1966, p. 85.
[98] So, too, did India, as is shown by T. Banerjee, *Internal Market of India, 1834–1900*, Calcutta 1966.

47

may not have been an adequate substitute, for the period following 1585 also saw an increase in the production of an inferior type of vegetable salt in the area of the middle Niger. Nevertheless, the biannual caravans which set out from Timbuctu to Taoudeni in the late nineteenth century commonly had a combined total of 25–30,000 camels, and carried about 4–5,000 tons of salt on the return journey. Slaves were employed at Idjil, Teghaza and Taoudeni to cut and load salt bars. The work was arduous and had to be performed in the most gruelling conditions: it was so dry at Teghaza that even some of the buildings were made of salt. Historians of Africa who are apt to praise great states and famous men should remember that the glittering courts of Ghana, Mali and Songhai were maintained at a considerable cost in human life.

Non-specialists may be surprised to learn that pre-colonial West Africa had a range of manufacturing industries which closely resembled those of pre-industrial societies in other parts of the world.[99] The composition of the manufacturing sector in West Africa, as in pre-industrial Europe, reflected the embryonic nature of the market, and was based on clothing, metal working, ceramics, construction, and food processing.

The most important of these manufactures was clothing, which consisted chiefly of cotton cloth, though silks, woollens and raffia cloth were produced in some localities. Cotton, a long-established crop in West Africa, was manufactured at a very early date, though it seems probable that the expansion of the industry began with the spread of Islam from the eighth century onwards. Muslim influence led to greater contact with the markets of the Arab world and Europe, and also stimulated domestic demand by introducing new and more exacting standards of dress. By the twelfth century cotton goods from the Western Sudan had become well known in Europe, so much so that the terms *bouracan* or *bougran*, which were derived from Mandingo words, were being used there to describe certain types of cloth.[100] All stages of the manufacturing process—ginning, carding, spinning, dyeing and weaving—were performed locally. At the close of the sixteenth century the city of Timbuctu, on the southern border of the Sahara, had twenty-six master tailors, many of whom employed between fifty and one hundred apprentices and workers. By the middle of the nineteenth century Kano (in what is now northern Nigeria) had become in influence, if not in organisation, the Manchester of West Africa. The famous traveller, Barth, advertised the town's achievements in the following way:

> There is really something grand in this kind of industry, which spreads to the north as far as Murzuk, Ghat, and even Tripoli; to the west not only to Timbuctu, but in some degree even as far as the shores of the Atlantic, the very inhabitants of Arguin [an island off the West African coast] dressing in the cloth woven and dyed in Kano; to the east all over Bornu, although there it comes into contact with the native industry of the country; and to the south it maintains a rivalry with the

[99] See, for example, L. A. Clarkson, *The Pre-Industrial Economy in England*, 1971, pp. 75–85.
[100] F.-J. Nicolas, 'Le bouracan ou bougran: tissu soudanais du moyen âge', *Anthropos*, 53, 1958, pp. 265–8.

native industry of the Igbira and Igbo, while toward the southeast it invades the whole of Adamawa, and is only limited by the nakedness of the pagan *sansculottes*, who do not wear clothing.[101]

Barth estimated that Kano's cloth sales amounted to at least 300,000,000 cowries a year in the 1850s, which was equivalent to about £40,000. There were, in addition, many smaller centres besides Timbuctu and Kano, each known for its speciality, which was based on producing cloth of a particular weight, design and colour.[102]

Hides and skins, and the leather goods made from them, were produced mostly in the Western Sudan, where the main centres of animal husbandry lay. Many of these products were exported and became known in Europe as 'Moroccan' leather, though in fact a proportion of the goods passing under this name originated in West Africa. Metal working, as noted earlier, was a long-established craft, and blacksmiths were especially important. At the beginning of the seventeenth century Jobson, an English traveller on the Gambian coast, observed that the smith 'makes their Swords, Assegay heads, Darts and Arrow heads barbed; and instruments of Husbandry, without which they could not live. Hee hath his Bellowes, small Anvill, and Cole of a red wood, which alone will give the heat to our Iron.'[103] Pottery was also a widespread craft, and provided the majority of the containers needed for liquids and foodstuffs. The elements of a construction industry existed too. Most dwellings were probably built by the household concerned with some assistance from neighbours and other kinsmen, but the erection and maintenance of substantial dwellings in large towns created a demand for more specialised groups of builders, plasterers and woodworkers. Finally, it is worth noting that the processing of staple foods and drinks for sale outside the household was a common, and predominantly female, activity in urban centres and on trade routes.

In the absence of a sufficient number of case studies of pre-colonial manufactures, it is impossible to set down a series of summarising and definitive statements regarding the organisation and location of West African industries. Nevertheless, some speculative comments are called for in order to suggest that 'primitive' industry, like 'primitive' agriculture, can be understood in formalist terms, and also to direct the attention of other scholars to this neglected subject.

Most craft production was on a small scale, and was based on the household unit. The majority of crafts were governed by guilds, which often represented one or more households.[104] Guilds exercised control over entry to a craft, methods of production, standards of workmanship and prices. Consequently, membership of a

---

[101] H. Barth, *Travels and Discoveries in North and Central Africa*, centenary ed., 1, 1965, p. 511. Barth was in Kano in 1851.

[102] For a comprehensive list of centres of cloth production in West Africa, see Sundström, *The Trade of Guinea*, pp. 147–86.

[103] Quoted in Basil Davidson, *The African Past*, Harmondsworth 1966, p. 204.

[104] For a detailed case study see P. C. Lloyd, 'Craft Organisation in Yoruba Towns', *Africa*, 23, 1953, pp. 30–44.

craft was usually inherited, though it was sometimes possible for outsiders to join a guild once they had completed an apprenticeship. The household employed little fixed capital and used its liquid resources to buy necessary inputs, such as raw materials and labour. The purchase of some raw materials was unavoidable, but there was scope for economising on labour costs. Hence the use of inexpensive family labour, and the preference found over a wide range of crafts (including cloth-working, gold-smithing and canoe-building) for slave rather than wage labour. The economics of small scale production can be illustrated by the example of ceramics. Pottery was a widespread craft because the necessary raw materials were readily available and easily worked, and because the transportation of hollow-ware was difficult (since there was a high risk of breakages) and costly (since the finished product took up more space than the constituent raw materials). It was virtually impossible to sustain a long distance trade in pottery, apart from a few, high quality items. Dispersal was sound policy because it avoided the diseconomies which centralisation would have brought. Since each unit of production catered for a restricted market, it made sense to limit the degree of specialisation. Hence pottery tended to be a part-time occupation, reaching a peak of activity during the dry season, when the clay was more easily fired, and when labour demands on the farm were light.[105] Equally, there was little point in investing in capital equipment. Consequently, even relatively simple pieces of machinery, such as the potter's wheel, were not used.

Industrial concentrations were most likely to be found where raw materials were comparatively rare and needed some initial processing before they could be transported, and where the existence of a nearby and substantial market reduced the cost of delivering finished goods to the consumer. The Kano cloth industry provides a good example of the application of these two conditions. Concentrated employment was favoured by the presence of the two principal raw materials, cotton and indigo, both of which were grown in the area, by proximity to a large domestic market in and around Kano itself, and by the highly efficient distributive network organised by Hausa traders, which secured access to markets in other parts of West Africa. In these circumstances the Kano cloth industry could support a number of specialised artisans and some sizeable units of production. Nevertheless, it would be a mistake to contrast the organisation of the Kano textile industry too sharply with that of smaller centres. Kano producers used the same narrow loom as was found in other parts of West Africa, and most cloth workers were semi-specialists, who operated independently or were co-ordinated in a putting-out and collection system. In the absence of cost-reducing technical innovations, Kano's prominence derived from the external economies which it enjoyed, together with the product differentiation (based on colour and pattern) which it achieved, rather than from genuine economies of scale within the manufacturing firm itself.

---

[105] Every generalisation has its exceptions, and it should be noted that there were specialised women potters in some areas.

3   The distributive system

The preceding discussion has emphasised the variety of pre-colonial systems of production and analysed their logical basis, but so far little has been said about output targets—the economic goals of productive activities. A consideration of the exchange sector should remedy this omission. It will be argued that the concept of a subsistence economy needs to be modified substantially to take account of the fact that exchange was widespread; that the organisation of trade and markets was both complex and efficient; that the channels of recruitment to, and the prestige rankings of, mercantile occupations demonstrate that the conventional distinction between ascribed (traditional) and achieved (modern) status has little connection with reality; that a general purpose currency and an embryonic capital market had evolved at an early date; and that established statements regarding pre-colonial transport systems have succeeded in entrenching a series of misconceptions about a subject which has yet to be fully investigated.

All the products considered so far, from neolithic rice to nineteenth-century cloth, were traded within West Africa. Descriptive evidence showing that exchange was widespread in the pre-colonial period is overwhelming, and refers to the greater part of the region, whether forest or savanna, whether influenced by Islam or animism, whether in areas controlled by large, centralised states or among small communities in which political authority was dispersed.[106] Quantitative data, unfortunately, are less plentiful, though a few estimates are available for the nineteenth century.[107] In the 1850s Barth reckoned that the trade of Kano amounted to about £100,000 a year; at the close of the nineteenth century the commerce of Timbuctu, then in decline, was estimated to be worth roughly £80,000 a year; and in 1900 Baillaud published a map showing some fifty towns (excluding those in Nigeria and the southern part of the Gold Coast) which between them had an annual trade of £1 million. The majority of households undoubtedly produced the greater part of the goods they required as consumers, but the pure, subsistence economy was an exception rather than the rule. Most households regarded trade as a normal and an integral part of their activities, and planned their production strategy accordingly. To grasp this point is also to reformulate the question of market growth in at least some underdeveloped societies. The problem ceases to be one of introducing exchange to closed, self-sufficient communities, where wants are limited and commercial institutions non-existent, and becomes the more realistic and interesting issue of

---

[106] Evidence representing a variety of disciplinary approaches is contained in Paul Bohannan and George Dalton, eds., *Markets in Africa*, Evanston 1962; Elliott P. Skinner, 'West African Economic Systems', in *Economic Transition in Africa*, ed. Melville J. Herskovits and Mitchell Harwitz, 1964, pp. 77–97; Lars Sundström, *The Trade of Guinea*, Lund 1965; Centre of African Studies, *Markets and Marketing in West Africa*, University of Edinburgh, mimeo., 1966; B. W. Hodder and U. I. Ukwu, *Markets in West Africa*, Ibadan 1969; Marvin P. Miracle, ed., 'Markets and Market Relationships', *African Urban Notes*, 5, 1970, pp. 1–174; and Claude Meillassoux, ed., *The Development of Indigenous Trade and Markets in West Africa*, 1971.

[107] I am grateful to Marion Johnson for the examples which follow.

identifying the constraints inhibiting the further development of an already established exchange sector.

Social scientists have given considerable thought to the problem of understanding the internal trade of pre-colonial Africa. The most publicised analysis of this subject is that proposed by Bohannan and Dalton, which is based on a distinction between the market place and the market principle.[108] Bohannan and Dalton have advanced a three-fold classification: first, societies which lack markets and in which market principles are hardly present; second, societies which have market places, but in which market principles operate peripherally; and third, societies in which the market place has declined, but in which market principles have become dominant. The first two categories are said to apply to Africa, while the last is typical of industrial societies. Communities of the first two types can be thought of as being multicentric, having distinct transactional spheres distinguished by different goods and services, and operating according to discrete principles of exchange. In multicentric economies the laws of supply and demand are less important in determining the terms of exchange than are principles of reciprocity and redistribution. The aim of economic endeavour is to 'convert' goods from one sphere (such as subsistence) to another (such as prestige) in order to achieve goals which are essentially social in character.

This is a subtle analysis, and it has stimulated, directly and indirectly, a great deal of further research. However, Bohannan and Dalton's classification will not be used here for the following reasons (which, because of limitations of space, will have to be stated briefly). The chief criticism is one, curiously, which has not been stressed before, possibly because most commentators have been economic anthropologists rather than historians. Although Bohannan and Dalton claim that their first two categories are applicable to 'traditional' societies in Africa, neither author has made more than brief use of sources which historians would regard as necessary to the analysis of the pre-colonial period. It so happens that during the past ten years historical research has shown that both the market place and the market principle were more important than Bohannan and Dalton allowed in their publication of 1962. Their claim that peripheral markets do not influence production decisions is at variance with the evidence. The extent to which market activity failed to mobilise the factors of production fully is better explained in terms of economics (technological limitations and constraints on demand) than in terms of social controls based on anti-capitalist values. Even if it is assumed that the market principle was in some sense peripheral, this insight turns out to be less helpful than it appears at first. The crucial problem is to find a way of measuring the degree of peripherality, but this, admittedly daunting, task is not one which Bohannan and Dalton have attempted. Their case rests on the assumption that there is a sharp contrast in the values governing multicentric and unicentric economies. However, this belief is based on ideal types rather than realities. It is not values and goals which distinguish pre-industrial from

---

[108] 'Introduction', to *Markets in Africa*, ed. Paul Bohannan and George Dalton, Evanston 1962, pp. 1–26.

industrial societies so much as the structure of the two types of economy, which provide different means of achieving what, in general terms, are similar ends. Principles of reciprocity and redistribution undoubtedly operated to some extent in Africa,[109] but they can also be found in industrial societies both in private and in public sectors. Moreover, industrial societies are concerned with social as well as economic values. The American millionaire remains at his desk not to make money, but to exercise power and to maintain his prominence in the community, or, in African parlance, to be regarded as a 'big' man. Similarly, a successful English businessman may well put money into a football club instead of opening a new factory. In short, *all* societies are to some extent multicentric, but until means are devised of distinguishing differences of degree this observation is of limited use.

The classification adopted here is a simple one based on a distinction between local and long distance trade. Local trade refers to transactions which took place within a radius of up to about ten miles of the area of production. This was the range which could be covered in one day by foot or by donkey, while still allowing time to exchange products and return home. Beyond this radius it was necessary to make arrangements for overnight stops, to reallocate work in the household, and sometimes to make use of professional carriers and commercial intermediaries. This distinction has been criticised, though mainly by those who have been influenced in varying degrees by the substantivist viewpoint.[110] However, it is worth pointing out, in anticipation of an additional objection, that classifications of trade, as of other economic and social institutions, are best judged according to their suitability for the particular purpose their advocate has in mind, rather than with reference to an ideal, comprehensive classification which will be fully revealed to the diligent scholar providing he searches hard enough. Having established that trade was widespread, the distinction between local and long distance commerce becomes helpful because it draws attention to differences in degrees of specialisation, in types of commercial institution, in the composition of the goods traded, and in the nature of consumer demand. In other words, instead of discussing constraints on the development of the market as a whole, as if the market were homogeneous, this distinction permits some refinement of analysis by making it possible to identify the blockages appropriate to each category of trade.

The first issue to be considered concerns the origins of local trade. Hodder has questioned the view that local exchange and local markets arose naturally in West Africa as a result of the complementary needs of communities which were in close proximity to each other, and has suggested instead that local trade was stimulated

[109] See, for example, Ronald Cohen, 'Some Aspects of Institutionalized Exchange: a Kanuri Example', *Cahiers d'Études Africaines*, 5, 1965, pp. 353–69.

[110] Richard Gray and David Birmingham, 'Some Economic and Social Consequences of Trade in Central and Eastern Africa in the Pre-Colonial Period', in *Pre-Colonial African Trade: Essays on Trade in Central and Eastern Africa Before 1900*, ed. Richard Gray and David Birmingham, 1970, pp. 2–5, and Claude Meillassoux, 'Introduction' to *The Development of Indigenous Trade and Markets in West Africa*, ed. Claude Meillassoux, 1971, pp. 67–8. However, it should be noted that these authors also qualify the argument advanced by Bohannan and Dalton.

primarily by long distance, and especially external, commerce.[111] This interpretation, it is said, helps to explain the existence of certain marketless areas in West Africa, and also the contrast with East Africa, where, so it is claimed, there was no comparable long distance trade in the pre-colonial period and less local exchange too. However, the historical evidence provides no clear justification for choosing between these two views. It will be argued here that local exchange needs were important in the creation of local markets, *and* that long distance trade had a stimulating effect on marketing activity at all levels. As for the contrast with other parts of the continent, recent research has indicated that the assumption that East Africa had little long distance trade is mistaken.[112]

Short distance trade resulted from the production strategy of local households, and from variations in the natural and human resource endowment of the microenvironment. The basic aim of most households was to secure the products needed to maintain their customary standards of living. In order to reach this target each household tried to plant the amount of crops needed for survival in what, from experience, was known to be a poor year. In planning for disaster, there would be more crops available in an average year than the household could consume. Sometimes these crops were stored for future use, but this was not always possible with perishable varieties. Sometimes they were consumed in harvest 'festivals', but there were limitations to the amount of food which one community could eat in a short period of time. Sometimes, if neighbouring villages lacked foodstuffs, local produce was traded. This type of trade can be thought of as a system of compensation, equalising losses experienced elsewhere. A surplus was planned, but trade was unpremeditated. This example has been cited to show that exchange potential was present even where production levels were governed by the siege mentality associated with pure, subsistence economies. A more typical case was that of households which regularly planned their production of foodstuffs and crafts with a certain amount of exchange in mind. Trade of this kind was made possible by the presence of complementary needs within regions which are sometimes regarded, wrongly, as being uniform. Variations in natural resources did not have to be profound for local trade to develop, though marketing activity was especially intense on the borders of ecological zones. Usually, it was not a question of sharply contrasting specialisms, but of a subtle shift of emphasis between adjacent areas with very similar economies. For example, one village might grow foodstuffs of a different variety or better quality than the next, or produce a particular colour or design of cloth. Human resources also lacked the homogeneity claimed in textbook generalisations about 'traditional' societies. The concept of the average household disguises the possibility, discussed earlier in this chapter, that wealth could be distributed in an unbalanced way even in a small community in an underdeveloped region. Inequalities meant that some members of the community could afford to trade, while

[111] B. W. Hodder, 'Some Comments on the Origins of Traditional Markets in Africa South of the Sahara', *Transactions of the Institute of British Geographers*, 36, 1965, pp. 97–105.
[112] Richard Gray and David Birmingham, eds, *Pre-Colonial African Trade: Essays on Trade in Central and Eastern Africa Before 1900*, 1970.

others needed to secure goods which they had failed to produce for themselves.[113]

Most local exchange was conducted in the market place, though Muslim women frequently traded within their compounds. A typical example of a local market near the Senegal river was described by Cadamosto, a Venetian sailor, in the fifteenth century.

> Hither repaired, with their wares, both men and women, for four or five miles about; and those who lived at a greater distance went to other markets nearer them. The great poverty of this people appeared in the goods found in these faires; which were, a few pieces of cotton-cloth, cotton-yarn, pulse, oil, millet, wooden tubs, palm mats, and everything else for the use of life.[114]

Towns were capable of generating a greater and more varied demand for local products. The expansion of the port of Lagos, for instance, set up demands which stimulated production in the hinterland.[115] This 'spread effect' is illustrated by the following list of African goods on sale in the nearby market of Ejirin in September 1892:[116]

Foodstuffs	Raw Materials	Livestock	Manufactures
Asala nuts	Cotton	Bullocks	Calabashes
Beans	Indigo	Ducks	Cotton cloth
Benniseed	Palm kernels	Goats	Pots
Egusi seeds	Potash	Guinea fowl	Soap
Farina		Horses	Yarn
Groundnuts		Pigeons	
Locust seeds		Sheep	
Maize		Turkeys	
Okra			
Palm oil			
Pepper			
Shea butter			
Yams			
Yam flour			

Of these thirty-one items, only two (palm oil and palm kernels) were important in overseas trade.

Markets were not distributed at random, nor was the timing of market days a matter of 'custom and impulse'. Continuous markets, that is markets which were in almost permanent session, were found mainly in large towns. Elsewhere, markets

---

[113] Polly Hill, 'The Myth of the Amorphous Peasantry: a Northern Nigerian Case Study', *Nigerian Journal of Economic and Social Studies*, 10, 1968, pp. 239–60.

[114] Thomas Astley, ed., *A New General Collection of Voyages and Travels*, 1745, p. 587.

[115] This example may be compared with that of London at an earlier date. See F. J. Fisher, 'The Development of the London Food Market, 1540-1640', *Economic History Review*, 5, 1935, pp. 46–64.

[116] C.O. 147/86, Carter to Ripon, 4 Oct. 1892, Public Record Office.

were held at intervals of between two and eight days, and occasionally longer.[117] Today, seven-day markets are the most common in West Africa as a whole, though four-day markets are more typical of the forest east of Ghana. Periodic markets were usually formed into rings or cycles, though the arrangement was by no means rigid and it also changed in the course of time, as some markets fell into disuse and others were founded. The frequency with which any one market was held depended on the number of markets in a particular ring. For example, in a ring containing just two markets each met on alternate days, and a two-day market week operated. The sequence of meetings was decided by the principle that 'proximity in space implies separation in time'.[118] That is to say, two markets which were part of a larger ring were unlikely to meet on consecutive days if they were only a short distance apart, because to do so might lead to needless duplication. Periodic markets were often held at places which were convenient to several settlements, but which did not coincide with any one of them. It was possible for a local market to attract several thousand people on the day it met, yet to be almost completely deserted during the rest of the week.

Periodicity was primarily a function of the volume and spatial distribution of purchasing power. Where effective demand was strong and concentrated in a small area, such as an urban centre, continuous markets predominated. Where demand was weaker and spread over dispersed settlements, periodic markets were the rule. The formation of market rings provided each community in a given area with easy and regular access to goods and services which it needed. At the same time the device which ensured that each market met at a specified interval kept the costs of collection and distribution to a minimum. Rotating markets, like systems of shifting and rotational cultivation, were an expression of the principle that the costs of permanence were not justified by the returns.

The traders involved in local exchange tended to be predominantly female, part-time, small scale, mobile and numerous. They were mainly female because local trade was a convenient adjunct to household and, in some societies, farming activities; they were part-time because trade was regarded as a supplement, though often an important one, to primary, domestic occupations; they were small scale because they lacked the capital to be anything else; they were mobile (except in the towns) because the most efficient way of connecting buyers and sellers was by bringing them together in periodic, rotating markets; and they were numerous because local trade was a generally accessible way of adding to farm incomes, since it required few managerial or technical skills and little capital.

[117] On periodic markets see Polly Hill, 'Notes on Traditional Market Authority and Market Periodicity in West Africa', *Journal of African History*, 7, 1966, pp. 295–311; B. W. Hodder, 'Periodic and Daily Markets in West Africa', in *The Development of Indigenous Trade and Markets in West Africa*, ed. Claude Meillassoux, 1971, pp. 347–58; and the comprehensive study by Robert H. T. Smith, 'West African Market-Places: Temporal Periodicity and Locational Spacing', in *ibid.*, pp. 319–46.

[118] Vernon G. Fagerlund and Robert H. T. Smith, 'A Preliminary Map of Market Periodicities in Ghana', *Journal of Developing Areas*, 4, 1970, p. 343.

It used to be thought that the employment of many hands increased distribution costs unnecessarily. During the colonial period expatriate officials and companies often complained about the large number of local traders, believing, with their Tudor predecessors, that 'middlemen' (by which they meant *other* middlemen) were 'Marchauntes of myschyefe that go betwixt the barke and the tree'.[119] However, it is now agreed that the distributive system was efficient, even if it did employ a multiplicity of intermediaries. There was no cheaper way of serving a market in which most consumers had low per capita incomes and were scattered in dispersed settlements. Competition in local trade was fierce because there were hardly any barriers to entry and few alternative employment opportunities. Consequently, profit margins were slender. Of course, there were some imperfections in the market, but these should be seen not as evidence of the 'primitive' nature of pre-colonial exchange, but as a reminder that perfect competition is an ideal which is rarely found in the real world, even in industrial societies. A variety of traders' organisations existed in West Africa, and these tried to exert a measure of control over prices and competition.[120] However, the indications are that the prices of most goods in local markets were determined mainly by supply and demand, and that the haggling skills of the parties concerned played an important part in deciding the exact price agreed in any single transaction. Traders' organisations had greater success in representing the interests of their members in negotiations with state authorities, and in helping to enforce regulations regarding weights and measures, and laws governing debt, contract and agency.[121] The indigenous distributive system was not made redundant by the 'impact of modern capitalism'. On the contrary, the skill, efficiency and adaptability of local traders assisted the rapid expansion of internal trade during the colonial era.[122]

The conditions which gave rise to local trade also set limits to its expansion.[123] On the supply side, pre-industrial costs of production meant that there was no way of reducing the selling prices of foodstuffs and crafts to the point where consumers could have afforded significantly greater quantities without any change taking place in average per capita incomes. It seems likely that a greater volume of goods could have been produced at constant unit prices with the factors already available, but constraints on the demand side meant that this happened only sporadically. The 'primitive' consumer was perfectly willing to depart from established consumption levels, but lacked the means of doing so. Variations in the resource base enabled a

---

[119] R. H. Tawney and Eileen Power, eds, *Tudor Economic Documents*, 3, 1924, p. 49.

[120] There is scope for further work on these organisations, especially those involving women traders.

[121] For a study of the most famous weights see Brigitte Menzel, *Goldweights from Ghana*, Berlin 1968. For information on indigenous commercial law in one area see A. G. Hopkins, 'A Report on the Yoruba, 1910', *Journal of the Historical Society of Nigeria*, 5, 1969, pp. 88–92.

[122] As is shown in Chapter 7, section 2.

[123] With more space and more information it would be possible to construct a detailed flow chart of local goods and services along the lines developed by Frederick Barth, 'Economic Spheres in Darfur', in *Themes in Economic Anthropology*, ed. Raymond Firth, 1967, pp. 149–74.

certain amount of trade to take place, but limitations to complementarity in a small area meant that it was usually possible for households to supply acceptable substitutes for most of the goods offered for sale. In other words, the kinds of goods which farmers were best able to produce and trade were already being produced and traded equally cheaply by those who were their potential customers. Consequently, the scope for exchange was limited and per capita incomes remained low. If per capita incomes had risen markedly, the proportion of the increase spent on foodstuffs would have declined, while that spent on manufactures, such as cloth, would have grown. As this development did not occur, the effective demand for craft products remained small. Consumers with net incomes above the average were able to spend more on manufactures, but there were too few of them in any one locality to induce producers to specialise and to introduce cost-reducing techniques.

Long distance trade can be regarded as an attempt by African entrepreneurs to overcome the limitations of local commerce. Constraints still existed on the supply side, because it was just as expensive to produce goods for long distance trade as for sale locally. On the demand side, however, long distance trade presented an opportunity of connecting social islands of purchasing power, that is consumers who, though only a small proportion of the total population, had sufficient wealth between them to support a market which was greater than that available to local traders in any one area. The less affluent majority participated in this commerce to a certain extent by using profits accumulated from local trading activities to purchase cheaper types of cloth and small quantities of essential items, such as salt. In general, however, long distance trade tended to cater for the needs of relatively high income groups because only prosperous consumers could afford to pay prices which took account of the scarcity value of items that were unavailable locally, and the greater handling costs and risks of carrying goods beyond the area of production.[124] These principles help to explain the composition and organisation of long distance trade not only in Africa, but also in other parts of the world, as the examples of the fur trade of pre-industrial Europe and the silk trade of the Far East clearly demonstrate.[125]

A complex network of trade routes had to be created in order to reach these geographically dispersed islands of relatively wealthy consumers. Some of the most important long distance routes were aligned on north–south axes, because these crossed major geographical zones, which, as noted earlier, ran from west to east in roughly parallel bands. Thus the pastoralists of the Sahara-savanna border traded livestock, dairy produce and salt with the cultivators of the savanna in return for millet and cloth. In turn, the savanna region traded livestock, salt, dried fish, potash and cloth with the peoples of the forest, from whom they received slaves, kola

---

[124] The assumption (criticised earlier in this chapter) that there were no marked inequalities of wealth in pre-colonial African societies makes it extremely difficult to explain the existence and longevity of long distance trade.

[125] See T. S. Willan, *The Early History of the Russia Company, 1553–1603*, 1956, and C. G. F. Simkin, *The Traditional Trade of Asia*, 1968.

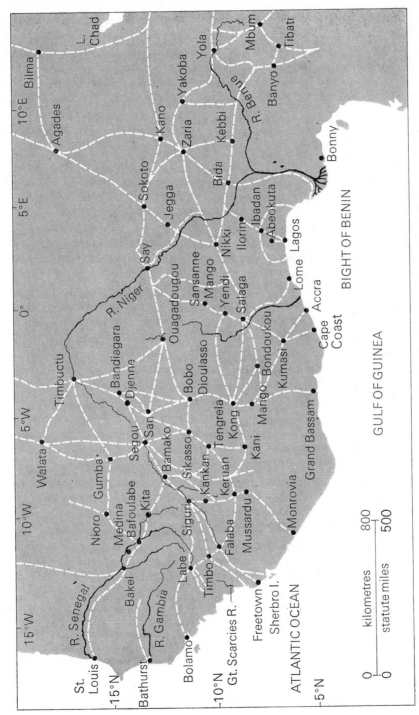

MAP 6. Major Trade Routes of the Western Sudan in the Nineteenth Century.

nuts,[126] ivory, ironware and cloth. Finally, producers in the forest sold various food-stuffs and manufactures to coastal settlements in exchange for fish and sea salt. There were other routes, however, which ran in a west–east direction, for complementary needs could arise quite easily within regions as large as the savanna and the forest. Slaves, dried fish and Kano cloth, for instance, were sold throughout the Western Sudan. There was also some movement of foodstuffs outside the locality of production: the great entrepôt of Timbuctu imported grain, vegetables and livestock from the twelfth century onwards, and in the fifteenth century there was a considerable trade in millet, rice, cotton and livestock within the empire of Mali. Similarly, slaves, rare beads and Yoruba and Ashanti cloth were traded throughout the forest.

The foregoing list of commodities and inter-regional connections makes it clear that simple, bilateral exchanges were the exception rather than the rule. Long distance trade in West Africa involved re-exports and multilateral relations, and was equally as complicated, protracted and risky as the better known triangular trade which spanned the Atlantic in the seventeenth and eighteenth centuries. Long distance commerce in Africa raises some fascinating, and as yet unanswerable, questions regarding the terms of trade and the balance of trade between various regions, the direction of money flows and their significance in settling debts outstanding on the trading account, and the ways in which the balance of payments between states and regions was affected by external commerce across the Sahara and Atlantic.[127]

The traders involved in long distance commerce were less numerous and more specialised than those whose activities were confined to local markets. This broad contrast needs further refinement, for it is clear that long distance traders were not all of one type. It is suggested here, by way of preliminary classification, that they can be divided, on the basis of size and specialisation, into four sub-groups.

First, there were target marketeers, that is occasional traders who made a few trips, usually during the dry season, with cloth, salt or kola nuts in order to acquire a specific sum of money for a particular purpose. These men usually provided their own finance, and also carried their own goods. Target marketeers were relatively unimportant, and their motivation was certainly not typical of long-distance traders as a whole.[128]

Second, there was a group of regular traders whose commercial operations were integrated vertically (at least initially) with a specialised type of productive activity. For instance, Kooroko blacksmiths from Ouassoulou (in southern Mali) built up stocks of implements and weapons, sold them when prices were particularly favourable, and used the proceeds to enter the salt and kola trades, moving alter-

---

[126] Kola nuts are a mild stimulant containing caffeine. They were (and still are) chewed to relieve tiredness and to overcome thirst. The most popular variety was *cola nitida*, which was grown in the forest from Guinea east to the Gold Coast. The main centres of demand lay in the Western Sudan, a dry region, and also one in which Muslim influence prohibited the consumption of alcohol.

[127] Clearly, these are subjects which deserve further research.

[128] Kwame Arhin, 'Atebubu Markets, *ca.* 1884–1930', in *The Development of Indigenous Trade and Markets in West Africa*, ed. Claude Meillassoux, 1971, p. 207.

nately north (for salt) and south (for kola nuts).[129] A further example is provided by the intricate exchanges conducted by the tobacco farmers of Katsina (in northern Nigeria) during the late nineteenth century.[130] These farmers grew tobacco, stored the crop for six or nine months until prices rose, and then sold it in Zinder and Agades (100 and 250 miles away). With the proceeds they bought cattle, sheep and goats, and then returned home. They set off again a few weeks later, when the animals had been fattened, this time travelling south to Ilorin, Ibadan and Abeokuta (between 375 and 450 miles from Katsina). They sold their livestock, and then went on to Lagos to buy kola nuts, which they disposed of on their return home. This was a complicated business operation, particularly since these farmer-traders had to leave their land during the rainy season, a time of maximum inconvenience, and entrust the harvest to relatives and slaves so that they could secure the highest price for their tobacco. These two examples demonstrate that production strategies *were* influenced by market principles during the pre-colonial period.

Third, there were highly specialised and substantial professional traders. These men had no direct control over the production of the goods they handled, but they did establish a degree of horizontal integration with respect to particular staples, partly by using kinsmen and slaves to staff a network of 'branches' along the main trade routes. In the nineteenth century the merchants of Djenne, a large town on the middle Niger, were said to have

> organised 'business firms' in the European sense of the word, which were provided with a routine and staff similar to our own. They established representatives in important centres and opened branches at Timbuctu. They sent out travelling agents who received percentages of the business they accomplished, and were, in fact, none other than 'commercial travellers'.[131]

The two leading groups of professional, long distance traders were the Dioula and the Hausa. The former were of Mande origin and were especially important in the western part of West Africa, though they traded south-east as far as the forests of the Ivory Coast, selling livestock, fish and cloth, and buying kola nuts and slaves. Hausa traders were dominant in the eastern part of West Africa, spreading out from their base in northern Nigeria as far south-west as the Gold Coast, where they exchanged salt, cloth and livestock for gold, kola nuts and slaves.[132]

[129] The Kooroko have now become more specialised as traders, and their activities are no longer closely tied to their original craft. See Jean-Loup Amselle, 'Parenté et commerce chez les Kooroko', in *The Development of Indigenous Trade and Markets in West Africa*, ed. Claude Meillassoux, 1971, pp. 253–65.

[130] Polly Hill, *Studies in Rural Capitalism in West Africa*, Cambridge 1970, pp. 141–5.

[131] Felix Dubois, *Tombouctou la mystérieuse*, Paris 1897, p. 174.

[132] There were also several other groups, such as the Diakhanke, who traded in the hinterland of Senegambia and were especially prominent during the period 1600–1850. See Philip D. Curtin, 'Pre-Colonial Trading Networks and Traders: the Diakhanke', in *The Development of Indigenous Trade and Markets in West Africa*, ed. Claude Meillassoux, 1971, pp. 228–39.

Fourth, there were official traders, who transacted business on behalf of the state. Given that the need for revenue was a common preoccupation of all governments, it is not surprising that some states tried to raise money by participating in long distance trade. In Ashanti official trade was conducted by functionaries such as the *batafo*; in Dahomey royal rights over trade were delegated to a group of quasi-official merchants in return for a share of the profits; and in the Mossi states large caravans were organised by senior officials. In their commercial dealings, these states can be thought of as substantial firms. Public enterprise had access to the capital needed for long distance trade, and it was also in a position to secure privileges which, in theory at least, gave official traders a competitive advantage over private merchants. State enterprise was sometimes responsible for major commercial innovations, as, for example, in the case of the Ashanti government, which played a leading part in the development of the kola trade in the nineteenth century.[133] Nevertheless, it seems unlikely that state traders conducted a larger share of long distance trade than did independent merchants. Indeed, in some cases, as among the Akan states of the southern Gold Coast, public authorities deliberately refrained from engaging in trade directly, not because they were insensitive to commercial opportunities, but because they judged it more advantageous to encourage private traders and then to tax them.[134] The imposition of tolls and market dues was undoubtedly a widespread means of raising revenue,[135] and being a relatively simple and virtually riskless exercise, it may well have been preferred, on the whole, to direct trading.

Directly or indirectly, trade seems to have been an important source of state income, particularly since 'feudal' rents derived from land were far less common in Africa than they were in medieval Europe. All West African states had a keen interest in encouraging trade. Prudent rulers kept in close touch with leading traders and mercantile organisations, and commercial policy formed a large part of state policy as a whole. Pre-industrial states in other continents may well have hindered the expansion of the market, as is sometimes alleged, by imposing bureaucratic controls on private enterprise, and by directing policy towards the attainment of spiritual rather than economic goals. These arguments have little relevance for West Africa.

It is worth while looking more closely at the organisation of long distance commerce to see how African businessmen dealt with the problems of handling goods, of dealing with 'foreign' customers, and of raising the capital required to invest in costly, long term ventures. A study of the solutions devised for these difficulties should provide some indication of the capabilities of indigenous entrepreneurs.

Long distance traders of all types banded together in caravans, which resembled armed convoys, having guards, porters and drovers, as well as a leader, a guide, a

[133] Ivor Wilks, 'Asante Policy Towards the Hausa Trade in the Nineteenth Century', in *The Development of Indigenous Trade and Markets in West Africa*, ed. Claude Meillassoux, 1971, pp. 130–33.
[134] Kwame Y. Daaku, 'Trade and Trading Patterns of the Akan in the Seventeenth and Eighteenth Centuries', in *The Development of Indigenous Trade and Markets in West Africa*, ed. Claude Meillassoux, 1971, pp. 168–81.
[135] Sundström, *The Trade of Guinea*, pp. 5–13, 61–5.

treasurer and a quartermaster.[136] Hausa caravans in the nineteenth century consisted of 1–2,000 people, most of whom were armed, and an equal number of donkeys. They travelled for five or six hours each day on well established routes, where water and food were known to be available, and sent out scouts to search for brigands and to negotiate for supplies. The round trip from Sokoto to Ashanti (a total of about 1,200 miles) took between six months and one year. Caravans were like slowly moving markets, selling some of their goods on the route and paying for foodstuffs and services as they went. Without them, long distance trade would have been impossible. However, there were diseconomies of scale which became apparent during the colonial period. With greater freedom of movement and more secure markets, long distance traders began to travel in small groups, an arrangement which gave them flexibility in timing departures and arrivals, offered them a wider choice of routes, and reduced their overheads, since it was no longer necessary to contribute towards the cost of guards and guides. Large caravans became redundant in the twentieth century, but long distance trade survived: it was merely reorganised in ways which were less readily identifiable.

The caravans of the pre-colonial period commuted ponderously between large entrepôts, many of which were located at points of overlap between different ecological zones. A line of these markets ran from west to east along the Sahara-savanna border, and included towns such as Segou, Djenne, Timbuctu, Gao, Sokoto, Katsina and Kano. A similar chain existed in the south on the borders between the savanna and the forest, and included Bouna, Bondoukou, Begho, Onitsha and the Ashanti markets of Salaga and Kintampo. These entrepôts were bulking and bulk-breaking centres, and also places where goods were transferred from one mode of transport to another. On arrival at the entrepôts, the caravan broke up and the traders made contact with specialised agents, who helped them dispose of their goods and buy other products for the return journey. The two most important agents were landlords and brokers.[137] The former were wholesalers, who provided storage for goods, pasture for livestock and accommodation for traders. The latter were commission agents and interpreters, who played a crucial role as intermediaries between buyers and sellers, though sometimes they traded on their own account as well. Many goods were sold in the market place, but negotiations over some of the more valuable items, such as gold and salt, usually took place in the house of the landlord or broker concerned. Landlords and brokers based their business on personal connections, and were concerned to build up a reputation for fairness and honesty. Clapperton, who visited Kano in the 1820s, noted that

> if a *tobe* or a *turkadee* [cotton garments for men and women respectively] purchased here is carried to Bornu or any other distant place, without being opened, and is

[136] For further information see N. Levtzion, *Muslims and Chiefs in West Africa*, Oxford 1968, pp. 23–5, and Paul E. Lovejoy, 'Long-Distance Trade and Islam: the Case of the Nineteenth-Century Hausa Kola Trade', *Journal of the Historical Society of Nigeria*, 5, 1971, pp. 537–47.

[137] Sundström, *The Trade of Guinea*, pp. 57–60; Polly Hill, 'Landlords and Brokers: a West African Trading System', *Cahiers d'Études Africaines*, 6, 1966, pp. 349–66. It should be noted that some agents acted both as landlords and as brokers.

there discovered to be of inferior quality, it is immediately sent back, as a matter of course—the name of the *dylala*, or broker, being written inside every parcel. In this case, the *dylala* must find out the seller, who, by the laws of Kano, is forthwith obliged to refund the purchase money.[138]

This arrangement suggests a degree of modernity which modern consumers themselves might well envy.

Three of the chief requirements of long distance trade were capital, credit and security. These needs encouraged a trend towards the control of a particular staple, market or trade route by a family, by a lineage or even by a whole ethnic group. This tendency resulted partly from the fact that mobilising funds and securing credit depended largely on personal, face-to-face relationships,[139] and partly from a recognition that integration had advantages of spreading risks over a number of investors, of providing reliable agents in distant places, and of strengthening the bargaining position of traders in relation to landlords and brokers. At the same time it seems likely, though this is hypothetical, that this method of raising funds ultimately limited the growth of a firm, for it was not always possible for a family, still less for larger units, to co-operate successfully. A shortage of capital in any one firm would tend either to increase the total number of firms engaged in a particular trade, or (if new competitors were excluded) to keep the volume of trade below the level of effective demand. Even where co-operation was achieved, expansion could still be impeded by rival organisations. For example, Hausa merchants were encouraged to buy kola nuts, but were prevented by the Ashanti from entering the areas of production. Lack of capital, combined with political interference, often meant that goods had to be handed over by one group of merchants to another at staging posts and entrepôts, thus giving rise to a system of relay trading.[140]

Successful integration required a formal moral code to sanction and control commercial relationships. The 'blueprint' for the formation of a moral community of businessmen was provided by Islam, which was closely associated with long distance trade in West Africa from the eighth century onwards.[141] Islam helped maintain the identity of members of a network or firm who were scattered over a wide area, and often in foreign countries; it enabled traders to recognise, and hence to deal readily with, each other; and it provided moral and ritual sanctions to enforce a code of conduct which made trust and credit possible. It was through Islam that Dioula and

---

[138] Quoted in Thomas Hodgkin, *Nigerian Perspectives*, 1960, p. 217.

[139] The successful businessman demonstrated his importance and credit worthiness by his open-handed manner and conspicuous generosity. It is typical of the ethno-centric judgements made about the underdeveloped world that these characteristics are regarded as evidence of improvidence, whereas in the European context they are cited as examples of shrewd business sense.

[140] Sundström, *The Trade of Guinea*, p. 54; Jean-Louis Boutillier, 'La cité marchande de Bouna dans l'ensemble économique Ouest-Africain pré-colonial', in *The Development of Indigenous Trade and Markets in West Africa*, ed. Claude Meillassoux, 1971, pp. 240–52.

[141] See Abner Cohen's outstanding contribution, 'Cultural Strategies in the Organization of Trading Diasporas', in *The Development of Indigenous Trade and Markets in West Africa*, ed. Claude Meillassoux, 1971, pp. 266–81.

Hausa merchants established the commercial networks, or diasporas,[142] which made them so prominent and successful in long distance trade. Diasporas of various kinds have been an important feature of migration and innovation in many parts of the world besides Africa, as the contrasting examples of Chinese traders in south-east Asia and white settlers in the British empire illustrate.

An additional perspective on these regional and inter-continental migrations is provided by the concept of the frontier, which was applied originally to the development of the American west in the nineteenth century.[143] This concept has been considered in relation to the history of Europeans in Africa,[144] but it has not been used to identify and analyse the cultural and economic frontiers which existed *within* the continent in the pre-colonial period. The analogy with nineteenth-century America cannot be pressed too hard, but it is by no means as far-fetched as it might seem at first sight. Caravans, like wagon trains, developed a pioneer ethic borne of shared risk and common purpose; they often led to the foundation of new settlements (*zongos*); and they expressed a competitive and acquisitive spirit, which manifested itself in a search for new sources of wealth, as well as in trade in established staples. Muslim traders converted and clothed the 'pagan sans-culottes' with all the zeal of the Faithful — Islam being as much the inspiration of capitalist enterprise in West Africa as the Protestant ethic (which was once thought to have exclusive rights in this sphere) was in parts of Europe. Further consideration of the concepts of diasporas and frontiers in African history might well prove useful in focusing on regional differences, on pressures towards the expansion of the market economy, and on the reasons inhibiting the further advance of established boundaries of exchange.

It is tempting to conclude that the foregoing analysis demonstrates that pre-industrial business organisation was entirely different from that of the modern commercial world. This temptation should be resisted. Differences, of course, existed, but these can easily be exaggerated. Kinship, it is said, is replaced by contract; ascription becomes less important than achievement; and businessmen acquire more respect and status. These familiar contrasts are attractive partly because of their clarity and simplicity, and partly because they express approved liberal and democratic sentiments. Whether they relate to the realities of either the pre-industrial or the industrial world is open to question.

In practice, a great deal of the most important business of the leading industrial states today is transacted on a basis of mutual trust and confidence.[145] Furthermore, the cohesiveness of influential sections of the business community is maintained by developing a value system which assists recognisability and reinforces trustworthiness.[146] Promotion to senior positions in merchant banks, insurance companies and

---

142 In Cohen's phrase, a diaspora is 'an ethnic group in dispersal'.
143 Frederick Jackson Turner, *The Frontier in American History*, New York, 1920.
144 W. K. Hancock, *Survey of British Commonwealth Affairs*, 2, part 2, 1942.
145 Stewart Macaulay, 'Non-Contractual Relations in Business: a Preliminary Study', *American Sociological Review*, 28, 1963, pp. 55–67.
146 Hugh Thomas, ed., *The Establishment: a Symposium*, 1959.

the Stock Exchange in the City of London is dependent on absorbing an ideology, based on a secularised version of the Christian ethic, which defines the rules of the game and provides instructions on how to play it. This ideology is acquired informally in the home and formally through the public school system. The exercises chosen for developing the qualities needed in later life are those which encourage members of the group to play together (to express social solidarity against outsiders), yet also to play competitively (to permit the emergence of leaders). The finished products can be recognised by their dress and accent, which provide a generally reliable guide to their behaviour. The identity of the group is reinforced by inter-marriage, which ensures that kinship ties remain significant in business relationships.

Social, as well as educational, entry qualifications severely limit the extent to which merit is rewarded by promotion in twentieth-century Britain. A recent study has shown that over one hundred years *after* the beginning of the industrial revolution 'leadership by inheritance applied in a great range of industrial activities', and that newcomers often found their advance blocked by family control.[147] In the case of the City of London recruitment is still restricted to members of the upper and middle classes, and preference is given to those who have been brought up in the Home Counties. Commercial leaders are chosen from within this minority group, not from outside it. In pre-colonial West Africa there was no lack of the will to achieve, and there was scope for traders of ability to make their way in commerce. Admittedly, those who became successful tried to entrench themselves and to ensure that their families had advantages which others lacked, but such aims are scarcely a peculiarity of the pre-industrial world.

Finally, it is worth noting that there is no evidence that businessmen were accorded a low status in pre-colonial Africa, or that they suffered from any other form of social discrimination. The indications are that successful merchants were highly regarded, as indeed they are today. Furthermore, it is mistaken to suppose that businessmen enjoy a notably superior status in advanced capitalist societies. Business occupations do not rank at the top of the status hierarchy even in the United States, and it is now clear that similarities in the occupational-prestige rankings of pre-industrial and industrial societies are much greater than used to be thought.[148]

Local trade, as explained earlier, had its own rationale, but it was also connected to long distance commerce through the sale of supplies to passing caravans and, to a small extent, through the distribution of the goods which they delivered. The network of long distance trade routes thus gave West Africa a tenuous economic unity, linking, and partially integrating, different geographical zones and ethnic groupings, and crossing many state boundaries. However, there were limitations to the development of a 'national' West African economy. The unity achieved through long

[147] P. L. Payne, 'The Emergence of the Large-scale Company in Great Britain, 1870–1914', *Economic History Review*, 20, 1967, p. 538.

[148] Robert W. Hodge, Donald J. Treiman and Peter H. Rossi, 'A Comparative Study of Occupational Prestige', in *Class, Status, and Power*, ed. Reinhard Bendix and Seymour Martin Lipset, 1967, pp. 309–21; and Robert W. Hodge, Paul M. Siegel and Peter H. Rossi, 'Occupational Prestige in the United States', in *ibid*, pp. 322–34.

distance commerce was incomplete because the trade itself was restricted in volume and because its principal effects were felt by a minority of the total population. Further consideration will be given to the question of constraints on the growth of this market in the final section of the present chapter, after the two remaining features of the distributive system, money and transport, have been examined.

It is often supposed that West Africa failed to develop a monetary system which was designed to facilitate exchange and could succeed in doing so. According to one view, 'primitive' trade was conducted by barter. Another interpretation admits that currencies of various types existed, but argues that they did not have the same properties or perform the same functions as modern money. In neither case was it possible for a capital market to develop, nor was there any need for a sophisticated institutional device of this kind. If one or other of these arguments is correct then an explanation of the limitations on commercial expansion must attach some weight to deficiencies in pre-colonial monetary systems.

There is no doubt that a proportion of the goods entering the market were exchanged by barter. A number of books refer to the so-called 'silent' trade or 'dumb' barter, which, supposedly, was an arrangement whereby goods were exchanged by altering quantities, but without verbal consultation as to price. This curious behaviour is in accord with the European image of quaint native life, and it is easy to believe that these tribal traders, having kept silent for so long, compensated by dancing and drumming even more vigorously than before. Reality, however, must intrude: the only scholar to investigate the various accounts of 'dumb' barter decided that the supporting evidence was so weak that it was necessary to resort to Gestalt psychology to explain why Europeans continued to believe in it![149] Barter aided by verbal communication was common, but it was not the dominant means of effecting exchange. Despite the evolutionist assumption that barter is the first stage in the emergence of a market economy, this method of trade is not necessarily associated with 'simple' societies, and it works efficiently if goods can be 'paired' easily. It is as well to remember that a substantial, and increasing, proportion of world trade today is conducted on a modified barter basis, whereby goods such as locomotives are exchanged for products such as coffee, and deficiencies are made up by cash payments or by vouchers redeemable elsewhere.[150] Africans were more familiar with this system in the pre-colonial period than they were with pure barter.

Since trade was widespread and involved multilateral relations, goods were not always readily interchangeable, and money was needed to facilitate exchange. A variety of currencies was in circulation in the centuries before colonial rule, the most important being gold, cowries, strips of cloth, and copper and iron rods.

Gold was current throughout much of the Western Sudan and also in central parts of the forest, such as Ashanti, from the eleventh century onwards and probably earlier. Gold currencies took two main forms: gold dust, which was transported in small bags and measured on a portable balance, and *mithqals* (an alternative name

[149] Sundström, *The Trade of Guinea*, pp. 22–31, 66–73.
[150] *The Times*, 26 January 1972, p. 19.

for dinars), which were in use both as coins and as units of weight for gold dust.[151] The *mithqals* minted at Nikki, in what is now northern Dahomey, are thought to have had an extensive circulation in the eastern half of the Western Sudan in the early nineteenth century.

Cowrie shells, for centuries the major export of the Maldive Islands, were used as currency in several parts of the world, including much of Africa. [152]They were first imported into West Africa via an overland route from North Africa and the Middle East, and were in use in the chief markets of the middle Niger from at least the eleventh century. Cowries spread west to Mauritania before the fifteenth century; east to Hausaland early in the eighteenth century, reaching Bornu in the second half of the nineteenth century; and south to the forest between the Ivory Coast and the Niger Delta, where they merged with cowries imported by European traders by sea from the sixteenth century onwards. Cowries were the most widespread currency in West Africa, and they continued to expand in area and in volume until the late nineteenth century, by which time they were used in all parts of the region except the Upper Guinea coast and its hinterland (from Senegal to Liberia), and eastern Nigeria.

Cloth money and metal currencies other than gold were found in many parts of West Africa, but were dominant only in areas where cowries had failed to penetrate. Cotton strips were especially important in Bornu in the eighteenth century and in parts of Senegambia, particularly among the Wolof, in the nineteenth century. Iron money of various kinds was used on the Upper Guinea coast, and copper rods and wires circulated in the eastern part of the Niger Delta and, before the eighteenth century, in Bornu.[153] The origins of these metal currencies have been the subject of a discussion which is noteworthy principally as a further illustration of the diffusionist hypothesis that all complex social phenomena found in sub-Saharan Africa must have originated elsewhere unless there is very clear proof to the contrary. However, it seems unnecessary to resort to theories of the Egyptian or Eastern provenance of metal currencies, since these could easily have been, and probably were, developed in West Africa itself.

The problem now arises as to how to interpret the function of these pre-colonial currencies. To classify them as 'transitional' currencies is useful in drawing attention to a category which lies between pure barter on the one hand and the monetary systems of advanced industrial societies on the other, but it has the disadvantage of grouping a wide range of currencies which may not share quite the same properties. A more helpful classification is that which divides transitional currencies into two types. First, there are general-purpose currencies, which are intended to assist liquidity, and which can be exchanged readily for all goods and services irrespective

[151] Marion Johnson, 'The Nineteenth-Century Gold "Mithqal" in West and North Africa', *Journal of African History*, 9, 1968, pp. 547–69.

[152] The authoritative study on West Africa is Marion Johnson, 'The Cowrie Currencies of West Africa', *Journal of African History*, 11, 1970, pp. 17–49 and 331–53.

[153] Manillas—horseshoe-shaped currencies made of copper and brass—are noted in Chapter 3, part 2, in connection with external trade.

of the social status of the parties concerned. The usefulness of these currencies can be judged by their efficiency in promoting 'modern' exchange. Second, there are special-purpose currencies, which are designed to control liquidity, which can be used to purchase only a limited range of goods, and which are not freely convertible with other currencies. These currencies should not be analysed as if they were agents of modernity, for they dominated societies where market principles were unimportant, and their main purpose was to solidify the social structure.

The chief problem is an empirical one; whether West Africa's pre-colonial currencies should be classified as general-purpose or as special-purpose money. According to the substantivist school, the transitional currencies of Africa were special-purpose currencies. This conclusion follows from the assumption that market principles were peripheral, and is also, so it is claimed, supported by historical evidence. The substantivist interpretation deserves close attention because it has been stated often and, on occasion, forcefully. Perhaps the best test of its accuracy is to see whether it meets Polyani's own precept that 'the fount of the substantivist concept is the empirical economy'.

Judged by this criterion, the basis of the substantivist case seems rather slender. Dalton's generalisations are derived mainly from a re-examination of a previous scholar's study of shell money on the Pacific island of Rossel.[154] It is relevant to observe in this connection that Pospisil and Epstein have shown that shell money *did* function as a general-purpose currency in the Pacific.[155] Bohannan's argument is drawn largely from his fieldwork among the Tiv, an important and interesting people, but one who number less than one per cent of West Africa's present population.[156] Latham's investigation of the historical sources relating to copper money demonstrates that Bohannan's interpretation does not apply to eastern Nigeria as a whole, and suggests that he may also have been mistaken with regard to the much smaller area occupied by the Tiv.[157] Copper rods were valid for all goods and services, and were split into small denominations (wires) in order to facilitate exchange. Polanyi's study of cowries is confined to southern Dahomey in the eighteenth century, and uses a limited selection of available sources.[158] Marion Johnson's comprehensive study has revealed important shortcomings in his work.[159] Cowries and gold formed a single currency system over a large part of West Africa, the

[154] George Dalton, 'Primitive Money', *American Anthropologist*, 67, 1965, pp. 44–65.

[155] Leopold Pospisil, *Kapauku Papuan Economy*, Yale 1963, and T. Scarlett Epstein, *Capitalism, Primitive and Modern*, Canberra 1968, pp. 19–26.

[156] Paul Bohannan, 'The Impact of Money on an African Subsistence Economy', *Journal of Economic History*, 19, 1959, pp. 491–503.

[157] A. J. H. Latham, 'Currency, Credit and Capitalism on the Cross River in the Pre-Colonial Era', *Journal of African History*, 12, 1971, pp. 599–605.

[158] Karl Polanyi, *Dahomey and the Slave Trade*, Seattle 1966, pp. 173–94. Polanyi's discussion contains a number of ambiguities, but it is only fair to note that his book had to be prepared for publication after his death.

[159] And also that Polanyi's views on the related question of the ounce trade need revision. See Marion Johnson, 'The Ounce in Eighteenth-Century West African Trade', *Journal of African History*, 7, 1966, pp. 197–214.

exchange rate between them sometimes being fixed and sometimes being left to float. The system was designed to assist trade, and it is no coincidence that it served an area where long distance commerce was particularly active. The success of the cowrie is readily explicable. Its size and shape made it easy to handle, convenient to count and impossible to counterfeit, while its durability meant that it could be stored safely for many years. Moreover, cowries, though often used as small change for gold, could be multiplied for accounting purposes by standardised units (strings, 'heads' and bags). Finally, it is worth noting that Ames has shown that Wolof cloth currency was available in standardised multiples, and was acceptable as payment for 'subsistence' and 'prestige' items.[160]

The foregoing review makes it clear that the major currencies of pre-colonial West Africa functioned as general-purpose currencies, and had the attributes of modern money. Each one acted as a medium of exchange, as a common measure of value, as a store of wealth and as a standard for deferred payment. This interpretation is fully consistent with the argument advanced earlier in this chapter that trade and market principles were more common in the pre-colonial era than some writers have thought. The concept of special-purpose money still retains its value as a theoretical tool, and doubtless examples can be found to illustrate the ways in which it operated.[161] Furthermore, it is only fair to point out that the general-purpose currencies of West Africa did not share precisely the same attributes: there is room for considering the merits of, say, cowries in relation to cloth; for examining the reasons underlying the boundaries between different currency areas; and for analysing the varied monetary functions of the state. However, the main conclusion still holds: the principal currencies of West Africa served to extend trade, not to obstruct it. The indications are that these currencies were adequate for the needs of the time. It was only in the nineteenth century, when they became less efficient, that they were replaced by the currencies of the industrial world.

The presence of extensive trade and general-purpose currencies provides grounds for supposing that pre-colonial West Africa also had a capital market. Sundström's evidence confirms that this was indeed the case.[162] It is suggested here (though mainly to prompt others to consider this neglected subject in more detail) that West African credit institutions can be divided, on the basis of their primary functions, into two groups. First, there were small credit associations, such as the Yoruba *esusu*, which were organised by kinsmen or by groups of friends, and were devoted mainly to social purposes, such as raising money for funerals. Second, there was a commercial capital market, which served economic needs at local and inter-regional levels. As far as local needs were concerned, it is important to emphasise, once again, that small communities were not necessarily homogeneous, and that it was possible for poorer members of society to become indebted to wealthier neighbours. The extent and

[160] D. W. Ames, 'The Use of a Transitional Cloth-Money Token Among the Wolof', *American Anthropologist*, 57, 1955, pp. 1016–23.

[161] Ration coupons and trading stamps are examples of special-purpose currencies in industrial societies.

[162] *The Trade of Guinea*, pp. 34–44.

causes of local indebtedness (especially its relationship to the availability of land) are subjects which require further research. At the inter-regional level, it is clear that professional traders often needed to finance their activities by securing credit, because their initial investment was high and returns were long delayed. Commercial capital was obtained from fellow merchants and from specialised bankers and money lenders. The large entrepôts had bankers who invested money on behalf of depositors and operated a system whereby credits could be transferred to third parties; exchange brokers, who also speculated in currency values; and a futures market in the main staples of long distance trade. Interest rates reflected the scarcity of capital and the risks involved in most lending operations, and were rarely less than 100 per cent per annum. Security was given in various ways, though most credit agreements were based on personal connections of the kind noted already with reference to the Dioula and Hausa. Usually, credit facilities were arranged in the presence of witnesses, and were guaranteed either by depositing bonds supplied by third parties, or by offering property (livestock, houses and land) as security. Poorer members of society often resorted to pawning as a means of guaranteeing the repayment of a debt. Pawning was a system by which the debtor or a nominee (usually a kinsman) worked for his creditor without payment until the debt was cleared. Legal sanctions were also employed, and most societies had rules which defined various types of loan and laid down regulations for recovering debts. This was true both of Muslim states in the Western Sudan, where the Koranic injunction against usurious loans had little influence on the operation of the commercial money market, and of the 'pagan' states in the forest zone, as, for example, among the Yoruba kingdoms.[163]

The remaining feature of the distributive system to be considered is transport. It is easy to locate sources which dismiss pre-industrial means of transport as primitive, but harder to find those which support this judgement by defining terms and by examining the costs and benefits of various means of carriage in the pre-railway age. As usual, the Dark Continent has suffered particularly in this respect, and the familiar statement that 'Africa south of the Sahara has never invented the wheel'[164] is commonly used as an index of the region's backwardness in comparison with other parts of the world. It will be contended here that general pronouncements about the primitive nature of pre-colonial transport disguise complex and important problems: in the first place, various meanings can be given to the adjective 'primitive' in the context of transport, and not all of them apply to Africa; secondly, since Europe did not invent the wheel either, it is not the independent origins of this device which require investigation so much as the factors governing the spread and adoption of technical innovations; finally, it is worth observing that to possess advanced technical knowledge is not necessarily to be on the road to economic development, as Needham's remarkable study of China has demonstrated.[165]

[163] A. G. Hopkins, 'A Report on the Yoruba', *Journal of the Historical Society of Nigeria*, 5, 1969, pp. 90–2.

[164] P. T. Bauer, *Economic Analysis and Policy in Underdeveloped Countries*, 1965, p. 47.

[165] Joseph Needham, *Science and Civilisation in China*, 1, Cambridge 1954. Other volumes have been published, and this immense study is still in progress.

Communications by land were based entirely on animal and human power. One of the greatest transport innovations of the pre-colonial era was the introduction of the camel. This extraordinary animal was the principal means of transport in the desert for almost two thousand years. It was present in North Africa in the first century B.C., and it became known throughout the Sahara during the early centuries of the Christian era. The camel was more efficient in desert conditions than were horses and oxen, which had been used previously, and its supremacy remained unchallenged until the coming of the motor car in the 1920s. Camels were bred specially for desert transport by nomads, such as the Tuareg, and could carry between 3 cwt and 5 cwt across the Sahara. The camel did not travel very far into the Western Sudan partly because it preferred the poorer fodder of the desert, and partly because it was susceptible to diseases, such as sleeping sickness. At northern entrepôts, such as Timbuctu, goods were transferred to donkeys and oxen, which were better suited to savanna conditions. Donkeys were the chief pack animal in the Western Sudan. They carried about 100 lb, which was substantially less than the amount carried by oxen, but donkeys were cheaper to buy and feed, they were faster, and they were more effective over rough terrain. Donkeys, like camels, were bred specially for transport purposes. Those raised by the Mossi had a particularly high reputation in long-distance trade, and were bought in Salaga by Hausa traders, who used them to carry kola nuts on their journey home. At the savanna-forest border markets, such as Salaga, goods travelling further south were transferred to porters, because the use of pack animals in the forest was restricted by a combination of trypanosomiasis and lack of pasture. Professional carriers, who were often slaves, could head-load 55–65 lb and cover an average of twenty miles a day.

Water transport was used where possible, for it was known to be the cheapest means of transporting bulky commodities over long distances. However, many West African rivers were hard to navigate: a number had dangerous rapids; some were flooded during the rainy season; and others lacked water in the dry season. Canoes were better able to deal with these difficulties than were other types of craft. West African canoes varied in size. Some were eighty feet or more in length and could carry as many as one hundred men.[166] Most canoes were propelled by paddles, though small sails were used in some areas. Commercial water transport was particularly important on Lake Chad, the Niger, the Senegal, sections of the Volta and numerous smaller rivers in the forest, and along the coast, especially where estuaries and lagoons provided shelter from ocean waves and storms. The busiest inland waterway was the middle section of the Niger, which linked Timbuctu to the commercial and administrative centres of Djenne (250 miles upstream) and Gao (about the same distance downstream).[167] Hundreds of craft were in use on this stretch of the river from the thirteenth century onwards and probably earlier. Some of these canoes carried twenty to thirty tons of merchandise, including foodstuffs as

---

[166] Robert Smith, 'The Canoe in West African History', *Journal of African History*, 11, 1970, pp. 515–33.

[167] M. Tymowski, 'Le Niger, voie de communication des grands états du Soudan occidentale jusqu'à la fin du XVIᵉ siècle', *Africana Bulletin*, 6, 1967, pp. 73–95.

well as the more luxurious items of long-distance trade. Water transport enabled the middle Niger complex to become one of the great centres of pre-colonial trade in Africa. It encouraged the growth of specialised occupations, such as building and operating canoes; it led to the development of specialised ports, such as Kabara, which served Timbuctu; and it contributed to the political and economic unity of the empires of Mali and Songhai.

The efficiency of a transport system can be analysed in three ways. By following this procedure it is possible to arrive at a clearer understanding of what is meant by backward or primitive means of communication. First, the physical availability of transport fixes the size of the market in geographical terms. West African transport certainly provided a wide coverage, joining caravans to periodic markets and offering, via head-loading, what was virtually a door-to-door service. Second, the freight capacity of the system determines the volume carried. At first sight it might seem that African transport was defective in this respect. Fortunately, this hypothesis can be tested against the example of the nineteenth century, when there was a massive increase in the volume of goods carried without any change taking place in established modes of transportation. Therefore, it seems unlikely that there was a shortage of freight capacity. Third, the cost of transport defines the depth of the market in social terms. In this instance there is no doubt that African modes of transport were deficient. Evaluating transport costs is a difficult task, but it is clear that the value added in long distance trade was considerable.[168] Head-loading was particularly expensive, and goods could be taken only a short distance by this means before the cost of transport exceeded the profit on sales. This explains why head-loading was used in long distance trade only in parts of the forest, where there was no alternative, and in cases where the carrier was a slave who was destined to be sold at the end of the journey. Foodstuffs and other items of everyday use could rarely be transported far beyond the area of production by any means of carriage. The case of Timbuctu is an exception which proves the rule, for the city was able to use the relatively cheap Niger route and could also pay for imported supplies from foreign trade earnings. Even so, in the nineteenth century the price of imported cloth at Timbuctu was two to three and a half times as great as it was on the coast. Kola nuts, which today are common items of consumption, were a luxury enjoyed by the relatively wealthy in the pre-colonial period. In the late nineteenth century one kola nut bought at Gonja, in the area of production, for five cowries sold for 250–300 cowries by the time it reached Lake Chad (about 1,250 miles away).[169]

The principal deficiency of African transport was its high cost. The question to be considered now is whether this drawback was made more serious by the absence of

---

[168] To assess transport costs accurately it is necessary to take account of the capital cost of a particular form of carriage, maintenance costs, the life expectation of a vehicle and its resale value, if any. Moreover, goods in transit in West Africa paid numerous tolls. This expenditure was reflected in the price of a product at its final destination, and needs to be differentiated from the cost of transport.

[169] C.O. 879/49, H. J. Reid, 'Memorandum on the British Possessions in West Africa', 12 May 1897, Public Record Office.

the wheel. It is possible to attribute the lack of wheeled transport to ignorance. However, there is now evidence that horse-drawn chariots or carts were crossing the Sahara some five centuries before the birth of Christ, and since West Africa remained in contact with the Arab world in subsequent centuries, it seems improbable that this explanation will suffice. Alternatively, it could be argued that Africans knew of the existence of the wheel, but, being rather slow-witted in comparison with the inhabitants of other continents, were unable to devise ways of using it to advantage. It will be contended here that this view is also inaccurate. It seems more likely that wheeled transport was not adopted either because it was inappropriate to West African conditions or because its greater cost was not justified by proportionately greater returns.

In two areas of West Africa environmental circumstances meant that there was little scope for wheeled transport. On the sand and rock of the Sahara the camel was a more efficient means of carriage, so much so that it replaced the wheel at an early date. In the forest the difficulty of keeping draught animals greatly reduced the value of wheeled vehicles. In the Western Sudan, however, both horses and oxen were present, and wheeled transport would have been possible. The problem in this case was that the gain from greater traction would have been nullified by the capital and maintenance costs of carts, wagons and draught animals, and by the slower rate of progress of wheeled vehicles. Since draught animals were not used on the farm, the cost of keeping them solely for transport purposes during the dry season was much higher than in other parts of the world, where there was scope for combining the two functions. The horse, the most powerful draught animal, was very expensive, needed a high intake of fodder and water, and succumbed easily to disease.[170] Horses were used in West Africa as cavalry and on ceremonial occasions, and they remain symbols of prestige today. The poor quality of the roads would have greatly reduced the efficiency of wheeled vehicles, and the cost of improving the road system would have been prohibitive, especially in an area where population was, in general, rather sparse. Pack animals predominated because they were relatively cheap to buy, inexpensive to operate and well suited to the terrain.

The foregoing argument can be tested against the evidence provided by one of the earliest systematic attempts to introduce wheeled transport into part of the Western Sudan.

In January 1905 the first cart convoy arrived at Zaria from Zungeru, and the difficulties due to having to rely solely on human porterage were temporarily obviated, though the carts were not able to continue running when once the rainy season set in. Every effort was made to organise an efficient system during the dry season of 1905–1906. Artificers and drivers had even been imported from India, and proved to be of greatest use; depots were established for supplies of fodder along the road; a veterinary surgeon was attached to the Department. In spite of

----

[170] On the relative merits of horses and oxen see A. Burford, 'Heavy Transport in Classical Antiquity', *Economic History Review*, 13, 1960, pp. 1–18.

all these efforts, however, the cart transport proved little less expensive than carriers.[171]

It seems reasonable to conclude that the absence of the wheel was a matter of decision rather than of chance or ignorance, and that the presence of wheeled vehicles in West Africa would not have reduced transport costs during the pre-colonial period.

Although the wheel is commonly regarded as a symbol of economic progress, it is as well to remember that wheeled vehicles did not achieve a decisive advantage over other forms of transport until the industrial revolution, with the development first of the railway and then of the motor car. Before that time, the use of wheeled vehicles in Europe was inhibited by many of the problems experienced in Africa. In eighteenth-century Spain, for example, pack animals, especially donkeys, were by far the most important means of transport, though ox-carts were available and were used to a certain extent.[172] The ox-cart carried three to four times as much as a large pack animal, but since it was costly to purchase and operate, and travelled at half the speed, it could not compete with donkey transport. Wagons did not become numerous in northern Europe until the sixteenth century, and even then they were used mainly for short-haul work. Until the roads were improved, pack animals remained the leading form of long-distance commercial transport on land. 'Long trains of these faithful animals, furnished with a great variety of equipment . . . wended their way along the narrow roads of the time, and provided the chief means by which the exchange of commodities could be carried on.' This statement could well apply to the Western Sudan in the pre-colonial period, though in fact it refers to England in the early eighteenth century.[173] The evidence suggests that while Africa's transport system was costly in relation to modern forms of transport, it was no more expensive than that which operated in other pre-industrial societies.

4 Internal constraints on growth

The domestic economy has been examined at length because of its overwhelming importance in the economy as a whole during the pre-colonial period and today, and because it is customarily regarded as the point of departure for countries wishing to achieve economic growth. Arguments about the means of attaining growth, and indeed about the desirability of doing so, are greatly influenced by assumptions about the characteristics of traditional economies, and by beliefs about the quality of life in the pre-industrial world.

This chapter has criticised some of the more widespread of these assumptions and beliefs, which have been characterised here as the myths of Primitive and Merrie

[171] Sir Charles Orr, *The Making of Northern Nigeria*, 1911, pp. 184–5.

[172] David R. Ringrose, 'Transportation and Economic Stagnation in Eighteenth-Century Castille', *Journal of Economic History*, 28, 1968, pp. 51–79.

[173] W. T. Jackman, *The Development of Transportation in Modern England*, 2nd ed., 1962, p. 141.

Africa. It has been shown that the pre-colonial, domestic economy was more varied than is often supposed, and that it included manufactures as well as a wide range of agricultural products. Output targets were geared not merely to subsistence needs, but also to trade, which was regular, widespread and of great antiquity. A survey of the principal economic activities has demonstrated that their history was far from static, that their organisation was efficient, and that Africans were receptive to new ideas, where these were suitable and profitable.[174] Several explanations of economic backwardness, ancient and modern, have been considered and rejected: it has been shown that geographical interpretations based on climate and on natural resources are unsatisfactory; that sociological explanations relating to family structure, social mobility, the status-hierarchy and supposedly anti-capitalist values are unacceptable; and that economic explanations concerning the efficiency of the labour force, the organisation of 'primitive' agriculture, communal land tenure and allegedly inadequate commercial institutions, are inapplicable. In short, there is a corpus of popular beliefs about African underdevelopment which needs to be jettisoned.

At the same time, it is clear that pre-colonial Africa was not moving in the direction of an indigenous industrial revolution. Pressures towards the expansion of the market coming from certain regions within West Africa and spear-headed by professional merchants, such as the Dioula and the Hausa, were unable to overcome the pressures towards self-sufficiency which were present throughout the area as a whole. The greater part of total output consisted of foodstuffs and other everyday necessities. These commodities could be traded locally, but not over long distances because transport costs prevented them from competing with acceptable substitutes, which could be produced on the spot in other areas. Local trade, by definition, served a market which was too small in terms of numbers of consumers and purchasing power to justify the introduction of cost-reducing innovations and greater specialisation. Moreover, the income-elasticity of demand for foodstuffs was low: if per capita incomes had risen, demand would have shifted away from foodstuffs and towards manufactured goods, such as textiles. In the absence of a general expansion of incomes, trade in commodities with the greatest growth potential depended on connecting social and geographical islands of purchasing power by means of long-distance trade. The problem here was that the costs of carriage were too great and the number of relatively affluent consumers was too small to permit the development of a mass market in manufactured goods. Consequently, the multiplier effects of long-distance commerce were limited. Freight charges per ton/mile were no more expensive in Africa than they were in other parts of the world, but transport costs were higher for each consumer served than in many other areas because the population was small and scattered. Underpopulation was critical in preventing market growth because it encouraged extensive cultivation, favoured dispersed settlement and generated strong tendencies towards local self-sufficiency. Where population was concentrated, it was partly for defensive reasons, and so was not indicative of

[174] This conclusion is in line with that advanced by Theodore W. Schultz, *Transforming Traditional Agriculture*, New Haven 1964, with the important qualification that 'traditional' agriculture in West Africa was not as changeless as Schultz suggests was generally the case.

developed exchange activities, and partly for commercial motives, in which case it was usually associated with slavery, and with a low level of purchasing power.

There were two possible escape routes from this situation. The first was through an increase in population, which would have altered the land–labour ratio, encouraged the adoption of more intensive forms of agriculture and provided a larger and more concentrated market. This is exactly what happened in Western Europe during the Middle Ages, though the reasons governing population changes in that period are little better understood than they are in the case of pre-colonial Africa.[175] The second escape route was through technical innovation, which would have increased the size of the market by reducing production costs. Technical innovation might have occurred in response to an increase in demand brought about by population growth (or by a rise in incomes among the existing population), or else to overcome shortages of supply, such as a lack of raw materials or of labour. In Africa no pressures or incentives existed on the demand side, while on the supply side the main deficiency, a shortage of labour, was dealt with by using slaves. This solution met the needs of the time, for though labour was scarce in relation to land, the capital required for technical innovation was even scarcer. Moreover, a reduction in production costs would not have cut distribution costs significantly because transport charges accounted for a large proportion of the retail price of goods entering long-distance trade. Africa needed to make a huge and virtually impossible leap: the continent required not merely the wheel, but steam and internal combustion engines as well.

To suggest these possibilities is not to argue that population growth and technical innovation would have brought about an indigenous industrial revolution in Africa. An expanding population might well have caused more problems than it solved, and West Africa might have been faced, ultimately, with a Malthusian situation. Technical advances might have been misapplied, or used merely to arrest a fall in living standards brought about by an increase in population. Cumulative economic growth allied to technical advance occurred in only one part of the pre-industrial world, namely north-west Europe. A unique departure from normality took place not because the economic and social structure of this small region possessed attributes which were totally lacking in other continents, but because, by a fortunate coincidence, long-run changes in factor prices made continuous innovation both necessary and rewarding. It was possible, from an early date, to begin to build a ladder to economic progress by means of small-scale, and interacting, technical inventions.[176] Other societies possessed much the same ingredients, but were unable to mix them in quite the same way. Commercial capitalism in West Africa failed to promote industrialisation because there was little scope for the development of an intermediate technology. Surplus trading profits were invested in slaves and luxuries, not because Africans were doggedly pursuing non-economic goals, but because of a lack of more profitable alternatives.

[175] Douglass C. North and Robert Paul Thomas, 'An Economic Theory of the Growth of the Western World', *Economic History Review*, 23, 1970, p. 11.
[176] See, for example, E. M. Carus-Wilson, 'An Industrial Revolution of the Thirteenth Century', *Economic History Review*, 11, 1941, pp. 39–60.

three

External trade: the Sahara and the Atlantic

Africa, like China, was not well known to the outside world before the nineteenth century, and information about the interior was the product of occasional visits from hardy travellers, such as Ibn Battuta—the Marco Polo of the tropics. However, the assumption that the continent was also isolated from external contacts, though it has served a useful purpose here in focusing attention on internal checks on the development of the market, is historically inaccurate and must now be discarded. In reality, West Africa had well established and highly organised external commercial links across the desert and the ocean. These highways, though slow and hazardous, connected the region to the international economy centuries before the industrial revolution enabled the major European powers to increase their penetration of the underdeveloped world. The fact that West Africa conducted an extensive foreign commerce is clearly relevant to the theme of stability and change in the market, for it is a matter of historical experience that societies which have been inhibited by domestic constraints have sometimes discovered a path to economic development through international trade.

The theory of economic growth through international trade is basically an application to nations and continents of the concept of specialisation, as set out originally by Adam Smith.[1] Where foreign trade has acted as an engine of growth, it has done so by establishing a link between societies whose resource endowment, whether natural or acquired, differs in certain important respects. In this situation, each of the societies concerned can supply goods which the other requires, yet cannot produce itself, or at least cannot produce as cheaply. Of the numerous factors affecting relative costs, transport has been particularly significant in the history of commerce between nations. One country may be able to produce a commodity more cheaply than another, but freight charges can easily cancel this superiority, and so prevent trade from taking place. However, given the necessary commercial institutions, political support and degree of success in overcoming the transport problem, the various parties will find it beneficial to specialise according to their particular comparative

[1] For expositions of the classical theory, and the elaborations made to it subsequently, see G. Harberler, *International Trade and Economic Development*, Cairo 1959, and Ragnar Nurkse, *Patterns of Trade and Development*, 1961. Some problems of current interest are considered in Hla Myint, *Economic Theory and the Underdeveloped Countries*, 1971.

advantage, and trade will develop. Rising incomes in the export sector lead to increased consumer spending and to further investment in productive enterprises. In this way the benefits of foreign trade spread to the rest of the economy. Typically, additional economic activity is generated through the provision of goods and services for the export sector and through the development of processing industries making use of imports. The result is the mobilisation of factors which, because or deficiency of demand, lack of necessary supplies, shortage of capital, or inadequate technology, were not fully used before. In practice, the strength of linkages between the foreign trade sector and the domestic economy is by no means the same in all cases, and one of the tasks of international trade theory is to measure and account for these differences by making a detailed examination of the structure of the export sector, of the volume and disposition of income derived from foreign trade, and of the capacity of the local economy to respond to external stimuli.

This chapter has a dual aim: to clarify what has long been a controversial aspect of West African history, namely the external slave trade, by making use of research which has been completed in recent years; and to analyse West Africa's external trade in terms of the model outlined above in order to identify the linkages which were established, and explain why their beneficial effects were so limited. To achieve these aims, the chapter has been divided into four parts. The history of trans-Saharan commerce will be outlined first of all, as this was the earliest branch of external trade to develop. Next will come a consideration of Atlantic commerce, with special reference to the notorious traffic in slaves. Then there will be an investigation of the reasons for the decline of these two trades. Finally, there will be an assessment of the consequences of external trade for Africa and (very briefly) for other parts of the world. Discussion of the new, replacement commerce, which arose in the nineteenth century, will be reserved for Chapter 4.

1 Trans-Saharan trade

Trans-Saharan trade between West and North Africa began as early as 1000 B.C., when the desert crossing was made by oxen and by chariots or carts drawn by horses. The trade was developed by the Carthaginians from about the fifth century B.C., and was given further impetus by the Romans three centuries later, following their expansion into North Africa and the subsequent introduction of the camel.[2] With the collapse of Roman rule in the fourth century A.D., the trade diminished, and may even have ceased altogether. It was not revived until after the Byzantine reconquest of North Africa in 533–35. The rise of Arab power from the seventh century onwards, though at first a destabilising influence on North African politics, eventually contributed substantially to the growth of trans-Saharan commerce. Arab merchants and missionaries were present in the Western Sudan from about the

[2] R. C. C. Law, 'The Garamantes and Trans-Saharan Enterprise in Classical Times', *Journal of African History*, 8, 1967, pp. 181–200.

second half of the eighth century,[3] and their influence grew after the Almoravid invasion of the negro empire of Ghana in 1077. The period which corresponds to the Middle Ages in European history was a flourishing time for trade on the Saharan routes, particularly from the middle of the thirteenth to the end of the sixteenth centuries. This period saw an upswing in demand for West African products in Europe and the Middle East, and at the same time a substantial increase in supply, which was greatly assisted by an era of settled government in North Africa and the Western Sudan.

The golden age of trans-Saharan trade is usually thought to have ended in the sixteenth century, as the expansion of sea-borne commerce led to a reorientation of trade routes towards the coast, and as the Western Sudan entered a long period of political instability following the overthrow of the Songhai empire by the Moroccan army in 1591. 'The story of the Moorish conquest,' concluded Bovill, 'remains one of the darkest chapters in the history of the continent.'[4] Indeed, in partial deference to this weight of authority, the Western Sudan disappears from many history textbooks after 1591, and only emerges two centuries later, when (the Moors having been suitably discomfited) the *jihads* (holy wars) of the early nineteenth century noisily claim attention. There are grounds for thinking that this interpretation exaggerates reality. In the first place, there is little evidence to show that the arrival of the Europeans on the West Coast had a dramatic or even an immediate impact on the economy of the interior. Trans-Saharan trade survived, and its value actually increased during the nineteenth century. The final decline did not set in until after 1875, as will be shown in Chapter 4. Secondly, research now in progress[5] makes it possible to suggest that the events of 1591 were not as traumatic as has been thought, and that the period which followed was not one of unchecked political anarchy and irreversible economic decline. It is likely that too much attention has been paid to changes in personnel among the rulers—a common bias in the writing of African history. For the great majority of the population, life probably went on very much as before; they merely exchanged one set of tax collectors for another.

It is worth underlining three points arising out of this historical survey. In the first place, it must be said that the deficiency of statistics is a serious handicap to any satisfactory interpretation of the rise and fall of trans-Saharan trade, and there is a need for caution over the use of what little information of this kind is available. Secondly, interpretations of fluctuations in the prosperity of trade at present rest on an incomplete understanding of the determinants of booms and slumps in this unusual commerce. Current explanations stress the importance of political factors, particularly stability and instability at the southern and northern ends of the trade routes. These explanations require qualification and elaboration. There are many examples

---

[3] Tadeusz Lewicki, 'L'état nord-Africain de Tahert et ses relations avec le Soudan occidentale à la fin de VIIIe et au IXe siècle', *Cahiers d'Études Africaines*, 2, 1962, pp. 513-35.

[4] Bovill, *The Golden Trade* . . . , p. 195. The Moors, presumably, took a rather different view. See also Mauny, *Tableau géographique* . . . , p. 441.

[5] Notably by N. R. Laurent of the School of Oriental and African Studies, University of London, and J. R. Willis of the University of California, Los Angeles.

in West African history (as in medieval Europe) where, contrary to all reasonable expectations, long distance trade managed to steer a way through even the most extreme political disturbances. Thirdly, as far as the initial effects of the European presence were concerned, it is more likely that new areas of production were stimulated near the coast than that the economy of the Western Sudan was undermined. The economic effects of the coming of the Europeans now require detailed investigation with reference to particular areas and specific items of trade, and the history of the Western Sudan in the seventeenth and eighteenth centuries needs to be rescued from its inappropriate association with the Dark Ages.

The variety of commodities traded was limited by two main considerations, apart from the low level of purchasing power in West Africa. To begin with, the length of the journey, which lasted from seventy to ninety days and sometimes longer, meant that highly perishable goods could not be taken across the desert. Next, all goods had to have a high value in relation to their weight. Freight charges across the Sahara added about 100–150 per cent to the cost of most items, but formed a much smaller proportion of the asking price of goods with a high value-weight ratio. Slaves, it is true, transported themselves, but they still had to be guarded and fed, and an allowance made for the fact that a proportion of them—an estimate for the nineteenth century suggests 20 per cent—died on the route. Trans-Saharan commerce reached its optimum point of organisational efficiency at an early date with the introduction of the camel, and no further internal or external economies were possible (or at least were achieved) until the coming of the motor car in the 1920s.

The commodities traded can be divided into two categories, though the line between them is not easily drawn. First, there were state necessities such as gold and slaves, which were sent north, and cowries, salt,[6] and weapons,[7] which journeyed south. These items played an essential part in maintaining the economic and political structures of the states which purchased them, whether in Europe, North Africa, the Middle East or West Africa. Gold and cowries were major currencies; slaves formed a sizeable proportion of the labour force and military strength in certain areas; salt was a dietary necessity; and military equipment, including cavalry horses, was vital to the preservation and extension of political power. Second, there were luxury items, such as expensive cloth, pepper, ivory, kola nuts, leather goods and, in the nineteenth century, ostrich feathers, which were carried north, and high quality

[6] As noted in Chapter 2, much of the salt imported into West Africa was brought by special caravans which were not involved in trans-Saharan trade. However, some salt was picked up on the way by south-bound caravans from North Africa.

[7] Foreign trade enabled West Africa to keep abreast of the main European developments in the techniques of warfare. Between the thirteenth and the sixteenth centuries Tlemcen (in North Africa) was the main entrepôt for the trade in sword blades, which came mostly from Marseilles, Bordeaux and Genoa. Guns were certainly present in parts of the Western Sudan before the Moroccan invasion of 1591, for they were used to guard caravans early in the sixteenth century. The military superiority which enabled Pizarro to topple the empire of the Incas in 1533 was not achieved with respect to West Africa until the nineteenth century.

textiles (especially those coloured with dyes not available locally), copper, preserved foodstuffs, glassware, beads and miscellaneous 'fancy goods', which were sent south. A proportion of the slaves exported from West Africa should also be classified as luxuries, and so should the valuable foreign slaves who were imported into the Western Sudan and kept in wealthy households mainly for prestige reasons.

Two items, gold and slaves, were important enough to require additional comment. The precise origin of the gold trade is uncertain, but it may date back to Carthaginian times or even earlier. Exports increased during the eleventh century, following the adoption of gold coinage throughout the Muslim world, and they received a further boost after 1252, when gold began to replace silver as Europe's main currency.[8] Between the eleventh and the seventeenth centuries West Africa was the leading supplier of gold to the international economy, and in the later Middle Ages accounted, according to one estimate, for almost two-thirds of world production. West African gold flowed to Cairo and the Middle East, where it helped to sustain Arab power until the end of the thirteenth century, when the basis of the monetary system changed to silver. African gold contributed to the functioning of the domestic economy in Europe, and also helped to settle international debts. In the later Middle Ages Europe needed bullion to pay for imports from the Far East because most of her exports were too bulky to be worth transporting such a long distance overland. The Italian merchants of Genoa, Florence and Venice had a favourable trade balance with North Africa from the end of the twelfth century, and so were able to import gold. This advantage, together with their geographical situation, enabled them to become the magnificent brokers of international trade. Control over the gold trade also assisted the expansion of Portugal and Spain in the fifteenth and sixteenth centuries, when Seville became, for a while, Europe's 'capital of gold'. Finally, the gold trade was important in Africa itself: it assisted the rise of the ports of North Africa from the end of the twelfth century, and it contributed to the wealth of the great states of the Western Sudan. On present evidence it would be unwise to conclude that there was a sharp decline in the trans-Saharan gold trade in the seventeenth century, even though gold was being sent to Europe by ocean routes. The overland trade, though greatly reduced, continued in the nineteenth century, when new sources of supply had been discovered and other means devised to settle the accounts of international trade.

With regard to the trade in slaves, it is important to note first of all that human beings were exported from West Africa long before the rise of the more publicised Atlantic traffic in the late fifteenth century. The trans-Saharan trade even antedates the spread of Islam in the seventh century, though it is unlikely to have been very large much before then, for in Carthaginian and Roman times demand was modest and other sources of supply more popular. The expansion of Arab power led to an increased demand for slaves in North Africa and the Middle East for use as soldiers,

---

[8] R. S. Lopez, 'Back to Gold, 1252', *Economic History Review*, 9, 1956, pp. 219–40; Andrew M. Watson, 'Back to Gold—and Silver', *ibid.*, 20, 1967, pp. 1–34.

labourers and servants.[9] This north-bound trade continued without serious disruption until the late nineteenth century, and in a clandestine way and on a much reduced scale it survived well into the twentieth century. The size of the trade is hard to assess. Mauny has estimated that the trans-Saharan routes may have carried as many as two million slaves in each century during the late Middle Ages.[10] More recently, Lewicki has concluded that twelve to fifteen million slaves passed through Cairo in the sixteenth century.[11] Since the majority came via Algiers and Tripoli, it is likely that a proportion of the total was sent across the desert from West Africa. These figures are astonishing, for, as Lewicki himself points out, his estimate for the sixteenth century alone approximates to that usually suggested for the whole of the Atlantic slave trade! Malowist, on the other hand, feels that Mauny's figures are exaggerated,[12] and Boahen, dealing with the early nineteenth century, has suggested that only about 10,000 slaves per annum were being exported north across the Sahara compared with approximately 70,000 being shipped west by the Atlantic routes.[13] Judgement on Lewicki's claim must await the full publication of his research. At present, the general assumption is that the trans-Saharan slave trade was never as important as the Atlantic trade. If this view is to be proved false, it will also be necessary to explain what happened to such large negro communities (assuming that they existed), for they appear virtually to have disappeared from North Africa and the Middle East today.

The expansion of trade, following the introduction of the camel and the subsequent spread of Islam, led to the development of a complex network of routes across the desert (Map 7). Moving from west to east, the most important of these were as follows: Ghana to Mogador and Fez via Awdaghost; Timbuctu to Mogador and Fez via Teghaza; Timbuctu to Tunis and Tripoli via Wargla, Ghadames and Ghat; Kano to Tunis and Tripoli via Agades, Ghat and Ghadames; and Bornu to Tripoli via Bilma and Murzuk. The most important route in Carthaginian and Roman times was that centred on Murzuk, the capital of Fezzan, which joined Tripolitania and Egypt with the Niger bend. In the period following the rise of Islam, the 'golden road' from Timbuctu to Morocco was considered, notably by Bovill, to have been outstanding. However, more recent authorities, such as Mauny, Ol'derogge and Boahen, are of the opinion that no single route achieved permanent dominance, and that there was a progressive shift of emphasis from western to eastern routes. This interpretation appears to be more acceptable, though care should be taken not to

---

[9] On this subject see the useful articles by Norman R. Bennett, 'Christian and Negro Slavery in Eighteenth-Century North Africa', *Journal of African History*, 1, 1960, pp. 65–82, and L. Valensi, 'Esclaves chrétiens et esclaves noirs à Tunis au XVIII⁰ siècle', *Annales*, 22, 1967, pp. 1267–88.

[10] Mauny, *Tableau géographique . . .*, p. 379.

[11] Tadeusz Lewicki, 'Arab Trade in Negro Slaves up to the End of the XVIth Century', summary of an unpublished paper in *Africana Bulletin*, 6, 1967, pp. 109–11.

[12] Marian Malowist, 'Le commerce d'or et d'esclaves au Soudan occidental', *Africana Bulletin*, 4, 1966, p. 60.

[13] A. Adu Boahen, *Britain, the Sahara, and the Western Sudan, 1788–1861*, Oxford 1964, p. 128.

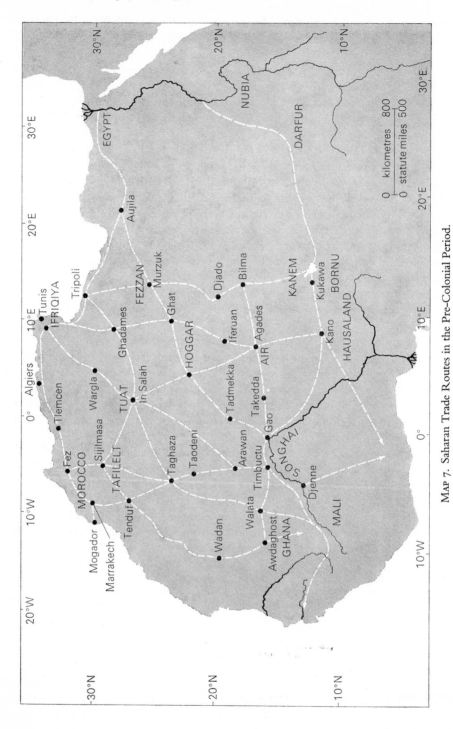

MAP 7. Saharan Trade Routes in the Pre-Colonial Period.

exaggerate either the rapidity or the extent of the eastwards movement. On this basis it can be said that the road from ancient Ghana was supreme up to about the thirteenth century; that the routes from Timbuctu predominated during the time of the empires of Mali and Songhai; and that those from Kano and Bornu became important from the seventeenth century onwards, the Kano route attaining particular prominence in the nineteenth century.

The organisational needs of trans-Saharan trade encouraged the development from very early times of centres of four main types, which were designed to minimise the difficulties of desert trade and to increase the efficiency of the distributive system.[14] First, there were the southern termini, such as Timbuctu, Kano and Kukawa. At these centres, which lay close to the desert, north-bound goods were packed and loaded, and south-bound goods were transferred and divided among smaller caravans for redistribution in other parts of West Africa. If camels were the 'ships of the desert', then these towns were their ports, and their hinterlands in the south stretched almost to the coast. Second, there were halting places on the routes, such as Teghaza, In Salah, Ghat and Agades (until it was replaced by Iferuan in the nineteenth century). These were desert oases, where camels, food and fresh water could be obtained. Third, there were points such as Sijilmasa (until it was destroyed in the late eighteenth century), Tenduf (which replaced it), Wargla and Ghadames, where caravans travelling north unloaded their goods, and those bound for the south gathered before departure. These places were located close to the northern fringe of the desert, where provisions could be bought, and guards, guides and camels hired Finally, there were the great northern termini, such as Mogador, Fez, Algiers, Tunis and Tripoli. These entrepôts were situated on or near to the North African coast, where sales and shipments to Europe and the Middle East were arranged.

Trans-Saharan commerce also required specialised and experienced personnel. It is sometimes said that the trade was dominated by Arab merchants, but this view needs to be treated with care because pre-colonial writers tended to refer, inaccurately, to all Muslims as Arabs. At present there is little precise information about the relative significance of various religious or ethnic groups. Arab merchants, properly defined, were undoubtedly very important, but Berbers, Jews and Negroes also played a major part in the trade, and on the north coast European merchants were to be found. Many of the large entrepôts, like 'free' ports in the other parts of the world, reserved quarters for foreign merchants, guaranteed their security and granted them special privileges. Thus expatriate firms were present in both North Africa and the Western Sudan long before they came to the West Coast. Of the other specialists who made a living out of trans-Saharan trade, the most important were desert colonists such as the Tuareg, whose livelihood was based on the camel and on the plunder or control of the trade routes. The exploitation of the opportunities presented by desert trade encouraged the development of marked economic and social

---

[14] I should like to acknowledge my debt here to Professor Adu Boahen's book, *Britain, the Sahara, and the Western Sudan, 1788–1861*, Oxford 1964, which contains by far the most detailed and reliable study of the trans-Saharan caravan trade yet produced.

inequalities in Tuareg society.[15] In the sultanate of Air (on the route north of Kano) Tuareg clans were divided into two basic groups: the nobles, who controlled the ownership and use of camels, and their vassals, who were restricted to herding goats. As early as the fifteenth century, specialisation and the division of labour had destroyed the pristine 'democracy of poverty' in this remote area, assuming, that is, that it had ever existed.

Long distance trade, with its considerable capital requirements and slow turnover, called for extensive credit facilities and careful investment. In 1825 Laing observed that the merchants of Ghadames 'calculate with profound nicety the expense of carriage to distant countries, duties, customs, risk, trouble, the percentage that their goods will bear, and even do business by means of Bills and unwritten agreements or promises.'[16] It is interesting to note that business arrangements which were very similar to the better known and much criticised 'trust system' of West Coast trade also operated in trans-Saharan commerce, and for the same reasons.[17] The need to mobilise capital and credit on a large scale was a barrier which tended to favour large firms in Timbuctu as in Whydah. It is to be hoped that historians of Islam in Africa will soon begin to extend their important work on religious and political matters, and investigate the little known merchant princes of the caravan trade.

Clearly, the Sahara was not, as once used to be thought, an impenetrable barrier isolating West Africa from the rest of the world. On the contrary, by a feat of daring the more impressive because it was repeated annually over many centuries, African and other merchants succeeded in creating an overland trade which, in size and organisation, deserves to rank with the most famous achievements of merchant venturers in the era before industrialisation removed the physical hardship from international commerce.[18] The desert crossing was extremely dangerous, and could be made only at certain times of the year. The traveller had to be prepared to risk sandstorms, lack of water, sharp variations in temperature (from day to night) and attacks from armed marauders. If he was not asphyxiated, dehydrated, frozen or disposed of by fellow humans, he could easily lose his way—with fatal consequences. Ibn Battuta, who made the desert crossing in 1352, recorded that he used to stray occasionally from the main caravan until the day when one of his party wandered off and never returned. 'After that,' he noted drily, 'I neither went ahead nor lagged behind.'[19] As late as 1910 over fifty people in the small outpost of Taodeni died of

[15] Johannes Nicholaisen, 'Political Systems of Pastoral Tuareg in Air and Ahaggar', *Folk*, I, 1959, pp. 67–131, and 'Ecological and Historical Factors: a Case Study from the Ahaggar Tuareg', *Folk*, 6, 1964, pp. 75–81.

[16] Quoted in Boahen, *Britain, the Sahara . . .*, p. 113.

[17] These arrangements were to be found in other parts of the world too. See, for example, E. S. Crawcour, 'The Development of a Credit System in Seventeenth-Century Japan', *Journal of Economic History*, 21, 1961, pp. 342–60.

[18] For purposes of comparison see Owen Lattimore's essay 'Caravan Routes of Inner Asia', in his *Studies in Frontier History*, 1962, pp. 37–72.

[19] Ibn Battuta, *Travels in Asia and Africa, 1325–1354*, translated and selected by H. A. R. Gibb, 1927, p. 318.

starvation owing to the delayed arrival of a caravan bringing food supplies. Today, most of the routes once trodden by traders, slaves and pilgrims have fallen into disuse. Those which remain carry the great lorries of modern commerce, and sometimes a few adventurous European tourists taking a motorised journey into the African past. Airborne pilgrims *en route* for Mecca now survey only briefly, and from a height of 30,000 feet, the terrain so familiar to generations of their pedestrian predecessors.

2   Trade across the Atlantic

Just as trans-Saharan commerce brought Africa into the international commerce of the Middle Ages, so, too, the development of an overseas trade from the late fifteenth century involved the continent in the creation of a new and extensive multilateral trading relationship, this time with the New World as well as with Europe. In the three centuries before the industrial revolution the focus of international trade moved from the Mediterranean to the Atlantic, from Venice and Genoa to Liverpool and Nantes. This momentous shift of economic power was the product of fundamental changes in the economic and technological basis of European society at the close of the Middle Ages, and was not initiated, as is sometimes implied, solely by the pioneering enterprise of the charismatic Prince Henry of Portugal, navigator extraordinary.[20] Furthermore, it would be quite wrong to assume that from the fifteenth century onwards sea-borne exports from West Africa consisted almost entirely of human cargo. When Jobson was offered slaves on the West Coast in 1620, he replied, disdainfully, that 'we were a people who did not deale in any such commodities, neither did we buy or sell one another, or any that had our owne shapes.'[21] The motive behind the first 'scramble' for Africa was undoubtedly economic, but it sprang from a desire to capture riches which were already known and valued in Europe.[22] The overseas slave trade came later.

Before the rise of legitimate commerce in the nineteenth century, the main exports from West Africa, apart from slaves, were gold, ivory, timber, dye-woods, gum, beeswax, leather and spices, notably peppers. These commodities sometimes supplemented the trade in slaves, but they were also treated as viable exports in their own right. Initially, the principal aim of the European merchant mariners was to gain control of the gold resources of West Africa. Hence some of the earliest and busiest coastal bases were in Senegal and the Gold Coast, close to the main centres of mining activity. In addition to their keen interest in minerals, the Europeans paid

[20] Though whether the African quest was undertaken by a Portuguese nobility anxious to rescue its declining fortunes, or whether it was wealth won from the trans-Saharan gold trade which encouraged an expanding Iberia to expand even further, is a matter which must be left for historians of Europe to decide.

[21] Jobson, *The Golden Trade . . .* , p. 112.

[22] For further details see Marian Malowist, 'Les fondements de l'expansion européenne en Afrique au XVᵉ siècle: Europe, Maghreb et Soudan occidentale', *Acta Poloniae Historica*, 18, 1968, pp. 156–79.

some attention to the agricultural resources of the continent.[23] An attempt was made to use West African products as substitutes for those from Asia, whose exports to Europe had fallen under Muslim control in the later part of the Middle Ages. It was for this reason that the Portuguese began to ship pepper from Benin in the fifteenth century. From the sixteenth century onwards efforts were made to develop the production of crops such as sugar, cotton and tobacco. These ventures anticipated experiments which were to be tried again, and on a greater scale, in the nineteenth century, but which meanwhile were to achieve much greater success in the West Indies and North America.

Even after the Atlantic slave trade had become well established, some parts of West Africa, particularly areas west of the Volta river, continued to conduct an important export trade in other commodities. Detailed information about the size and value of this commerce is hard to find at present, though according to one estimate about two-fifths of the income of the Royal African Company at the end of the seventeenth century came from sales of goods other than slaves.[24] Gold was by far the most valuable of these products, and was still the principal overseas export of the Gold Coast at that time, even though the region had also become a major supplier of slaves. It was only in the latter part of the eighteenth century that the situation changed, and Gold Coast exporters then sold slaves to European merchants in exchange for gold. Further west still, in Sierra Leone, exports such as camwood, ivory and beeswax were worth more than shipments of slaves until at least the middle of the eighteenth century. Another prominent example of an area where trade in natural products was of considerable importance was Senegambia, which developed initially as a centre for the gold trade. Later on, slaves were exported, but significant quantities of other goods were handled as well, as Abdoulaye Ly has made clear.[25] Gum was the major export from the Senegal Valley and the Mauritanian coast in the seventeenth and eighteenth centuries,[26] and beeswax was as important as slaves in the overseas trade of Casamance (southern Senegal) during the same period. Both products had pharmaceutical and industrial uses, gum being especially significant as a raw material in the manufacture of textiles. Finally, it is interesting to note that Europeans sometimes acted as middlemen in African interregional trade, employing their ships to expand existing local markets and occasionally to create markets where none existed before. In the fifteenth century, for example, the Portuguese exported slaves from Benin and sold them on the Gold Coast for gold. Two centuries later they were using kola nuts from Sierra Leone to buy slaves in Senegambia. In the seventeenth century, too, the Dutch shipped cloth and beads from Benin to the Gold Coast, and in the eighteenth century Bristol slavers

[23] Marian Malowist, 'Les debuts du système de plantations dans la période des Grandes Découvertes', *Africana Bulletin*, 10, 1969, pp. 9–30.

[24] K. G. Davies, *The Royal African Company*, 1957, pp. 179–80.

[25] *La compagnie du Sénégal*, Paris 1958.

[26] This question has been dealt with by André Delcourt, *La France et les établissements français au Sénégal entre 1713 et 1763*, Dakar 1952.

bought and sold rice, guinea corn, millet and yams as they made their way along the coast.

It is worth summarising the comments made so far, as they have often been underplayed in the past,[27] and they need to be borne in mind during the discussion of the Atlantic slave trade which follows. First, the Europeans who came to West Africa in the fifteenth and sixteenth centuries were interested mainly in goods other than slaves. Second, this commerce continued even after the overseas slave trade was well under way. Third, there were marked regional differences in West Africa depending on the nature of trade with the Europeans. Fourth, European shipping services encouraged the growth of a new kind of long distance coastal trade in West Africa. Finally, it may be useful to point out that further research is needed into the subject of trade in non-slave products. Future work will undoubtedly lead to a more varied view of what is now considered as the era of the Atlantic slave trade, and it will also modify the way historians interpret developments in the nineteenth century, when an export economy based entirely on 'legitimate' goods was created.

The Atlantic slave trade is perhaps the most discussed episode in the economic history of West Africa, and is certainly the only one known to that notional being, the general reader. Unfortunately, most of the popular books which appear regularly on this subject, though they may succeed in giving the more dramatic aspects appropriately epic treatment, rarely contribute anything new in the way of facts or ideas. Few make full use of the available secondary sources, and some perpetuate old-fashioned views of Africa among a reading public which, understandably, is not in touch with the latest developments in African studies.[28] Age and repetition have combined to entrench both myths and truths to such an extent that it is hard now to tell one from the other. Fortunately, some valuable studies of particular aspects of the Atlantic slave trade have been carried out recently, and it is certain that this subject will look very different in a few years' time. In the pages which follow an attempt will be made to summarise and comment on the main themes as they appear at present, and to explore a few of the problems which, hopefully, future research will reveal as significant. The discussion will begin by briefly outlining the main sources of demand for labour, and will then consider how the supply of slaves was organised, dealing first with the European side of the trade, and second with the situation on the West Coast itself. No apology is made for mentioning regions other than Africa, for the slave trade cannot be understood without reference to the international setting within which it grew, flourished and declined.

Some Africans had been bought by Europeans from the beginning of their contact with the West Coast in the fifteenth century, notwithstanding Jobson's lofty indifference towards this type of commerce. In the sixteenth century a few slaves were used by the Portuguese to work sugar plantations on islands just off the coast of

[27] An important exception is the study by Walter Rodney, *A History of the Upper Guinea Coast, 1545–1800*, Oxford 1970, ch. 6.

[28] An outstanding exception to these critical generalisations is Basil Davidson's *Black Mother*, 1961, though inevitably this book has been overtaken to some extent by research carried out during the last ten years.

West Africa, and others were exported to South America to mine the silver which was discovered there in the 1520s. However, the demand for slave labour was not very great at this time, and the export trade was unimportant. The rapid expansion of the Atlantic trade began only in the middle of the seventeenth century, as a result of the rise of sugar plantations in the West Indies.[29] This development revolutionised the economy of the Caribbean. Until about the 1650s the main export from the West Indies had been tobacco, which was grown on a small scale by a few European settlers.[30] Sugar, however, was pre-eminently a planters' crop, and it required land, capital, and labour on a large scale. The land was there already; the capital came from Europe; and, in the event, the labour came from Africa, not because the continent was overpopulated, but because no other cheaper source of suitable manpower was readily available. The indigenous inhabitants of the Americas had been tried and found wanting, and many of the European pioneers on this particular frontier of the New World chose to cultivate land for themselves elsewhere, especially in Virginia and Carolina, where tobacco was becoming an important export crop. To retain a free labour force where there was abundant land and alternative employment opportunities would have meant paying high wages. Cheap and subservient labour was preferred and was probably essential. Besides being relatively inexpensive and readily available (thanks to the efficiency of the Afro-European delivery system), negro labourers had a higher survival rate in the West Indies, and therefore had a cost advantage over potential competitors in the labour market. The advantage was a result of their greater immunity from diseases such as yellow fever and malaria, and had nothing to do with the alleged inability of the white man to work in a tropical climate.[31] And so the venturers who had originally sailed to West Africa primarily to trade in gold stayed on to supply labourers for the new sugar plantations of the Caribbean.

The eighteenth century was the golden age of prosperity for the West Indies, the time when the Islands became the chief suppliers of sugar to Europe. The principal centres of production were Jamaica, a British possession, and St Domingo, which belonged to France. According to Sheridan, about two-thirds of all the slaves shipped to the Caribbean worked on sugar plantations, and in the highly specialised economy of Jamaica no less than 84 per cent of the slaves (160,000 out of 190,000) were employed in the sugar industry in the 1770s.[32] Other crops, such as coffee, cotton, indigo and tobacco, were grown, but sugar remained by far the most important export. The expansion of sugar production was stimulated by a rise in demand in Europe

[29] D. A. Farnie, 'The Commercial Empire of the Atlantic, 1607–1783', *Economic History Review*, 15, 1962, pp. 205–18.

[30] A. P. Thornton, 'The Organization of the Slave Trade in the English West Indies, 1660–1685', *William and Mary Quarterly*, 12, 1955, pp. 399–409.

[31] This point has been elaborated by Philip D. Curtin, 'Epidemiology and the Slave Trade', *Political Science Quarterly*, 83, 1968, pp. 190–216.

[32] R. B. Sheridan, 'The Commercial and Financial Organization of the British Slave Trade, 1750–1807', *Economic History Review*, 11, 1958, p. 249, and 'The Wealth of Jamaica in the Eighteenth Century: A Rejoinder', *ibid*, 21, 1968, p. 49.

following an increase in the consumption of tea and coffee; by a growth in the capacity of the sugar processing industry, which had caught up with supply by about the middle of the eighteenth century; and by government support, which underpinned the structure of Atlantic trade. From 1651 to 1854, for example, producers in the British colonies in the West Indies were protected by the imposition of heavy duties on foreign sugar entering the United Kingdom. In the second half of the eighteenth century the French government offered bounties to slave ships leaving France for Africa, and made an additional payment for every slave they landed in the French West Indies. This concern is understandable when it is realised that by 1789 about two-thirds of French maritime exports went to her colonies in the West Indies, and that sugar was the most valuable commodity sent to France from overseas. Sugar was also the largest single item imported into England in the eighteenth century. The average annual value of sugar imports rose nearly four times from £630,000 in the period 1699–1701 to £2,364,000 in the period 1772–74. Between 1714 and 1773 imports from the West Indies averaged about 20 per cent of the annual value of all imports into England. Commercially, the Caribbean had become more important to England than Asia, and was second only to trade with Europe. To Malachi Postlethwayt, a spokesman of mercantilist orthodoxy, the British Empire was a 'magnificent superstructure of American commerce and naval power on an African foundation'.[33] His summary cannot be bettered.

The importance of the various Western powers engaged in trade with Africa was largely a reflection of their changing political positions in Europe.[34] Portugal was the leading foreign power in West Africa in the fifteenth and sixteenth centuries; the Dutch presence became significant in the seventeenth century; and England and France dominated the eighteenth century. One useful index of the relative positions of the major powers is provided by the number of slaves handled by each at the height of the Atlantic trade.[35]

Slave exports from West Africa by the three major powers, 1701–1810

England	2,009,700
France	613,100
Portugal	611,000
	3,233,800

England's supremacy is clearly demonstrated: she alone was responsible for about two-thirds of the total number of slaves shipped by the three leading powers. Her pre-eminence in West Africa was one striking illustration of the more general growth of her foreign trade in the eighteenth century, and of the global dominance of her

[33] Quoted in Eric Williams, *Capitalism and Slavery*, 1964 edn, p. 52.
[34] Further information about the political rivalries of the great powers in West Africa can be found in J. D. Fage, *A History of West Africa*, 1969, chs 3 and 4.
[35] Philip D. Curtin, *The Atlantic Slave Trade: a Census*, Madison 1969, p. 211.

navy. Britain's ascendancy was not seriously challenged until the close of the nineteenth century, when French troops began their long, dusty march across what Lord Salisbury was to refer to, ironically, as the 'light' soils of the Western Sudan. It is sometimes said that French power in West Africa deteriorated in the second half of the eighteenth century. However, it is important to realise that England's supremacy was the result of the relatively quick pace of her commercial expansion, and was not brought about by an absolute decline in French commerce with West Africa, though France still relied on Holland and Britain for many of her trade goods. Indeed, the tempo of French activity in this part of the world actually increased after 1763, following Choiseul's efforts to develop Africa to compensate for the loss of Canada, and to free the French West Indies from dependence on British ships for supplies of slaves. The position of the Portuguese is especially noteworthy. Far from declining in the early seventeenth century, as is commonly supposed to be the case, their commercial hold remained strong long afterwards. Admittedly, Portugal's share of slave shipments declined as the eighteenth century progressed, but it revived again during the first half of the nineteenth century, when the trade entered its final, and far from negligible, phase.

Before the nineteenth century the European powers were represented in West Africa by large, state-chartered companies and by individual traders rather than by regular soldiers and professional administrators. Chartered companies were prominent during the early phase of sea-borne trade with West Africa, and especially during the seventeenth century. These companies were given trading monopolies over various sections of the African coast in return for fulfilling certain obligations. In the Netherlands the leading officially-sponsored firm was the Dutch West India Company (1621), which, besides having interests in the Caribbean, was also active along the West African coast during the seventeenth century. The most important French companies were the Compagnie des Indes Occidentales (1664), founded by Colbert on ideas formulated by Richelieu, the Compagnie du Sénégal (1673), and the Compagnie du Guinée (1684). The principal English concern was the Royal African Company (1672), which succeeded the aptly named and unbusinesslike Royal Adventurers into Africa (1660). The presence of joint-stock companies in some branches of foreign commerce was mainly a result of the desire of subscribers to share the risks of African trade, which was notorious for its uncertainty, though in part it was also a response to the capital requirements of long distance trade, especially the need to invest in fixed capital, such as forts and ships. The state issued charters because it saw the companies as useful agents of foreign policy, and, hopefully, as a means of enriching the rulers too. The promoters sought government patronage as a means of attracting capital and eliminating competition. Interdependence was the basis of mercantilism: the power of the state was increased by measures designed to achieve a favourable balance of trade; at the same time particular interest groups sought to use state power as a means to private gain.[36] In the context of the inter-

---

[36] Charles Wilson, *Profit and Power: a Study of England and the Dutch Wars*, 1957, p. 153. On mercantilism see D. C. Coleman, ed., *Revisions in Mercantilism*, 1969.

national rivalries of the seventeenth century, the chartered companies can be seen as protagonists in the struggle between conflicting national, mercantilist policies which aimed at controlling not only African trade, but the commerce of the Atlantic, and, ultimately, of Europe.

The chartered companies were more impressive in their plans than in their achievements. It is clear from the specialist works of Davies, Delcourt and Ly that the companies shared much the same defects. In the first place, they were unable to attract sufficient capital. French merchants were traditionally wary of putting their money into government companies, which consequently required subsidies from public and court funds. English merchants were more prepared to invest in chartered companies, but they rarely acquired large holdings, and were quick to switch their money to alternative uses if more profitable opportunities arose. Second, the companies had large overheads in the shape of officials and forts, and they sometimes had to carry extensive burdens of defence. Third, they were unable to secure staff of sufficient quality, and their employees also failed to identify their interests with those of the firm, with the result that mismanagement and private trading by company servants seriously hindered the efficient conduct of business. Fourth, the companies were required to meet specific obligations, such as supplying a fixed number of slaves each year, and so had to continue trading irrespective of the conditions operating at the time. It was this problem which led the Compagnie du Sénégal into difficulties after 1679. Finally, the chartered companies were attacked by a variety of interests which opposed their monopoly powers. These included traders who were kept out of the areas under the jurisdiction of the companies; manufacturers, who were dissatisfied with restricted outlets for their goods; colonists (especially in the West Indies), who objected to the terms on which they exchanged their products for consumer imports; and the political opponents of monarchical power, who saw the chartered companies as symbols of the royal prerogative. By about 1700 it was clear that the chartered company, though not yet eliminated, had little future in West African trade. Financially, the chartered companies were failures. They were asked to perform the most difficult of all commercial feats, the reconciliation of the capitalist ethic with public duty, an expectation which survives today only in certain nationalised industries. Their main achievements were as frontier agencies of the old colonial system, opening up markets which others were to exploit more effectively later on.

It used to be customary for historians to contrast the mercantilist restrictions of the seventeenth century with the development of free trade in the eighteenth century. This interpretation can no longer stand without qualification. It is true that the monopoly powers of the chartered companies were dismantled during the course of the eighteenth century, but the process was a gradual one, and most of the companies managed to struggle on until about the middle of the century or even later. At the same time, it should be noted that, in practice, private traders had played an important part in West African trade even in the seventeenth century. From the outset the companies had been unable to make exclusive use of their monopoly powers. They had found it necessary to issue 'passports' or licences to private traders, and they had also been forced to tolerate interlopers, who traded in their territories without permission. In more general terms, it would be quite wrong to equate the decline of the chartered companies with the rise of free trade, at least in the sense that this concept came to be used in the nineteenth century. It has been shown that the eighteenth century saw a marked *increase* in high level duties on goods imported into England, and that this change in the tariff structure had the effect of protecting domestic manufactures.[37] Whether they realised it or not, at the close of the eighteenth century Adam Smith and his disciples were attacking a comparatively recent development in commercial policy, and not a tariff structure inherited from the era of mercantilism.

The shift to free trade was therefore somewhat limited. As far as West African commerce was concerned, it took the form of a relative increase in the importance of private traders and a relative decline in the position of the chartered companies. This change was not the outcome of a mighty confrontation between conflicting economic philosophies, but was made for practical business reasons. The chartered companies, which had not been successful even in the conditions of the seventeenth century, were quite unable to cope with the expanded scale of the slave trade in the eighteenth century. The private traders prospered because they had smaller overhead costs (a lower ratio of staff to turnover and less money tied up in overseas bases); they enjoyed a much greater degree of personal supervision on the West Coast, which meant they could respond more quickly to changing circumstances; and they were unhampered by public obligations and government directives, and so could trade when, where and on what terms they chose.

The success of the private traders was to be seen in the spectacular rise of the two greatest European centres of the slave trade, Liverpool and Nantes. In the eighteenth century English ships carried about two-thirds of the total number of slaves sent across the Atlantic from West Africa, and French ships roughly one fifth of the total. Liverpool and Nantes each accounted for no less than half of these national totals and sometimes considerably more. In view of the marked concentration of trade on these two ports it is worth while saying a little more about them, especially since Liverpool's role in the Atlantic slave trade has been curiously neglected by modern scholars (the most recent study being an unpublished and little used M.A. thesis),[38] while the part played by Nantes, though well covered by the researches of Gaston Martin, Jean Meyer and Père Rinchon, is usually by-passed in works by English historians.[39]

---

[37] Ralph Davis, 'The Rise of Protection in England, 1689–1786', *Economic History Review*, 19, 1966, pp. 306–17.

[38] J. E. Merritt, *The Liverpool Slave Trade from 1789 to 1791*, University of Nottingham M.A. thesis, 1959.

[39] Gaston Martin, *Nantes au XVIIIᵉ siècle: l'ère des négriers (1714–44)*, Paris 1931; Jean Meyer, 'Le commerce négrier nantais (1774–1792)', *Annales*, 15, 1960, pp. 120–29; and Père D. Rinchon, *Pierre-Ignace-Liévin van Alstein, capitaine négrier*, Dakar 1964. Other work on Nantes by Meyer and Rinchon, and by Everaert and Maugat is listed in the bibliography.

By 1712 the Royal African Company was in an advanced state of decay, and London, the headquarters of the company and the main English slave port in the seventeenth century, was fast losing control of the African trade. Bristol, which began slave trading in the 1690s, was the principal beneficiary of the decline of her rival, but her own supremacy lasted for only three decades, reaching a peak between 1725 and 1735.[40] Liverpool's participation in the slave trade also began in the late seventeenth century, but it was not until the 1730s that her involvement became significant. Within ten years Liverpool had become the leading slave-trading port in Europe, a position which she retained until 1807, when it became illegal for British subjects to engage in the African slave trade. By 1750 Liverpool's ships were carrying over half the slaves exported from Africa in English vessels, and from then on the trade expanded until the American War of Independence (1776–83), which struck the port a hard blow. In 1779 only eleven ships left Liverpool for Africa, which figure was the lowest in the history of the trade (1730–1807). With the conclusion of peace there was a revival of trade: in the 1790s Liverpool's merchantmen were transporting between 25,000 and 50,000 slaves across the Atlantic each year, which was roughly three-quarters of the total handled by English ships. In 1798 a record number of 149 vessels left Liverpool for the African coast. These fluctuations illustrate the extent to which Atlantic commerce, with its long, perilous trade routes and widely separated markets, was affected by hostilities between the great powers, and particularly by naval warfare. What the figures do not reveal is the ability of shipowners to adapt to these crises. Some sought compensation by sending their vessels to friendlier waters; others took to privateering.

Liverpool's dominance owed something to geographical advantages. The port was more favourably situated for trade across the Atlantic than was London, and in time of war it was less harassed by French privateers than either London or Bristol. More important still, however, was Liverpool's position as the chief entrepôt of an expanding hinterland, which covered not only Manchester, but more distant centres such as Sheffield and Birmingham. Part of London's early success in trade to Africa was the result of her proximity to Europe, for down to the middle of the eighteenth century over half the goods sent to Africa from the United Kingdom were re-exports of items obtained from Holland, Sweden and other countries on the Continent. In the second half of the century the position changed, and between two-thirds and three-quarters of the goods destined for Africa were manufactured in the United Kingdom. Liverpool became the main outlet for these new industrial products. Relatively low internal transport costs enabled the port to ship cotton goods, hardware and guns more cheaply than any of its competitors, an advantage which was strengthened by the completion of the Bridgewater canal in 1772. The value of the link with Manchester first became apparent in the second quarter of the eighteenth century, when there was a boom in exports of Manchester goods to Spanish America. Once the African trade was under way, Manchester manufacturers gave considerable help

[40] Bristol's role in the slave trade has been well covered by P. D. Richardson, *The Bristol Slave Trade in the Eighteenth Century*, University of Manchester M.A. thesis, 1969.

4*

to Liverpool slave merchants by granting them credit for up to eighteen months. This facility was particularly valuable in a trade which required a substantial outlay of capital (largely because of the amalgamation of mercantile and shipping functions), and an ability to await returns on investments (because of the length of time involved in completing transactions spanning several continents).

Finally, part of Liverpool's success must be attributed to the 'ruthless efficiency' of her merchants, a feature stressed by specialist works on the history of the port, but one which is difficult to evaluate. Ruthlessness may well have had the edge over efficiency: Liverpool slavers had lower running costs than their Bristol rivals, but this was not because they carried fewer hands or more slaves per ton, but because they paid their crews lower wages.[41] Liverpool slave traders came from all sections of society, and had many other interests besides African commerce. They counted in their ranks landowners, manufacturers, tradesmen, merchants in other branches of overseas trade, and a number of ships' captains, such as the famous Billy Boats, a self-made man who eventually became an independent shipowner. Their ventures were financed from private savings, from the profits of other business activities (including past slaving expeditions), and from credits granted by banks and manufacturers. As the century advanced, there was a trend towards concentration among the slave-trading firms. By the 1780s and 1790s the trade was dominated by about ten firms, all conducting a regular trade, and each having roughly a dozen partners, who were often members of the same family. In the period 1789–91, for example, the seven largest firms undertook over half the total number of slaving ventures. There was a second, and numerically larger, group of slave traders, which consisted of small, speculative investors, many of whom had only 1/32 share in a voyage. It is clear that the rise of private traders did not represent a shift from large scale to small scale operations. This is not surprising, for many of the problems (of raising capital and spreading risks) which had led to the creation of joint-stock companies in the seventeenth century were still present in African trade long after the monopolist concerns had lost their charters.

The case of Nantes presents some interesting comparisons and contrasts with that of Liverpool. Nantes began slave trading in the 1690s, and expanded her activities by acquiring concessions from the monopoly companies. In 1716 Nantes was one of four French ports which were permitted to deal freely in slaves, and from the 1720s she became the leading slave-trading port in the country. By the middle of the century her ships transported about 10,000 African captives a year across the Atlantic, which was over half the total carried by French vessels. Gaston Martin argued that this was the time of peak prosperity for the port, and that a permanent decline set in after 1774. However, recent work by Meyer and Everaert has shown that the downturn was only temporary, and that there was a boom between 1783 and 1792, when ships from Nantes delivered more slaves than in any other decade of the eighteenth century. In this period Nantes sent out an average of thirty-five slavers a year as

---

[41] Lower wages may also have reflected a difference in the supply price of labour in the two regions.

against twenty-one a year between 1749 and 1755. Moreover, the tonnage of the vessels used in the trade increased towards the close of the century. This extension of Gaston Martin's pioneering study demonstrates that the fluctuations experienced by Nantes before 1792 were much the same in timing as those felt by Liverpool. The chief cause in both cases was warfare between the great powers. It is also clear that there was no absolute decline in slave trading at Nantes in the second half of the century. However, it is true to say that there was a *relative* decline, as slaving became proportionately less important to Nantes than other branches of foreign commerce, and as rival ports began to participate in the slave trade on a greater scale than in the first half of the century. By the 1780s, Nantes, though still dominant, was followed closely by Le Havre, Bordeaux, La Rochelle and Honfleur, all of which expanded their slave trading activities after 1763.[42] La Rochelle, for example, turned to slaving in an attempt to secure compensation for the loss of the Canadian fur trade.

Nantes, like Liverpool, owed much of her success to a special connection, though it was one of a rather different kind. Nantes had close ties with the Compagnie des Indes (1719), a gigantic concern which played an important, if erratic, part in French foreign trade until it was dissolved in 1767. Nantes, one of the Compagnie's main centres in France, enjoyed advantages in obtaining goods for shipment to West Africa, especially cotton manufactures from India, which were a staple of the trade. Nantes also acted as a carrier for the Compagnie, and was given certain tariff concessions on shipments to the French West Indies. The relationship between Nantes and the Compagnie des Indes illustrates the dangers, noted earlier, of adopting a simplistic view of the rise of free trade in the eighteenth century, for the private traders of the port, though formally opposed to monopoly, in practice gained a great deal from their association with a privileged company. It is no coincidence that the ascendancy of Nantes began to be challenged in the second half of the eighteenth century, when there was a marked increase in competition among French slave traders.

In Nantes, as in Liverpool and Bristol, slave traders came from varied backgrounds, though the majority were already in business as shipowners or merchants before they took to slaving. In Nantes, too, the distinction between mariner and merchant was often hard to define. The career of Pierre van Alstein (1733–93) shows that the captain of a slave ship had to be a good businessman as well as a good navigator. Consequently, it was not hard for a successful captain to attain a more desirable status, that of a *bourgeois gentilhomme*. Van Alstein began his career at Nantes in 1748, became a captain in 1758 at the age of twenty-six, and retired thirty years later. In common with other slave captains, he received only a small fixed wage

---

[42] Information about these ports can be found in the following works, all of which deserve to receive more attention from historians of Africa: J. Cl. Bénard, 'L'armement honfleurais et le commerce des esclaves à la fin du XVIIIe siècle', *Annales de Normandie*, 10, 1960, pp. 249–64; Pierre Dardel, *Navires et marchandises dans les ports de Rouen et du Havre au XVIIIe siècle*, Paris 1963; G. Rambert, *Histoire du commerce de Marseilles*, 6, de 1660 à 1789, les colonies, Paris 1959; and H. Robert, 'Les trafics coloniaux du port de La Rochelle au XVIIIe siècle', *Mémoires de la Société des Antiquaires de l'Ouest*, 4, 1960, pp. xii–211.

and relied heavily on commission for boosting his income. Between 1748 and 1768 van Alstein's total earnings amounted to 26,000 livres, which was not a vast sum, but his last three expeditions (1768–84) enabled him to increase this figure ten-fold, and by the time he retired he had made a fortune of about 300,000 livres. Far from being treated as an outcast, van Alstein became a wealthy bourgeois, a respected, modest and religious man. The fact that a slave trader could become a pillar of French provincial society is an interesting comment on the values of the eighteenth century, and one which highlights the need to make a clear distinction between relative and absolute standards when making historical judgements.

Voyages from Nantes were financed in much the same way as those from Liverpool and Bristol, that is by groups of about twelve subscribers using their savings, past profits, local credit, and—in the case of the French port—capital from Paris. In the middle years of the century the slave trade was concentrated in a few hands. Scarcely fifty merchants were engaged extensively in the trade, and three families alone were responsible for financing over half the vessels leaving Nantes on slaving expeditions. However, in the second half of the century there was a movement away from specialisation, and the pattern became one of a larger number of merchants equipping proportionately fewer slaving ventures. This trend was partly a result of the Seven Years War (1756–63), which greatly increased the risks of the trade, and partly a reflection of the reorientation of commerce at Nantes towards the close of the century, when slaving became just one aspect of a merchant's business rather than his sole concern.

Research into the organisation of Europe's overseas trade in the eighteenth century has led, in recent years, to a revival of interest in the routes followed by slave ships. Historians of Africa have not shown much awareness of the debate on this subject, and have tended to adhere to the traditional notion of the triangular trade, as established in the earliest textbooks of imperial history. According to the conventional view, the African trade was organised in three stages, in which vessels left Europe for the West Coast to sell consumer goods and to buy slaves, then sailed to the West Indies to exchange slaves for sugar, and finally returned home to dispose of sugar and to settle their accounts. The accuracy of this description has been questioned, and it has been suggested that the triangular trade existed only in the early days of the Atlantic slave trade, when relatively little sugar was being sent to Europe, and that for the greater part of the eighteenth century slaves and sugar were two distinct trades.[43] This suggestion has encouraged historians to re-examine the conventional approach, which certainly oversimplifies reality. At the same time, however, the revised interpretation cannot be accepted as it stands because it rests on a set of *prima facie* arguments rather than on empirical evidence.

The view adopted here is that Merritt and others are mistaken in claiming that the triangular trade was exceptional in the eighteenth century, but correct in implying that it was far from being the only, or always the most important, means of conduct-

---

[43] J. E. Merritt, 'The Triangular Trade', *Business History*, 3, 1960, pp. 1–7, provides a summary of views expressed earlier by other writers.

ing Atlantic commerce. With regard to the first point, evidence from Bristol, Nantes and Honfleur, in particular, shows that the classical triangular trade was still quite normal in the eighteenth century. As to the second point, it is equally clear that the transportation of slaves and sugar cannot be understood simply in terms of the triangular trade alone. A number of direct routes were very important, though they have rarely been sufficiently emphasised. A direct route between Europe and Africa was followed by ships trading in non-slave products, notably gold and gum. In addition, there were direct routes to the West Coast across the Atlantic from North America, the West Indies and Brazil, which were used by colonists trading rum and tobacco for slaves.[44] Finally, there was a very busy route between Europe and the West Indies. This was used by fleets of merchantmen, which came from Europe with supplies for the Islands, and returned home carrying a substantial proportion of the sugar crop. The volume of traffic on this route is indicated by the fact that, in 1789, 116 ships left English ports for Africa, whereas no less than 449 left for the West Indies. Liverpool, which was dominant in the slave trade, had roughly equal shares with London and Bristol in the sugar trade. Nantes was the chief importer of sugar into France, but several other ports, including Rouen, Le Havre, Marseilles and St Malo, conducted a considerable direct trade with the Caribbean. In the case of St Malo, Le Corre has estimated that for every ship engaged in the triangular trade in the late seventeenth century fifty went straight to the West Indies.[45]

Whether a vessel returned home from the West Indies with ballast or sugar was a decision which, from the slaver's point of view, depended largely on the availability and price of produce. At the same time, there were good reasons why an additional, specialised fleet was required to carry sugar on the last leg of the triangular voyage. In the first place, slave ships were not entirely adequate as transporters of tropical produce. They were not built to carry hogsheads of sugar; they were often in an unseaworthy condition when they reached the Caribbean; the irregularity of their arrival meant that planters could not be certain of evacuating their crop at the right time; and, perhaps most important of all, the expansion of the sugar industry set up a demand for freight which exceeded the physical capacity of the ships arriving from Africa. Secondly, by the middle of the eighteenth century the increasing use of bills of exchange enabled accounts to be settled quickly, and made the exchange of sugar for slaves less of a necessity.[46] There is some evidence that the slave traders put up the price of slaves to compensate for returning in ballast, but they also gained from the new arrangement to the extent that payment in bills enabled them to make a faster turnaround. Thirdly, the development of close ties between planters and metropolitan sugar merchants during the eighteenth century tended to reinforce direct trading links, with the result that captains of slave ships often found that the

[44] On the latter see Pierre Verger, 'Mouvements de navires entre Bahia et le golfe de Bénin (XVIIIᵉ–XIXᵉ siècles)', *Revue Française d'Histoire d'Outre-Mer*, 55, 1968, pp. 5–36.

[45] A. Le Corre, 'Le grand commerce malouin en 1686–1687', *Annales de Bretagne*, 3, 1958, pp. 275–331.

[46] On the use of bills of exchange in Atlantic commerce see S. G. Checkland, 'Finance for the West Indies, 1780–1815', *Economic History Review*, 10, 1958, pp. 461–9.

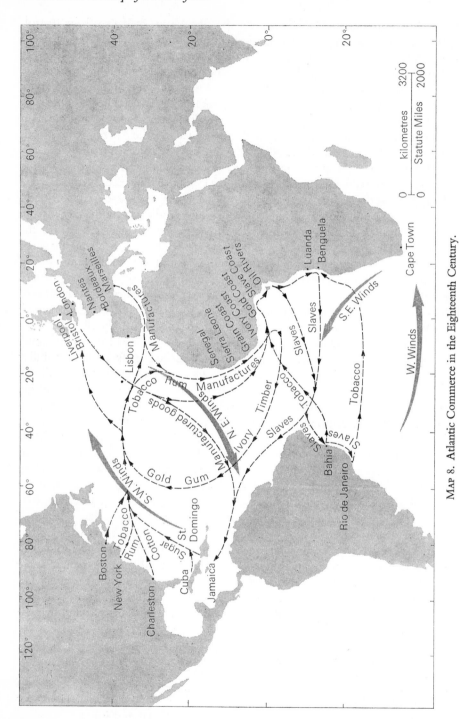

MAP 8. Atlantic Commerce in the Eighteenth Century.

planters had made alternative arrangements for shipping produce to Europe. Increasing specialisation in the slave and sugar trades lowered the investment requirements for entry into Atlantic commerce, reduced the risks of trade, and speeded the turnover of capital, since the direct trip to the Caribbean could be completed in about six months, whereas the triangular trade took a year or even longer. It was for these reasons that the merchants of Marseilles, for example, preferred to concentrate on direct trade to the West Indies, in spite of official efforts to encourage the port to participate in the slave trade.

The African side of the Atlantic slave trade will be considered in three parts. These will consist of an assessment of the numbers involved, a discussion of the 'production' of slaves, and an examination of the organisation of the coastal wholesaling centres. The important question of the consequences of the slave trade will be reserved for the final section of this chapter.

A review of historical opinion on the numbers of slaves exported from Africa to the Americas provides a classic example of how the repetition of untested statements can create an almost unshakable orthodoxy. Figures derived ultimately from the well-intentioned, but prejudiced, guesswork of nineteenth-century abolitionists have been passed on, endorsed and elaborated right down to the present day. The totals cited by the majority of writers range from 15–20 million African slaves imported into the Americas, to 18–24 million shipped from Africa, the difference being accounted for by losses on the way. Fortunately, Professor Curtin, with characteristic originality, has recently carried out a meticulous investigation of the available evidence—an historical exercise which may seem obvious, but is so only in retrospect.[47] His main conclusion is that established estimates greatly exaggerate the scale of the Atlantic slave trade. In Curtin's view the total number of African slaves reaching the Americas, the Atlantic islands, and Europe amounted to 9,566,000, of whom all except 175,000 were landed in the New World. This total, which is about half the mean of the figures usually cited, is not to be treated as a set figure 'to be repeated in the textbooks'.[48] It is to be used rather as an indication of a range of possibilities, which extend from a minimum figure of 8,000,000 to a maximum of 10,500,000.[49] If 15 per cent is added, as seems a reasonable average, to allow for losses during the voyage, then the total number of slaves exported from Africa was about 11 million, which again is about half the figure commonly cited. In theory a further percentage should be added to allow for deaths caused by slave raiding expeditions in Africa, but at present it is impossible even to guess at what this amount might be.

Curtin's data also supply important information about the chronological development and geographical incidence of the slave trade. As to the first, the figures of slaves reaching their destinations can be broken down in the following way:[50]

[47] Philip D. Curtin, *The Atlantic Slave Trade: a Census*, Madison 1969. But for the timely publication of Curtin's book, the present writer would also be counted among the unquestioning majority.

[48] Curtin, *The Atlantic Slave Trade*, p. 86.

[49] Curtin, *The Atlantic Slave Trade*, p. 87.

[50] Curtin, *The Atlantic Slave Trade*, p. 268.

Slave imports into the Americas and Europe, 1451–1870

1451–1600	274,900
1601–1700	1,341,100
1701–1810	6,051,700
1811–1870	1,898,400
	9,566,100

These lower totals are consistent with the emphasis given in this chapter to trade in products other than slaves, and they confirm that the boom in slave exports coincided with the expansion of sugar production in the Caribbean during the eighteenth century. No less than 80 per cent of all slaves landed in the New World were transported between 1701 and 1850. The figures for the nineteenth century demonstrate that the slave trade remained significant even after it had been outlawed by Britain, the greatest slave-trading nation, a point which the imperial school of history, with its emphasis on Wilberforce's triumph in 1807, never really explained.

With regard to areas of supply, Curtin's figures indicate that rather more slaves were exported from places south of the Cameroons, especially the Congo and Angola, than is customarily assumed. A calculation made on the basis of Curtin's data suggests that about 6,300,000 slaves (55 per cent of the total shipped across the Atlantic from Africa) came from West Africa.[51] Slaves were not exported in identical proportions from all parts of the West Coast. Indeed, in the eighteenth century the region between Senegal and the Ivory Coast played a relatively unimportant part in the Atlantic slave trade, and the principal area of export was the shorter stretch of coast running from the Gold Coast east to the Cameroons. In the 1780s, when the Atlantic trade was at its peak, annual exports from various sections of the coast were as follows:

Senegambia	2,200	Gold Coast	10,000
Sierra Leone	2,000	Slave Coast to Benin	12,500
Grain and Ivory Coasts	4,000	Niger Delta to Cameroons	22,000
	8,200		44,500

From these figures it can be seen that the area from the Gold Coast to the Cameroons accounted for 82 per cent of all slaves shipped from West Africa at this time. The region west of the Gold Coast may have been rather more prominent in the early days of the trade, but it should also be remembered that far fewer slaves were exported before 1700 than later on. There were successive shifts of emphasis within the major regions of supply. Thus the slave trade tended to spread eastwards from the Gold Coast after the middle of the seventeenth century, with the result that by 1800 the most important section of the coast was the sub-division from Benin to the

[51] J. D. Fage, *A History of West Africa*, 1969, pp. 84–8.

Cameroons. The Atlantic slave trade provides further evidence of regional economic differences in West Africa during the pre-colonial era.

Figures relating to the destinations of slaves shipped across the Atlantic confirm that the Caribbean and South America were the two leading reception areas.[52]

Destinations of African slaves exported across the Atlantic, 1451–1870

Old World (Europe and the African Islands)	175,000
North and Central America	651,000
Caribbean Islands	4,040,000
South America	4,700,000

However, the extent of the dominance of the Caribbean and South America has not been appreciated: these areas between them accounted for 91 per cent of all slaves shipped across the Atlantic, the leading importers being Brazil, Haiti, Jamaica and Cuba. North America, notwithstanding its current racial problems, received less than 7 per cent of the total.

The Atlantic slave trade still remains one of the greatest migrations of all time. However, it is clear that many of the generalisations commonly made about this controversial phase of African history will need to be reassessed in the light of Curtin's evidence. His research is bound to stimulate a lively debate; it is to be hoped that it will also be a profitable one.

The production, or, more accurately, the harvesting of slaves was one of the biggest commercial ventures launched in Africa during the pre-colonial era. Unfortunately, detailed information about this appalling form of business enterprise is lacking at present, and as yet little attention has been paid to the economics of the slave-producing firm. Many of the remarks which follow are deliberately speculative, and are designed to prompt others to consider this subject at greater length than is possible here.

To begin with, little is known about the geographical and social origins of the slaves shipped from Africa. The few pioneering attempts to grapple with the former problem have confirmed the broad regional divisions noted earlier, and have stressed the impossibility of generalising further at this stage.[53] For the moment, all that can be said is that the sources of supply included well populated regions in the immediate hinterland of the ports of shipment, and sparsely populated areas located far from the major centres of trade. The importance of the latter may well have been exaggerated in the past, for a recent study has shown that in one prominent case the sparseness of the population was the result not so much of slave raiding as of the general inhospitality of the environment.[54] It is probable that the relative significance of both types

[52] Curtin, *The Atlantic Slave Trade*, pp. 88–9, 268.

[53] Philip D. Curtin and Jan Vansina, 'Sources of the Nineteenth-Century Atlantic Slave Trade', *Journal of African History*, 5, 1964, pp. 185–208; Curtin, *The Atlantic Slave Trade*, ch. 4; Walter Rodney, 'Upper Guinea and the Significance of the Origins of Africans Enslaved in the New World', *Journal of Negro History*, 54, 1969, pp. 327–45.

[54] Michael Mason, 'Population Density and "Slave Raiding"—the Case of the Middle Belt of Nigeria', *Journal of African History*, 10, 1969, pp. 551–64. See also the further discussion by M. B. Gleave and R. M. Prothero, 'Population Density and "Slave Raiding"—a Comment', *Journal of African History*, 12, 1971, pp. 319–24, and Mason's reply, *ibid*, pp. 324–7.

of catchment area changed through time, as it seems likely that their initial selection was related to features such as the size, distribution and defensive capability of the population, which were bound to alter. It is even possible that major producers established a regional cycle of exploitation, in much the same way as farmers alternate arable and fallow land, though this suggestion may exaggerate the extent to which slaving was an operation amenable to long term 'development' planning.

As to the social origins of the Africans shipped across the Atlantic, it used to be thought that the Europeans simply drew on an existing pool of slave labour in Africa. Originally, this interpretation appears to have gained currency as a half-hearted justification of the slave trade, the argument being that if slaves were already present in Africa then it was not quite so wicked merely to transfer them to another continent. This view appears to imply that Africans kept paddocks full of slaves in the fourteenth century in the hope that one day the West Coast would be discovered by the Europeans, who would then purchase this carefully accumulated and super-fluous labour force. However, Walter Rodney's study of the Upper Guinea coast has shown that there was no servile class simply waiting to be exported,[55] and work carried out on the more important slave-exporting area east of the Ivory Coast tends to support this view. Admittedly, there were various economically and socially subordinate groups, including slaves, in many West African societies long before the coming of the Europeans, but these developed, as was shown in Chapter 2, in response to local needs, and were not surplus to domestic requirements. With the advent of the Europeans, members of these groups may well have been among the first to be sold, though of course this would have happened only if the profit on their sale abroad exceeded their value to their owners or employers in Africa. As the trade expanded, however, it became necessary to secure a massive increase in the numbers of slaves and other saleable subordinates. The indigenous rulers then set about creating a class of unfree Africans, with the result that by the close of the eighteenth century there was indeed a servile group which was more numerous and more closely defined than in the sixteenth century. It seems reasonable to suppose that the bulk of the eleven million people shipped from Africa were not members of an established slave population, but ordinary farmers and their families, who were deprived of their liberty by fellow Africans in response to external demands.

There were various ways of securing slaves, including raiding, warfare, collecting tribute, kidnapping, purchasing, and disposing of criminals, real and alleged. It appears that the majority of slaves were gathered through raids, warfare and tribute, all methods which impinged on other societies. Raiding and warfare were effective means of direct action, while tribute was a type of extortion used by a dominant power to secure a specified number of slaves from a satellite state or village. The methods employed by the latter varied, but usually included raiding. By the stand-ards of the time slave raiding and trading were operations which required consider-able labour and capital, and so tended to be financed and directed by a few, substantial entrepreneurs who concentrated their efforts in carefully planned drives.

[55] *A History of the Upper Guinea Coast, 1545 to 1800*, Oxford 1970.

As Barbot noted in the late seventeenth century, slaving was 'the business of kings, rich men, and prime merchants, exclusive of the inferior sort of blacks. . . .'[56] Labour was needed to assemble a band of raiders, and capital to pay for equipment, guides, agents, tolls, and for the maintenance of retainers and captives. Moreover, a slave was indivisible, and his value was such that transactions were handled by large dealers, and not by petty traders. Firms which were only just big enough to overcome these barriers can be thought of as marginal; they had no reserves for dealing with unforeseen circumstances, and they were more likely to be liquidated. Once the minimum conditions for entry had been met, the optimum size of the firm could vary to some extent according to the number of slaves required, the distribution of settlement, and the defensive capacity of the people who were to be raided.

Fundamentally, the external slave trade existed only because the return on exports was greater than on employing labour in the domestic economy. If this had not been the case a much larger number of slaves would have been retained for use in Africa itself. The cost of gathering slaves was the same for both markets, and the cost of moving them to local markets was often as high as the cost of transferring them to coastal entrepôts. It was mainly the price paid for them which differed, and this difference reflected the greater productivity of labour in the Americas. The export price of slaves never rose to the point where it became cheaper for Europeans to turn to alternative sources of supply, and it never fell to the point where it caused more than a temporary check to the trade. Consequently, Africa was able consistently to undercut all other potential suppliers. Production and wholesaling remained in indigenous hands mainly because the African delivery system, despite inevitable disputes and occasional breakdowns, was flexible and efficient enough to supply the slaves required at a price the Europeans were prepared to pay. The remarkable expansion of the slave trade in the eighteenth century provides a horrific illustration of the rapid response of producers in an underdeveloped economy to price incentives. The interaction of supply and demand merits further consideration because it raises some interesting questions about the historical development of the trade. For example, it is possible that part of the increase in the price paid for slaves in the eighteenth century resulted from a growing scarcity of labour resources and from better defensive arrangements on the part of those who had become frequent targets of slave gathering expeditions. In other words, slave suppliers may have experienced increasing marginal costs as a result of the growth of external diseconomies which, given the extent of slaving, were inevitable. It is hard to see how producers could have adjusted successfully to this situation: once the minimum conditions of entry had been met, there appear to have been few important economies of scale to slaving operations, and consequently little scope for reducing the internal costs of the firm.

The political implications of economic activities are not a major concern of this book. Nevertheless, two aspects of this question need to be mentioned here. First, it is clear that the growth of foreign trade encouraged the expansion of some states, such as Dahomey and Oyo, and also changed their structure, with the result that

---

[56] Quoted in Basil Davidson, *The African Past*, Harmondsworth 1966, p. 213.

contractual relationships became more important than kinship.[57] In these states slaving was either in the hands of a small, wealthy oligarchy, or else was a state monopoly. The firm acquired political functions; conversely, the state acted like a huge corporation. The chartered companies operated by Europeans in the seventeenth centuries must have been easily recognisable to Africans, whose own export activities were organised in much the same way. The parallel draws attention to an important general point, namely that the Atlantic slave trade was made possible by an alliance of two groups, European shippers and African suppliers, who agreed, in effect, to exploit the less powerful peoples of the Continent. The trade may have been initiated by Europeans, but it cannot be understood simply in terms of their role alone. Second, care must be taken not to over-simplify the relationship between trade and politics. It would be mistaken to imply that the slave trade was a necessary condition for the formation of large, centralised states in West Africa.[58] Benin, for example, developed independently of the slave trade,[59] while other areas, such as the Niger Delta, conducted a substantial foreign trade, yet did not produce major states, still less empires.[60] Clearly, additional motives and means, non-economic as well as economic, need to be explored if African state-building movements are to be understood.

When a sufficient number of slaves had been collected, they were marched to coastal entrepôts and sold to dealers, who held them pending shipment. Between Senegal and the Gold Coast the exchange of slaves was on a fairly casual basis, and ships put in at various places where they had access to the shore, in the hope of buying slaves rather than in the certain knowledge of being able to do so. From the Gold Coast eastwards, however, the trade was highly organised, and the slavers usually made for recognised centres. These included European forts on the Gold Coast, where many of the chartered companies had their headquarters, and large African ports of call, such as Whydah, Badagri, Lagos, Bonny and Old Calabar. In purpose and organisation the West Coast entrepôts may be compared not only to the great 'ports' of the desert, such as Timbuctu, but also to the great European centres, such as Liverpool and Nantes. Their chief function, whether controlled by Africans or Europeans, was to act as wholesaling depots, though they also performed the subsidiary, but necessary, task of supplying slave vessels with provisions for the long voyage across the Atlantic. The entrepôts helped to synchronise exchanges between slave gatherers, shippers and employers, so that slaves were delivered to the West

---

[57] This point has been developed by I. A. Akinjogbin, *Dahomey and its Neighbours, 1708–1818*, Cambridge 1967. On Oyo see Peter Morton-Williams, 'The Oyo Yoruba and the Atlantic Trade, 1670–1830', *Journal of the Historical Society of Nigeria*, 3, 1964, pp. 25–45.

[58] E. J. Alagoa, 'The Development of Institutions in the States of the Eastern Niger Delta', *Journal of African History*, 12, 1971, pp. 269–78.

[59] James D. Graham, 'The Slave Trade, Depopulation, and Human Sacrifice in Benin History', *Cahiers d'Études Africaines*, 5, 1965, pp. 317–34.

[60] This question has been explored by Patrick Manning, 'Slaves, Palm Oil and Political Power on the West African Coast', *African Historical Studies*, 2, 1969, pp. 279–88, and E. J. Alagoa, 'Long-distance Trade and States in the Niger Delta', *Journal of African History*, 11, 1970, pp. 319–29.

Indies at harvest time (December to June), when they were most wanted. The majority of slavers visited the West Coast between October and March, which was when the entrepôts were at their busiest.[61] By holding stocks in anticipation of demand, the wholesaling centres attracted a regular business and enabled slave ships to achieve a rapid turnaround. Naturally, this service was not provided free of charge, and it was accepted that trade at the entrepôts involved paying either customs duties or higher prices for slaves, and sometimes both. However, excessive charges could be countered by transferring to another port or by trading outside the entrepôts. These possibilities helped to stabilise relations between wholesalers and shippers.

Two of the leading entrepôts were Whydah and Old Calabar. Whydah achieved prominence in the last quarter of the seventeenth century, and remained a centre of the slave trade until about the middle of the nineteenth century.[62] As an entrepôt without any profound natural advantages, Whydah was particularly susceptible to external influences. Trade suffered after 1727, when the town was captured by Agaja, the King of Dahomey, and again after 1774, when Oyo decided to send its slaves to the nearby market of Porto Novo. Whydah was also seriously affected, along with many other entrepôts, by interruptions caused by the American War of Independence and by the Napoleonic Wars. English vessels shipped 14–15,000 slaves a year from the port in the 1680s, and exports remained at about this level until 1727. Thereafter a gradual decline set in. In 1776 about 10,000 slaves were exported, and this figure was halved by the end of the century. However, business revived after 1810, when England and Portugal agreed to allow Whydah to continue as a centre of the slave trade.

The Dahomeyan conquest was important because it led to the integration of producing and wholesaling activities, though Whydah still depended on additional suppliers, such as Oyo. This merger was not planned, for Agaja's initial aim in 1727 was to *stop* the slave trade.[63] However, Agaja soon discovered that he needed European support to counter the political threat from Oyo, and it was then that he became involved in slaving. Under Dahomeyan rule the slave trade became a state monopoly, and a governor was installed at Whydah to see that business conduct conformed to official regulations and to ensure that the prescribed taxes were paid. In practice, however, the slave trade was dominated by an oligarchy headed by the king, and not simply by the monarch alone. Dahomeyan kings found it advantageous to lease some of their royal privileges to senior chiefs, just as European rulers found it politically advisable to grant concessions to their nobles. Some chiefs were allowed to participate directly in slave raiding and trading, while others received a percentage of the taxes derived from foreign commerce.

[61] This was also the dry season, when Europeans experienced fewer health risks.

[62] For further information see Rosemary Arnold, 'A Port of Trade: Whydah on the Guinea Coast', in *Trade and Market in the Early Empires*, ed. Karl Polanyi, C. M. Arensberg and Harry Pearson, Glencoe 1957, pp. 154–76, and Simone Berbain, *Le comptoir français de Juda (Ouidah) au XVIIIᵉ siècle*, Paris 1942.

[63] However, it should be noted that there is not complete agreement over this interpretation.

Old Calabar was a leading slave port for nearly two hundred years (1650–1841), and as late as 1828 was said to be shipping 6–8,000 slaves a year.[64] Its history was less spectacular than Whydah's because it was never dominated by a large state, such as Dahomey, a kingdom which achieved notoriety in Europe as a result of publicity given to the allegedly unenlightened despotism of its rulers and to the exotic exploits of its Amazonian warriors. Old Calabar was founded by Efik settlers in the sixteenth century, before trade with Europe began. The economy was by no means self-sufficient even at that time, and the local inhabitants exchanged fish and salt for yams and palm produce, which were obtained from the north. When the external demand for slaves reached the eastern edge of West Africa, the Efik established themselves as wholesalers, exploiting the natural advantages of their estuarine site, and excluding all rivals from direct trade with the Europeans. The Efik occasionally launched slave raids, but mostly bought slaves from other suppliers, especially the Aro, and by the eighteenth century they had a network of market contacts which stretched two hundred miles inland.

The development of the slave trade had a profound effect on Efik institutions. In the first place, economic inequalities became more pronounced as a result of the varying success rates of households participating in foreign trade. Secondly, the accretion of immigrants, mostly slaves, who were used as retainers, led to an unequal numerical expansion of the original Efik household units. Thirdly, there was a trend towards greater social differentiation as freemen took steps to secure the superiority of their status over that of slaves and other subordinate newcomers. Because slave buying and wholesaling were activities which required considerable capital, commercial success came to depend very largely on access to credit granted by the Europeans. As a result, trade and political power became concentrated in the hands of a small oligarchy, in much the same way as at Whydah, Liverpool and Nantes. There were about a dozen important African dealers in Old Calabar in the middle of the eighteenth century. The number was reduced to three by the end of the century, and to one early in the nineteenth century. The survivor, Duke Ephraim, was the greatest trader, the sole collector of customs duty, and, effectively, ruler of the town. The Efik never established a highly centralised monarchy on the Dahomeyan model, but they did set up a conciliar institution of federal kind, which was known as *Ekpe*. This institution developed early in the eighteenth century in response to the need to integrate the new social groupings in the town. *Ekpe* was particularly important as a debt-collecting agency, ensuring the viability of the credit system, and, through this, the continued success of the port. *Ekpe* was dominated by freemen, and especially by the heads of the principal lineages, who used it to reinforce their monopoly of credit facilities and of commercial and political patronage. It was a device which the leading worthies of Liverpool would have recognised, and perhaps even envied.

The relationship between European and African at their meeting points on the West Coast was not that of employer and employee, but that of two complementary

---

[64] The best study of Old Calabar is A. J. H. Latham, *Old Calabar, 1600–1891: the Economic Impact of the West upon a Traditional Society*, University of Birmingham Ph.D. thesis, 1970.

and more or less equal trading partners, whose mutual business interests were cemented by a mixture of goodwill and extensive credit obligations. The position of African wholesalers was very similar to that of landlords and brokers in internal trade, in that they provided accommodation, acted as interpreters, and linked buyers and producers. Pursuing this analogy, it might be said that the European purchaser was in much the same position as the indigenous 'stranger' who placed himself under the protection of an African landlord.[65] The two groups formed what Christopher Fyfe has aptly called a 'moral community', which was held together not only by obvious economic ties, but also by cross-cultural links, which helped to create a climate of understanding and trust. Some Africans, for example, became Christians, just as, in a different context, the great traders of the Western Sudan had become Muslims. Conversely, Europeans became members of some African institutions, such as *Ekpe*, the Efik council, and secured representation in others, such as the *Poro* society in Sierra Leone. Verbal communication was assisted by the development of a form of pidgin-English, and also by the rise of a group of mulatto traders and agents. These men became important commercial and cultural intermediaries in the seventeenth and eighteenth centuries, particularly in Senegambia, Sierra Leone and the Gold Coast.[66] Their role may be compared to that of the comprador class which arose in the Far East in the nineteenth century, following the growth of intercontinental and inter-cultural business connections.[67] To cite evidence of collaboration between Europeans and Africans is not to deny that crude and unscrupulous methods, including force, were used by both sides from time to time, but to point to an aspect of commercial relations which, though significant, has not been given much prominence in general studies of the Atlantic slave trade.

The co-operative element in Afro-European business transactions helps to explain the operation of what has become known in the literature as the credit or trust system. It was common practice for Europeans to advance goods against deliveries either if slaves were unavailable immediately, or to book supplies for the following season. Guarantees were sometimes given in the form of hostages or moveable property, but it was quite normal for the purchaser to trust the wholesaler with advances which often amounted to several thousand pounds sterling. Eyo Nsa (*c.* 1740–1820) of Old Calabar became known to European merchants as Willy Honesty, such was his reputation for trustworthiness and reliability. Two comments need to be made about the trust system, which has been condemned by generations of European commentators on the grounds that it encouraged improvidence on the part of susceptible and morally vulnerable 'natives'. First, credit would not have been so widespread if it had not been needed to finance part of the operations of slave dealers and suppliers. Since the export sector continued to require injections of foreign

[65] V. R. Dorjahn and C. Fyfe, 'Landlord and Stranger: Change in Tenancy Relations in Sierra Leone', *Journal of African History*, 3, 1962, 391–7.

[66] Margaret Priestley has made a careful and most useful study of one such family, the Brews, in *West African Trade and Coast Society*, Oxford 1969.

[67] Yen-p'ing Hao, *The Comprador in Nineteenth-Century China: Bridge between East and West*, Oxford 1970.

capital, it is not surprising that the credit 'system' survived the abolition of the slave trade, was a prominent feature of the colonial economy, and exists today in the form of international loans and 'suppliers' credits'. Second, more remarkable than the alleged iniquities of the trust system was the extent to which it operated satisfactorily, especially in view of the cross-cultural nature of business transactions. That the system remained workable over several centuries was a tribute to the practical value of the moral community created by dealers and shippers. It was customary, for example, for African wholesalers to accept responsibility for bad debts incurred by unscrupulous or unfortunate traders to whom they had passed on advances of cash or goods. At the same time, it would be wrong to leave the impression that defaulters were solely of one race and colour. As John Newton, a prominent slave trader, observed in 1788: 'When I have charged a Black with unfairness and dishonesty, he has answered, if able to clear himself, with an air of disdain, "What! do you think I am a White Man?" '[68]

Besides organising the sale and shipment of slaves, the coastal entrepôts also supervised the storage and distribution of the goods received in exchange. Detailed information about the commodities imported into West Africa during this period is lacking at present. However, it seems clear that the leading items can be grouped under a few main headings, and that these remained unaltered for the duration of the Atlantic slave trade.

The leading import was cloth, which was in steady demand in an underdeveloped economy.[69] Textiles of all kinds accounted for between half and three-quarters of the goods sent to West Africa from Rouen and Le Havre in the eighteenth century, and it is likely that shipments from other leading European ports were of much the same order of magnitude. In the seventeenth and eighteenth centuries cotton goods from Bengal were particularly prominent, and it is interesting to reflect that on the eve of the industrial revolution Europe still conducted a sizeable re-export trade in Indian manufactures. In the second half of the eighteenth century, however, this trade was adversely affected by the disorder which followed the collapse of the Mogul Empire, and by competition from imitations produced in Holland, France and England. By the late eighteenth century European textiles, especially cottons, which had become more important both in volume and value than woollen goods, were replacing Bengal cloth, though it was not until about the 1820s that the latter became insignificant in West African trade. Guns and gunpowder were probably next in importance after cloth, and represented about one fifth of the value of cargoes shipped from England to Africa in the eighteenth century. The demand for munitions was partly a function of their role as inputs in the 'production' of slaves, and partly a result of the need to make adequate defensive arrangements against slave raids. However, guns and gunpowder were not causally related to the beginnings of the Atlantic slave trade, for imports of these items did not become substantial until after the trade was well established. Initially, the Dutch were the principal suppliers,

[68] Quoted in Christopher Fyfe, *The Sierra Leone Inheritance*, 1964, p. 74.

[69] J. Fourneau and L. Kravetz, 'Le pagne sur la côte de Guinée et au Congo du XVᵉ siècle à nos jours', *Bulletin de l'Institut d'Études Centrafricaines*, 7–8, 1954, pp. 5–21.

but after the middle of the eighteenth century English manufacturers became dominant. Hardware, principally utensils and tools, was probably third on the list of leading imports. Other well-known trade goods were salt, beads, bar iron, gin and brandy, all of which came from Europe, and tobacco and rum, which were shipped from the Americas. Contrary to popular belief, cheap gin, though it may have been the drink of the English poor, was not a widespread stimulant, solace or currency in Africa at this time.

There was considerable variety within these main categories of imports because there were many different types of cloth, guns and hardware. At the end of the seventeenth century, Bosman, the distinguished Dutch trader, estimated that at least 150 items were required for trade on the Gold Coast alone. The variety of the import trade has often been seen as proof of the unpredictable psychology of 'primitive' consumers. Yet there were sound commercial reasons why ships entering West Coast entrepôts resembled floating supermarkets. In the first place, the trade was highly competitive and the Europeans found it necessary, and often to their advantage, to bargain for slaves by varying the goods offered, as well as by altering their price. Secondly, the slavers were unable to predict the state of the African market in any detail, and by the time they had reached the West Coast they were a long way from their sources of supply. There was no point arriving with a boat load of guns, for instance, and nothing else, if these had just been delivered by a previous vessel. Thirdly, European critics often overlooked the fact that African purchasers on the coast were not final consumers, but wholesalers, who required a wide range of goods because they had to supply a sizeable market over a long period of time. Finally, the absence of an internationally acceptable currency on the West Coast made it relatively difficult to substitute one item for another, so having as many goods as possible (and having them in different quantities) increased the facility of transactions.

It would be wrong to suppose that exchange at the entrepôts was conducted simply by barter. Imports into West Africa also included a number of currencies, such as cowries, manillas, iron bars, copper rods and silver dollars, and these, together with gold, were used in part or full exchange for slaves. The difficulty of evaluating slaves in terms of assorted trade goods and commodity currencies led to the development of various units of account, such as the mythical 'bar', the 'sorting', and the 'ounce'.[70] The bar became a unit of account in the seventeenth century, principally in Senegambia and eastern Nigeria; the sorting made its appearance at the same time, and was used mainly between the Gold Coast and the Cameroons, though it was also found in some western parts of the coast, such as Sierra Leone; the ounce was introduced into the Gold Coast early in the eighteenth century, and was adopted at Whydah in the 1760s. These units were adapted from indigenous systems of currency and accountancy, and provide a further illustration of the way in which Europeans fitted in with African trading customs. Originally, the bar was simply an iron bar of

[70] Marion Johnson, 'The Ounce in Eighteenth-Century West African Trade', *Journal of African History*, 7, 1966, pp. 197–214.

differing lengths and weights, while the trade ounce was applied to goods exchanged on the Gold Coast for one ounce of gold. At the same time, the slavers were anxious to adapt these units to the needs of external trade because they offered a solution to one of the main problems of barter, that is calculating in advance the likely profitability of a particular transaction. By adding together the proposed selling prices of diverse trade goods and expressing them in units of account, the European traders could begin to build a margin of profit into the import trade.

European traders were content to remain on the coast not only because of the difficulty and cost of moving inland, but also because the system of slave gathering and wholesaling devised by Africans proved efficient, and was therefore acceptable. The African response to external demands has been explained here in terms of universalist or formalist assumptions because African economic behaviour in the export sector is recognisable as approximating to that of contemporary western economic man. This approach contrasts with the substantivist viewpoint, and in particular with Karl Polanyi's stimulating analysis in *Dahomey and the Slave Trade*.[71] Space does not permit a lengthy review of Polanyi's account of what he calls an 'archaic' economy. It must suffice to say that his book has serious omissions in its historical sources, and that it does not satisfactorily define or apply certain characteristics of the archaic economy, particularly the concepts of 'administered' trade and 'redistribution'. Nevertheless, Polanyi's work, as always, provokes further thought. One idea, which others might like to consider, is that the principles of administered trade and redistribution are more typical of independent African states today than of states in the pre-colonial era. Administered trade (in the shape of large public corporations) has become an ideological commitment, while redistribution (in the shape of patronage and job creation) has grown to be a political necessity since the rise of the mass party.[72]

3   The abolition of the external slave trade

In 1807 it became illegal for British subjects to engage in the slave trade, and in 1833 the institution of slavery was abolished in all Britain's imperial possessions. In spite of these measures, substantial numbers of slaves were transported across the Atlantic after 1807. This paradox was the result first of the development of new centres of demand, especially in Cuba and Brazil (for the production of sugar and coffee) and to a small extent in the southern states of North America (for cotton growing), and second of the difficulties of giving practical effect to the new laws without the full co-operation of other interested nations. However, having abolished her own share of the trade, it was in Britain's interest to see that others followed suit. The campaign for abolition then moved into a new phase of long and hard international bargaining. Sustained diplomatic pressure led to the passage of anti-slavery legislation by other

---

[71] Seattle 1966.

[72] For some perceptive reflections on parallel lines see Aristide R. Zolberg, *Creating Political Order*, Chicago 1966, pp. 134–45.

nations in Europe, North Africa, the Middle East and the Americas during the first three-quarters of the nineteenth century. Three of the more significant events were the rapid decline of the Brazilian slave market from the 1850s, the elimination of the Cuban slave trade in the 1860s, and Lincoln's decision in 1862 to co-operate with Britain on the slavery issue, a move which was dictated largely by his desire to deprive the southern states of a possible ally. Other measures adopted included the deployment of an anti-slavery squadron in West African waters,[73] and the annexation of certain key ports on the West Coast in an attempt to stop the trade at its source. The year 1807 may mark the end of an era, but it was a rather protracted ending. Not until the close of the 1860s was the Atlantic slave trade suppressed and the trans-Saharan slave trade reduced to negligible proportions.

The problem of why Britain, the most important slave-trading nation, took the lead in condemning the Atlantic traffic is a matter of considerable controversy. For a long time this radical change of policy was attributed to the influence of a group of dedicated reformers led by Granville Sharp, Thomas Clarkson and William Wilberforce. The classic statement of this view was presented by Sir Reginald Coupland in *The British Anti-Slavery Movement*, first published in 1933.[74] Coupland explained with great lucidity, and with that sense of the onward march of history which characterised the 'Whig' school of history, just how vested interests were destroyed by a combined non-conformist and humanitarian pressure group. Coupland and the other imperial historians, 'the chaplains on the pirate ship', were given a rough passage by Eric Williams, a West Indian historian (now Prime Minister of Trinidad and Tobago) in his book *Capitalism and Slavery*, which appeared in 1944. According to Williams, the slave trade was abolished primarily for economic reasons. When the industrial capitalism of the nineteenth century began to replace the purely commercial capitalism of the eighteenth century, it became necessary to destroy the sugar monopoly of the West Indies as a step towards dismantling the *ancien régime* of mercantilist restrictions and establishing a new order of free trade and economic efficiency. The role of the humanitarians, he claimed, had been 'grossly exaggerated by men who have sacrificed scholarship to sentimentality and, like the scholastics of old, placed faith before reason and evidence.'[75]

Both interpretations are open to criticism. Coupland was stronger on narrative than on explanation; he made no serious attempt to understand the economic aspects of abolition; he failed to account adequately for the continuation of the slave trade

---

[73] The anti-slavery squadron freed only about eight per cent of the total number of slaves shipped from Africa in the period after abolition. However, the navy's presence had a deterrent effect which was much greater than this figure indicates. A recent study suggests that about 825,000 additional slaves (an increase of forty-three per cent) would have been transported from Africa to the Americas between 1811 and 1870 had there not been an African squadron. See E. Phillip LeVeen, *British Slave Trade Suppression Policies, 1821–1865: Impact and Implications*, University of California at Berkeley Ph.D. thesis, 1971.

[74] Although in many ways Frank J. Klingberg's *The Anti-Slavery Movement in England*, New Haven 1926, is a superior book.

[75] Williams, *Capitalism and Slavery*, p. 178.

after 1807; and he had a rather simplistic view of the composition and operation of the abolitionist pressure group. Against Williams it has been said that he failed to fit his argument into an acceptable chronological pattern; that he exaggerated the importance of industrial interests as a compulsive force demanding, and achieving, abolition; and that he misinterpreted the part played by Pitt, and, later, by Palmerston, and also the attitude of the abolitionists towards the sugar duties.[76] Nevertheless, the general thesis put forward in *Capitalism and Slavery*, though it requires modification, comes much closer to understanding the problem than does Coupland's book. An examination of abolition in France and England shows that anti-slavery agitation was able to succeed when it did only because by the end of the eighteenth century the basis of the old colonial system had been undermined by a number of developments which were primarily economic in character.

In France, as in England, there was a long history of propaganda against slavery and the slave trade.[77] Montesquieu, for example, had advanced an economic argument against slavery (based on its alleged inefficiency) as early as 1748. In 1788 the French 'humanitarians' founded the Société des Amis des Noirs in order to press for abolition more effectively. Yet the decline of the French slave trade was the result of changes which were largely independent of domestic agitation. First, a profound split developed in the second half of the eighteenth century between French planters and the metropolis. The *colons*, in debt and resenting it, dissatisfied with the French tariff system, and suspicious of policies which prevented the development of colonial manufactures, could no longer be relied on to stand firm, even against abolitionist forces. Second, there was a relative decline in the importance of the slave trade at Nantes in the late eighteenth century, with the result that the town was less committed to defend the trade than it had been fifty years earlier. It is true that other French ports had become involved in the trade, but slaving remained a very minor part of their total activities. Third, and most important of all, in 1792 there was a major slave revolt in St Domingo which disrupted production in what, by that time, was the most important sugar island in the Caribbean. Two years later, France abolished slavery in her colonial possessions in a vain attempt to bring the revolt under control. These events led to the rapid decline of the French slave trade. Napoleon restored the institution of slavery in 1802, and he also tried to re-establish the slave trade, but this reversal of policy proved unsuccessful. Indeed, the Napoleonic Wars disrupted French Atlantic commerce still further.[78] In 1815 the restored monarchy agreed, under pressure from Britain, to stop French subjects from trading in slaves, though Nantes, the last of the great French slaving ports, still carried on a clandestine traffic in slaves until the close of the 1820s. It is not surprising that the anti-slavery movement in France gained so little momentum when it was also

---

[76] Roger T. Anstey, 'Capitalism and Slavery: a Critique', *Economic History Review*, 21, 1968, pp. 307–20.

[77] David Brion Davis, *The Problem of Slavery in Western Culture*, Cornell 1966.

[78] François Crouzet, 'Wars, Blockade, and Economic Change in Europe, 1792–1815', *Journal of Economic History*, 24, 1964, pp. 567–88.

regarded as being anti-patriotic.[79] Not until 1822, when the energetic Duc de Broglie took command, did the French 'humanitarians' begin to acquire political influence.[80] Even so, it was only in 1848 that slavery was abolished, this time permanently, in all French colonial possessions.

The case of England was analogous to that of France to the extent that changing economic circumstances in the West Indies and in the metropolitan slave ports seriously weakened her traditional commercial interests in the Atlantic. After the middle of the eighteenth century the British sugar islands entered a long period of decline, which was marked by falling profits, slave rebellions, and, above all, by competition from newer and richer areas of production, such as Cuba, Brazil, and St Domingo. (Ironically, the revolution in St Domingo helped to prop up the British sugar islands for another fifteen years.) The British West Indies also declined relatively as a market for British goods, and by the end of the century Latin America had become more important. Thus it was becoming hard to justify the tariff advantages which the Islands enjoyed, and sugar importers and manufacturers began to look for newer and cheaper sources of supply to serve the expanding metropolitan market. At the same time, the planters had difficulty in presenting a united front in defence of their interests. The increased cost of slaves in the late eighteenth century caused a number of planters to encourage their slaves to breed, with the result that by about 1800 they were far less dependent on imports. Consequently, there was a division between those who were virtually self-sufficient and were prepared to make concessions to the abolitionists in order to prevent the development of competitors, and those who were opposed to compromise because they had a continuous need for fresh supplies of slaves.

At the English end of the trade, Liverpool, the principal slave port, had become less dependent on slaving by the close of the century. Admittedly, Liverpool's slave trade had expanded, but capital had also begun to move into other fields; into industry, and into branches of trade which had become more important than slaving.[81] The interests of the outports had always been varied, and they could reallocate their resources more easily than could producers in the West Indies. Those who had backed the planters in prosperity began to leave them in adversity. Defections opened the way for the growth of abolitionist feeling in Liverpool itself.[82] Bristol's overseas commerce was showing signs of a general decline at the end of the eighteenth century. In 1793 there was a serious economic crisis, which hit the port's African and

[79] This theme is developed in a neglected article by Y. Debbasch, 'Poésie et traite; l'opinion française sur le commerce négrier au début du XIXᵉ siècle', *Revue Française d'Histoire d'Outre-Mer*, 48, 1961, pp. 311–52.

[80] Serge Daget, 'L'abolition de la traite des noirs en France de 1814 à 1831', *Cahiers d'Études Africaines*, 11, 1971, pp. 14–58.

[81] The profitability of the cotton trade, for example, compared favourably with the slave trade by the end of the century. See F. E. Hyde, B. B. Parkinson and S. Marriner, 'The Cotton Broker and the Rise of the Liverpool Cotton Market', *Economic History Review*, 8, 1955, p. 80.

[82] Jean Trepp, 'The Liverpool Movement for the Abolition of the English Slave Trade', *Journal of Negro History*, 13, 1928, pp. 265–85.

American interests, and bankrupted many of the leading slave traders. From then on Bristol ceased to provide active opposition to the abolitionist movement.[83] The London financiers, who, as creditors of the planters, had a disguised interest in slavery, were eventually won over by the offer of compensation, for much of the £20 million allocated to the slave owners in 1833 found its way back to the capital city.

The developments outlined above weakened the economic basis of the old colonial system, and made possible a radical change of policy. Pitt's death in 1806 was followed by the formation of a cabinet which was prepared to press ahead with anti-slavery legislation, and the Act prohibiting British subjects from engaging in the slave trade was passed in the following year. Those who expected the immediate extension of this measure were to be disappointed. At length, the abolitionists, no longer prepared to wait in hope, reorganised their movement in 1830. The bill providing for the abolition of slavery was presented to a reformed Parliament, and was passed in 1833. Duties on sugar imports were equalised in 1851 in accordance with Russell's Sugar Act of 1846. The British West Indies then entered a long and difficult period of economic and social reconstruction.

It would be wrong to think that the political opportunities presented by these economic changes were grasped simply and solely by a group of 'humanitarians', defined rather vaguely as men of goodwill seeking to alleviate the suffering of others, or else, as in many books, not defined at all. Some of the anti-slavery agitators were far from disinterested, and few of the selfless men were radicals espousing the cause of the downtrodden. Scrupulous in their concern for property rights, adamant in their defence of the social and political status quo, and totally unmoved by the industrial 'slavery' which existed around them, Wilberforce and the abolitionists were a less romantic and more complex band than they have often been depicted.[84] Yet, precisely because of the kaleidoscopic nature of the movement, there was room in it for some who did stand for reform of a more fundamental kind. James Cropper, for example, a Quaker businessman and the greatest importer of East Indian sugar into Liverpool in the early nineteenth century, found in the abolitionist cause a perfect fusion of his idealistic and material aspirations.[85] He, and others like him, representatives of a developing industrial society and of a new economic philosophy, stood in sharp opposition to the old order of bounties and monopolies, and, to some extent, to the royal authority which upheld them. Abolition was not, as Fox told the House of Commons in 1789, 'a question between humanity on the one side and interest on the other', but an issue between two opposing coalitions of interests, each with its own ideology.

---

[83] Peter Marshall, *The Anti-Slave Trade Movement in Bristol*, Bristol 1968, pp. 21–4.

[84] Indeed, it has been argued by Ford Brown in *Fathers of the Victorians*, Cambridge 1961, that the abolitionist movement became dominated by evangelical reformers who selected an issue (slavery) which would arouse support for their moral crusade, without at the same time involving them in domestic issues.

[85] See the excellent articles by David B. Davis, 'James Cropper and the British Anti-Slavery Movement, 1821–1823', *Journal of Negro History*, 45, 1960, pp. 241–58, and 'James Cropper and the British Anti-Slavery Movement, 1823–1833', *ibid.*, 46, 1961, pp. 154–73.

4 International trade and economic growth

It remains to assess the economic consequences of West Africa's external trade in terms of the model outlined at the beginning of the chapter. The two main branches of trade, over the Sahara and across the Atlantic, can be considered jointly for this purpose because their structural similarities, based on the nature of the goods traded and the organisation of production and wholesaling, were more important than their differences, which were mainly of direction and size. The external effects will be outlined first of all, and then the repercussions on Africa itself will be examined.

The chief effect of the overseas slave trade in the New World was to populate and develop the abundant land resources of the Americas and the West Indies. The trade in negroes was the first great human migration across the Atlantic; as such, it provides a striking historical example of international factor mobility, albeit of an enforced kind. The subsequent fortunes of these reluctant colonists are closely identified with the social and political history of the Americas. The type and degree of assimilation achieved in the nineteenth and twentieth centuries varied greatly from region to region.[86] In some countries, such as Argentina and Brazil, the absorption of 'strangers' was harmonious and fairly complete,[87] while in others, notably the United States, the passage of time served to entrench marked economic, social and political distinctions between settlers of different races. The legacy of the African slave trade remains the major domestic issue facing the world's richest and most powerful state.

With regard to Europe, most attention has been focused on the profits of the slave and sugar trades, and on the economic consequences of the re-investment of these profits. Nevertheless, at present there is little precise information about the amount of capital accumulating from African and Atlantic commerce or about its subsequent investment role. Many voyages, triangular and direct, were outstandingly successful, and these have tended to attract the eyes of historians. However, it must be remembered that the rate of profit had to take account of the slow turnover of capital and the very real risk of total loss in the future.[88] It is clear that large investors could easily lose as well as win a fortune in the slave trade, and that small subscribers tended to make modest gains by steady, but slow, accumulation, on much the same scale and in much the same way as in other branches of commerce. When these qualifications have been made, it remains true that the slave and sugar trades brought great wealth to the principal entrepôts, such as Liverpool and Nantes, and to many of their leading citizens. It is impossible to account for the economic vitality of these ports in the eighteenth century, their physical and demographic expansion, and the

---

[86] Herbert S. Klein, *Slavery in the Americas: a Comparative Study of Virginia and Cuba*, Oxford 1967.

[87] For an interesting account of continuing cultural interaction following the resettlement of Africans in the Americas see Pierre Verger, 'Nigeria, Brazil and Cuba', *Nigeria Magazine*, Oct. 1960, pp. 113–23.

[88] F. E. Hyde, B. B. Parkinson and S. Marriner, 'The Nature and Profitability of the Liverpool Slave Trade', *Economic History Review*, 5, 1953, pp. 368–77.

remarkable overflow of money into cultural activities, without stressing the causative, though not exclusive, role of Atlantic commerce. It is equally clear that the prosperity of the ports had beneficial linkage effects in their hinterlands. Examples of investment in the domestic production of goods for the export sector were to be found in the impetus given to the cotton industries of Manchester and Nantes, to the gun trade of Birmingham, and to the production of linen and hardware in Rouen. Examples of the expansion of industries which made use of imports of raw materials were to be seen in the sugar refineries of Liverpool, London, Bristol, Nantes and Orleans, and in the gum processing works of Nantes and Paris. It should be noted, too, that importing and exporting activities provided a stimulus to service industries, such as shipping and banking.

African and Atlantic commerce undoubtedly brought substantial gains to individuals and to certain regions. It does not follow, however, that the 'triangular trade made an enormous contribution to Britain's industrial development', or that the 'profits from this trade fertilized the entire productive system of the country.'[89] In the first place, any stimulus which foreign trade gave to domestic production resulted from links with other parts of the world besides Africa and the Americas. It is as well to remember that Europe alone accounted for over half the value of England's foreign commerce in the eighteenth century. Secondly, it is mistaken to suppose that there was a simple, one-way relationship between trade and industry. The connection between Liverpool and Manchester shows not only that overseas trade assisted the growth of manufacturing, but also that manufacturers helped to finance trade. Thirdly, by concentrating on foreign trade, Williams and others have tended to under-estimate the part played by the home market, which was of central importance in the early phase of industrialisation as a source of factor supply and of consumer demand.[90] A fourth objection has been raised recently in a criticism of R. B. Sheridan, whose approach is broadly in accord with that of Eric Williams.[91] It has been suggested that the profits of the British sugar trade came from the high prices which resulted from tariff preference, and that if the trade had not been subsidised in this way consumers would have been better off and capital attracted to the West Indies would have been invested more profitably at home. On this view colonies were, as Adam Smith alleged, a drain on the mother country. The first part of the argument is well founded. It seems probable that the British taxpayer was indeed subsidising an imperial venture which mainly benefited a relatively small interest group. However, the second part of the argument breaks down, as do many other stimulating counter-factual, or hypothetical, propositions, because it is impossible to know now what the position would have been if tariff protection had

[89] Williams, *Capitalism and Slavery*, p. 105.

[90] See *The Growth of English Overseas Trade in the Seventeenth and Eighteenth Centuries*, ed. W. E. Minchinton, 1969, pp. 36–52.

[91] Robert Paul Thomas, 'The Sugar Colonies of the Old Empire: Profit or Loss for Great Britain?', *Economic History Review*, 21, 1968, pp. 30–45. See also Sheridan's subsequent article, 'The Plantation Revolution and the Industrial Revolution, 1625–1775', *Caribbean Studies*, 9, 1969, pp. 5–25.

not existed, and it is easy to think of plausible alternatives to those suggested by Professor Sheridan's critic.

On present evidence, quantitatively imprecise though it is, it can be concluded that African and Atlantic commerce did assist English economic growth in the eighteenth century, but that it was by no means the sole, nor even the most powerful, propellant of the first industrial revolution. Eric Williams's thesis may require qualification, but it must be acknowledged that in originality of argument and liveliness of presentation his book sets standards which few historians attain, and for this reason it will continue to command respect.

The effect of international trade on Africa is a subject which has provoked a number of vehement and usually condemnatory historical judgements. It is widely believed that foreign trade, and particularly the slave trade, retarded the economic development of Africa, and may even have prevented the continent from achieving an indigenous industrial revolution. These interpretations have been influenced, understandably, by concern over the morality of the traffic in human lives, and by hostility to what is felt to have been colonial exploitation. The starting point of the analysis advanced here will reverse the customary approach: instead of beginning with the assumption that foreign trade delayed the development of Africa, and then looking for supporting evidence, it will be supposed that foreign trade should have benefited the continent in the ways suggested by the model outlined at the start of this chapter. This standpoint, which some readers may find uncongenial, can be ustified in two ways. In the first place, it is the historian's job to take account of bias of all kinds, including his own. If historians are now willing to attack the many absurd ideas which Europeans have held about Africa, then they should also be prepared to undertake the less palatable task of assessing the influences currently shaping their own attitudes towards controversial problems such as the slave trade. Secondly, the approach adopted here does not necessarily lead to conclusions which are entirely different from those commonly held, but it may help to distinguish between sound and unsound arguments cited in support of present orthodoxy.

International trade undoubtedly brought benefits, at least to some of the parties concerned. Africans who controlled the production and wholesaling of exports, whether gold, gum or slaves, gained a great deal from foreign commerce. In 1750, for example, the King of Dahomey had a gross revenue of about £250,000 from overseas sales of slaves. A proportion of export earnings was spent on goods such as cloth, hardware and salt, which helped to raise living standards. The prosperity of the large entrepôts on the coast and on the desert margin created some additional employment opportunities for traders and transporters, and also for farmers, who supplied foodstuffs to towns, caravans and slave ships. If the Western Sudan had not conducted a thriving export trade, fewer kola nuts would have been produced in the forests of Ashanti.

Nevertheless, the multiplier or 'spread' effects of foreign trade were far less pronounced in West Africa than they were in Europe, and the economy was not transformed, at least in a way conducive to further development. There were four main reasons why Saharan and Atlantic commerce failed to overcome existing obstacles to the expansion of the market. First, the export trade was confined to staples which required little diversification of existing methods of production and no significant additional commercialisation of factors in West Africa. Second, the import trade consisted of consumer goods which needed hardly any further processing, and so provided few opportunities for productive investment in the domestic economy. Third, the distribution of incomes, combined with the relatively high cost of imports, prevented the emergence of a mass market based on cheap manufactures. Purchasing power was concentrated among a restricted group of wealthy consumers because the conditions of entry into export production and wholesaling favoured large concerns, and offered little scope for the majority of the population. Since the openings which did exist were often filled by slaves and other dependants, no sub-stantial, independent, wage-earning group was able to develop. The high price of imports was the result of pre-industrial costs of production and transport. Fourth, the size of export proceeds was too small to stimulate either a wide range or a large number of new enterprises. One estimate suggests that West Africa's sea-borne trade was worth about £4 million a year at its peak in the late eighteenth century. This figure was only about a quarter of the average annual value of total imports and exports in the period 1901–1905. Even so, it was not until the middle of the twentieth century, after a further, massive, fifteen-fold increase in overseas trade between 1906–1910 and 1955–1959, that Nigeria, Ghana and Senegal succeeded in generating a mass market which was capable of supporting local manufacturing activities of a modern kind.[92]

So far the analysis has concentrated on the reasons why external trade failed to act as a leading sector. It remains to examine the argument that international trade, and the slave trade in particular, positively retarded the economic development of the continent.

Some of the more sweeping claims which have been made in support of this view need to be treated with caution. First, it is sometimes said that the terms of trade (that is the price received for exports in relation to the price paid for imports) exploited or cheated Africans. It is unlikely that this charge can be sustained. Demand for slaves was strong, and there was keen competition among buyers. Moreover, once Euro-pean slavers had reached West Africa they were committed to trade, and to do so as quickly as possible. Suppliers, on the other hand, often had a local monopoly of slaves, and their position was reinforced by the fact that prospective purchasers had no certain knowledge that conditions would be better elsewhere. Furthermore, the cost of temporarily withholding supplies was not a crippling one. Slaves could be made to maintain themselves as subsistence farmers if necessary, and though they were, like other capital assets, liable to physical deterioration, they did not depreciate very rapidly. If, meanwhile, they reproduced, their owner reaped what might be

---

[92] The question of size is particularly relevant in considering trade in goods other than slaves. Shipments of commodities such as gum and ivory were potentially more fruitful than exports of human beings, but it was not until the nineteenth century, after the industrial revo-lution, that world demand for tropical raw materials underwent a marked expansion. The consequences of this development are considered in the next chapter.

called an unplanned profit. Second, it is often suggested that the import trade consisted of shoddy goods. Evidence in support of this proposition is limited mainly to imports of guns, some of which were not proved or bored. However, it is improbable that the bulk of imported goods was sub-standard, and it is even less likely that Africans would have put up with poor quality wares for very long. Concern over the terms of trade and the quality of imports derives mainly from a feeling that consumer goods were not items of 'real' value, the implication being, presumably, that African states should have taxed foreign luxuries and adopted a vigorous policy of import substitution. This, to say the least, is an unhistorical point of view, for it ignores both the aims of the rulers themselves, and the domestic obstacles to the development of a different kind of commerce.

Third, it is often alleged that foreign imports led to the decline of local industries. This claim will be familiar to historians of the underdeveloped world, and especially to those with knowledge of India, which has been the subject of a long debate on this question. Just as the European middle classes are always rising, so, too, traditional crafts in other parts of the world are continually being ousted. In the case of West Africa no general evidence has been presented in support of the claim. Many indigenous manufactures, such as cloth and pottery, remained important, and it seems more likely that the market was enlarged (in terms of the volume and range of goods) than that foreign imports replaced domestic craft products. Fourth, it is sometimes stated that slaving expeditions caused widespread devastation. It is indeed highly likely that slave raids increased the number of wars and made life insecure, but again little research has been carried out to indicate the extent of the resulting disruption. Meanwhile, the continuous history of internal trade, the regional variations in the incidence of slave raiding, and the recent, lower estimates of the volume of slave exports suggest that this point should not be made without qualification.

Finally, it is necessary to consider the effect of the export of labour on the course of African development. Once again, the information necessary for judging this issue, as opposed to guessing about it, is not available at present. It is obvious enough that the immediate and most acute losses were suffered personally by the six million or so unwilling West Africans who were shipped across the Atlantic, by the much smaller number who were exported across the Sahara, and by those who were killed or maimed in the process of slave-gathering operations. However, emigration, even on this scale, was not necessarily a serious setback for the economy. The main difficulty in analysing this question is that so little is known about the size of the population during the pre-colonial period. One estimate, based on the admittedly suspect procedure of using twentieth century data to reconstruct the distant past, suggests that the total population of West Africa may have been around 25 million in 1700, in which case the rate of loss during the eighteenth century, when the overseas slave trade was at its height, was about 0·2 per cent per annum.[93] As this figure was

[93] J. D. Fage, *A History of West Africa*, pp. 85–7, and the same author's article 'Slavery and the Slave Trade in the Context of West African History', *Journal of African History*, 10, 1969, pp. 393–404.

roughly equal to the rate of natural increase, it can be said that in numerical terms the chief effect of the export of labour between 1700 and 1800 was to keep the population static. What would have happened if the Africans shipped abroad had remained in Africa is now a matter of speculation. For the external slave trade to have been an economic disaster, it is necessary to postulate that West Africa would have achieved a major economic breakthrough before the nineteenth century if the supply of man-power had not been diminished by the amount specified. The evidence available does not support this hypothesis, and it is hard to see how the retention of those slaves sent abroad would have caused the economy to develop along significantly different lines. In the late nineteenth and early twentieth centuries, however, when the economy began to expand very rapidly, there was undoubtedly a serious shortage of labour in many part of West Africa, and it could be argued that at that point the pace of advance would have been faster if the slave trade had not retarded the growth of population.

It is possible that the aggregate approach disguises some of the consequences of the export of labour. It is conceivable, for example, that those regions which were most involved in slaving operations were affected particularly severely. In practice, however, areas such as Senegambia and the seaboard between the Gold Coast and the Cameroons, though prominent in the slave trade, were the leading zones of export growth during the era of 'legitimate' commerce. Alternatively, it could be held that shipments of slaves involved qualitative losses which are masked by the figures for total exports. Since about two-thirds of the slaves exported were males, it is possible that their removal might have affected female occupational roles. How-ever, generalisation on this issue is difficult, partly because of lack of information, and partly because the division of labour between the sexes was by no means the same in all West African societies. If those sold abroad possessed scarce technical or entrepreneurial skills, then the consequences of their emigration might have been far greater than a consideration of numbers alone would suggest. However, it seems probable that the majority of enslaved Africans were ordinary farmers, who were engaged mainly in subsistence and local exchange activities. Other things being equal, the principal effect of their removal would have been to reduce total output, but by an amount which was matched by a fall in demand.

It is quite clear that international trade, though long established and efficiently organised, failed to act as an engine of growth in West Africa, though the more extreme claims regarding the destructive effects of Atlantic and Saharan commerce have yet to be proved. The export sector, besides being comparatively small, established few beneficial links with the rest of the economy. The result was that the gains from international trade were severely limited, quantitatively, geographically and socially. Export growth produced a type of 'enclave' development, which had few connections with the domestic economy.[94] The analogy with the mining and plantation enclaves of the twentieth century cannot be taken too far. Nevertheless,

---

[94] Benjamin Higgins, 'The Dualistic Theory of Underdeveloped Areas', *Economic Develop-ment and Cultural Change*, 4, 1956, pp. 99–115.

the West African enclaves of the eighteenth century, like those of the modern world, were characterised by the importation of superior skills and technology, by a pattern of income distribution that inhibited the growth of the market, and by a pronounced leakage of foreign trade earnings. The first characteristic was to be found in European control of ocean navigation. The second could be seen in the contrast between slave labour and a wealthy élite.[95] The third characteristic was present in the exchange of export earnings for manufactured consumer imports, and in the repatriation of the profits made by foreign firms. Early in the nineteenth century the French traveller, Caillié, observed that in Timbuctu many Moors 'are engaged in trade, and like Europeans repair to the colonies in the hope of making their fortunes, usually return to their own country to enjoy the fruit of their industry.'[96]

If foreign trade is to act as a leading sector, it has to overcome the limitations associated with enclave development. The chapter which follows will try to show how and when the export trade of West Africa began to establish close links with the domestic economy.

[95] The West African case can be compared, in this respect, to the cotton plantations of the American south in the nineteenth century. See Alfred H. Conrad and John R. Meyer, *Studies in Econometric History*, 1965, pp. 223–33.

[96] R. Caillié, *Travels to Timbuctu*, 1830, 2, p. 53.

four

The economic basis of imperialism

Once the European powers had decided to abolish the external slave trade, West Africa was faced with the problem of developing alternative exports. The outcome was a period of transition and experimentation, which is customarily referred to as the era of 'legitimate' commerce in order to distinguish it from the illegal trade in slaves. This chapter will try to establish two conclusions about West African history in the nineteenth century. First, it will be argued that the structure of legitimate commerce marked an important break with the past and signified a new phase in the growth of the market, a phase which can be seen as the start of the modern economic history of West Africa. This argument contrasts with the traditional view, which stresses continuities with the past and the ease of the transfer to legitimate trade. Second, it will be suggested that the strains involved in creating this economy, combined with fluctuations in its performance, are central to an understanding of the partition of West Africa in the last quarter of the nineteenth century. This proposition, too, is intended to be set against current interpretations, most of which hold that imperialism was the product of political motives stemming from Europe. For these two reasons the analysis of legitimate commerce and partition has been combined in one chapter.

These are large claims, and they require some initial elaboration before the historical evidence is presented. The main structural features of the new commerce will be outlined first of all. The foreign trade statistics will then be used to support the theoretical argument, and to indicate the relationship between commercial fluctuations and the economic and political history of West Africa in the nineteenth century. Finally, the development of legitimate commerce will be considered with reference to specific African and European interests in order to demonstrate how the interaction of these groups produced the partition of West Africa. Two points need to be borne in mind in evaluating the argument of this chapter. First, the economic theme is emphasised here partly because this book is concerned with economic history. It is argued that economic motives are a central and neglected feature of partition, not that they provide a complete explanation of it. Second, in relating the economic theme to the timing of partition, it is important to remember that though the tensions caused by structural change were felt in West Africa from the early nineteenth century, they became acute only in the last quarter of the century, when they were aggravated by a serious downturn in the terms of trade.

1   The economy of 'legitimate' commerce

There is no novelty in saying that slaves and palm oil are commodities with obvious physical differences. What has not been appreciated fully is that these differences had far-reaching consequences for the structure of the export economy. The main features of the new economy can be analysed by making use of staple theory, which has been developed specifically to explain the particular type of growth stemming from diversification around a well-defined export base.[1] Staple theory has grown up and been applied chiefly in North America and Australia.[2] These are countries of recent, European settlement, which at critical stages of their economic growth have relied on primary exports, such as fur, wheat and wool, to stimulate the expansion of the domestic market. The aspects of the theory which are especially relevant to the West African case are those which stress the economic consequences of the physical properties of the staple and the type of linkages which it establishes with the rest of the economy.

The physical properties of the staple are important because they influence the factor combination and the nature of returns to scale. In the case of West Africa the basic point is a simple one, which may explain why it has not engaged much interest: the vegetable oils which became staple exports in the nineteenth century could be produced efficiently and on a small scale by households possessing little capital, employing family labour, and using traditional tools. Palm products and ground-nuts, unlike slaves, were divisible into very small units, each of which was of low value per unit of weight, yet was still marketable and yielded a return in the same season. Land, moreover, was cheap and readily available. Admittedly, the new exports could also be produced on sizeable estates, but the few farmers who did so simply increased their inputs of land and labour without securing any of the econo-mies of large scale production because there was little scope for substituting machin-ery for labour, and few advantages to centralised management. Large producers were not particularly inefficient, but they no longer had a monopoly of the export market.

This change in the structure of export-producing firms was a key event in African history. The capital and labour requirements of slave raiding and trading had encouraged the rise of a relatively small group of large entrepreneurs, many of whom became the rulers or senior officials of great states in the Western Sudan and in the forest. Producing and selling palm oil and groundnuts, on the other hand, were occupations in which there were few barriers to entry. Legitimate commerce therefore enabled small-scale farmers and traders to play an important part in the

---

[1] A good introduction to staple theory can be found in Melville H. Watkins, 'A Staple Theory of Economic Growth', *Canadian Journal of Economics and Political Science*, 29, 1963, pp. 141–58.

[2] It should be added that staple theory is generally thought to be inapplicable in cases where export growth occurs in indigenous, subsistence economies. However, the reasons given in support of this view rest on assumptions about 'traditional' societies which have been criticised earlier in this study (Chapter 2).

overseas exchange economy for the first time. In so far as firms of this type and size are the basis of the export economies of most West African states today, it can be said that modernity dates not from the imposition of colonial rule, as used to be thought, but from the early nineteenth century.

The character of the staple also influences the nature and strength of the linkages between export activities and the domestic economy. In an underdeveloped economy dominated by an indigenous society linkages tend to be weaker than in an area of recent settlement, such as North America, where there were special advantages of capital and modern skills in the nineteenth century. Nevertheless, the linkages created by legitimate commerce were much stronger than those set up previously by Saharan and Atlantic commerce.[3]

The new export trade saw a marked increase in the commercialisation of labour and land in Africa, instead of, as in the eighteenth century, the export of one factor of production (labour) and the comparative neglect of another (land), except for domestic needs. Support for this contention can be found in the migration of peoples from the Western Sudan to the 'groundnut coast' of Senegambia, and in the influx of newcomers into the forest in search of the wealth which could be won from the palm tree. An idea of the scale of the new, legitimate enterprise is provided by an estimate that in 1892 no less than 15 million palm trees were in production for the export market in Yoruba country alone.[4] The expansion of legitimate commerce also provided additional employment opportunities in export-processing, even though the methods in use remained technically simple.[5] Admittedly, it was not until the coming of railways and roads that areas in the interior could participate in export production. Nevertheless, a start had been made: after 1900 the colonial rulers simply carried further a process which was already under way.

The import trade still consisted of manufactured consumer goods. However, as a result of the industrial revolution, the consumer imports of the nineteenth century were mainly cheap, mass-produced goods, which offered large numbers of inconspicuous Africans opportunities of material improvement and of emulating the superior, inherited status enjoyed by a minority of their compatriots. To the extent that the revolution of rising expectations is an identifiable phenomenon, then it can be said to have started in West Africa early in the nineteenth century. Furthermore, it is worth observing at this point that imports of cheap manufactures provide a more favourable base for the introduction of modern industries than imports which contain a high proportion of luxuries. If the market for imports grows, then there may well come a time when it is feasible and profitable to manufacture some of these goods on the spot instead of buying them from other countries. This time came in parts of West Africa after 1945.

[3] The discussion which follows should be compared with the conclusions reached in the previous chapter, pp. 119–23.

[4] *Kew Bulletin*, 1892, p. 208.

[5] Female labour appears to have been particularly important in preparing groundnuts and palm produce for export. The division of labour between the sexes is a subject which merits further research.

The change in the quality of consumer imports was made possible not only by cost reductions on the supply side, but also by a shift in the distribution of incomes in Africa. As a general proposition, it can be said that the more equal the distribution of incomes, the smaller the demand for luxury items and the greater the demand for cheap, mass-produced goods.[6] Down to the nineteenth century the distribution of incomes from foreign trade had been very uneven, and purchasing power had been concentrated in a relatively few, large units. With the development of exports of vegetable oils, earnings from overseas commerce began to be spread over many small units of consumption, and incomes achieved greater equality.[7] The evidence for the nineteenth century suggests that imports were being distributed more widely, socially as well as geographically. Furthermore, and again in contrast to the period before the nineteenth century, the size of export proceeds increased as a result of the growth of demand for tropical raw materials and of West Africa's ability to meet that demand. Goods other than slaves were exported before the nineteenth century, but were unable to generate much additional income because the demand for them was still limited. The expansion in the volume and value of trade in the nineteenth century also gave a further stimulus to service industries, especially those providing transport and accommodation, and it led to the development of market gardening to supply foodstuffs to the larger commercial centres.

It is necessary now to show that the statistics of overseas trade are consistent with the argument advanced so far. In particular, the value and volume of trade should show an upward trend; the character of staple exports should conform in detail to the specifications which have been outlined in brief; and the dominant European powers on the West Coast should be those best fitted to supply manufactured goods and to process tropical raw materials.

Although the details of the transition to legitimate commerce are not yet known, it would seem that on the whole West Africa did not experience a prolonged period of economic crisis, principally because many areas were able to export legitimate goods and slaves side by side down to about the middle of the nineteenth century. It is clear that there was a remarkable expansion in the value of overseas trade in the second quarter of the century. Newbury, who has carried out some much-needed research on West African trade in the nineteenth century, has estimated that the total value of the overseas commerce of the region in legitimate goods alone amounted to a minimum of £3½ million a year in the early 1850s.[8] This figure may be compared with Fage's estimate that at the end of the eighteenth century, at the height of the Atlantic slave trade, West Africa's overseas commerce was worth about £4

---

[6] R. E. Baldwin, 'Patterns of Development in Newly Settled Regions', *Manchester School of Economic and Social Studies*, 24, 1956, pp. 161–79.

[7] This change is analogous to the distinction between the cotton economy of the American south, where plantations were dominant in the nineteenth century, and the wheat belt of the west, where the typical unit was the small, family farm. See Douglass C. North, 'Agriculture and Regional Economic Growth', *Journal of Farm Economics*, 41, 1959, pp. 943–51.

[8] C. W. Newbury, 'Trade and Authority in West Africa from 1850 to 1880', in *Colonialism in Africa, 1870–1960*, ed. L. H. Gann and Peter Duignan, 1, *The History and Politics of Colonialism, 1870–1914*, Cambridge 1969, pp. 76–9.

5*

million a year.[9] In the second half of the century trade expanded roughly four times, and by 1901–1905 amounted to about £15 million a year. The rate of growth was not even throughout this period, and it was to be dwarfed by the expansion which occurred during the colonial era. Nevertheless, it was great enough to support the proposition that the new economy was also a much bigger economy. It is worth emphasising that European commercial involvement in West Africa was expanding rather than diminishing, as this is a factor which has not been taken into account by historians who have argued that economic motives were of little significance in the partition of West Africa.

No useful comparison of volumes can be made between legitimate commerce and the slave trade. However, the main point to note with regard to the volume of trade in the nineteenth century is that West African societies had to adjust in a relatively short time to the immense physical task of transporting huge quantities of low value, bulky commodities. Imports of palm oil into the United Kingdom from West Africa reached 1,000 tons in 1810, 10,000 tons in 1830, over 20,000 tons in 1842, over 30,000 tons in 1853, and over 40,000 tons in 1855. Even this expansion was dwarfed in the second half of the century, when there was a rapid growth in shipments of groundnuts, and a still more dramatic rise in overseas trade in palm kernels. Two examples will illustrate the size of the increase. Exports of groundnuts from Senegal rose from virtually nothing in the 1840s to an average of 29,000 tons a year in the period 1886–1890, while exports of palm kernels from Lagos, one of the great slave ports in the 1840s and 1850s, reached an average of 37,000 tons in the same period. The palm oil trade failed to maintain its early rate of progress, but exports still averaged about 50,000 tons a year between 1860 and 1900. The organisation required for moving, let alone producing, tonnages of this magnitude provides some indication of the skill and adaptability of African entrepreneurs.[10] The return trade in imported goods also involved transporting much greater quantities than ever before. For instance, the quantity of cotton goods (measured by the yard) exported from the United Kingdom to West Africa increased thirty times in the short period between 1816–1820 and 1846–1850.[11] The increase was partly a reflection of the rise in the value of trade, but was mainly an outcome of the industrial revolution in Europe and of the shift in the social composition of demand in Africa arising out of the structure of the new export economy. It is safe to conclude that the volume of exports and imports expanded considerably as a result of the rise of legitimate commerce and the decline of the external slave trade.

Vegetable oils, as noted already, became the staples of legitimate commerce. Palm oil was the pioneer export early in the nineteenth century, and it was joined by palm kernels and groundnuts in the second half of the century. The fact that these products already grew in West Africa, where they were traded and consumed as foodstuffs, helps to explain why the end of the Atlantic slave trade did not cause a complete

---

[9] Fage, *A History of West Africa*, pp. 91–2.

[10] The subject of internal transport in the pre-colonial period still awaits investigation.

[11] Calculated from C. W. Newbury, 'Credit in Early Nineteenth-Century West African Trade', *Journal of African History*, 13, 1972, pp. 83–4.

disruption of overseas commerce, though it does not mean that the transition was entirely smooth. The expansion of exports of palm products and groundnuts was a response to industrial growth in Europe, which led to a rise in the demand for oils and fats. Palm oil was used in the production of soap, lubricants and candles. Soap was required for cleansing the population in the growing urban centres; lubricants were needed to oil the new machinery, especially the railways; and candles were in demand for lighting the expanding towns and factories. Manufacturers, happily uniting material and moral motives, urged the public to 'buy our candles and help stop the slave trade'.[12] Palm kernels, though jointly produced with palm oil, were not exported at first, and a large proportion were not used at all, even in West Africa.[13] This was not because the African producer was fickle, or because his wants could be satisfied from the sale of palm oil alone, but because there was little demand in Europe for palm kernel oil, which had a different chemical composition from the oil extracted from the outer part of the fruit. Only in the late nineteenth century was it found possible to employ kernel oil in the manufacture of margarine, then a new product, and to process the residue for cattle food. Groundnuts were used mainly in the manufacture of cooking oil and soap. Other commodities, many of which had been shipped abroad before the nineteenth century, continued to be exported after abolition. The most important of these were gum from Senegal, gold from the Gold Coast, and timber, ivory and cotton from various parts of the forest zone.

Four items accounted for about three-quarters of the value of all imports into West Africa. These were textiles (a classification covering a wide range of cotton and woollen goods), spirits (especially rum and gin), salt and iron. Other prominent items were hardware, tobacco, guns and gunpowder.[14] Textiles remained the leading commodity, as in the eighteenth century. In Senegal, for example, one popular variety alone (known as 'guinea' cloth) accounted for no less than 25 per cent of the value of total imports during the third quarter of the nineteenth century. At Lagos (about 1,800 miles away) textiles of all kinds averaged 44 per cent of total imports in the period 1880–1892. Similarities between the types of goods imported before and after the end of the external slave trade should not be allowed to disguise some important differences: by the middle of the nineteenth century the quantity had increased greatly, and (as will be pointed out) the price per unit had declined.

On the European side of the trade, Britain and France continued to be the most important foreign powers on the West Coast, as they had been in the eighteenth century. Liverpool dominated the new trade, just as it had the old, and was by far the largest importer of palm oil in Europe. Nantes underwent a decline in the nineteenth century, but Bordeaux and Marseilles, the ports which took its place, both had long-standing connections with Africa. Most of West Africa's groundnut exports were

---

[12] Quoted in Allan McPhee, *The Economic Revolution in British West Africa*, 1926, p. 31, n. 2.

[13] Though some were used in Africa for fuel.

[14] Rum and tobacco imports dwindled in the last quarter of the nineteenth century following the decline of trade with America and Brazil, the two principal suppliers.

shipped to France, where they enjoyed tariff advantages over certain other vegetable oils, including palm oil. The most striking aspect of the national distribution of trade was the pre-eminence of Britain.[15] In 1868 a French consul estimated that Britain and France shared four-fifths of Europe's trade with West Africa, and that two-thirds to three-quarters of this total was in the hands of Great Britain. Furthermore, as much as 70 per cent of Britain's trade in the period 1860–1880 was conducted with areas outside her few, small colonies. France's trade, by contrast, was centred on her traditional base and colony of Senegal, which accounted for between half and three-quarters of her total trade with West Africa during the same period. A new feature of the second half of the century was the rapid growth of German commerce. By the 1880s Hamburg was said to handle nearly one third of all West Africa's overseas trade.[16] This expansion was the result of three factors: the rise of the palm kernel market, which was dominated by Hamburg because German farmers were the main buyers of cattle cake, and because the Dutch were the largest manufacturers of margarine; the ability of Hamburg to supply cheap liquor; and the development of steamship services between Germany and West Africa.

The abolition of the Atlantic slave trade and the rise of legitimate commerce were events which undoubtedly favoured Britain, the first industrial nation. She, above all others, was in a position to cater for the mass market which was beginning to emerge in West Africa, though her supremacy was being challenged in the late nineteenth century by new competitors. No other foreign powers were of any account in West Africa apart from Britain, France and Germany. The Danes sold their Gold Coast forts to the British in 1850, and the Dutch followed suit in 1872. The Portuguese, once the great innovators of European enterprise in Africa, had difficulty in maintaining even one tiny colony (Portuguese Guinea). All three countries had been overtaken by a world in which industrialisation had become the basis of commercial and political power.[17]

The rapid expansion of overseas commerce has tended to overshadow the history of West Africa's external trade across the Sahara. It is commonly supposed that by the nineteenth century this trade was only a fraction of the value it had attained in the golden age of the sixteenth century. Professor Boahen, for example, has suggested that total trade on the trans-Saharan routes amounted to no more than about £125,000 a year in the first half of the nineteenth century.[18] However, the defic-

[15] Newbury, 'Trade and Authority in West Africa from 1850 to 1880' in *Colonialism in Africa, 1870–1960*, ed. L. H. Gann and Peter Duignan, 1, *The History and Politics of Colonialism, 1870–1914*, Cambridge 1969, pp. 79–80.

[16] K. Vignes, 'Étude sur la rivalité d'influence entre les puissances européennes en Afrique équatoriale et occidentale depuis l'acte général de Berlin jusqu'au seuil du XXᵉ siècle', *Revue Française d'Histoire d'Outre-Mer*, 48, 1961, p. 14.

[17] Shortage of space has caused this rather cavalier treatment of minority expatriate interests, each of which is worthy of study in some detail. There was also an interesting trade between North America and West Africa which has been investigated and, indeed, virtually discovered by George E. Brooks, *Yankee Traders, Old Coasters and African Middlemen*, Boston 1970.

[18] A. Adu Boahen, *Britain, the Sahara, and the Western Sudan, 1788–1861*, Oxford, 1961, p. 131.

iencies in the evidence for both the sixteenth century and the early nineteenth century are so great as to make calculations and comparisons a matter of guesswork. Recent research indicates that the old caravan routes still had a surprising amount of life left in them in the second half of the nineteenth century. To begin with, it is now apparent that trans-Saharan trade was *not* seriously affected by competition from goods brought by sea until the very end of the century. Indeed, Manchester textiles were carried across the Sahara and achieved a wide distribution. As late as 1869, for example, the town of Ilorin was said to be commercially nearer the Mediterranean (some 2,000 miles to the north) than it was to the Bight of Benin, even though the port of Lagos was only about 150 miles away.[19] Secondly, in the most detailed examination of the trade figures yet attempted, Newbury has shown that the total value of trans-Saharan trade actually increased from the 1840s, and reached a peak in 1875, when it was worth around £1,500,000.[20] It was only after this date that a slow and final decline set in. Thus the Sahara developed its own brand of 'legitimate' commerce. Because of transport limitations, however, the overland routes failed to develop a sizeable export trade in bulky, low value goods, and the boom in the third quarter of the century was based partly on the ephemeral demand of the Victorian world for ostrich feathers.[21] Even with this boost to the trade, trans-Saharan commerce was worth only a fifth of the value of the West Coast's seaborne trade in 1875.

Economic development by way of staple exports can be a precarious and lengthy process. Changes in supply and demand can set back the progress of the staple, retard the development of the economy as a whole, and have serious social and political repercussions. West Africa's raw material exports entered a wide range of manufacturing processes, and the price paid for them and the volume required tended to vary in accordance with the level of business activity in industrial Europe. West African producers had to accept the world price as given because they were unable to control the volume of palm produce and groundnuts placed on the market, and because the industrial countries could buy alternative, competing products from other underdeveloped regions. By the mid-nineteenth century the days when West Africa enjoyed a monopoly as the sole supplier of labour to the plantations of the Americas were over, and the silent imperialism of the steamship was beginning to bring vegetable oils and substitute products from other continents besides Africa.

The identification of fluctuations in West Africa's external trade is a matter of considerable historical importance. The progress of the new economy of legitimate commerce is best charted by changes in the terms of trade of West African export producers: the net barter terms provide an index of the import-purchasing power of a unit of exports, and the income terms measure the import-purchasing power of

[19] A. Millson, 'Yoruba', *Manchester Geographical Society Journal*, 7, 1891, p. 92.

[20] C. W. Newbury, 'North African and Western Sudan Trade in the Nineteenth Century: a Re-evaluation', *Journal of African History*, 7, 1966, pp. 233–46.

[21] These decorated the hats of Victorian ladies in much the same way as they had adorned the ostriches themselves. African traders may well have wondered at the strange values of the white man, who was prepared to sell manufactured cloth for such an item, and for such a purpose!

total exports.[22] Insufficient data are available at present to enable precise calculations to be made, but the general trends are clear enough, and are confirmed by the evaluation of contemporary observers. It is hoped that others will find this subject important enough to carry out the research needed to improve the provisional and approximate analysis presented here.[23]

Information on the early nineteenth century is particularly sparse. However, as far as the main staple, palm oil, was concerned, prices on the West Coast and in Europe appear to have pursued an upward trend, with the exception of falls in 1844–1846 and 1851–1852, reaching a peak in 1854–1861, when the Liverpool price stood at around £45 per ton. At the same time, the prices of manufactured goods imported into West Africa fell dramatically as a result of the industrial revolution. By 1850 staple items cost half and in some cases only a quarter of what they had at the start of the century. Consequently, the barter terms of trade moved in favour of primary producers. Since the volume of exports was rising during the first half of the century, the income terms also improved. The result was a period of prosperity for West African trade. Indeed, since 1800 West Africa has experienced only three periods when both barter and income terms have moved sharply in favour of producers for at least ten years. The first period played an important part in establishing the new commerce; the second, from 1900–1913, helped to install the colonial rulers; and the third, from 1945–1955, was a phase of expanding expectations and economic diversification which was associated with the end of the colonial era.

In all situations of historical change there are elements of continuity. During the first half of the nineteenth century, when legitimate commerce was in its infancy and was also comparatively prosperous, producers and traders were encouraged to believe that the transition from the slave trade would be an easy one. Initially, various features of commerce on the West Coast were simply carried over from the eighteenth century. For example, a number of established European traders and African producers managed to adapt from the old trade to the new; some of the minor exports of legitimate commerce continued to be shipped after abolition just as they had been before; the credit or trust 'system' survived and expanded, in spite of repeated complaints from those who thought that it was morally reprehensible and economically risky; sailing ships remained in use on routes between Europe and Africa; and business was still transacted by means of barter and 'transitional' currencies, such as cowries and manillas. Above all, the effort to stop the slave trade and to establish legitimate commerce, though it led to voyages of exploration, to missionary enterprise, and to a slightly greater degree of official activity on the West Coast, did not bring about any major alterations to the political map. Because an adjustment was made to the economy without causing an immediate and total upheaval, traders and officials felt confident that casual and limited political commit-

[22] These terms are introduced here briefly, and are dealt with at greater length in Chapter 5, where the data available are sufficient to justify more extended treatment.

[23] Mention should be made of Patrick Manning's excellent special study, *An Economic History of Southern Dahomey, 1880–1914*, University of Wisconsin Ph.D. thesis 1969, which contains a thorough investigation of the overseas trade of that particular region.

ments could be maintained, much as they had been in the eighteenth century. The European frontier did not extend inland; it did not even cover all parts of the coast. There was no partition of Africa in 1807 or 1833.

The position changed considerably in the second half of the century. The boom came to an end in 1861, and there was a depression between 1862 and 1866, when the European price for palm oil fell to around £32 per ton. Although prices revived in 1866–1867, they never again reached the peaks of 1854–1861. On the contrary, they underwent a serious decline from an average of £37 per ton in 1861–1865 to £20 a ton in 1886–1890, the lowest on record since the early days of the trade. Thus in twenty-five years prices were cut by nearly 50 per cent. There was a very slight improvement in the 1890s, but it was not until 1906 that prices regained the levels achieved in the 1850s. Palm kernel prices fell by about a third from roughly £15 per ton in the 1860s to just over £10 in the period 1886–1890. Groundnut prices at Rufisque in Senegal also fell by roughly a third from 25 to 27½ francs per 100 kilos in the period 1857–1867 to around 15 francs in the period 1877–1900. In both cases, there was no recovery until after the turn of the century. There were two main causes of this fall, though there were several contributory factors, such as reduced ocean freight rates. First, there was an increase in the supply of mineral and vegetable oils following the discovery of petroleum resources in the United States in the 1860s, and the entry into the market of Indian groundnuts and Australian tallow after the opening of the Suez Canal in 1869. Second, European demand for a wide range of raw materials, including oils and fats, was checked in the last quarter of the nineteenth century with the advent of the so-called Great Depression.[24]

There is little systematic information available about the local prices of goods imported into West Africa in the second half of the nineteenth century. The trend was probably a downward one, reflecting the fall in freight rates, an increase in competition on the West Coast, and continuing improvements in industrial efficiency. However, it is certain that the substantial price reductions of the early nineteenth century were not repeated, and that any decline which occurred was relatively slight and also gradual.[25] In the third quarter of the nineteenth century, when export prices fell particularly sharply, the barter terms of trade moved decisively against primary producers.

The question now arises as to what extent and in what sense an increase in the volume of exports can be said to have compensated for this adverse movement in the barter terms of trade. The broad trend, as noted earlier, was a rising one, but with few exceptions expansion levelled off in the late 1870s and in the 1880s, and in some cases the volume of exports actually declined. A few examples will illustrate how widespread this experience was: in the Niger Delta palm produce exports showed no

[24] The best recent analysis of what in some respects was a non-event, is S. B. Saul's *The Myth of the Great Depression, 1873–1896*, 1969, though this study analyses the problem from a British, rather than from a European, point of view.

[25] See Lars G. Sandberg, 'Movements in the Quality of British Cotton Textile Exports, 1815–1913', *Journal of Economic History*, 28, 1968, p. 19.

clear upward movement in the 1870s and 1880s, and there was a decrease at Opobo during the period 1887–1893; at Lagos, one of the major centres of legitimate commerce, there was a slight, but indecisive, trend towards expansion in the 1870s and 1880s; on the Gold Coast oil and kernel exports were almost static from 1886–1900; on the Ivory Coast palm oil exports fell sharply in the mid-1880s; and in Sierra Leone the picture was much the same. The position with regard to groundnuts was very similar; shipments from Gambia declined in the 1870s and 1880s; and in Senegal exports reached a plateau in the late 1870s which was not substantially exceeded until about the turn of the century. Even in cases where the volume of exports rose to the extent that total earnings were maintained, producers were still not as well off in the 1880s as they had been earlier. In the absence of technical improvements in agriculture or in internal transport during the second half of the century, a rise in the volume of exports could be achieved only in one of two ways: first, by existing producers deciding to increase their labour inputs, thus reducing net incomes by cutting down on leisure or other activities, or by paying for additional labour services; and second by expanding the total number of independent producers, thus causing the average per capita incomes of export producers to fall.

It seems likely that the income terms of trade either declined or maintained a precarious stability during the last quarter of the century. Even in the latter case there is a strong probability that the real income of the average export producer was reduced.

The foregoing analysis has referred to the major staples of overseas trade. However, it is important to realise that the late nineteenth century was also a time of crisis for minor staples and for trans-Saharan trade. The Senegalese gum trade declined in the second half of the century as a result of the development of chemical substitutes and the growth of competition from Egyptian gum. Gold exports from the Gold Coast were static, cocoa exports were negligible, and rubber exports did not expand until the 1890s. The Western Sudan was affected in the nineteenth century by a series of political upheavals stemming from the *jihads* (holy wars), which were launched by the protagonists of a revived Islam. The nature of these revivalist movements is still a subject of dispute.[26] Their economic influence appears to have been conservative, except, possibly in the case of Senegal. At best they preserved traditional agricultural and trading activities; at worst they perpetuated archaic economies based on plunder, tribute and slavery. To these troubles was added another, namely the decay of trans-Saharan trade, which declined after 1875, and was reduced to a trickle by 1900. Initially, this slump was the result of slackening demand in Europe, but by the end of the century the desert trade had also been seriously affected by the

---

[26] The Russian scholar, D. A. Ol'derogge, has argued that the *jihad* in northern Nigeria was primarily a protest of Hausa and Fulani commoners against oppression by the ruling class. So far, this view has not made much impression, at least on British scholars. However, Ol'derogge's interpretation deserves attention, not least because testing his theory involves writing the history of ordinary Africans, as opposed to that of prominent religious and political figures, and this is surely highly desirable. On the *jihad* in Senegambia see Martin A. Klein, *Islam and Imperialism in Senegal*, Edinburgh 1968.

disintegration of the slave system which supported the oases, and by competition from ocean routes, which could deliver manufactured goods more cheaply.

The evidence indicates that West Africa's external trade experienced a crisis in the last quarter of the nineteenth century. Export producers had become caught in a staple trap: the barter terms of trade had turned against them, and attempts to increase the volume of exports had either failed or, where successful, had contributed to a further decline in the terms of trade, with the result that growth had become self-defeating. Within a relatively short space of time primary producers and traders came under severe pressure to develop alternative exports and to adopt cost-reducing innovations. This 'general crisis' of the late nineteenth century led to strains, misunderstandings and conflicts between all those, Europeans as well as Africans, who in varying degrees had become dependent on legitimate commerce for their livelihood. The expansion in the volume of overseas commerce in the second half of the nineteenth century, combined with the adverse movement in the terms of trade, led to the modification or abolition of many of the early features of legitimate commerce that had been inherited from the time of the external slave trade, and also caused the European powers to discard the assumptions governing their traditional policy of limited intervention in West Africa. Just as pronounced booms have had a marked effect on the course of West African history, so, too, have serious slumps. Since the beginning of legitimate commerce there have been two periods of ten years or more when the barter terms of trade have moved against export producers *and* when the income terms have either fallen or remained static. The first period of depression was in the last quarter of the nineteenth century, and helped to bring the Europeans into Africa. The second period, covering the years 1930–1945, helped create the movement which was to expel them.

2   Economic motives in partition

Imperialism is seen here as a process of interaction and, ultimately, conflict between the industrialised nations and the underdeveloped world. To analyse this process parallel analyses are required, the first dealing with intra-group relations, that is among African producers, traders and politicians on the one hand, and among European manufacturers, traders and politicians on the other; the second covering inter-group strategy, that is between Africans and Europeans at what, broadly, can be called the national level. The principal difficulty, apart from the problem that there is considerable controversy about the role of the Europeans, is that so little is known about the part played by Africans both in assisting and in opposing the invasion of their continent. The argument presented here is by no means complete, but it does try to establish and explore a framework of analysis which it is hoped will lead to further, more detailed research.[27] This framework is in three different

---

[27] In this respect the analysis is a response to the plea made by J. D. Hargreaves in an important article written more than ten years ago, 'Towards a History of the Partition of Africa', *Journal of African History*, I, 1960, pp. 97–109. For the most recent statement of Professor

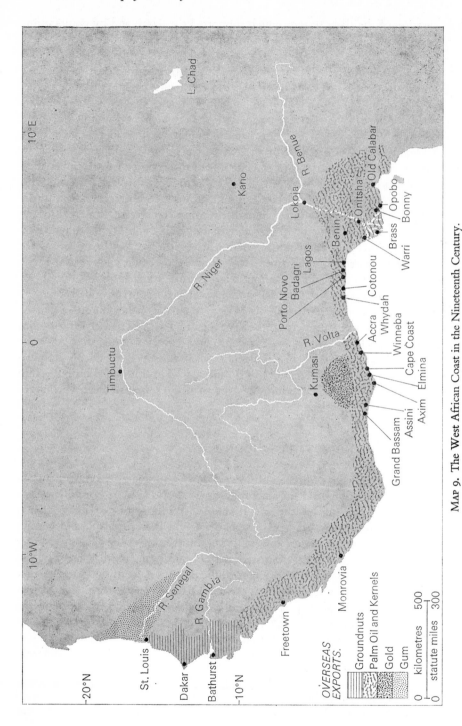

MAP 9. The West African Coast in the Nineteenth Century.

sections, all of which are concerned with the implications of the economic structure created by legitimate commerce: the first will consider problems of supply and their effect on intra-group relations on the African side of the frontier; the second will focus on problems of demand and their effect on intra-group relations on the European side of the frontier; and the third section will examine how the economic crisis of the late nineteenth century affected inter-group relations at the national level, and led to the decisions to move the established frontier inland, that is to partition West Africa.

It was by no means easy to develop satisfactory substitutes for the Atlantic slave trade, even though some of the staples of legitimate commerce were already grown in West Africa, and the terms of trade favoured primary producers in the second quarter of the nineteenth century. With the benefit of hindsight, historians have been able to point, justly, to the success of palm produce and groundnuts. For contemporaries, however, legitimate commerce was a long, precarious experiment, an era of fluctuating fortunes which held out no guarantees for the future. This explains why European interests, official and private, thought it necessary to tangle with a series of risky ventures in tropical agriculture. In the 1820s, for example, the French undertook an ambitious agricultural project in Senegal.[28] The main idea behind this scheme was to grow in Africa, and with African labour, the crops which had been produced on slave plantations in the Americas. A model farm was established, several crops, including cotton and indigo, were tried out, and new techniques of irrigation and ploughing were introduced. The experiment was abandoned in 1831 as a result of mismanagement, lack of capital, and ignorance of tropical conditions. In the 1840s British commercial interests established a model farm at Lokoja on the Niger, but this, too, was a failure.

The next important wave of experiments occurred just after the middle of the century, and was prompted by a cotton famine in Europe arising out of the American Civil War. Attempts were made to grow cotton at various points on the West Coast, such as Senegal, southern Nigeria and the Gold Coast.[29] In the 1860s the French still thought that Senegal was destined to become a leading exporter of cotton. Again they were disappointed. Many previous errors were repeated, and American production recovered far more quickly than had been anticipated. Above all, the Senegalese farmer, envisaging a rather different future for his country,

Hargreaves's own view see his contribution 'West African States and the European Conquest', in *Colonialism in Africa, 1870–1960*, ed. L. H. Gann and Peter Duignan, I, *The History and Politics of Colonialism, 1870–1914*, Cambridge 1969, pp. 199–219. I should like to acknowledge my debt to Dr Martin Klein, Dr Patrick Manning and Dr C. W. Newbury, who (though they may not be fully aware of it) have caused me to re-think my ideas on this subject over the past few years.

[28] Roger Pasquier, 'En marge de la guerre de sécession: les essais de culture du coton au Sénégal', *Annales Africaines*, 1955, pp. 185–202.

[29] Plantation agriculture on the Gold Coast, where experiments sponsored by the Basel Mission were of great importance, has been studied by Kwamina B. Dickson, *A Historical Geography of Ghana*, Cambridge 1969, pp. 120–32.

preferred groundnuts to cotton because they were more profitable. A greater degree of success was achieved at Abeokuta in south-west Nigeria, though there, too, cotton exports dwindled in the 1870s.[30] The promoters found that they were unable to compete in international markets, partly, it is interesting to note, because of the high cost of free African labour. The final phase of experiments came in the 1880s as a result of declining profits in the palm produce trade. Many proposals were put forward to remedy the problem, and several of the more feasible were tried out. Arthur Verdier, a prominent French merchant, began coffee plantations in the Ivory Coast; the Royal Niger Company started plantations of cocoa, coffee and rubber in the Niger Valley; and the colonial administration established botanic stations at Lagos (1887) and on the Gold Coast (1889).

These experiments have implications which extend beyond the local details given above. As a record of early European endeavours in tropical agriculture, they are important for geographers and botanists, as well as for historians. They also represent an interesting stage in the development of economic policy, for they stand mid-way between the mercantilist concept of colonies serving the needs of the mother country, and the realisation of this ideal in the different circumstances of the twentieth century. Furthermore, these nineteenth-century debates over the means of achieving agricultural progress anticipate the controversy which arose in the colonial period between the protagonists of peasant and plantation crops. For historians the schemes are especially noteworthy because they expressed the realisation that the external slave trade would not simply die of its own accord, and that a positive effort was required to find substitute exports. Many of those engaged in this search were energetic and commercially-minded Christians, who were intent on converting the soul of Africa as well as its economy. These men, the militant arm of the abolitionist movement, saw it as their mission to carry the moral convictions and economic optimism of the industrial world into the Dark Continent.

The most important and successful experiments, however, were those undertaken by Africans themselves, without European supervision, indeed frequently without expatriate officials and traders knowing what was happening. It is not always realised just how varied the export economy was in some parts of West Africa during the era of legitimate commerce. At Freetown, for instance, timber accounted for about 70 per cent of all exports by 1829; by 1860 timber exports had almost disappeared, and the main items of overseas trade were gold, palm oil and groundnuts, each of which accounted for about 20 per cent of total exports; by the 1880s these three products had also declined, and palm kernels had become the dominant export.[31] It was in the 1880s, too, and as a direct result of the economic problems of the period, that Africans began cocoa farming in the Gold Coast and southern Nigeria, achieving results which none of the European 'experts' could emulate. These examples

[30] J. B. Webster, 'The Bible and the Plough', *Journal of the Historical Society of Nigeria*, 2, 1963, pp. 418–34.
[31] P. K. Mitchell, 'Trade Routes of the Early Sierra Leone Protectorate', *Sierra Leone Studies*, 16, 1962, pp. 204–17.

illustrate that African responses to changing returns on their exports were flexible and rapid, given the natural resources at their disposal and the technical constraints operating in the nineteenth century, notably in internal transport.

Palm oil, palm kernels and groundnuts, the main staples of legitimate commerce, were produced and delivered to the coast entirely through indigenous enterprise. Yet because of the widespread assumption that the transition to legitimate commerce was easy and uneventful, some basic questions about the historical development of these crops have still to be asked. For example, few historians have appreciated that palm oil was not a homogeneous commodity. Some regions, such as south-west Nigeria, produced a soft quality oil which fetched a high price; others, such as the Gold Coast, supplied a harder oil which was less in demand. These distinctions deserve further consideration, for they are likely to supply much-needed information about the resource base of the various export regions, about differences in methods of preparation, and about the motives for developing alternative exports, such as why the Gold Coast expanded cocoa production at an earlier date than did Nigeria. Similarly, not enough attention has been paid to the fact that palm kernels did not simply join palm oil as an additional export, but were developed largely to compensate for the decline of the latter in the second half of the nineteenth century. Yet some regions exported a much greater proportion of kernels to oil than did others, though both products were in joint supply. This, too, is a difference which needs exploring further, for it may provide a clue to important problems, such as the extent of internal trade in palm oil, and the ability of various parts of the coast to adjust to the decline of staple exports in the late nineteenth century. Finally, more thought needs to be given to the remarkable 'do it yourself' character of staple export production, in which each man became an entrepreneur in his own right, albeit on a modest scale. Traditional economic frontiers were broken down through the initiative of African migrants and settlers, who colonised and developed previously underused land, and in doing so brought about changes in settlement patterns, farming practices, land tenure, and in the role, status and size of the labour force engaged in export production.[32] This is a theme of epic proportions, which still awaits epic treatment.

European demand for vegetable oils had far-reaching economic, social and political consequences in West Africa, though it is important to stress that these were not identical in all parts of the region. Ultimately, it should be possible to define and classify the various areas of West Africa according to the precise type of adaptive challenge which confronted them, and the nature of their responses to it. At present it is hard to do more than sketch the outlines of a complex regional map. Three categories will be suggested here by way of preliminary analysis.

---

[32] On migration see Marion Johnson, 'Migrants' Progress', *Bulletin of the Ghana Geographical Association*, 9, 1964, pp. 4–27, and 10, 1965, pp. 13–40; and R. K. Udo, 'The Migrant Tenant Farmer of Eastern Nigeria', *Africa*, 34, 1964, pp. 326–39. On land tenure see Akin L. Mabogunje, 'Some Comments on Land Tenure in Egba Division, Western Nigeria', *Africa*, 31, 1961, pp. 258–69. The expansion of 'peasant' exports in the twentieth century is dealt with in Chapter 6.

First, there were areas which experienced a decline in the staple export, slaves, without securing adequate compensation in the form of new products. This was particularly true of those parts of West Africa which were either unsuitable for growing palm trees and groundnuts, or were too far from the coast for export production to be remunerative. The Western Sudan, with its famous trans-Saharan commerce in decline after 1875, was a case in point, for palm produce and groundnuts were bulky items with a low value to weight ratio, unlike slaves, which could be traded profitably over long distances. Second, there were areas which had not been involved in the external slave trade to any great extent, and which were presented with new openings in the export sector. This was the case along parts of the coast between Senegal and the Ivory Coast, which began to export vegetable products in the nineteenth century. Third, there were areas in which the change to legitimate commerce meant a shift from the production of slaves (at least as an export commodity) to the production of vegetable oils. This applied to Senegambia and to most of the forest from the Gold Coast eastwards. There is considerable justification for concentrating on the third category, apart from the convenient fact that it happens to be the best documented. Not only was this extensive region by far the most important supplier of legitimate exports, despite its close involvement with the Atlantic slave trade,[33] but it was also from points within this area that the Europeans launched their invasion of the interior at the close of the century.[34]

Three aspects of the economic history of this region will be considered here. First, its general development as an export centre will be outlined; next, the position of export producers will be investigated with particular reference to the fortunes of the large entrepreneurs who had dominated production during the time of the Atlantic slave trade; finally, the situation of the coastal wholesalers will be examined, using the Niger Delta as a case study.

The supply of West African palm produce came from an area which stretched from Guinea to the Cameroons, though the most important source lay in the eastern section from the Gold Coast to Old Calabar. The prominence of this sub-division was the result of the abundance of its oil-palms, which occurred naturally in a broad belt lying close to the coast,[35] and of the network of lagoons and inland waterways stretching from Porto Novo to Old Calabar, which made it possible to transport produce relatively cheaply. In the period immediately after 1807 the leading centre

[33] In some cases (Old Calabar and Whydah are two obvious examples) it is clear that the overseas slave trade developed entrepreneurial skills and commercial institutions which greatly assisted the rise of legitimate trade. However, it would be wrong to infer that the slave trade was in any sense necessary to the successful expansion of legitimate commerce. Everything that is known about African enterprise in internal trade in the pre-colonial period strongly suggests that indigenous societies would have produced the required number of wholesalers and traders, and in a short space of time, even if the Atlantic slave trade had never existed.

[34] At the same time, it is worth while pointing out that areas in the second category also experienced some of the difficulties of economic transition. See E. A. Ijagbemi, 'The Freetown Colony and the Development of "Legitimate" Commerce in the Adjoining Territories', *Journal of the Historical Society of Nigeria*, 5, 1970, pp. 252–6.

[35] Many palm trees were also planted deliberately.

of production in West Africa was Old Calabar, which shipped well over half the total palm oil imports entering Great Britain. In the 1830s Old Calabar was joined, and for a while overtaken, by Bonny, further west in the mouth of the Niger Delta. In the 1840s exports from the Delta as a whole averaged 15–20,000 tons per annum, which was equivalent to about three-quarters of total oil imports into the United Kingdom. Bonny's supremacy lasted until the 1870s, when its suppliers and outlets were captured by the nearby port of Opobo following a political coup. After the middle of the century other centres sprang up, and the Niger Delta, though still very important, no longer completely dominated the West African oil trade. The geographical and quantitative expansion of legitimate commerce was closely associated with the decline of the Atlantic slave trade, for until about the 1860s slaves still competed successfully with palm oil at several points along the coast, especially at Whydah and Lagos. By the third quarter of the century palm produce was the leading overseas export along a broad stretch of the West Coast. During the last twenty years of the century oil and kernels accounted for over 70 per cent of the value of total exports from the Gold Coast, over 80 per cent at Lagos and over 90 per cent in Dahomey and the Niger Delta. A remarkable transformation of the export economy had been achieved in a comparatively short space of time.

Groundnuts, an annual crop, were grown for export in a region which extended from Senegal to Sierra Leone, though as they prefer sandy soils and a long, reliable dry season, Senegambia became by far the most prominent area of production. Transport costs made it uneconomic to grow the crop for export very far inland, so the main areas of production, as in the case of palm oil, lay near the coast. The small British colony of Gambia was the earliest focal point of the trade, partly, it is interesting to note, as a result of purchases made by American traders.[36] In the 1820s about 90 per cent of Gambia's exports consisted of beeswax and hides. Groundnuts were exported for the first time in the 1830s, and by the middle of the century they accounted for two-thirds of all exports. A proportion of the groundnuts shipped from Gambia were grown in areas which would have made use of ports in neighbouring French territory, except for the fact that an export duty was levied on agricultural exports from Senegal until 1855. With the removal of this duty, exports from Senegal greatly increased. By the last quarter of the century the export trade of Senegambia was as dependent on groundnuts as that of the forest was on palm produce. The main areas of production were Casamance south of Gambia, and Cayor to the north. (However, further north still, around St Louis, the export trade relied principally on gum, as it had in the days of Atlantic commerce.) The groundnut trade, like the palm oil trade, saw the conversion of former slave ports into centres of legitimate commerce. Kaolack, for example, became a large centre for the groundnut trade from the 1860s onwards.[37] A great deal of additional historical research needs to be carried out on most aspects of legitimate commerce, but

---

[36] Brooks, *Yankee Traders, Old Coasters and African Middlemen*, pp. 184–9.

[37] A. Dessertine, 'Naissance d'un port: Kaolack, des origines à 1900', *Annales Africaines*, 1960, pp. 225–59.

especially on the development of groundnut production. Fouquet, Pelissier, and others have made substantial contributions to the study of Senegalese groundnuts in the modern context, but the economic history of the crop remains to be written.

In some parts of the underdeveloped world the requirements of the industrial nations were consistent with the maintenance of the established social and political order. Britain's demand for Argentinian beef, for example, strengthened the position of an already existing class of large landowners in that area, since cattle rearing was most efficient on sizeable units of land.[38] Peaceful economic integration was also associated with a policy of political neutrality in Latin America, though it was not the only reason for it. In West Africa, on the other hand, the accidents of geography and history which enabled small farmers and traders to participate efficiently in overseas commerce posed acute problems of adaptation for the traditional warrior entrepreneurs who had co-operated so profitably with European slavers during the days of the Atlantic trade. African rulers experimented with a number of modes of adaptation to their new situation, and these can be classified according to their negative or positive character. Four of the most important, which were adopted singly or in conjunction, will be dealt with here.

The first negative response was to continue exporting slaves in defiance of the ban imposed by the European nations. Little is known at present about the relative profits of slaving and legitimate commerce, but it seems that few African slave exporters turned willingly to the new trade, even though the terms of trade were more favourable in the second quarter of the century than they were to become later on. This reluctance may be taken as an indication that for established exporters the costs of legitimate commerce (in terms of diminished political power as well as of cash income) outweighed the returns. The predicament of Ghezo, the ruler of Abomey, was duplicated in other parts of the West Coast:

> The state which he maintained was great; his army was expensive; the ceremonies and customs to be observed annually, which had been handed down to him from his forefathers, entailed upon him a vast outlay of money. These could not be abolished. The form of his government could not be suddenly changed, without causing such a revolution as would deprive him of his throne, and precipitate his kingdom into a state of anarchy.[39]

As for the palm oil trade, that was 'a slow method of making money, and brought only a very small amount of duties into his coffers'. Ghezo's support of the slave trade ceased only with his death in 1858. After the withdrawal of European nations from the Atlantic trade, the shipment of slaves was handled mainly by Brazilian merchants, such as Domingo Martinez, who operated in the Bight of Benin between

[38] H. S. Ferns, 'Latin America and Industrial Capitalism—The First Phase', *Sociological Review Monograph*, 11, 1967, pp. 18–20.

[39] Brodie Cruickshank's report of 1848, quoted in C. W. Newbury, *The Western Slave Coast and its Rulers*, Oxford 1961, p. 51.

1833 and 1864.[40] The Brazilians were eventually eliminated by the naval squadron, by the closure of foreign slave markets, and by their own inability to procure the necessary European trade goods. By the end of the 1860s the overseas slave trade had been reduced to a trickle. Responding to the new trade by trying to perpetuate the old was no longer possible.

Next, African rulers attempted to bolster their fortunes by means which were familiar to pre-industrial governments throughout the world, namely by employing armed strength to plunder and to exact tribute from their neighbours. The kings of Senegambia used this tactic as an outlet for the energies of their hard-drinking, hard-fighting warrior élite (*tyeddo*); Ashanti mixed force with diplomacy in order to control, or secure access to, the wealth of the coastal peoples; the kings of Dahomey made annual incursions into Yoruba country; and the Yoruba states themselves fought a series of wars in which economic goals were prominent. Military operations, and, perhaps more important, the constant threat of them, led to the abandonment of fertile land, and to the creation of broad areas of neutral territory between hostile states. They perpetuated conditions which were inimical to the growth of the petty capitalism that had been fostered by legitimate commerce. They dramatised what may be called the crisis of the aristocracy in nineteenth-century West Africa, a social and political crisis stemming from a contradiction between past and present relations of production. They were a last resort, and, as such, represented the ultimate failure of the *ancien régime* to adapt peacefully and efficiently to the demands of the industrial world.

The first of the two positive modes of adaptation was for former slave suppliers to develop an export trade in legitimate goods. Some of them became employers rather than exporters of slaves, and they used servile labour to harvest palm trees, to grow groundnuts and to transport produce to markets. The rise of legitimate commerce, far from bringing about the abolition of domestic slavery, increased the demand for cheap labour in Africa itself, and so perpetuated a service industry (the supply of slaves) which was detrimental to the long-term development of the natural resources of the region. The result was the growth of a small group of large export producers in areas which were near enough to the coast for the transport of bulky goods to be a feasible proposition. In Dahomey and some of the Yoruba states, for example, the rulers and important chiefs established large palm oil estates worked by slave labour. However, these men now had to face competition at their palace gates from a multiplicity of small, efficient farmers who were only partly committed to the overseas market, but who supplied the greater part of the produce shipped to Europe in the second half of the nineteenth century. The large producers found that they were unable to influence local export prices simply by controlling production, as they had done previously, yet at the same time they themselves were highly vulnerable to changes in the prices paid for produce by European merchants on the coast, since a sizeable part of their total incomes was derived from export earnings.

[40] David A. Ross, 'The Career of Domingo Martinez in the Bight of Benin, 1833–64', *Journal of African History*, 6, 1965, pp. 79–90.

States which were not situated close to the coast had great difficulty in making constructive adjustments to legitimate commerce. Ashanti, however, is an interesting example of a partially exceptional case.[41] Faced with a severe crisis early in the nineteenth century, the rulers of Ashanti responded by expanding their export trade to the north, selling kola nuts and buying cattle and slaves. Demand in the Hausa states had grown following the *jihads* of the early nineteenth century because kola was an approved stimulant in Muslim communities, which were denied alcohol. Supplies were increased partly by gathering kola nuts from wild trees, but mainly, it appears, through the establishment of plantations worked by slave labour.[42] Good fortune, commercial skill and a highly efficient system of government helped Ashanti to adjust to the central economic problem which it faced in the nineteenth century. Yet some important questions still have to be answered before the response of Ashanti can be counted as an unqualified success. In the first place, not enough is known about the total value and the rate of profit of the northern trade to say whether its expansion in the nineteenth century fully compensated for the diminution of exports to the south. It has to be remembered that the size of the internal market was still severely limited by transport costs, and that the decline of trans-Saharan trade after 1875 might well have affected purchasing power in the north. Secondly, Ashanti still depended on the coast for supplies of munitions, salt and cotton goods, which came through satellites, such as the Fante states. These states now produced palm oil and kernels for export, and no longer relied on Ashanti for supplies of slaves for shipment overseas. Thus it is likely that there was, from the Ashanti point of view, an unfavourable shift in the balance of economic power. What is certain is that the attempt to reassert control over the Fante in the second half of the century brought Ashanti closer to conflict with the British. Finally, more research is needed into the potentially disintegrative elements within the Ashanti state: the implications for her long-term economic welfare and political stability of the existence of marked inequalities of wealth, the growth of the slave labour force, and the frustration of the merchant class, whose development was deliberately restrained, lest private enterprise should harm the national interest, as conceived by the king.[43]

The second positive mode of adaptation was for traditional rulers to recognise the small producers as a serious new force, and to give them an increased stake in a

[41] Very few historians of Africa can match Ivor Wilks's achievement in reconstructing the history of Ashanti. See, for example, 'Ashanti Government', in *West African Kingdoms in the Nineteenth Century*, ed. Daryll Forde and P. M. Kaberry, 1967, pp. 206–38, and his study of the 'war' and 'peace' parties in *Political Bi-polarity in Nineteenth-Century Asante*, Centre of African Studies, Edinburgh 1971.

[42] Ivor Wilks, 'Asante Policy Towards the Hausa Trade in the Nineteenth Century', in *The Development of Indigenous Trade and Markets in West Africa*, ed. Claude Meillassoux, 1971, pp. 124–41.

[43] Some important work on these topics is being undertaken by K. Arhin. See, for example, 'The Structure of Greater Ashanti', *Journal of African History*, 8, 1967, pp. 65–85, and 'Aspects of Ashanti Northern Trade in the Nineteenth Century', *Africa*, 40, 1970, pp. 363–73.

reformed political system. For example, Lat Dior, the ruler of Cayor in Senegal, tried to forge an alliance with the groundnut farmers of his state in the 1870s in an attempt to counterbalance the power of the traditional military estate. However, support could not always be relied on, and aspirations, once encouraged, tended to multiply. The small producers used their new wealth to purchase, among other items, guns, and with these they could threaten the rulers who sought their co-operation.[44] The new generation of export producers in West Africa had every reason to be wary of encouragement from their superiors, for rulers who allowed independent producers to develop did so in the hope of taxing their wealth. Not surprisingly, this aim became a cause of friction, particularly in the last quarter of the century, when profits from the export trade were reduced to a minimum. Further-more, taxing small producers posed serious practical problems. Collecting tolls from a convoy of slaves travelling on an established route was easy enough, but, as the Aro of south-east Nigeria found, levying duties on palm oil was an entirely different matter, for oil was produced and traded in small quantities at many diverse points. Thus the attempt to accommodate the new capitalist class and secure the incomes of traditional rulers was a difficult operation.

The negative responses may have helped to prevent a sudden decline in incomes, but were ultimately self-defeating. The positive responses achieved better results, but were still not wholly successful. The difficulties of the progressive rulers arose first from an internal conflict of interest stemming from a basic change in the structure of export-producing firms, and second from the fact that they were unable or unwilling to make the necessary adjustments in the time allowed by impatient and often unsympathetic foreigners. For a while it seemed that there was a chance of stabilising the existing frontier between Europeans and Africans on the West Coast, but in the last quarter of the century the indigenous rulers were called on to make concessions over such matters as railways, internal tolls and slavery, which they judged, quite rightly, would undermine their political independence. At that point the dialogue over peaceful coexistence came to an end. Possessing fewer internal assets, and experiencing at the same time greater external pressures, the modernising aristocracies of West Africa were less able to control their future than were their revolutionary counterparts in Japan after 1868.[45]

As a general proposition, it can be said that the traditional unit of trade was less affected by the structural changes brought about by legitimate commerce than was the traditional unit of production. This was because large wholesalers were still necessary, whether the commodities to be handled were slaves or palm oil, whereas large producers were not. Many established entrepôts, such as Whydah, Lagos, Bonny and Old Calabar, substituted palm oil for slaves and survived as major ports right down to partition, and in some cases beyond. Their rulers continued to levy

[44] These developments are discussed by Martin Klein in 'Slavery, the Slave Trade, and Legitimate Commerce in Late Nineteenth-Century Africa', *Études d'Histoire Africaine*, 2, 1971, pp. 22–4.

[45] A brief survey of this aspect of Japanese history is given in Thomas C. Smith, 'Japan's Aristocratic Revolution', *Yale Review*, 5, 1960–1, pp. 370–83.

traditional taxes on visiting ships, and their leading merchants received credit and goods on a larger scale than ever before. Even the old trading premises survived: after abolition, the barracoons (warehouses where slaves were kept pending shipment) were used to store the new, legitimate exports. Although the entrepôts were not affected in precisely the same way as producers in the hinterland, it does not follow that they were not affected at all by the development of legitimate commerce, or that they found it any easier to establish a lasting and satisfactory relationship with their European customers. On the contrary, African rulers had to struggle in the nineteenth century to control destabilising forces which threatened the cohesion of the entrepôts, and sometimes their very existence. Some indication of the nature of these forces is necessary for an understanding of the degrees of solidarity and disunity exhibited by the middlemen states when faced with increased European pressure towards the close of the century. The best illustration of their problems is provided by the history of the area centring on the Niger Delta, which has been the subject of some important research in recent years.[46]

Legitimate commerce presented opportunities to a new generation of traders, as well as producers, because it gave employment to a greater number of intermediaries, who were needed to collect export crops and to distribute manufactured goods. Entry into small scale trade was easy because there were few barriers of capital or skill. The result was that existing wholesalers faced more competition than they had in the past, though this is not to imply that such rivalry was unimportant during the time of the Atlantic slave trade. The new traders won their most striking success in the Niger Delta. Virtually all the 'city states', as Dike has called them, experienced serious political unrest between 1850 and 1875, as slaves and ex-slaves challenged the authority of the established wholesalers and rulers. This movement was personified by Ja Ja, the former slave who rose to a position of economic importance in Bonny in the 1860s, but whose social origins prevented him from attaining the highest political office. In 1869 Ja Ja founded his own state at nearby Opobo, thus conferring on himself the political power which he felt his commercial success deserved. The career of Nana Olomu, the leading figure in Itsekiri trade and politics in the 1880s, provides another striking example of how advancement was becoming based on commercial achievement rather than on inherited status, though Nana's social origins were less humble than Ja Ja's, and he was able to further his political ambitions in his home territory.[47] Ability put a man in a strong position; ability *and* acceptable family connections made him almost unassailable.

Indigenous commercial institutions in the Delta states were not entirely immune from change, and were affected by the alterations in personnel. At Bonny and

[46] The major studies are K. O. Dike, *Trade and Politics in the Niger Delta, 1830–1885*, Oxford 1956; G. I. Jones, *The Trading States of the Oil Rivers*, Oxford 1963; Obaro Ikime, *Merchant Prince of the Niger Delta*, 1968; and A. J. H. Latham, *Old Calabar, 1600–1861: the Economic Impact of the West upon a Traditional Society*, University of Birmingham Ph.D. thesis, 1970.

[47] On the problems of economic transition among the Itsekiri see P. C. Lloyd, 'The Itsekiri in the Nineteenth Century: an Outline Social History', *Journal of African History*, 4, 1963, pp. 207–31.

Kalabari, for example, the rise of men whose success was a result of trading ability rather than of ascribed social position had repercussions on the traditional canoe 'house' (a compact and well organised trading and fighting corporation capable of maintaining a war canoe) because increased social mobility led to a greater turnover of commercial and political authority. Jones has analysed the history of these states in the nineteenth century in terms of a developmental cycle, which started with the expansion of a canoe house, moved on to a phase of political accretion, in which several houses coalesced, and culminated in varying degrees of disintegration, as unity broke down. For present purposes it might also be useful to think of the economic aspects of this cycle in terms of the theory of the firm, whereby a successful company expands, takes over its rivals, and achieves a local monopoly, only to find that its dominance is undermined from within, as managers leave to start their own businesses, and challenged from outside, as new competitors move in to try and secure a share of the monopoly profit.

Certain qualifications to the foregoing analysis have to be made, even at the risk of complicating the story. In the first place it should be noted that legitimate commerce speeded social change in the trading states, but did not initiate it, for social 'upstarts' had also found scope for their talents during the days of the Atlantic slave trade.[48] Secondly, some states escaped slave revolts, and in others slave risings were not always movements of the downtrodden against their masters. In Kalabari, for example, class conflict was minimised by integrating mechanisms which helped to assimilate slaves into society.[49] In Old Calabar slave risings were partly demonstrations in support of established, rival political factions, and so served a functional purpose in reinforcing the status quo. Finally, care must be taken not to romanticise the careers of the famous Delta traders. Some scholars, understandably anxious to write African rather than Imperial history, have seen in these men the forerunners of the nationalist movements which developed in the colonial period. This interpretation bestows on the actors a motive and sense of purpose which they themselves would have had difficulty in recognising. The leaders of the Delta states were great traders, and they certainly fought hard to maintain their independence, but their world view did not extend much beyond their local commercial interests, their vision of social justice did not include the emancipation of their own slaves, and they resisted African as well as European rivals with the true impartiality of *homo economicus*.

Besides the problem of internally-generated instability, the entrepôts faced an additional complication which did not affect the producers directly, namely the physical presence of commercial agents from the Western world. In the second half of the nineteenth century the growth of a bulk trade, combined with the advent of the steamship, led the European merchants to set up many more shore bases. With

[48] See, for example, Kwame Y. Daaku, *Trade and Politics on the Gold Coast, 1600–1720*, Oxford 1970, ch. 5.
[49] Robin Horton, 'From Fishing Village to City State: a Social History of New Calabar', in *Man in Africa*, ed. Mary Douglas and Phyllis M. Kaberry, 1969, pp. 37–58.

the merchants came missionaries and educated African ex-slaves. This development was a serious threat to the position of the ruling oligarchy in the entrepôts. In contrast to the era of the slave trade, when European visitors tended to be sailors first and traders second, the newcomers were permanent and competitive wholesalers. Furthermore, the presence of an expatriate community, however small, had important political consequences. It acted as a magnet for the disaffected, from slaves seeking freedom to disgruntled members of the local oligarchy looking for external support for battles which they could not win on their own. Since the European merchants were the main suppliers of credit, whatever action they took, whether Machiavellian or innocent in intent, was bound to have repercussions on the internal political situation, either confirming the power of the existing rulers or building up the claims of rivals.

Potentially the most serious destabilising influence was the possibility of a serious trade depression, an event which would have affected the large wholesalers in much the same way as the large producers because both depended on foreign trade for their livelihood. Indeed, it could be argued that the middlemen were even more vulnerable than the producers since some of the entrepôts relied on local imports for their basic supplies of food, and they nearly all lacked an alternative means of maintaining their incomes. A crisis in foreign trade would intensify internal rivalries by fostering disputes over the allocation of shares in the export trade, over the prices to be asked and given, and over the distribution of reduced profits. It would also increase external pressures. On the one hand, European traders would try to pay less for produce and charge more for manufactured goods; they would become more closely concerned as creditors of faltering and bankrupt African wholesalers; and they would be tempted to give support to families and houses which appeared more capable of safeguarding their interests than did the existing rulers. On the other hand, the wholesalers would run into difficulties with their hinterland customers, as they tried to pass on the price changes which they themselves had been forced to accept. While trade remained prosperous these tendencies, though present, were held in check. In the last quarter of the century, however, there was a radical change in the situation.

African producers and wholesalers were not alone in facing problems of adaptation in the nineteenth century. Commercial interests on the European side of the frontier were also profoundly affected by the expansion of overseas trade and by the change in its character following the rise of legitimate exports. Two developments in particular helped to bring about a fundamental reorganisation of West African trade after 1850, resulting in a greater degree of competition, the final liquidation of eighteenth-century commercial practices, and the beginnings of a recognisably modern organisational structure for the expatriate firms. The first development, in terms of chronology, concerned ocean transport, and the second involved alterations to the media of exchange used on the West Coast. Just as there were reactionary, as well as progressive, elements on the African side of the frontier, so, too, contrary to what might be supposed, there were those among the European community who did their best to convince themselves and their customers that the industrial revolution had never occurred.

In the first half of the nineteenth century, the products of legitimate commerce were carried to Europe by sailing ships, and the leading trading firms all possessed ocean-going vessels. The Bordeaux firm of Maurel et Prom kept a sizeable fleet of three-masted ships in service on the route to Senegal between the 1830s and the 1880s, and other large merchants, such as the London firm of F. & A. Swanzy, which traded to the Gold Coast, followed this practice. However, shortly after the middle of the century the technical development of the steamship reached a point where it could begin to compete successfully with sail.[50] The African Steam Ship Company was formed in England in 1851 and began a regular service to the West Coast in the following year. This firm was joined by another, the British & African Steam Navigation Company in 1868, first as a rival and then as an associate. The British Lines were the most important serving West Africa, but other European interests were also represented. In France a consortium of Bordeaux and Marseilles firms ran steamships to parts of West Africa in the 1870s before the formation of the Fabre-Fraissinet line in 1889, and in Germany the merchant house of Woermann began to run steamers to the West Coast in the 1870s, before the establishment of the Woermann-Linie in 1886. During the third quarter of the century the West African carrying trade was converted to steam, and by the 1870s the sailing ship was playing a secondary and diminishing role. In 1880 the number of sailing vessels entering Lagos harbour, for example, was about a third of the number of steamers and represented only one sixth of the tonnage of the latter.

The second change centred on the decline of the main transitional currencies, and on an increase in the circulation of modern money (especially British and French silver coins) in the key exporting areas.[51] In the present state of knowledge it is hard to make firm generalisations about this process, but three points can be established. First, the change was under way *before* the advent of colonial rule, though the timing varied at different points along the West Coast. In the second half of the nineteenth century iron and copper currencies and cowries underwent a serious depreciation, and by the close of the century had ceased to play an important part in external trade. Francs were used extensively in the groundnut trade as early as the 1850s, and florins and shillings became the main media of exchange for palm produce during the last quarter of the century. Second, it seems clear that the decline of these currencies was closely associated with a fall in the cost of supplying them to West Africa. In Europe technical advances made it possible to manufacture manillas and iron currencies more cheaply, and in Africa new resources of cowrie shells were

[50] Technical supremacy, however, did not come until the 1880s. See Gerald S. Graham, 'The Ascendancy of the Sailing Ship, 1850–85', *Economic History Review*, 9, 1956, pp. 74–88. Further information about the beginnings of steamship services to West Africa can be found in P. N. Davies, 'The African Steam Ship Company', in *Liverpool and Merseyside*, ed. J. R. Harris, 1969, pp. 212–38, and in a neglected article by Emile Baillet, 'Le rôle de la marine de commerce dans l'implantation de la France en A.O.F.', *Revue Maritime*, 135, 1957, pp. 832–40.

[51] For further details see A. G. Hopkins, 'The Currency Revolution in South-West Nigeria in the Late Nineteenth Century', *Journal of the Historical Society of Nigeria*, 3, 1966, pp. 471–83, and a more comprehensive article by Marion Johnson, 'The Cowrie Currencies of West Africa', *Journal of African History*, 11, 1970, pp. 331–53.

discovered on the East Coast around the middle of the century. Improvements in ocean transport made it possible to deliver all these currencies at reduced cost. European merchants, competing with each other for the purchase of produce, began to flood the West African export market with transitional monies. Over-issue undermined confidence and led to a fall in exchange rates with other currencies. By the 1880s traders in some centres needed porters to headload their small change, in much the same way as workers in Germany needed suitcases to carry home their weekly earnings following the depreciation of the mark in the 1920s. Third, the collapse of transitional currencies undermined the barter system, which was closely associated with it, and the mythical ounce and bar trade too, though again little is known at the moment about this aspect of African monetary history.[52]

In the long run the advent of the steamship and the introduction of modern money brought advantages to those engaged in overseas trade, principally because they assisted the expansion of the market. Without these innovations West Africa would certainly have become uncompetitive in international trade. The steamship was cheaper per ton/mile than sail, and this was a vital consideration at a time when the West African export trade had become centred on bulky vegetable products, which, as noted earlier, were of low value per unit of weight compared with slaves. The steamer was also faster than sail; in the middle of the century sailing ships took about thirty-five days to reach West Africa, but by 1900 the steamer had reduced this time by half. The speed of the steamship made it possible to transport a wider range of perishable goods, and it enabled traders to complete their transactions more quickly, thus helping them to economise on capital. Finally, the steamship, being less dependent on natural conditions than was sail, could guarantee regularity of service. Fore-knowledge of the steamer's arrival enabled traders to purchase and prepare goods for shipment. Greater readiness reduced the time spent in port, and so lowered running costs.

Modern money helped to increase the number and variety of possible transactions. British and French silver coins were almost perfect substitutes, that is to say they were acceptable for virtually all goods and services. Africans who were paid in silver coin for their produce received units of general purchasing power instead of a packet of goods and transitional currencies. Export earnings could be diverted more easily to domestic uses, or could be spent on imported goods supplied by a variety of firms. African producers and traders had more freedom of choice: they were no longer tied to the firm which bought their produce, and they enjoyed greater independence from rulers who previously had exercised a degree of central control over export sales and over the distribution of foreign trade earnings. It was no coincidence that francs and shillings spread in areas where legitimate exports were developing most quickly, and it was no coincidence either that low denomination coins were in great demand, for they were an indication of the growing importance of small producers

[52] Further work is also needed to clarify the consequences of the decline of transitional currencies for African societies, particularly for fixed income groups and those wealthy enough to hold stocks of money. It would also be interesting to know whether a depreciating exchange rate assisted exports in the 1860s and 1870s.

and traders in the new export economy. These men were not innocents who had a modern money economy thrust upon them by rapacious expatriate firms; they embraced the new system willingly because it gave them the means of striking a better bargain.

In the short run, however, the steamship and modern money had a profoundly unsettling effect on West African trade. Essentially, they can be regarded as external economies which made it easier for newcomers to enter West Coast commerce. The result was a marked increase in competition in the second half of the nineteenth century. With the arrival of the steamship, the trader whose resources were very limited could hire a small amount of cargo space for a short period of time. Merchants trading to West Africa did not need to buy a ship of their own, nor did they have to join a consortium to charter one. Few of the established firms, apart from Woermann, were able to convert to steam, partly because the initial capital investment needed to build an ocean-going steamer was much greater than that required for a sailing vessel, and partly because more working capital was needed to finance the expansion of legitimate commerce.[53] The result was that trading and carrying became separate activities, and the established firms were less able to keep control of new entrants than in the days when they also monopolised shipping space. Moreover, and this is a feature which is often overlooked, the steamer also concentrated competition at the ports of call, in contrast to the days of sail, when ships could adapt their schedules to meet varying market conditions. Evidence of increasing concentration was to be seen in the expansion of a few favoured centres, such as Dakar, Freetown and Lagos, and, ultimately, in the decline of well-known trading stations, such as St Louis, Cape Coast, and Opobo.

The commercial effect of the steamship has been commented on by McPhee and subsequent writers, but the consequences of monetary change have not been fully appreciated. The steamer brought new traders to the coast, but it could not help them to trade once they had arrived. As long as barter and transitional currencies remained firmly entrenched, newcomers were at a severe disadvantage, for they had to master the complexities of a pre-industrial monetary system, itself a serious barrier to entry; they had to acquire these strange currencies, in some cases from the established firms; and they had to be prepared to engage both in importing and in exporting. For example, a new trader hoping to sell cotton goods would have to take produce in exchange, since transitional currencies were not an acceptable means of payment in Europe. Cash payments made it possible to separate the two trades, and enabled firms to specialise in one or other if they wished. This specialisation reduced the capital required for entering West African trade and encouraged competition. No wonder the old-established European firms, far from trying to 'entangle Africans in the web of a money economy' strove to maintain the barter system for as long as possible. In this respect some of the 'natives' of Liverpool and Marseilles were far more conservative than those in the hinterlands of Dakar and Lagos!

[53] C. W. Newbury, 'Credit in Early Nineteenth-Century West African Trade', *Journal of African History*, 13, 1972, pp. 81–95.

Evidence of increasing competition can be seen in the appearance of two new groups of traders in the second half of the century. First, there were progressive European merchants who had little or no previous connection with West Africa, but who established themselves by taking advantage of the steamer and of cash transactions. For example, Cheri Peyrissac began as a clerk at St Louis (Senegal) in 1862, and later built up a large independent import and export business based on manufactured goods and groundnuts; the Hamburg industrial concern of G. L. Gaiser expanded into West African trade in 1869 in order to secure supplies of palm produce for its oil mills, and was one of the first firms to develop a cash trade; the Manchester firm of John Walkden & Company started to trade with West Africa in 1868 as a mail order business, supplying manufactured goods on commission; and John Holt, a Liverpool merchant, broke into the Niger Delta trade in the 1870s, and later established branches in other parts of what was to become Nigeria.[54] Many of the older firms tried to adapt to legitimate commerce, but very few lasted until the end of the century. They had every incentive to adjust to the new conditions because they had sunk capital into African trade, they had spent years building up connections, and many of them were creditors of African suppliers. Thus John Tobin, a Liverpool slave trader, pioneered the palm oil trade in the Niger Delta early in the century. However, firms of this type were nearly all eliminated by the steamship and by the collapse of barter. Perhaps the most spectacular rearguard action was that fought by F. & A. Swanzy, which, with Forster & Smith, dominated the overseas trade of the Gold Coast in the early 1850s. Swanzy's reaction to the advent of the steamer was not to modernise their business, but to try to establish a local monopoly of palm oil supplies. Unfortunately for them, the producers retaliated by successfully boycotting the firm between 1858 and 1866.[55] Swanzy's managed to survive, but the firm declined in importance. The steamer, it could be said, had taken all the wind out of their sails.

The second new group of merchants were Africans, consisting mainly of liberated slaves and their descendants, men who grew up in settlements such as Freetown and Libreville, where they were converted to Christianity, took European names, and received some education from expatriate missionaries. These merchants, in sharp contrast to their slave-trading predecessors, were noted for their Victorian dress, bourgeois values and commitment to legitimate commerce. It was intended that they should form the nucleus of an African middle class, which would develop the continent's economy and uplift its spiritual life. Although numerically a small group, these liberated Africans had considerable importance in the second half of the nineteenth century. Many of them returned to their homelands, and so made their presence felt in most of the main urban centres on the West Coast. Furthermore, since they became lawyers, civil servants and missionaries, as well as merchants,

[54] On Gaiser and Holt see Ernst Hieke, *G. L. Gaiser: Hamburg—Westafrica*, Hamburg 1949; and Cherry J. Gertzel, *John Holt: a British Merchant in West Africa in the Era of Imperialism*, University of Oxford D.Phil. thesis, 1959.

[55] Freda Wolfson, 'A Price Agreement on the Gold Coast—The Krobo Oil Boycott, 1858–1866', *Economic History Review*, 6, 1953, pp. 68–77.

their influence spread over a wide occupational front. Essentially, their role was that of cultural intermediaries, men who straddled the frontier between Europe and Africa, interpreting, in the broadest sense of the word, one to the other. Europeans often referred to them, contemptuously, as 'trousered Africans', and Africans have criticised them for behaving as Uncle Toms. However, thanks to the painstaking work of Christopher Fyfe and others, it is now appreciated (or at least it should now be appreciated) that these were men of genuine dignity and considerable historical significance.[56] They performed an important function in introducing the Western world to Africa, yet they were by no means as alienated from their indigenous culture as has been alleged. They demonstrated to sceptical Europeans that Africans were not barbarians, and they were among the first to proclaim that Africa had a history of its own.

Helped by the steamer and by the transition to cash payments, these merchants mostly became low-cost, import specialists, acting either as independent whole-salers and retailers, or as agents selling goods on commission for manufacturing firms in Europe. Some were involved in the export trade, but the import business was preferred because it required less capital and also spread investments over a wider range of goods than the produce trade, which in addition experienced considerable short-run price fluctuations. Before 1900, when trading conditions once again began to favour large firms, a number of African merchants owned businesses which were as large as some of the European firms, though of course the latter were much smaller than they were to become in the twentieth century. Business profits tended to be attracted into property and education, two assets which continued to appreciate during the nineteenth and twentieth centuries irrespective of political changes.

One of the most outstanding of this new generation of Africans was Richard Blaize (1845–1904), who left Freetown in 1862 and made his business career in Lagos.[57] Blaize reckoned that he had earned the greater part of his fortune during the 1860s and 1870s, and was appalled by the narrow profit margins which ruled towards the end of the century. In the 1880s he built a new house and shop, which still stand on the Marina, and he also acquired 'a landau and pair of greys with which he drives out occasionally—footman and coachman on the box'. In 1896 a European official estimated that Blaize was worth about £150,000, which is a large sum even today, when the value of the pound sterling is far less than it was in the nineteenth century. Blaize's business, like that of most of his African contemporaries, died with him. However, the Blaize Memorial Institute, which was founded soon after his death with money left by him for that purpose, still flourishes, and contributes to what are now regarded as important functions, namely encouraging local manufacturing activities and providing Africans with technical training.

These two groups of merchants will be considered in more detail in Chapter 6. The main point to record in the present context is that there were pronounced

[56] Christopher Fyfe, *A History of Sierra Leone*, Oxford 1962. See also Arthur T. Porter, *Creoledom*, Oxford 1963, and Margaret Priestley, *West African Trade and Coast Society*, 1969.

[57] A. G. Hopkins, 'Richard Beale Blaize, 1854–1904: Merchant Prince of West Africa', *Tarikh*, I, 1966, pp. 70–9.

economic rivalries among firms on the European side of the frontier, just as there were among African suppliers. Competition between European firms was character-ised by bouts of co-operation and conflict which bore some resemblance to the accretion-fission cycle experienced by the canoe houses of the Niger Delta. Typic-ally, a newcomer trying to become established in one of the West African markets would begin by fixing his prices at levels which were more attractive than those of the established firms. These firms retaliated, and a price war followed. If this failed to drive out the new entrant, a compromise was eventually reached which allowed him to trade in the area on the understanding that competition was kept within 'reasonable' bounds. However, usually it was not long before the equilibrium was upset once again, either by the defection of an existing firm, or by the arrival of another outsider.

The trend was undoubtedly towards greater efficiency. In order to survive, firms had to adjust to the advent of the steamship, and to the development of cash trans-actions, and they also had to make internal improvements, as did John Holt, by employing better staff and by buying manufactures in bulk where possible. By the last quarter of the century evidence from the Gold Coast, Dahomey, Lagos, the Niger Delta and Old Calabar indicates that profit margins had been greatly re-duced. The commercial practices of the eighteenth century had finally disappeared, and the merchants, though not all of them realised it, were, in terms of business history, on the brink of the twentieth century, when wholesalers became accustomed to relying on narrower margins and on a much larger turnover. In 1875, however, the import and export market was still confined to a few coastal enclaves, and no additional cost-reducing innovations were possible within the existing political framework.

The adverse movement in the terms of trade in the last quarter of the nineteenth century had a serious effect on those engaged in the difficult process of adapting to legitimate commerce. Normal, non-violent commercial relationships started to break down, and the 'moral community' of traders, already under some strain, began to dissolve. The trade depression intensified rivalries within the various interest groups and between African producers on the one hand, and European firms on the other. Essentially, the dispute was over the distribution of reduced profits. The decline in the barter terms of trade affected the European firms in West Africa as well as primary producers. Initially, it was these firms which received lower prices for produce in Europe, and it was up to them to try and pass on reductions to their African suppliers. The extent to which they were successful depended on the balance of commercial power in individual West African markets. Not surprisingly, there was a fierce struggle in the late nineteenth century as each party sought to control the local market and to dictate terms to the other.

Evidence from various parts of the West Coast suggests that there were five main aspects of this struggle. None was entirely new, but each became more pronounced during the last quarter of the century. First, there were malpractices, such as diluting palm oil and misrepresenting the quality and length of cloth, which both sides adopted in an attempt to secure a better bargain than could be contrived by legitimate means. Second, there were demarcation disputes over functions and areas of influence. For example, some European firms, such as the Royal Niger Company, tried to move inland in the hope of buying export crops more cheaply from the producers than from the coastal wholesalers.[58] These moves often provoked retaliation, as when traders from Brass destroyed the Niger Company's base at Akassa in 1894. Similarly, some Africans tried to sell their oil direct to Europe. It was Ja Ja's threat to bypass the European middlemen in this way that was largely responsible for his expulsion from Opobo in 1887. Third, there were serious disputes, common everywhere at times of depression, and aggravated in the African case by the depreciation in the value of transitional currencies, about the repayment of the advances which European firms had made to African suppliers. Fourth, there were deliberate interruptions to the supply of produce. The Moors withheld supplies of gum in 1885–1886, the Yoruba closed their export markets at one time or another during the 1880s, and the Itsekiri held up palm oil exports in 1886–1887. The aim in all cases was to force European merchants to accept the suppliers' terms of sale, a policy which was to be repeated in the 1930s, when West Africa's foreign trade underwent its next great crisis. Finally, there were arguments about escaped slaves, many of whom sought refuge in the European colonies on the coast. Large scale African producers and traders resented the loss of their human capital, especially at a time when trade conditions dictated that slave labour should be fully exploited.

The outcome was a compromise which affected both parties adversely, and so satisfied neither. Africans were hit at a time when they were unable to achieve economies in production and transportation, and Europeans were hit at a time when their profit margins had already been reduced by increased competition. In these unprecedented circumstances the merchants, though traditionally suspicious of moves to expand the role of government, which they associated with increased regulations and additional taxes, began to press for a more active policy.[59] What is more, they also displayed an unaccustomed willingness to accept higher taxation to pay for action taken on their behalf. In making this decision, the merchants were undoubtedly influenced by the fact that the cost of coercion had been greatly reduced in the late nineteenth century by the invention of two daunting pieces of military equipment, the Gatling gun and the Maxim gun.

The merchants' call for action was backed, and indeed, often led, by colonial administrators.[60] Ambitious officials were well aware that posts in West Africa were rarely springboards to fame even at the best of times, and that a trade depression was scarcely the ideal setting for a distinguished career. They were charged with the task of protecting trade, yet when diplomacy failed, as it frequently did, they were unable to influence the policies of the African states which were the main trading partners

[58] See J. E. Flint's important study, *Sir George Goldie and the Making of Nigeria*, 1960.

[59] Information about mercantile pressures can be found in many of the items listed in the bibliography: see especially Aderibigbe, Dike, Dumett, Flint, Hopkins (1968), Latham, and Newbury (1959, 1968, 1969 and 1972).

[60] C. W. Newbury and A. S. Kanya-Forstner, 'French Policy and the Origins of the Scramble for West Africa', *Journal of African History*, 10, 1969, pp. 253–76.

of the European colonies. The administration's difficulties were increased at a time of depression because the colonies had overheads (in the shape of public debts and staff) which were fixed, and incomes which, because they were dependent on customs revenues, were either static or declining. In their own career interests and in the cause of duty, local officials decided that a radical change of policy was required. The missionaries, too, acting on their traditional postulate about the relationship between commercial prosperity and the progress of Christianity in Africa, urged the metropolitan governments to adopt more positive policies. Their views were of some significance in the nineteenth century, though ironically the missions were to be overtaken by the rush of events which they had helped to encourage. In the colonial period the missionaries found themselves pushed to one side, and they became, in political terms, mere clerical notes in the margins of empire.

There was some confusion about what was meant by an active policy, and there was a certain lack of realism about what it was expected to achieve. In broad terms, however, the merchants and officials made five main demands, though the stress laid on each varied at different parts of the West Coast. First, there was a call for the imposition of law and order in places such as Senegal, the Gold Coast, Yorubaland and the Niger Delta, where inter-state conflict was thought to be interrupting the supply of produce and the distribution of manufactured goods. Second, there were widespread complaints against the coastal middlemen, who were blamed (in much the same way as Africans were later to blame the expatriate firms) for using their monopolistic powers to impose one-sided trading contracts. Some European firms wanted to end the 'unproductive middleman system'; others were prepared to make use of a reformed trading organisation providing internal free trade was established. Third, there was pressure for the abolition of the tolls levied by African states. This issue was important because the European merchants were concerned not simply to increase the volume of produce on offer, but to see that export crops were delivered to the coast as cheaply as possible.

The last two demands were more positive. The fourth request, for example, was for the construction of railways. The railway, the White Hope of the nineteenth century, was thought to be capable of transforming the economies of West Africa, just as it had those of Europe. In 1879 the French adopted an ambitious scheme for building a railway line from Senegal into the interior, and in the 1890s the British made similar plans for their colonies. Finally, there was a realisation that the time had come to advance the frontier of expatriate trading influence by creating a much larger market for European goods than had ever existed before. Some expatriate firms, as Gertzel has pointed out, were still content to remain on the coast, either because they were willing to work through a reformed middleman system, or because they lacked the capital to set up branches inland.[61] Others, however, and especially the large firms, were now prepared to move inland once the government had cleared the way. A bigger turnover was needed if profits were to grow; firm

[61] Cherry J. Gertzel, 'Relations between African and European Traders in the Niger Delta, 1880–1896', *Journal of African History*, 3, 1962, pp. 361–6.

political boundaries were required to prevent trade from falling into the hands of other European rivals; and new products had to be found to re-establish the prosperity of the export trade. France and Britain hoped that there was more than fool's gold in the interior, and that some of the fabled wealth of the Western Sudan would rub off on them.

It is now necessary to take a closer look at the policies of the three main European nations with interests in West Africa, because ultimately it was decisions made by them which led to the partition of the continent. As far as Great Britain was concerned, her trading success appeared to support the anti-colonial arguments of Adam Smith and his followers, and it was certainly hard to see what Britain could gain by creating colonies in West Africa when she already dominated trade without them. In contrast to a once popular view, Britain's policy makers were not itching to establish colonies throughout the world.[62] Britain's chief aim in West Africa was to maintain free trade without political involvement, and to persuade France and Germany to do the same. Free trade, though sometimes presented as a high-minded principle capable of bringing prosperity with honour to the comity of nations, was in reality a passport to British supremacy. In conditions of 'equal' competition Britain was likely to dominate most world markets because she could produce and transport manufactured goods more cheaply than could any of her rivals. Given this advantage, it is understandable that Britain was unlikely to initiate a forward policy.

At the same time, it is important to remember that the maintenance of the status quo in West Africa depended on factors which were largely beyond Britain's control. If Britain's European rivals decided not to co-operate in upholding her supremacy, or if there was a serious threat to trade as a result of developments on the African side of the frontier, then Britain might be forced to change her traditional policy, for she had a moral obligation to support her traders in international markets. The obligation was not binding in all cases, and it had to be judged in relation to the wider, national interest, but it was a factor to be considered in the formulation of policy. In 1865 a Parliamentary Committee had recommended withdrawing from several parts of the West Coast, but by the 1880s it was realised in the metropolis that Britain's commitments were too large for disengagement to be possible.

Superficially, French policy appeared to have much in common with that of Great Britain. France, like Britain, wanted to develop a flourishing and peaceful trade with West Africa, and she was willing to work through indigenous authorities where possible.[63] From the 1830s she began to move towards a liberal tariff regime on the West Coast, and she also exercised a degree of political restraint which, broadly speaking, kept her in step with Britain. Yet it is now recognised that France

[62] Two of the best studies of British policy towards Africa are Ronald Robinson and John Gallagher with Alice Denny, *Africa and the Victorians*, 1961, and John D. Hargreaves, *Prelude to the Partition of West Africa*, 1963. For a global perspective see D. C. M. Platt, *Finance, Trade and Politics in British Foreign Policy, 1815–1914*, Oxford 1968.

[63] On French policy see Henri Brunschwig, *French Colonialism, 1871–1914: Myths and Realities*, 1966, and, for more detail on West Africa, Bernard Schnapper, *La politique et le commerce français dans le Golfe de Guinée de 1838 à 1871*, Paris 1961.

took the initiative in the 'scramble' for West Africa. Gallagher and Robinson have argued that it was a political crisis in Egypt in 1882, a rebuff for France, which caused her to adopt a more aggressive policy in West Africa, but so far this view, stimulating though it is, has not been confirmed by the research it has helped to inspire. Brunschwig has explained French expansion in terms of a search for national prestige, but this interpretation is not quite as helpful as it seems at first sight, since without close definition the phrase 'national prestige' becomes a vague and all-embracing concept. It will be suggested here that there was an important economic motive in French imperialism, and that France altered her policy not because her basic aims had changed, but because she came to realise that different means were required if they were ever going to be achieved. This conclusion did not come as a sudden flash of insight. It was a gradual acknowledgement of long-standing facts, namely that with the passage of time the disparity between French and British economic progress and global influence had increased rather than diminished, and that France was also being overtaken in Europe by German industrial and military power.

France had long-standing, global commercial ambitions, but few of these had been realised. Where she laboured, it seemed, Great Britain collected the rewards. India and Canada were lost to Britain in the eighteenth century, and France herself was defeated in Europe in 1815 after a series of wars which played a large part in retarding her economic development in the nineteenth century.[64] Britain, by contrast, emerged from the Napoleonic Wars with her industrial revolution already under way. Since the victors of Waterloo then pressed the French into declaring the slave trade illegal, it is not surprising that France viewed abolition as the final move in a British plot to destroy what was left of her Atlantic commerce. Any illusions that France had recovered her former power by the middle of the nineteenth century, at least in Europe, were shattered by the defeat which she suffered at the hands of Germany in 1870.

France was anxious to emulate Britain's industrial progress, which, according to some observers, was closely related to the growth of her trading and political influence overseas. Africa was regarded as a hopeful starting point for a French recovery because it was reasonably close to Europe, it had long-standing connections with France, and, above all, it was still largely unclaimed—except, of course, by Africans. Senegal was re-occupied in 1817, and some fortified posts were established at Assinie, Grand Bassam and Gabon in the 1840s. These moves, together with the conquest of Algeria in the 1830s, gave some momentum to the notion that France had an imperial destiny in Africa: the idea of linking West and North Africa was current in Paris long before the British began talking of joining the Cape to Cairo. Yet France gained no spectacular successes. The fortified posts, as Schnapper has

---

[64] See two essays by F. Crouzet, 'England and France in the Eighteenth Century: a Comparative Analysis of Two Economic Growths', in *The Causes of the Industrial Revolution in England*, ed. R. M. Hartwell, 1967, pp. 139–74, and 'Wars, Blockade and Economic Change in Europe, 1792–1815', *Journal of Economic History*, 24, 1964, pp. 567–88, which between them revise many of the standard views about the French economy in the late eighteenth and early nineteenth centuries.

shown, achieved very little, and the expansion of legitimate commerce benefited Britain more than any other European power. Only in Senegal was there some basis for optimism. French commercial interests there had been saved by the fortuitous development of the groundnut trade, and also by the adoption of measures which limited the entry of foreign traders. Even in the mid-nineteenth century France had not allowed herself to be mesmerised completely by Britain's advocacy of the free trade cause. During the last quarter of the nineteenth century she was to move even closer to protectionist policies, and in doing so was to undermine the basis of Britain's position in West Africa.

France, unlike Britain, had an incentive to upset the status quo in West Africa. She did not want to provoke Britain by a direct challenge, but she still had plenty of room for manoeuvre, for it was the weakness as well as the strength of the British position that her commercial supremacy had not been accompanied by the large scale annexation of territory. French imperial policy in the late nineteenth century was driven by a potent combination of forces: on the one hand by a fear that British economic expansion, spearheaded by Manchester textiles and backed by the world's strongest navy, would frustrate her ambitions once again; and on the other by an optimism about the wealth of Africa which had not been equalled since the Moroccans trekked hopefully across the desert in 1591.

German interests in West Africa will be noted briefly in order to explain their influence on the policies of the two major powers.[65] The German presence became a factor of some weight in the deliberations of London and Paris during the last quarter of the century, when, as has been pointed out, Hamburg merchants were rapidly expanding their share of West African trade. German firms were concentrated at some sensitive points: in Liberia, which was flanked by British interests in Sierra Leone and French interests in the Ivory Coast; in what was to become Togoland, a thin wedge of territory between the Gold Coast and Dahomey, centres of British and French activity respectively; in Dahomey itself, where they had succeeded in capturing the greater part of the region's overseas trade by the 1880s; and in what were to become Southern Nigeria and the Cameroons, which coincided with Britain's major trading interests in Lagos, the Niger Delta, and Old Calabar. In the 1880s the German government made an increasing show of protecting its traders on the West Coast, partly as a result of direct mercantile pressures, and partly as an offshoot of a campaign for tariff protection started by industrialists in response to the onset of the Great Depression.[66] Britain and France regarded the German presence as a serious threat to their own West African interests, and feared that a forward move by her might result in the exclusion of their trading firms from the unclaimed markets of Africa. For France, already worried about British commercial dominance, this new danger appeared to justify a more decisive, forward policy; for Britain,

[65] For further information see *Britain and Germany in Africa: Imperial Rivalry and Colonial Rule*, ed. Prosser Gifford and William Roger Louis, New Haven 1967.

[66] Hartmut Pogge von Strandmann, 'Germany's Colonial Expansion under Bismarck', *Past & Present*, 42, 1969, pp. 140–59; and Hans-Ulrich Wehler, 'Bismarck's Imperialism 1862–1890', *Past & Present*, 48, 1970, pp. 131–9.

6*

slowly waking up to the fact that the era of *laissez-faire* might not last indefinitely, it meant that she had to consider defensive action against two ambitious rivals, not just one.

The demands made by British and French merchants were very similar, but rivalry between the European powers meant that they did not co-ordinate their policies to produce a joint invasion of Africa, though gentlemen's agreements were occasionally made with regard to specific areas. On the contrary, the economic crisis between 1875 and 1900 intensified the antagonism between Britain and France, and led to competition for African territory. There were two main features of this rivalry. The first was characterised by a more aggressive element in the relationship between British and French firms. The foundation of the Compagnie Française de l'Afrique Équatoriale in 1880 and the Compagnie du Sénégal in the following year marked a new phase in French efforts to break into richer and predominantly British markets in West Africa.[67] These firms started trading in the Niger Delta, quickly established branches as far as the River Benue, and threatened to expand further still into what is now northern Nigeria. This enterprising exercise of the rights of free trade caused Britain some initial embarrassment. However, the French could not compete for long against the might of the National African Company, which bought out the French firms in 1884.[68] This episode demonstrated that British supremacy could not be challenged successfully by purely commercial means, at least by France. The French did not give up their hopes of penetrating the interior from the Guinea coast, but future efforts were to be launched from bases in their own colonies of Dahomey and the Ivory Coast, and were to be directed by soldiers rather than by traders.

The second feature of Anglo-French commercial rivalry was growing friction over areas of customs jurisdiction and levels of tariffs. The economic crisis of the late nineteenth century intensified the search for revenue, and led officials to extend the boundaries of their colonies, sometimes with, but usually without, instructions from the metropolis. These moves caused serious disputes, as rival administrations, expanding laterally along the coast, met each other, as they did for example in the area of Sierra Leone, on the Gold Coast, and at the frontier between Dahomey and Lagos. At the same time France began to adopt differential tariffs in West Africa as a means of increasing revenue and assisting her trade. The shift to a more protectionist policy was mainly a result of pressure from French metallurgical, textile and chemical industries, which had difficulty in competing with British products in world markets.[69] Many of the traders in centres such as Nantes, Bordeaux and Marseilles were opposed to protection to begin with, but were won over in the 1880s. Differential tariffs were imposed in Senegal in 1877 and in the Ivory Coast in 1889. Britain, of course, protested that these actions were contrary to the principles of free trade. The

[67] C. W. Newbury, 'The Development of French Policy on the Lower and Upper Niger, 1880–98', *Journal of Modern History*, 31, 1959, pp. 16–26.

[68] This firm began life as the United African Company in 1879, became the National African Company in 1882, and finally turned itself into the Royal Niger Company in 1886.

[69] C. W. Newbury, 'The Protectionist Revival in French Colonial Trade: the Case of Senegal', *Economic History Review*, 21, 1968, pp. 337–48.

French replied that tariffs in British colonies already had a differential effect because they were high on certain goods, such as brandy and wine, which were mainly French, and low on textiles, which were mainly British. By the 1880s the concept of free trade in West Africa was coming under attack, and the weak spots in Britain's empire of informal rule were being revealed.

In Britain, France and Germany West African affairs were taken up by specialised organisations, such as chambers of commerce, and by an assortment of more broadly-based imperial movements which were developing rapidly in the last quarter of the nineteenth century.[70] The chambers of commerce in Liverpool, Manchester, Bordeaux, Marseilles and Hamburg publicised African problems in the press, lobbied local members of parliament, and made direct contact with leading figures in the government. Outside the chambers of commerce African questions were drawn into a variety of campaigns: some dominated by economic interest groups which, without necessarily having any specific involvement in Africa, were agitating in France for protectionist measures, and in Britain for what, more circumspectly, was called 'fair' trade;[71] others led by politicians who saw imperialism as a means of saving Europe from socialism; and others still, headed by geographers, journalists, intellectuals and sundry eccentrics, who were beginning to talk in somewhat mystical terms about the relationship between empire and national greatness. Of course, the imperial movement was by no means united. Some industrialists wanted colonies in order to create guaranteed markets for their exports, but others were indifferent to colonial expansion because in the late nineteenth century, with the terms of trade moving against primary producers, they were able to buy raw materials cheaply.

It is clear that further research is needed to identify all the channels of communication which existed between the men on the spot in Africa and those who formally announced decisions in London and Paris, and to evaluate the extent to which politicians were susceptible to pressures from pro-imperial interest groups representing what might be called the 'unofficial mind' of imperialism.[72] At present it can be said that governments were subjected to considerable and increasing pressures in the later nineteenth century, and that these pressures were more effective in France than in Britain because French businessmen were less divided by entrenched commitments to free trade, and were more inclined to put their faith, if not always their investments, in imperial expansion.

What seems beyond dispute is that those in power in France were more inclined to take notice of imperial pressure groups than were those in Britain. Under the Third

[70] Bernard Semmel, *Imperialism and Social Reform*, 1960.

[71] The best general study is still B. H. Brown, *The Tariff Reform Movement in Great Britain, 1881–95*, New York 1943. For a case study of one area see R. J. Ward, *The Tariff Reform Movement in Birmingham, 1877–1906*, University of London M.A. thesis, 1971.

[72] Two interesting local studies are John F. Laffey, 'The Roots of French Imperialism in the Nineteenth Century: the Case of Lyon', *French Historical Studies*, 6, 1969, pp. 78–92, and W. Thompson, *Glasgow and Africa: Connexions and Attitudes, 1870–1900*, University of Strathclyde Ph.D. thesis, 1970.

Republic the political influence of provincial businessmen increased, and a group of leaders emerged, such as Freycinet, Jauréguiberry and Rouvier, who were prepared not merely to be influenced by others, but actually to direct the movement for colonial expansion.[73] In Britain, by contrast, policy-makers in both parties were reluctant to admit that circumstances had altered, and that attitudes would have to change too. In the 1880s British policy was still based on two established notions: first, an unrealistic optimism about the possibility of equalising tariffs and preserving free trade, an optimism which France was happy to encourage while her troops advanced inland; and second, a belief in the value of appeasement, that is the distribution of other peoples' territories in the hope of stabilising an inherently unstable situation. Since the facts refused to change, no matter how long British politicians kept their eyes closed, it was the politicians themselves who eventually had to modify their traditional attitudes towards empire. By the 1890s both Liberals and Conservatives were beginning to recognise that a more active policy was required if any of Britain's traditional spheres of influence in West Africa were to be preserved. It would be a mistake to think that Joseph Chamberlain came, like a bolt from the blue, and created, single-handed, a new attitude towards imperial affairs. Nevertheless, it was not until he became Colonial Secretary in 1895 that Britain had a Rouvier of her own.

By the time Britain had decided that a more positive policy was needed, the partition of West Africa was well under way. In 1879 the French began to advance across the Western Sudan from Senegal, reaching Bamako (six hundred miles inland) in 1883, Timbuctu in 1893, and Lake Chad (two thousand miles from Dakar) in 1900. At the same time, the invasion forces branched south, striking deep into the Fouta Djallon (later part of French Guinea), the Ivory Coast and Dahomey, and meeting the northwards advance of French troops from the Guinea coast. As a result of this strategy, tight boundaries were drawn around the coastal settlements of Gambia, Sierra Leone and Liberia. In the mid-1880s Germany made two relatively unambitious forward moves, one into Togo (between the Gold Coast and Dahomey), and one into the Cameroons (on the eastern flank of the Niger Delta). By the mid-1890s France had successfully claimed the greater part of West Africa, and Britain was left with the task of defending her two most important interests; the Gold Coast and what was to become Nigeria. The former, as Dumett has shown, was saved for Britain mainly as a result of mercantile pressure.[74] Kumasi, the Ashanti capital, was captured in 1896, and expansion further north gave Britain a sizeable colony. In the case of Nigeria, it was again successful mercantile agitation in the 1890s that kept the French out of Yorubaland and the Lower Niger.[75] Conspicuous in the latter area

[73] C. M. Andrew and A. S. Kanya-Forstner, 'The French "Colonial Party": its Composition, Aims and Influence, 1885–1914', *The Historical Journal*, 14, 1971, pp. 99–128.

[74] R. A. Dumett, *British Official Attitudes to Economic Development on the Gold Coast, 1874–1905*, University of London Ph.D. thesis, 1966, pp. 149–80.

[75] A. G. Hopkins, 'Economic Imperialism in West Africa: Lagos, 1880–92', *Economic History Review*, 21, 1968, pp. 580–606, and Flint, *Sir George Goldie*, chs 10, 11 and 12.

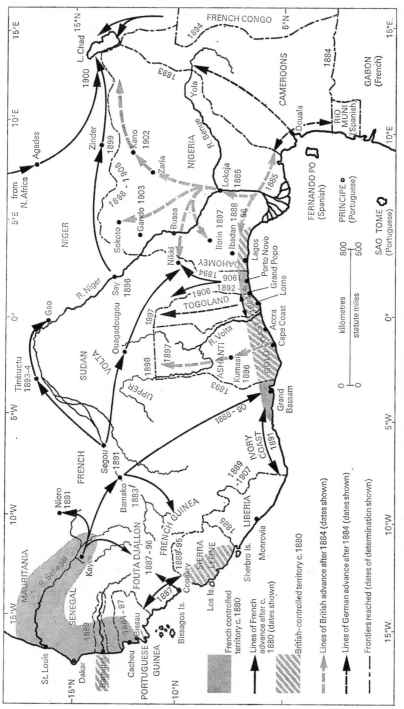

MAP 10. The Partition of West Africa.

was the Royal Niger Company, which, in the classical manner of chartered companies, used administrative as well as commercial weapons to drive out its competitors, English as well as French. By 1900 the partition of West Africa was over.

3 An explanation of imperialism in West Africa

The invasion of West Africa occurred in such a short space of time, and marked such a radical break with past policy, that historians have been tempted to fasten on specific military or diplomatic events as causes. Some writers have emphasised the importance of the Egyptian crisis of 1882, or of the Berlin Conference of 1884–1885. Others have drawn attention to the rise of particular military and political figures, men who were keen to do more than merely chalk hopeful arrows on departmental maps. A number of names come to mind: the French Prime Minister, Freycinet; his Minister of Marine, Admiral Jauréguiberry; the British Secretary of State for the Colonies, Joseph Chamberlain; and men on the spot, such as Archinard, Gallieni, Goldie and Lugard. These events and these men undoubtedly played a part, and in some cases a very important part, in determining the timing and the nature of the partition of West Africa, but their responsibility for causing it was of much the same order as that of the unfortunate Archduke Franz Ferdinand, whose assassination sparked off the First World War. The central problem is to clarify the circumstances which enabled these prominent politicians and soldiers to make a mark on history where others before them, men of similar ambitions, such as Faidherbe and Glover, had been frustrated.

This chapter has tried to show that the solution to this problem lies in the economic history of the nineteenth century. Economic motives do not constitute a complete analysis of imperialism, but there is considerable justification for concentrating on them here because on the whole they have been neglected in the past. This neglect is understandable in view of the current dominance of political and diplomatic interpretations of imperialism, but it has the fundamental disadvantage of abstracting from West African realities. Trade first brought the Europeans to Africa in the fifteenth century, and trade remained the basis of their relations with the continent from then onwards. It is the economic historian's task to see whether, and, if so, in what ways, commercial ties were related to the scramble for Africa.

What happened to Africa was part of a global confrontation between the developing and the underdeveloped countries in the nineteenth century, though the nature of the interaction between them, and its outcome, varied in different parts of the world. The economic expansion of Europe in the nineteenth century had a profound and destabilising effect on West Africa because it changed the structure of export production and involved the region in the trade cycle of the new, industrial economy. The Afro-European alliance which had made the external slave trade possible and profitable started to dissolve early in the nineteenth century. A new generation of African producers and traders began to develop outside the limits of the old, foreign trade enclaves, but was unable to establish a completely satisfactory partnership with merchants on the European side of the frontier. In some cases difficulties arose because of obstruction from traditional rulers, but even where the indigenous authorities were willing to co-operate, and achieved a measure of success in doing so, there were limits to the concessions which they were prepared to make. In the event, time was also against them. During the early, prosperous phase of 'legitimate' commerce, each side could afford to tolerate the economic imperfections (real and alleged) of the other, and it seemed possible that economic integration could be achieved by informal means. But the serious decline in the terms of trade in the last quarter of the nineteenth century upset the precarious balance which maintained the frontier between Europe and West Africa. Those on the European side of the frontier had no further scope for improving their efficiency, and they now feared that West Africa, with its pre-industrial transport system and its numerous tolls, was in danger of becoming, by international standards, a high-cost producer. Those on the African side of the frontier decided that if modernisation meant railways, the end of internal customs duties and the abolition, for whatever reasons, of slavery, then it also meant the end of their political independence. At that point they decided to resist and to defend their sovereignty, though there were some who, for reasons which have been indicated, were less than wholehearted in their opposition to European demands.

The economic depression transmitted by the industrial nations caused England, France and Germany to come into conflict with each other, as well as with African states. Their rivalry was partly a reflection of shifts in the balance of economic and political power in Europe following industrialisation, and partly the outcome of particular problems which arose during the Great Depression. These problems affected interest groups in the leading industrial states, as well as merchants trading to the West Coast. The extent to which interest groups succeeded in generating a forward policy depended on the strength of the pressure they exerted and on the responsiveness of those in power at the time. Reasons have been advanced under both headings to explain why, in the case of West Africa, it was France rather than Britain which took the initiative. The resolution of the problems which led to partition can be seen in the creation of colonial economies in the first half of the twentieth century.

It is for future research to elaborate and improve the analysis advanced here, and also to modify it, where necessary. The aim of this chapter has been to establish a framework of analysis which contains the main variables, but not, it must be stressed, to rank them in a fixed order of importance applicable to every point on the West Coast. At one extreme it is possible to conceive of areas where the transition from the slave trade was made successfully, where incomes were maintained, and where internal tensions were controlled. In these cases an explanation of partition will need to emphasise external pressures, such as mercantile demands and Anglo-French rivalries. At the other extreme it is possible to envisage cases where the indigenous rulers adopted reactionary attitudes, where attempts were made to maintain incomes by predatory means, and where internal conflicts were pronounced. In these cases an explanation of imperialism will need to place more weight on disintegrative forces on the African side of the frontier, though without neglecting external factors. Current contributions to the study of nineteenth-century imperialism frequently fail either to take adequate account of interests and attitudes on the indigenous side of the frontier with the Western world, or to organise local case studies in such a way as to permit systematic comparisons with other parts of other continents. The typology established here, based on the identification and interaction of interest groups, may prove useful in understanding the decisions which regulated the frontier between the industrial powers and the Third World in the nineteenth century.

five

An economic model of colonialism

The colonial era has ceased to be regarded as the sole substance of African history, and there are sound reasons for thinking that colonial rule itself had a less dramatic and a less pervasive economic impact than was once supposed. Little more than half a century elapsed between the end of the partition of West Africa and the beginning of independence. The first fifteen years of this period were devoted to pacifying recalcitrant peoples, the last fifteen years were spent trying to cope with African nationalism, and the intervening years provide plenty of evidence of the super-ficiality and impermanence of colonial rule, even though this was the time when the rulers themselves believed that their paternal control would remain unchallenged for several centuries.

Nevertheless, a good case can still be made out for according the colonial era separate treatment on economic as well as, more obviously, on political grounds, quite apart from the organisational necessity of allotting enough space to treat, with some pretence at adequacy, the vast amount of description, analysis and polemic which this period had generated. Essentially, and expressed in terms of the main theme of this study, colonialism marked a new, and, broadly speaking, expansionist phase in the evolution of the modern market economy: its main achievement was to remove the constraints which had hindered the development of the export sector in the nineteenth century. Of course, the colonial economy also had its limitations in terms of inherent deficiencies and of expectations which it aroused, yet seemed incapable of satisfying. As the colonial period advanced, the limitations appeared, in the eyes of African participants and an increasing number of sympathetic foreign observers, to outweigh the advantages, and the expectations began to find political expression. The colonial economy was not, however, a changeless economy, and it started to acquire important new features (notably a substantial public sector and modern manufacturing plant) shortly before the coming of independence in the period 1957–1960. The beginning of this novel, and still uncompleted, phase in West Africa's economic history (and its relation to the process of decolonisation) serves as an appropriate terminal point for the present study.

The purpose of this chapter is to provide a synoptic view of the evolution of the colonial economies of West Africa between 1900 and 1960. It will first present an economic model of colonialism, which is intended to carry further the analysis begun in Chapter 4, where the rise of legitimate commerce was considered in terms of staple theory, and it will then outline the statistical basis for charting the progress of the export economy. The aim of this approach is to provide analytical and chronological anchorage points for the detailed discussion which follows in Chapters 6 and 7.[1]

1 Open and closed economies

The analytical framework adopted here is derived from a model formulated by Professor Dudley Seers, originally with reference to Latin America.[2] Seers suggests that countries whose exports are heavily dependent on primary products can be placed in one of two categories, known as 'open' and 'closed' economies. An open economy was already beginning to emerge in West Africa in the second half of the nineteenth century, and it developed fully in the first half of the twentieth century. Before considering the main structural features of this type of economy, three preliminary points need to be borne in mind. First, notions of open and closed economies are ideal types, which approximate to reality but which are not identical to it. Some general modifications will be incorporated into the discussion which follows, and specific qualifications will be made in the next two chapters. Second, Seers was interested primarily in the transition to a closed economy. This was a phase of evolution which did not occur in West Africa until around the time of independence, and then only in a few countries. The interpretation presented here will use the concept of an open economy to analyse the colonial period as a whole, and not merely its final years. Third, Seers was concerned almost exclusively with the export sector. This pre-occupation will also be followed in Chapter 6 of the present work, but in Chapter 7 the analysis will be enlarged to take account of internal economic activities. It is hoped that these amendments will assist an understanding of the historical development of the West African economy, without at the same time doing an injustice to Seers's original schema.

Countries in the open phase of development have the following principal characteristics.[3] First, they export a limited range of agricultural and mineral products in exchange for a variety of manufactures, chiefly consumer goods. Second, expatriate interests usually dominate one or more sectors of the economy. In West Africa this domination was especially marked in overseas (but not internal) trade. Third, the major industrial powers are able to exert considerable influence on economic policy,

---

[1] Students requiring an explanatory economics text to accompany this and the following two chapters are advised to consult H. W. Ord and I. Livingstone, *An Introduction to West African Economics*, 1969.

[2] Dudley Seers, 'The Stages of Economic Development of a Primary Producer in the Middle of the Twentieth Century', *Economic Bulletin of Ghana*, 7, 1963, pp. 57–69.

[3] It must be emphasised that this paragraph, and the two which follow, present a formal statement of an ideal-type rather than a description of historical reality.

and in the case of colonies are able to control it completely. The chief aim of expatriate policy is to assist the flow of primary products, and to keep the door open for the sale of manufactured goods. Hence tariffs are kept low, though differential duties and quotas are sometimes imposed in order to restrict the entry of goods manufactured by rival industrial powers. Otherwise, there are few, if any, restrictions on the volume of imports apart from the limit set by the purchasing power of local consumers. Fourth, the metropolitan power aims at minimising its fiscal obligations, and expects its colonies to balance their budgets without external assistance. Fifth, an open economy has a monetary system which is an appendage of that of the major power, while banking arrangements are concerned mainly with financing the activities of the expatriate firms. The system assists the development of trade with the major power, without involving that power in any monetary responsibilities towards its colony or satellite trading partner.

The long-term rate of growth in an ideal-type open economy is determined by two major variables; the size of export proceeds and the income-elasticity of demand for imports (that is, the degree of responsiveness of demand for imports to changes in income). Export proceeds form a high proportion of national income, though far less than do earnings from internal economic activities, and are commonly subject to pronounced fluctuations.[4] Instability results on the one hand from variations in supply caused, typically, by changes in the weather and by adverse political conditions,[5] and on the other from factors governing the demand for tropical agricultural products in the industrial countries. West African countries have to accept the world price as given, even though they supply a considerable proportion of the cocoa, palm produce and groundnuts entering international trade. Cocoa prices are especially affected by changes in the size of the harvest, while palm produce and groundnut prices are greatly influenced by the fact that these commodities are to some extent substitutes, and so compete against each other (and against alternative oils and fats) in the world market. At the same time, the prices of all West Africa's agricultural exports reflect changes in the level of incomes in the industrial countries, as determined by the general state of business activity. A large proportion of the incomes which producers derive from exports is spent on imported consumer goods. Demand for imports tends to be highly income-elastic for three main reasons. In the first place, as incomes rise the proportion of the increase spent on manufactures grows, while that spent on food undergoes a relative decline.[6] Second, consumer tastes in the key importing areas are influenced to a considerable extent by standards set by advertising, by Westernised Africans and by the expatriate community.

---

[4] Though the degree of instability experienced by the underdeveloped countries should not be exaggerated. See Jagdish Bhagwati, *The Economics of Underdeveloped Countries*, 1966, pp. 58–64.

[5] The importance of variations on the supply side has been stressed by Alasdair MacBean, *Export Instability and Economic Development*, 1966.

[6] For a specific investigation of this tendency see Rowena Lawson, 'Engel's Law and its Application to Ghana', *Economic Bulletin of Ghana*, 5, 1962, pp. 34–46.

Third, manufactured goods have to be imported because the open economy has few modern industries of its own.

Thus, the open economy responds readily to external influences. Any increase or decrease in export earnings will be accompanied by a roughly parallel movement in expenditure on consumer imports. Quantitative changes occur easily enough, but qualitative, structural transformation is far more difficult. The circularity of the system is reinforced by restrictions on the volume of investment, which is limited by the level of export earnings, by the tendency for capital to be leaked abroad, by the cautious nature of bank-lending policy, by the colonial tradition of maintaining a balanced budget, and by the conservative attitude of the large expatriate firms. Such investment as there is in an open economy tends to be directed into the existing export sector rather than towards new projects outside it.

Although Seers was not concerned in his original article to explore possible variations in types of open economy, it is important for present purposes to recognise that certain distinctions can be made, and that these are necessary for a more precise understanding of the way in which a particular kind of open economy functions. One striking difference is that between economies in which export production has an indigenous base, as was the case in colonial West Africa, India and Burma, and those where the export sector is dominated by expatriate mining or plantation enterprises, as in parts of Central and East Africa, and in South-East Asia.[7] This difference corresponds roughly to Hancock's distinction between traders' and settlers' frontiers, though it should be remembered that export production can be controlled by expatriate interests, as in the Congo, without necessarily being associated with large-scale white settlement. These two categories of open economy display marked contrasts in the size of the units of production, in the sources of capital supply, in the complexity of technology, in the numbers employed in the export sector, and in the distribution of export proceeds.[8] Above all, their ability to generate additional productive employment in the domestic economy is by no means the same. In West Africa, where 'peasant' production dominated the export sector, the foreign-trade multiplier was stronger and the capacity for structural change greater than in some other parts of the world, where the classical, enclave economy developed.[9] The economic distinction between peasant and plantation economies is profound enough to have far-reaching social and political consequences. For example, because there were at most only about 130,000 transient Europeans in the whole of West Africa at any one time, racial conflict was minimised. In comparison with many other parts of

[7] Two excellent studies of East Africa, which are invaluable for comparative purposes, are Cyril Ehrlich, 'The Uganda Economy, 1903–1945', and C. C. Wrigley, 'Kenya: the Patterns of Economic Life, 1902–1945', both in *History of East Africa*, 2, ed. Vincent Harlow and E. M. Chilver, 1965, pp. 395–475 and pp. 209–64 respectively.

[8] For an early statement of these differences see H. W. Singer, 'The Distribution of Gains Between Investing and Borrowing Countries', *American Economic Review*, 40, 1950, pp. 473–85. For a broader and more recent survey see Hla Myint, *The Economics of the Developing Countries*, 1964, chs 3 and 4.

[9] This proposition is developed in Chapter 7.

the world, the political struggle which arose towards the close of the colonial era was on the whole orderly and evolutionary. In contrast to Rhodesia, there was no movement to keep Nigeria white. Knowledge of these differences must affect the evaluation of foreign rule in the underdeveloped world, and must throw serious doubts on the wisdom of attempting to generalise about the costs and benefits of colonialism without close reference to the particular region concerned. The question of why the traders' rather than the settlers' frontier should have dominated West Africa is thus no mere antiquarian issue. A reappraisal of the problem will be made in the chapter which follows.

Closed economies, though still heavily dependent on exports of primary products, are distinguished, as their name implies, by the adoption of measures designed to diminish their reliance on external influences and to assist diversification. First, expatriate dominance of some sectors of the economy is subjected to regulations of varying kinds, ranging from controls over the issue of profits, to nationalisation, and even expulsion. Second, though external interests may still bring pressure to bear on the government, economic policy is more firmly in the hands of the indigenous authorities. Increased independence is reflected in the imposition of exchange controls, which are designed to stem the leakage of capital overseas, and in the adoption of import restrictions, which are aimed at encouraging domestic manufacturing activity and non-factor services. Third, closed economies usually have their own monetary system headed by a central bank. This means that the supply of money can be increased without an equivalent amount of foreign exchange having to be acquired first of all, that a contra-cyclical policy can be operated to moderate the effects of extreme booms and slumps, and that the techniques of deficit financing can be used for development purposes.

The transition to a closed economy in West Africa followed the attainment of political independence in the period 1957–1960, though not all countries have been able to close their open economies, and some have not been concerned to do so. Two comments about the process of transition need to be made at this point. First, political independence was itself closely linked to a particular stage in the development of the open economy. It will be argued in Chapter 7 that the motivation and timing of the movement for political independence were related to the inability of the colonial system to cope with the demands made upon it. It is important to stress that this failure did not occur simply because the open economy was immobile and unresponsive, popular though this view might be. On the contrary, the West African variant of this economy showed some ability to raise incomes and finance diversification, especially in the period after the Second World War. The problem was rather that African expectations were expanding too fast to be contained within a colonial system, whatever its attributes. Second, the history of West Africa since independence has demonstrated that the closed economy is not necessarily a means to economic progress. The closed economy brings new possibilities, but with these come new dangers: exchange controls may discourage investment; import restrictions combined with the operation of an independent monetary system may lead to shortages of consumer goods and to inflation; and political pressures for development may induce the new rulers to make concessions in the form of wages, jobs and contracts, which in turn may lead to external debts and to internal inefficiencies.[10]

2   The performance of the open economy, 1900–60

The history of the open economy in West Africa will now be outlined by surveying the statistical data relating to the value and volume of overseas commerce, the direction of trade, the nature of the main exports and imports, the geographical location of the export sector, and the terms of trade. These figures are subject to quite a wide margin of error, as indeed are all statistics relating to the underdeveloped world. Nevertheless, they provide an indispensable guide to the recent economic history of West Africa, and one, moreover, which is not readily available in secondary publications. Only a summary view is attempted here; it is hoped that other economic historians will soon begin to explore the relevant primary sources in greater detail.[11]

It is clear that there was a substantial growth in the value and volume of overseas trade, and that the period of colonial rule gave a considerable boost to an economy which, as argued in Chapter 4, was already beginning to expand, but which appeared to have reached its ceiling in the last quarter of the nineteenth century. However, it is not easy to measure changes in the real value of trade. The figures usually cited by historians fail to take account of the fall in the value of sterling and the franc in the twentieth century, especially after 1914. If some very approximate adjustments are made to the uncorrected money values recorded in the primary sources, then it appears that in real terms the value of West Africa's overseas trade increased about fifteen times between 1906–1910 and 1955–1959. The rate of expansion, though uneven, was certainly rapid, being about four times as great as in the preceding period of comparable length between 1850–1855 and 1901–1905. Imports tended to follow the path taken by exports for the greater part of the colonial era. Deficits in the visible balance of trade were possible, and were almost the rule in French West Africa after 1925. Until 1945 these deficits were small, and were met by capital transfers from the metropolis, so that the overall balance of payments was in surplus. After the Second World War, however, the relationship between visible import and export values became far more tenuous, and imports began to exceed exports by a considerable amount,[12] a development which was made possible by greater capital aid from external sources, and by the expenditure of reserves built up in the 1940s and 1950s. The change in the composition of the balance of payments indicates that the open economy was no longer operating in its purest form.

[10] An important case study of these tendencies can be found in Douglas Rimmer, 'The Crisis in the Ghana Economy', *Journal of Modern African Studies*, 4, 1966, pp. 17–32.

[11] The evidence which follows has been derived mainly from Board of Trade, League of Nations and United Nations publications, details of which are given in the bibliography.

[12] After 1945 in the case of French West Africa, and after 1955 in the case of the British territories.

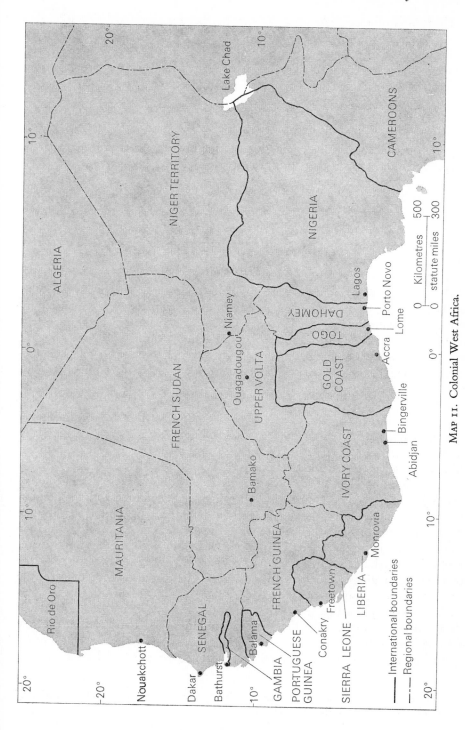

MAP 11. Colonial West Africa.

The volume of overseas trade grew about ten times between 1906–1910 and 1955–1959.[13] Two of the most spectacular increases were Gold Coast cocoa exports, which rose from a few hundred tons a year in the 1890s to 305,000 tons in 1936/1937, a figure which was not exceeded until 1959/1960, and groundnut products from Senegal, which averaged around 50,000 tons in the 1890s, and reached a peak of 723,000 tons in 1937. Until about 1945 import and export volumes tended to move together, but after the Second World War imports were on the whole greater than exports, as Figure 2 illustrates with reference to French West Africa. This trend was the result of a change in the composition of the import trade to include a larger proportion of heavy capital goods and ancillaries, such as cement and petrol.

Trends in the direction of overseas commerce are not easy to assess precisely, mainly because of the difficulty of accounting for re-exports. In broad terms, however, it can be said that the trade of the colonies became increasingly oriented towards the ruling power in the period following partition, though in the eyes of the more fervent protectionists and fair traders the immediate results were not entirely satisfactory.

In 1898 about 40 per cent of the total trade of French West Africa was conducted with France. By 1930 this figure had crept up to about 50 per cent, chiefly as a result of the expansion of the Senegalese groundnut industry, which was dominated by French merchants and by French markets. France also remained the most important trading partner of the tiny, British colony of Gambia, again because she bought virtually the whole of the groundnut crop. However, in some of her own colonies, such as Guinea, the Ivory Coast and Dahomey, France had only a minor share of total trade. It was not until the 1930s, with the adoption of protectionist measures, that commercial ties between France and her West African colonies as a whole were greatly strengthened. Between 1935 and 1960 roughly 75 per cent of the total trade of French West Africa was conducted with France. This gain, which was especially marked in the case of exports to West Africa, was made largely at the expense of Britain and other countries in the sterling zone.

After about 1900 Britain conducted more trade with her West African colonies than with other parts of West Africa. This alignment contrasted with the position in the nineteenth century, though of course it should be remembered that the size of these colonies had increased as a result of the partition of Africa. Between 1900 and 1930 Britain supplied about 75 per cent of British West Africa's imports and received approximately 50 per cent of her colonies' exports. There was still room for other trading nations within the British empire: German firms in particular made good use of the opportunities presented by the expansion of British rule in West Africa, especially through their domination of the palm kernel trade. Although these firms were expelled from the British colonies during the two World Wars, they showed remarkable resilience in re-establishing themselves thereafter. The imposition of quotas in the 1930s helped Britain to maintain her share of the import trade

---

[13] The expansion of exports from Nigeria, whose products were broadly representative of West Africa as a whole, is shown in Figure 1.

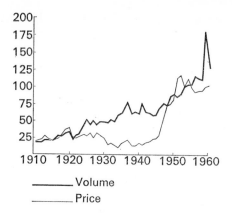

Figure 1. Nigeria: Indices of Export Volume and Price, 1911–60.
(base 1953 = 100)

(Source: G. K. Helleiner, *Peasant Agriculture, Government, and Economic Growth in Nigeria*, Homewood, Illinois 1966, table IV-A-2, pp. 494–5.)

Figure 2. French West Africa: Indices of the Volume of
Overseas Trade, 1925–55.
(base 1949 = 100)

(Source: J.-J. Poquin, *Les relations économiques extérieures des pays d'Afrique noire de l'union française, 1925–1955*, Paris 1957, tables IV and V, pp. 24 and 27.)

to West Africa, and the Second World War effectively eliminated competitors in the export trade, with the result that by 1945 Britain, like France, accounted for about three-quarters of the total overseas commerce of her West African colonies. Unlike France, however, Britain's dominance became less marked in the later 1940s, and by 1960 she was responsible for only about half the imports and half the exports of her possessions in West Africa. It is interesting to note that in the import trade the main beneficiary of Britain's decline was Japan, the country whose competitive threat to the Lancashire textile industry had been an important motive for the introduction of the quota system before the Second World War.

The growth of the export sector was based principally on agricultural and forest products, most of which were either established staples, such as palm oil, palm kernels and groundnuts, or had been introduced in an experimental way before the expansion of European rule, as was the case with cocoa and coffee. There were a few exceptions, such as mineral exports from Sierra Leone, but these qualify the generalisation rather than disprove it. Evidence regarding the composition of exports, it is suggested, supports the argument developed in the previous chapter that the chief purpose of colonial rule was to speed a process of economic change which was already under way. Indeed, for some colonies, notably Gambia and Dahomey, there is a sense in which it can be said that the era of legitimate commerce survived virtually untouched throughout the colonial period! Even in Liberia, the one independent country in West Africa, the nineteenth-century pattern of trade was not disturbed until the 1940s, when rubber came to dominate the export list. To the extent that there was some diversification of exports, then it affected the huge Federation of French West Africa less profoundly and at a later date than it did the three main British colonies.

In the first half of the colonial period (1900–1930) about three-quarters of the value of all overseas exports from French West Africa were derived from groundnuts (50–60 per cent), which were farmed in Senegal, and palm products (15–20 per cent), which came mainly from Dahomey. These two exports underwent a relative decline in the second half of the period (1930–1960), and especially after the Second World War. In the 1950s groundnuts and groundnut oil still accounted for about 30 per cent of total exports, but palm products had fallen away to about 5 per cent. The decline was the result of the expansion of coffee and cocoa exports from the Ivory Coast. Coffee production was of little importance before the Second World War, but it developed rapidly after 1946, and in the 1950s accounted for 25–30 per cent of all exports from the Federation. Cocoa exports increased more slowly, and rose from about 10 per cent to about 15 per cent of the total during the same period. At the time of independence in 1960 the two older staples and the two newer ones together accounted for roughly 75 per cent of all exports. Mineral exports were insignificant during the colonial period, and in 1955 were responsible for only 4 per cent of total export values. Nevertheless, by the late 1950s it was clear that minerals, especially iron ore from Mauritania and bauxite from Guinea, would become increasingly important in the era of independence.

In British West Africa palm products accounted for about 50 per cent of the value of total exports at the beginning of the period of colonial rule, dropped to about 33 per cent by 1930, and fell away to approximately 15 per cent in the 1950s. Before 1930 this decline was almost entirely the result of the rise of the Gold Coast cocoa industry, which expanded very quickly during the first three decades of the twentieth century, and by the close of the 1920s was responsible for 80 per cent of all exports from the colony. Cocoa has remained dominant ever since, though gold—one of the oldest exports—enjoyed a brief revival in the 1930s, following a price rise in world markets. Two other important innovations in the 1910s and 1920s were the development of Nigerian cocoa and groundnut exports, which between them accounted for about a quarter of all exports from Nigeria in the later 1920s, though palm produce still supplied half the total. In the second part of the colonial period the two new products continued to make progress at the expense of the traditional staples, with the result that by the late 1950s cocoa provided about 20 per cent of all Nigerian exports, groundnuts and groundnut oil a further 20 per cent, and palm products about 25 per cent. In Sierra Leone there was a more dramatic change in the 1930s. Palm products, which until then had formed about 70 per cent of total exports, declined rapidly as a result of the exploitation of diamond and iron-ore deposits. Mineral exports, negligible in 1930, formed 45 per cent of total exports in 1934, and by the close of the decade had reached over 60 per cent, a figure which, after some fluctuations, was attained once more in the 1950s.

Minerals were always of greater significance in British than in French West Africa, even without taking into account the contribution made by Sierra Leone. In the late 1920s tin represented about 10 per cent of the value of all Nigerian exports, and gold, diamonds and manganese were each about 5 per cent of Gold Coast exports. All these products had declined slightly by the end of the colonial period, but the discovery of new resources, notably Nigerian oil, indicated that minerals were certain to be important in the future development plans of the more fortunate countries.

The composition of the import trade presents some interesting continuities and contrasts with the pre-colonial era, though these cannot be measured with great precision because the categories by which imports were classified were altered from time to time and also varied between British and French colonies.[14] Manufactured consumer goods were still the chief import, as in the nineteenth century, and textiles, principally cotton goods, but including an increasing proportion of man-made fibres, such as rayon, remained the leading single item, accounting for about a third of the value of total imports into French West Africa and about a quarter of total imports in British West Africa in the period down to the Second World War. At the same time, two long-established staples lost their former prominence. Imports of guns and ammunition were curtailed after the partition of Africa, when the colonial authorities took steps to ensure that the chief means of coercion were kept in their own hands. Next came the decline of the liquor trade after the First World War. A

[14] There are also many minor frustrations, which will be familiar to those who have wrestled with the *Blue Books* and similar publications. Imports of motor vehicles, for example, though easily counted, were sometimes listed in terms of their total tonnage only. This formula doubtless served some obscure purpose of the Customs and Excise Department, but it gives the historian a severe headache.

combination of reasons was responsible for this: hostilities cut off Hamburg, the main source of supply, from West African markets; an increase in the circulation of British and French currency diminished the demand for liquor as a medium of exchange; the colonial powers, somewhat tardily, introduced measures to limit the trade by raising customs duties and by imposing higher standards on the quality of imported spirits; and consumer tastes, influenced by the availability of a wider range of goods, became more sophisticated.[15]

Several new items began to appear in the import lists during the early part of the colonial period. Imports of food, especially rice, fish, sugar, flour and salt, began to increase in the inter-war years, particularly in Senegal, the Gold Coast, Nigeria and the Ivory Coast, where some export producers and urban workers were no longer self-sufficient, and where the development of the overseas exchange sector had led to a demand for a higher quality and more varied diet.[16] After the Second World War the rapid expansion in the number of Europeans in French West Africa (from about 30,000 in 1946 to about 100,000 in 1960) contributed to this trend, for they were the main consumers of imported foodstuffs. By the end of the colonial period manufactured consumer goods and foodstuffs between them accounted for about 60 per cent of the value of all imports into French West Africa, and about 45 per cent in the case of British West Africa. After the Second World War, however, the import lists of the wealthier colonies showed an increasing shift to capital goods, such as machinery and motor vehicles, to semi-finished products, and to raw materials. This was a significant development because it indicated that in the 1950s, on the eve of independence, the open economy was showing signs of diversification.

The frontiers of trade were pushed back by this export-led development, so that by 1960 the area directly involved in production for the overseas market was very much larger than it had been in the nineteenth century. All the same, it is important to emphasise that most exports were drawn from a small part of the total area covered by West Africa, and that the contributions made by various regions also remained more or less constant throughout the colonial period. British West Africa, for example, though only a third of the size of French West Africa, supplied an average of 72 per cent of the value of total exports from West Africa as a whole, while the French colonies accounted for only 25 per cent of the total. The remaining territories (Liberia and Portuguese Guinea) were left with a mere 3 per cent.[17] Moreover, there was a considerable degree of concentration within the British and French territories. Nigeria and the Gold Coast were responsible for 90–95 per cent of total exports from the four British possessions, a figure which was equivalent to 37 per cent and 29 per cent respectively of all West African exports. Thus the trade of Nigeria alone was far more important than that of the whole of French West Africa, which was roughly

[15] The liquor trade is a profitable subject of future research, whether it is considered as a commercial undertaking, as an ideological controversy, or as an issue in international politics.
[16] W. B. Morgan, 'Food Imports of West Africa', *Economic Geography*, 39, 1963, pp. 351–62.
[17] The two German colonies of Togo and Cameroon were occupied by the Allies during the First World War, and in 1919 they were each split into two parts and placed under British and French mandate.

on a par with the Gold Coast.[18] In French West Africa itself two colonies, Senegal and the Ivory Coast, were pre-eminent, supplying between them about 75 per cent of the total exports from the Federation during the whole of the colonial period. Senegal was the leading centre in the first half of the twentieth century, but after the Second World War the Ivory Coast's foreign trade expanded rapidly, with the result that by the 1950s the two colonies were of approximately equal importance.

Many parts of West Africa which lay outside the main export-producing regions were able to participate in the colonial economy by supplying necessary inputs into export activities, such as labour. Other areas, however, were scarcely touched even by indirect economic influences, and some may well have suffered an absolute fall in living standards as a result of colonial rule. Mauritania, for example, with its traditional export, gum, in decline, found an imperfect substitute in trading foodstuffs (fish, millet and livestock) to Senegal. The area around Lake Chad is another instance of a part of West Africa which experienced the decline of an important traditional activity without at the same time receiving adequate compensation in the form of new opportunities. The Buduma, who inhabit the territory south of Lake Chad, originally arrived there without any knowledge of water transport, but they adopted the techniques of the people they subjugated, and by selling slaves were able to buy expensive wooden canoes from the distant forest region to the south. This superior means of transport enabled them to dominate much of the Lake Chad region. However, colonial rule brought the internal slave trade to an end. The prosperity of the Buduma declined, and they were forced to adopt cheaper reed skiffs, which are still in use today. The example of the Buduma, paddling their inferior skiffs and reflecting nostalgically on prosperous days gone by, serves as a reminder that market expansion was not a universal phenomenon in twentieth century West Africa.[19]

The pre-eminence of four colonies, Nigeria, the Gold Coast, Senegal and the Ivory Coast, points to a considerable degree of continuity with the past, for all of them had been centres of legitimate commerce in the nineteenth century, and the first three had been prominent earlier still in the days of the Atlantic slave trade. The overwhelming dominance of Nigeria and the Gold Coast is additional evidence that the British, with luck allied to judgement, were more determined and at the same time more subtle in the defence of their West African interests in the nineteenth century than is often suggested. Certainly, any assessment of French supremacy based simply on a comparison of the size of the territories ruled by the two great powers is very misleading. Finally, it is worth observing that considerable regional inequalities exist in West Africa, though without there being any marked dualism between the so-called 'traditional' and 'modern' sectors of the economy. Inequalities were present in the pre-colonial period, but colonial rule often accentuated and occasionally altered regional differences. Local disparities are sometimes ignored in

---

[18] However, if exports are related to population, then the Gold Coast ranks above all other colonies in West Africa.

[19] The Buduma's loss was others' gain: for a discussion of the ending of internal slavery see Chapter 6, part 2.

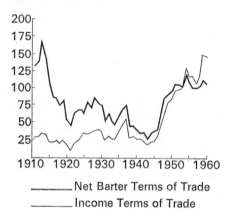

Figure 3. Nigeria: Terms of Trade, 1911–60.
(base 1953 = 100)

(Source: G. K. Helleiner, *Peasant Agriculture, Government, and Economic Growth in Nigeria*, Homewood, Illinois, 1966, table IV-A-6, p. 500.)

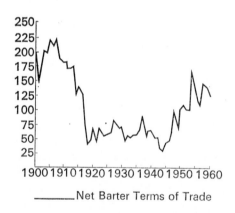

Figure 4. Gold Coast–Ghana: Terms of Trade, 1900–60.
(base 1953 = 100)

(Source: Stephen H. Hymer, 'The Political Economy of the Gold Coast and Ghana', in *Government and Economic Development*, ed. Gustav Ranis, New Haven 1971, pp. 136–7.)

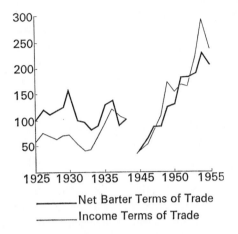

Figure 5. French West Africa: Terms of Trade, 1925–55.
(base 1938 = 100)

(Source: J.-J. Poquin, *Les relations économiques extérieures des pays d'Afrique noire de l'union française, 1925–1955*, Paris 1957, p. 135.)

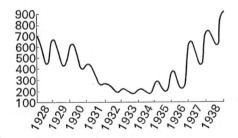

Figure 6. French West Africa (including Togo):
Bank Notes in Circulation, 1928–38.
(in millions of francs)

(Source: Huguette Durand, *Essai sur la conjoncture de l'Afrique noire*,
Paris 1957, graph XXII, p. 119.)

the debate about the alleged 'widening gap' between the living standards of the advanced and the underdeveloped nations.[20]

A historical survey of the terms of trade of West African export producers comes as near as is possible to providing a film of the performance of the open economy, though, since some of the reels are missing, the result is necessarily jerky and incomplete. The net barter terms of trade, that is the ratio between the indices of average export and import prices, measure changes in the quantity of imports which can be derived from a given unit of exports. The income terms of trade, that is the barter terms of trade multiplied by an index of the volume of exports, provide information about the total import-purchasing power of the country concerned.[21] In evaluating trends in the terms of trade the following points have to be borne in mind: first, the indices measure changes in relation to one base year rather than absolute gains and losses; second, they do not take account of alterations in the quality of imports and exports; and third, because the indices are derived from averages they tend to disguise the behaviour of individual commodities. In the 1930s, for example, the export trade of Sierra Leone changed its character, but the indices at present available for West Africa do not take this particular shift fully into account.

The three principal sources are Helleiner's data on Nigeria, which are presented in Figure 3, Hymer's figures for the Gold Coast (Fig. 4), and Poquin's important, yet virtually unused, work on French West Africa (Fig. 5). Since the trade of Nigeria, the Gold Coast and French West Africa included all the main items of West Africa's external commerce, there is reason to think that composite indices relating to these areas are broadly representative of the region as a whole. In the analysis which follows, the three main sources have been supplemented by evidence relating to the period 1900–1911, by Cox-George's work on Sierra Leone between 1914 and 1945, by Bauer's material dealing with the Gold Coast between 1935 and 1951, and by Berg's survey of real income trends in West Africa from 1939 to 1960.[22]

Taking the period 1900–1960 as a whole, it is clear that economic progress in the underdeveloped world was largely dependent on circumstances affecting the major industrial powers. Particularly outstanding in this connection was the impact of what, in terms of the theory of international trade, must be called fortuitous events, notably the two World Wars. More orthodox movements, such as the transmitted effects

---

[20] The emphasis given here to differences within regions and countries (in addition to the obvious comparison between national and colonial units) is paralleled by recent studies of English and American history at critical points of economic development. See, for example, E. A. Wrigley, *Industrial Growth and Population Change*, Cambridge 1961, and Douglass C. North, 'Agriculture and Regional Economic Growth', *Journal of Farm Economics*, 41, 1959, pp. 943–51.

[21] For a fuller explanation of these terms see Ord and Livingstone, *An Introduction to West African Economics*, pp. 363–7, and, more generally, Gerald M. Meier, *The International Economics of Development*, New York and London 1968, pp. 41–65.

[22] N. A. Cox-George, *Finance and Development in West Africa*, 1961; P. T. Bauer, *West African Trade*, Cambridge 1954, pp. 410–21, and Elliot J. Berg, 'Real Income Trends in West Africa, 1939–1960', in *Economic Transition in Africa*, ed. Melville J. Herskovits and Mitchell Harwitz, 1964, pp. 199–238.

of Juglar cycles of under nine years, are harder to discern. With regard to the controversy about the long term prospects of primary producers in the underdeveloped
world, the evidence available does not lend decisive support to either optimists or
pessimists.[23] The barter terms of trade fluctuated around a falling trend from 1913–
1945, but then recovered between 1945 and 1960. The income terms of trade, though
clearly affected by changes in the barter terms, tended to move upwards, reflecting
the general expansion of export volumes during the twentieth century. By the close
of the colonial period, West Africa's total import-purchasing power was about four
times as great as it had been at the beginning of the century. Allowing for the fact
that the population had roughly doubled during the same period, it can be said that
average per capita importing capacity was twice as high in 1960 as in 1900. Not all
export earnings went straight to the producers, and the distribution of benefits was
also uneven geographically and socially. Nevertheless, it is certain that Africans
gained considerably from participating in international trade.

A more detailed historical analysis of the terms of trade can be made by dividing
the period 1900–1960 into the following five sections: 1900–1913, 1914–1921, 1922–
1929, 1930–1944 and 1945–1960. It will be argued here that there is a significant relationship between these five phases and the general economic and political history of
the region, though no simple, mechanistic interpretation is intended. It is hoped that
the connections briefly noted in the ensuing analysis will be explored more fully by
others, and by political scientists as well as by economists and historians.

The period from 1900 to 1913 was marked by a steady improvement in the barter
terms of trade of African producers. Since the volume of exports was expanding at
the same time, the income terms of trade also rose, finally pulling the economy out
of the slump which had affected it so seriously in the late nineteenth century. This
favourable trend had three main consequences. First, it helped to reconcile Africans
to colonial rule, and so made the task of the new administrations much easier than it
would otherwise have been. Second, it made possible the financing of development
projects, notably railways, which were necessary if the economy was to expand
beyond the limits set by nineteenth-century conditions of export production. Third,
it induced more Africans to enter the export market, and so led to a further growth
in the volume of exports, and to plantings of tree crops which were to bear fruit in
the 1920s and 1930s. Developments between 1900 and 1913 were not quite as smooth
and uneventful as the foregoing summary may suggest. The partition of West Africa
ended in an atmosphere of bonanza, as traders and producers hoped for a lucky strike
to compensate for the lean years they had endured. At the turn of the century there
was a minor gold rush in the Gold Coast, and, more prosaically, a rubber boom,
which resulted from the discovery of wild rubber trees in parts of the forest zone
from Guinea to Nigeria. When the gold rush came to an end, which it did very
quickly, when most of the rubber trees ceased to be worth tapping, and when the
first geological surveys dispelled some of the more fanciful hopes of those whose

---

[23] These prospects depend, of course, on the development of new exports, as well as on
price movements affecting existing exports.

judgement had been seriously affected by a consuming desire to get rich quickly, then the great majority of West African export producers settled down soberly to a slower, harder grind towards prosperity.

These favourable trends were interrupted by the First World War. The barter terms of trade declined as a result of the shortage and consequently the high price of imported goods. Export expansion was checked by the closure of some European, especially German, markets, and by a lack of shipping space. The outcome was a fall in the income terms as well. In 1919 West Africa participated briefly in the post-war boom, but then suffered severely in the slump of 1920–1921, which was signalled by a dramatic collapse of export prices. These years saw the elimination of many smaller import and export firms, European as well as African, and the consolidation of the position of a few large concerns. The fluctuations of the period revealed to a new generation of Africans the extent to which their fortunes depended on external forces. They in turn demonstrated their disenchantment with colonial rule by organising protests in the main centres of trade. The First World War had serious consequences for West Africa: it was an unpleasant foretaste of the greater conflict of 1939–1945, which was to have an even bigger impact on the tropical colonies.[24]

In 1922 there began a recovery which lasted until 1929. The barter terms of trade improved, though they were not as favourable as in the pre-war years, and the income terms also revived as a result of a rise in the volume of exports. The exact degree of recovery is hard to judge. According to Helleiner, Nigeria's total importing capacity was only slightly greater in the late 1920s than it had been just before the First World War. In the absence of technical advances in agriculture, the capacity to import was maintained only by increased inputs of labour and land. Existing export producers had to work harder, and new producers had to be attracted into the export sector. The latter development was made possible by the arrival of the motor lorry, which enabled new areas of export production to be opened up. All that can be said at present, pending further, more detailed investigation, is that the recovery of 1922–1929 was a limited one, and that most export producers were unlikely to have experienced any marked improvement in their living standards.

From 1930–1944, the barter terms of trade declined once more, apart from a brief recovery in 1935–1937, and during the Second World War reached their lowest point of the century. More remarkable still, the income terms also showed a downward trend (though again there was a limited recovery in the mid-1930s) in spite of the fact that there was some expansion in the volume of exports.[25] The Second World War had a much more serious effect on West Africa than did the world slump of the 1930s because of an acute shortage of consumer imports and because of the abrupt closure of many export markets in Europe. French West Africa, having

[24] Some of the effects of the First World War have been explored in a valuable article by Michael Crowder, 'West Africa and the 1914–18 War', *Bulletin de l'IFAN*, B, 30, 1968, pp. 227–45. See also Cox-George, *Finance and Development in West Africa*, ch. 8.

[25] An interesting illustration of the depressive effects of this trend can be seen in Figure 6, which plots the fall in currency circulation in French West Africa, and also demonstrates the extent of seasonal variations in the size of the money economy.

declared for the Vichy government in 1940, found itself blockaded by the Allies, and so was particularly badly affected. By the end of the war West Africa's total importing capacity was lower than at any time since 1900 (with the possible exception of 1921), though population and public debts had both increased greatly since the beginning of the century. The adverse trends of the period 1930–1944 had two principal consequences. In the first place, investment was curtailed and ambitious projects postponed. Retrenchment was the theme, safety first the motto, and indirect rule the philosophy cut to suit the narrow cloth of the time. The main exceptions to this generalisation arose, perversely, during the Second World War, when a few schemes, such as the development of a harbour at Monrovia, were undertaken to aid the Allied war effort. Secondly, the long period of economic hardship led to the rise of a movement which was eventually to bring colonial rule to an end. This movement had its beginnings in the economic crisis of the 1930s, and, as a result of the Second World War, it became more widespread, more articulate, and ultimately irresistible.

After 1945 there was a rapid and unexpected improvement in the barter terms of trade brought about by a revival in demand for tropical products, which were required to assist the post-war recovery of Europe, and later to meet the need for raw materials during the Korean war. The upward trend levelled off in the second half of the 1950s, but the barter terms still remained more favourable than at any point since the period before the First World War. The volume of exports grew at the same time, slowly at first, but then more swiftly in the 1950s, with the result that the total importing capacity of West Africa achieved record levels. Several important developments were closely associated with this final, and generally prosperous, phase of colonial rule. First, there was a rapid, and seemingly irreversible, expansion of the public sector. Second, there was a revival of confidence and a renewed inflow of investment, just as there had been in the period 1900–1913, which also followed a time of economic slump and political crisis. Third, while the growth in the volume of exports was achieved mainly by established means, it also resulted from an increase in agricultural productivity brought about by the adoption of insecticides, fertilisers and better quality seeds. Fourth, in the 1950s the expansion of the market reached the point where large-scale manufacturing could begin. Finally, this phase saw the end of colonial rule. On the one hand the colonial powers felt a need to placate and reward colonial subjects who had endured the hardships of the war effort; on the other hand, Africans were more organised and better financed than they had been, and could make sure that the required concessions were forthcoming.

The analysis of the colonial period which follows is divided into two chapters, each corresponding to a stage in the history of the open economy. Chapter 6 will examine the construction of the open economy. Accordingly, the main focus will be on the first half of the colonial period (1900–1930), but subsequent events will be dealt with if they contributed to the maintenance of the open economy in its classic form. In contrast, Chapter 7 will concentrate on the difficulties experienced by the open economy and on the alterations which were made to it in the second half of the colonial period (1930–1960). Accordingly, the chief emphasis will be on disfunctional developments, that is those which tended to modify the open economy. Most historical accounts of the colonial period have followed the political divisions established by the major powers, and have dealt, in turn, with British and with French West Africa. This procedure is not suitable for the thematic, economic analysis proposed here. Chapters 6 and 7 will treat the economies of French, British, German and Portuguese West Africa as a whole, on the grounds that the similarities between them in terms of structure and evolution were more marked than the differences, though these will be noted wherever they were important. This approach has two secondary advantages: it includes Liberia, a country which, though politically independent since 1847, developed a typical open, export economy in the twentieth century; and it may also help to break down the insularity which academics have inherited from their colonial past.[26]

[26] The adverse effects of this insularity continue to be felt. For example, French scholars write about the Senegalese groundnut industry, but rarely mention northern Nigeria, and British scholars discuss the monetary system of British West Africa without making any reference to the system operating in the neighbouring French colonies.

six

Completing the open economy

This chapter is devoted to an analysis of the open economy during the first half of the colonial era. The evidence is organised around two themes which are central to the economic history of the period. The first theme is the introduction of the economic and political institutions which were needed to complete the structure of the open economy. The second theme concerns the way in which the component parts of the open economy combined to activate domestic resources and to expand West Africa's overseas trade.

Two alternative views are commonly expressed about the development of export economies during the early part of the colonial period, though other, less prominent, interpretations can easily be found. The first, and more traditional, argument makes the colonial government primarily responsible for introducing and managing economic change. This belief has led, in turn, to two opposed schools of thought. One suggests that Africans were tutored, in the event swiftly and efficiently, by a benign, though necessarily paternal, regime. McPhee, for example, told the story of *The Economic Revolution in British West Africa* (1926) very much from this official standpoint.[1] The other also emphasises the role of the administration, but disputes the idea that colonial rule was beneficial to Africans, and criticises official policy for disrupting and exploiting allegedly stable and prosperous traditional societies. This approach can be found in Suret-Canale's *Afrique noire occidentale et centrale: l'ère coloniale, 1900–1945* (1964).[2] The second, more recent, view has been advanced in different contexts by a number of development economists, and is concerned primarily with the mobilisation of land and labour resources in the indigenous economy. This approach is very different from that of McPhee and Suret-Canale; it bypasses the historical problem of the costs and benefits of colonial rule, and it seeks chiefly to analyse the contribution made by Africans to the process of export expansion.

Both views have their merits, but neither is acceptable without some modification. The first, though it has the advantage of paying attention to detail and chronology, is particularly suspect because it underplays the role of Africans themselves, while the conclusions it reaches about the welfare consequences of colonial rule over-generalise

---

[1] See also Alan Pim, *The Financial and Economic History of the African Tropical Territories*, Oxford 1940.

[2] Now in translation under the title *French Colonialism in Tropical Africa, 1900–1945*, 1971.

on a limited amount of frequently ambiguous evidence. The second view is more sophisticated and reflects recent trends in development economics, but it tends to exaggerate the ease and simplify the process of growth by suggesting that colonial development was essentially a matter of taking up the slack in existing, underutilised resources—in much the same way as a prefabricated building can be erected by persuading enough men to pull on a rope. What is required for present purposes is an approach which combines the historical depth of the first view with the analytical strength of the second.

The central problem is to identify and evaluate the main formative influences on the open economy. The particular difficulty lies in striking a balance between causes, when the nature of the evidence is such that these cannot be measured with great precision. For example, any book which claims to be based on recent research is bound to stress the contribution made by indigenous producers and traders. At the same time, however, care must be taken not to dismiss the history of European enterprise in West Africa as the unfashionable preoccupation of those who have failed to keep up with the somewhat exhausting pace of change in African studies.[3] A preliminary classification suggests that the chief formative influences can be divided into two broad categories; imported and indigenous. The former were significant in four areas: economic policy, transport, the distributive system, and money and banking. The latter can be analysed in terms of land and labour inputs. In brief, it will be argued that imported, colonial influences were in varying degrees necessary to the completion of the open economy, but were not a sufficient cause of it, and that it was indigenous entrepreneurs, by accepting and creating market opportunities, who ensured that export production did in fact expand.

These two categories will be dealt with in turn, though it will become evident that there was considerable interaction between them. The organisation of the chapter will have so take account of this overlap: for instance, while dealing with externally-induced changes in the distributive system it will be convenient to examine the position of Africans as well as of Europeans; similarly, in discussing the indigenous utilisation of land resources, it is appropriate at that point also to look at colonial policy regarding plantations and mines.

1   The expatriate role

It is customary for historians to contrast the attitudes of the two major colonial powers towards the business of government. The French approach is said to have been characterised by centralisation, administrative rigidity, and assimilationist

[3] Non-specialists may be under the impression that European activities have been fully investigated. This is not the case. For example, no one has written an economic history of the railway systems in West Africa, and there have been hardly any studies of expatriate trading, mining and plantation enterprises, or of official economic policy. These are important subjects, and it would be unfortunate if research students avoided them for fear of being thought old-fashioned in their approach to African history.

tendencies. Britain's policies, on the other hand, are usually thought of as being based on the delegation of authority, on political empiricism, and on the toleration of diverse indigenous institutions. Differences between the policies of the two colonial powers undoubtedly existed, and were almost certainly perpetuated by a notable lack of inter-colonial contact and co-operation. Nevertheless, the contrast was stronger in principle than in practice, and as far as economic policy was concerned France and Britain had more in common than is often appreciated.[4]

Economic policy was limited both in its philosophy and in its techniques. Governments were not envisaged as playing a central and dynamic part in developing the estates they had acquired, and in any case they had little of the necessary expertise at their disposal. This is not surprising. At a time when the ideas of Keynes and Beveridge had still to make their mark in Europe, it was unlikely that the economic principles which were applied to the colonies would differ markedly from those in force at home. The leading colonial civil servants were political officers, and there were few economists in government service. Those most closely involved with the economy tended to be practical men, such as agricultural and forestry experts, who, though recognised by their superiors as being necessary, were at the same time peripheral to what was regarded as the main task of government. These men went through their careers with much the same degree of obscurity and status deficiency as, for example, the staff of the Ministry of Transport still experience in Britain in relation to their counterparts at the Foreign Office.

Once pacification had been achieved, government activity reverted to its traditional role; the art of light administration. In economic affairs the political officers merely acted as Great White Umpires, ensuring that the rules were observed, not that they were changed. The general belief, inherited from the nineteenth century, was that private enterprise and the free play of market forces would lead to international specialisation based on the comparative advantage of the nations concerned, and that this would promote economic growth by bringing about a more efficient allocation of factors of production. Development by this means, so it was held, would be to the advantage of all parties. Of course, the main purpose of having colonies in West Africa was to secure a profitable trade for the mother country, and in some cases tariff regulations were devised to see that this happened.[5] All the same, it was necessary to make sure that some of the gains from international trade accrued to Africa because, in the last resort, if Africans remained poor they could not afford to buy manufactured goods. The belief that colonial rule should be based on co-operation and mutual interest rather than on crude exploitation found comprehensive expression in Lord Lugard's book *The Dual Mandate in British Tropical Africa* (1922). The concept of the dual mandate, which admirably combined philosophical largesse with financial economy, became acceptable rather later in France (according to British writers anyway) than it did in England, though with the publication of

[4] For a complementary view regarding similarities of administrative and educational policy see M. Semakula Kiwanuka, 'Colonial Policies and Administrations in Africa: the Myths of Contrasts', *African Historical Studies*, 3, 1970, pp. 295–315.
[5] Tariff policy is discussed in greater detail in Chapter 7.

Albert Sarraut's influential work *La mise en valeur des colonies françaises* in 1923 it can be said to have found a small niche in the official mind of French colonialism.

A few attempts were made to swim against the still powerful tide of *laissez-faire* thinking, but they were never wholly successful. At the turn of the century Joseph Chamberlain talked boldly about developing the tropical estates of the British Empire, but his schemes for financial aid were either blocked or whittled away by the Treasury.[6] The world which Gladstone had so recently departed was to continue to feel his influence in the field of public finance until well into the twentieth century. Two more plans of development were put forward immediately after the First World War. These were reflections of recent experience, both of the increased role which governments had been forced to assume during the war, and of the hastily awakened appreciation of the economic importance of the colonies at a time when the metropolis was under siege. Governor Guggisberg formulated a ten-year plan for the Gold Coast covering the period 1919–1928, and involving the expenditure of about £25 million, mainly on improving the transport system.[7] This plan, which was to be financed out of the colony's own resources, and therefore caused no alarm among Treasury officials in London, was cut back as a result of the years of indifferent trade in the early 1920s. However, there were some important achievements, notably the completion of the Accra to Kumasi railway line in 1923, the building of a deep water harbour at Takoradi, which was finished in 1928, and the construction of about 3,000 miles of motor roads. In France, Albert Sarraut, a former Governor-General of Indo-China and Minister of Colonies, put forward a similar, though more extensive, scheme of public works in 1921.[8] His plan, which was designed to exploit the resources of the Empire more fully, also had to be severely modified as a result of the post-war slump and the failure of Germany to pay reparations. Nevertheless, some projects were advanced: the Thiès–Kayes section of the Senegal railway was completed in 1923, improvements were made to Dakar harbour, and a start was made on a plan to irrigate the Middle Niger. All these schemes were designed to complete the structure of the open economy. Their aim was to expand the export economy, in contrast to current development plans, which are concerned mainly with growth in other sectors of the economy.

The prevailing view of the role of government in the economy found characteristic expression in the principles underlying colonial finance. The basic aim was self-sufficiency. As far as the British colonies were concerned, Earl Grey's famous dictum, enunciated in 1852, still held true: 'the surest test for the soundness of measures for the improvement of an uncivilised people is that they should be self-supporting'. In France budgetary reforms were adopted in 1900 which gave the colonies a greater degree of fiscal autonomy, but which also required them to pay their own way.

---

[6] S. B. Saul, 'The Economic Significance of "Constructive Imperialism",' *Journal of Economic History*, 17, 1957, pp. 173–92.

[7] D. K. Greenstreet, 'The Guggisberg Ten-Year Development Plan', *Economic Bulletin of Ghana*, 8, 1964, pp. 18–26.

[8] Suret-Canale, *Afrique noire*, pp. 350–60.

From 1904 to 1957 the colonies were linked in a Federation (with its capital at Dakar) which controlled the collection and distribution of nearly all indirect taxes.[9] The main aim of the Federation was to ensure that the rich colonies (Senegal and the Ivory Coast) paid for their poor relations, thus preventing the latter from becoming a drain on the metropolis. The four British colonies in West Africa remained financially independent of each other, and the two smaller territories (Sierra Leone and Gambia) had to receive support from Britain when they ran into financial difficulty.

To achieve financial self-sufficiency, both British and French colonies relied mainly on revenue from customs duties, which accounted for about two-thirds of total revenue for the greater part of the colonial period.[10] The proportion was even higher before the First World War, but it declined as a result of the expansion of direct taxes, such as head tax and income tax, and the growth of revenue from public investments. Nearly half the revenue was spent on the salaries and pensions of expatriate officials, a fact which helps to explain the introspective nature of official attitudes in the critical period between the two World Wars: at a time when discontent was brewing in Africa, government records seem to be dominated by information about promotions and pensions. Another large slice of public income went to repay the capital and interest on loans raised for development purposes. In the case of Nigeria this item rose from 14 per cent of total revenue in 1926 to 33 per cent in 1934. The amount left for the economic departments, such as agriculture and forestry, was minute. Furthermore, the official budget was subject to large and unpredictable variations of the kind which were typical of open economies. Revenue was most likely to grow during a trade boom, which meant that spending from current income could expand only fitfully. In the event of a slump, however, expenditure could not be reduced very easily because of the high proportion of fixed outgoings on salaries and debt repayments. The result was that the fiscal burden grew more onerous when trade was depressed, and was particularly heavy during the period 1930–1945.

There were two additional sources of public finance; grants-in-aid and loans. Grants-in-aid did not amount to large sums, and they were of no general importance in colonial development programmes. They were used selectively to help out colonies such as Gambia and Sierra Leone, which occasionally ran deficits, and to assist in emergencies, such as the need to increase defence expenditure during the First World War. Public loans, floated on the stock markets of London and Paris, were much more important. All the same, Frankel's pioneering study has shown that investment in tropical Africa in the period before the Second World War was very limited compared with what was required, what was to come in the future, and what was already being invested in other parts of the world.[11] Gross public and

[9] C. W. Newbury, 'The Formation of the Government General of French West Africa', *Journal of African History*, I, 1960, pp. 111–28.

[10] For a detailed case study see Sir Alan Pim, 'Public Finance', in *Mining, Commerce, and Finance in Nigeria*, ed. Margery Perham, 1948, pp. 225–79.

[11] S. H. Frankel, *Capital Investment in Africa*, 1938, and Suret-Canale's comments on his figures in *Afrique noire*, pp. 205–14.

7*

private foreign investment in West Africa amounted to about £147 million in the period 1870–1936. Approximately 50 per cent of this sum was public investment, which was mostly spent developing the transport system, notably railways. Regional disparities were marked: only about one fifth of total investment in West Africa (roughly £30 million) was placed in French territories; the rest went to the smaller, though more populous, British colonies. The ability to raise loans depended entirely on the resources of the colonies themselves, which helps to explain why the differences between rich and poor colonies increased rather than diminished with the passage of time. The borrowing capacity of the colonies, like the size of their current revenues, fluctuated with the trade cycle. The result was that down to 1945 investment tended to follow rather than cause growth, and capital flows magnified the effects of booms and slumps instead of reducing them.

Given the economic philosophy and financial stringency of the early colonial period, there was little scope for basing development policy on anything other than the well-tried Victorian principle of self-help. The validity of this conclusion is illustrated by government policy towards the important questions of commerce, land and labour. These three subjects will be examined in detail later, and are mentioned briefly at this stage simply to indicate the orientation of official thinking. With regard to commerce, the administrations created free trade areas within each colony, and then allowed market forces to operate more or less without restraint. An indulgent attitude towards the expatriate trading firms is understandable when it is remembered that these firms had been in the forefront of the clamour for government intervention in West Africa at the close of the nineteenth century. As to land, British and French policy confirmed African rights, and encouraged the development of an indigenous class of independent export producers. In the case of the labour force, colonial policy aimed at permitting, and sometimes even encouraging, mobility, so that key areas could secure an adequate supply of workers. Only in the field of transport, as will now be shown, was official enterprise dominant. For the rest, lack of techniques and personnel, lack of money, and lack of commitment to the idea of active government involvement in economic affairs meant that the colonial authorities played a less prominent part in creating the open economy than is sometimes thought.

According to Lord Lugard, 'the material development of Africa may be summed up in one word—Transport'.[12] One-word summaries of complex problems cannot be expected to achieve a high degree of accuracy. Nevertheless, it remains true that economists invariably assign modern transport facilities an important place in bringing about economic growth. W. W. Rostow, for example, has claimed that railways were the most important single cause of industrial 'take-off' in North America, Germany and Russia, and that they were very influential elsewhere, notably in England.[13] It is not hard to see why this should have been the case. Modern transport has the effect of discounting space, that is to say it moves goods

[12] *The Dual Mandate in British Tropical Africa*, p. 5.
[13] W. W. Rostow, *The Stages of Economic Growth*, Cambridge 1960.

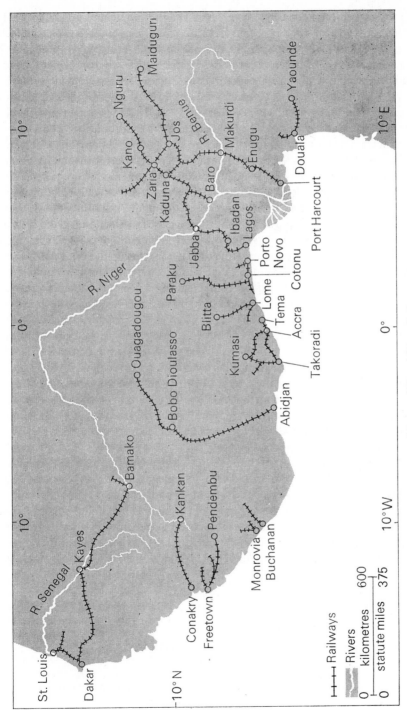

MAP 12. West African Railways.

Railways
Rivers
kilometres
statute miles

and people over longer distances faster and more cheaply than was possible previously. This innovation has had profound consequences. It has released capital and labour tied up in traditional transport operations for more productive employment elsewhere; it has led to the rise of new resources, such as coal and iron, which are basic to industrial development; and it has stimulated the export sector, which in turn has generated capital for internal investment. In view of the real and alleged significance of modern transport in the development of West Africa, it is surprising that economic historians have conducted so little research into the subject.[14] The survey that follows will concentrate on internal innovations, namely railways, harbours, motor transport and waterways. Improvements in ocean transport, principally the change from sail to steam, have been outlined already in Chapter 4.

Plans for the construction of railways in West Africa had been canvassed by private promoters since at least the middle of the nineteenth century.[15] Spacious in conception, obscure in purpose, and all too clearly astronomical in cost, these schemes required, and failed to obtain, government support. However, with the advent of a serious economic crisis in the last quarter of the nineteenth century, commercial interests and government officials became convinced that railways were needed to maintain West Africa's competitiveness in international markets. The construction of railways began in the 1880s and concluded in the 1920s at the end of the first phase of colonial rule. The ideas of private sponsors quickly became government property. The French aimed to drive east from Senegal and capture the Western Sudan, which could then be linked with lines from North Africa and from the southern coast of West Africa, thus enabling France to control the greater part of Africa west of Egypt and the Congo. British policy was on the whole less ambitious, being based on the maintenance of existing spheres of influence, though the possibility of a line which would run from southern Nigeria up to Lake Chad and beyond to Egypt was considered at the turn of the century during a mood of temporary euphoria.

The present railway map of West Africa clearly reflects these half-realised projects. The three main developments were in Senegal, the Gold Coast and Nigeria. The Senegal railway was begun in 1881, and after several changes of plan and many delays Dakar was finally joined to Bamako (a distance of 720 miles) in 1923.[16] On the Gold Coast a line from Sekondi to Kumasi was finished in 1903, another from Accra to Kumasi was ready in 1923, and a third completed the triangle by joining the two coastal ports in 1927. In Nigeria the principal line was begun at Lagos in 1896 and

---

[14] The starting point is still McPhee, *The Economic Revolution*, ch. 3. For one of the few recent case studies see Jacques Mangolte, 'Le chemin de fer de Konakry au Niger (1890–1914)', *Revue Française d'Histoire d'Outre-Mer*, 55, 1968, pp. 37–105. The only comprehensive account of railways in tropical Africa is that by André Huybrechts, *Transports et structures de développement au Congo: étude du progrès économique de 1900 à 1970*, Paris 1970.

[15] Olufemi Omosini, 'Railway Projects and British Attitudes Towards the Development of West Africa, 1872–1903', *Journal of the Historical Society of Nigeria*, 5, 1971, pp. 491–507.

[16] The construction of this line over a period of fifty years is an epic which certainly merits a study of its own.

reached Kano (a total of 711 miles) in 1911. A second line, joining Port Harcourt in eastern Nigeria to Kaduna via Enugu and Jos, was completed in 1926. There were shorter railways running from Freetown to Pendembu (completed in 1906); Lome to Atakpame (1913); Conakry to Kankan (1914); Cotonu to Parakou (1936); and Abidjan to Bobo Dioulasso (1936). By 1940 West Africa had a total of 5,200 miles of railway line, which was divided roughly equally between the British and French colonies.

Although the French experimented at an early stage with railway construction by private contract (and the British were nearly persuaded to do the same), in the event virtually the whole of the West African railway system was built by the colonial governments and with public capital.[17] There seem to have been three main reasons for this exceptional degree of official entrepreneurship. First, building railways in territories which had been acquired not only recently, but by force, raised a number of potentially explosive issues regarding land rights, labour supplies and, ultimately, political control. French and British governments felt that all these matters were best kept in official hands. Second, from the outset the railways had a military and administrative function as well as an economic one. Colonial governments had a close interest in the direction of railway routes and in the timing of construction because they wanted to be able to move soldiers and officials to key points as quickly as possible. Finally, private contractors and investors did not rush to build railways in West Africa. Those who did come forward wanted subsidies or other concessions, and frequently proved to be inefficient. Capital requirements were high because the railways had to serve a wide and sparsely populated area. Furthermore, some lines had to be built in anticipation of demand and not simply in response to it. Their ultimate profitability was not guaranteed, and in any case was certain to be a distant event. Where private capital was wary, government enterprise became necessary.

Harbour improvements were closely related to programmes of railway construction.[18] The steamship had already begun to expose the limitations of West African ports, many of which could not cope with vessels larger than traditional sailing ships. The steamer, however, did not have a marked effect on export production, whereas the railway did. By 1900 it was clear that existing harbours were unable to handle the volume of produce that the railway was capable of delivering. As a result, substantial alterations were made to the major ports beginning around 1900 and continuing throughout the colonial era. In some places, established centres, such as Dakar, Lagos and Freetown, were improved. Elsewhere, entirely new ports, such as Port Harcourt and Takoradi, were developed. The result was the decline of smaller centres, such as Badagri, St Louis and Old Calabar, and the increasing concentration of the export trade on a few, large ports served by railways. In the 1930s no less than 65 per cent of the total tonnage of French West Africa's overseas trade passed through Dakar. Takoradi on the Gold Coast and Lagos in Nigeria were

[17] For a comparative study (of Dahomey, Togo and south-west Nigeria) see C. W. Newbury, *The Western Slave Coast and Its Rulers*, Oxford 1961, pp. 141–7.

[18] A collection of case studies of the development of West African ports can be found in B. S. Hoyle and D. Hilling, eds, *Seaports and Development in Tropical Africa*, 1970.

equally dominant. The leading European ports for West African trade remained, as in the nineteenth century, Liverpool, Bordeaux, Marseilles and Hamburg.

Once the early, superficial talk about 'tapping the wealth of the interior' had vanished into the hot, tropical air, it became apparent that the influence of the railway was restricted to a small area on either side of the track. Large numbers of widely dispersed producers had not been brought into the export economy because the cost of taking their crops to the railway station would still have been too high in relation to the price obtainable. Before 1918 there were very few all-weather roads in West Africa outside the towns. The reason for this was simple: the motor car was a new invention, and the type produced at that time was slow, expensive, and so heavy that it tended to devour the roads it travelled on. Contrary to what might be assumed, at that time few officials or expatriate firms saw any future for the motor car in the underdeveloped world. In 1907, for example, the British Cotton Growing Association recorded its opinion that with regard to West Africa 'metal roads and motor transport are, as far as one can judge, a mistake'.[19] In the 1910s the pioneers of commercial passenger and freight services were Africans, the most prominent of whom was a Nigerian named W. A. Dawodu.

Prevailing attitudes were rendered as obsolete as the early vehicles themselves by the introduction of faster, cheaper and lighter Ford models, which reached West Africa in 1918. In 1923 the first motor car crossed the Sahara from Algeria to Timbuctu, an epic journey, though it was soon to become a commonplace one. By 1930 commercial haulage firms were operating in and around the main centres of economic activity in West Africa and the Sahara. By 1940 French West Africa had about 10,000 vehicles compared to a mere sixteen in 1913. The expansion of motor transport in British West Africa was even faster: in the 1920s the vehicles imported by the Gold Coast and Nigeria were double the number and twice the tonnage of those entering the French colonies.[20] The importation and operation of motor transport was in the hands of private firms, both African and European. Road building, however, was undertaken mainly by the colonial governments, which on the whole planned routes to feed the railways rather than to compete with them, though in West Africa, as in other parts of the world, there was a growing rivalry between the two systems of transport after the Second World War. It is important to note that Africans whose needs were not met by the official road-building programme, and who could command the necessary resources, also contributed to the new infrastructure. The cocoa farmers of Nigeria and the Gold Coast, for example, built their own roads and bridges in the 1910s and 1920s and ran fleets of motor lorries to speed the evacuation of their crop. The framework of the present West African road system, without which the expansion of motor transport could not have taken place, was erected in the 1920s and 1930s. For some officials and local communities the construction of a road to join the outside world was the outstanding

[19] C.O. 520/55, British Cotton Growing Association to Colonial Office, 8 August 1907, Public Record Office.

[20] For a case study, see A. M. Hay, 'The Development of Road Transport in Nigeria, 1900–1940', *Journal of Transport History*, n.s., 1, 1971, pp. 95–107.

event of their time, an historical and personal drama that has been captured by Joyce Cary's evocative novel, *Mister Johnson* (1939).

The development of inland waterways was on a modest scale, principally because the Europeans found, as Africans had found before them, that river transport was severely hampered by rapids and by marked seasonal variations in the water level. However, relatively simple improvements, such as the clearing of existing waterways, stimulated the local economy in some areas, as, for example, in parts of southern Nigeria. Not surprisingly, the main innovation, the use of paddle steamers, occurred on stretches of water such as the Niger, the Benue and the Senegal, which Africans had already made into well-known highways. Although steamers were owned mainly by private firms, some attempt was made to co-ordinate river and rail transport. The Senegal railway, for example, though it ended at Bamako, linked up there with the Middle Niger, thus connecting Dakar with Timbuctu and Gao. At the same time, however, traditional canoe transport occasionally provided serious and unforeseen rivalry for the railways, as in the case of the Lagos line, which had difficulty attracting traffic during its first ten years of operation because of competition from canoes on the river Ogun.

West Africa, along with other parts of the world, benefited from modern transport in many of the ways predicted by the classical economists. Freight rates were greatly reduced. In 1909 the cost of head-loading ranged from 3s 1d to 5s per ton/mile on the Gold Coast, depending on the commodities carried. Hand carts and cask rolling cost from 1s 2½d to 1s 11d. The charge by rail averaged 11¼d in 1903, but dropped to between 4d and 7½d in the 1920s, while the motor lorry cost as little as 3d per ton/mile in 1930. These dramatic reductions had two main effects. First, in substituting machinery for human power, modern transport encouraged a more efficient combination of factors of production by releasing scarce labour resources for other employment, by increasing mobility, and by spreading information about market opportunities. Europeans moved into the interior; Africans travelled to cocoa and groundnut farms, and to the towns. Second, the fall in the cost of transport was an external economy which accelerated the expansion of the export sector by making production profitable over a wider area and for a larger number of farmers, and which permitted the development of new resources, such as the coal deposits found near Udi in eastern Nigeria in 1909. Railways and roads pushed back and reshaped the traditional frontiers of trade. The arrival of the Lagos railway at Kano in 1911, for example, was an event of great significance in African commercial history. It marked the final decline of the old, north-facing, trans-Saharan trade, the reorientation of the markets of the interior towards the coastal ports, and the coalescence of two centres of exchange which, in previous centuries, had been in only sporadic contact with each other.

The foregoing assessment of the impact of modern transport requires qualification, both to avoid the sweeping character of traditional interpretations, which have tended to follow the spirit of Lord Lugard's pronouncement on this subject, and to take account of recent research, such as Fogel's study of North America, which has shown that the importance of railways in economic development can easily be exaggerated.[21] Four main reservations should be borne in mind in the case of West Africa. In the first place, generalisations about the effects of modern transport often refer, at least by implication, to the area as a whole. Yet Liberia had no harbour or motor roads until the 1940s, and no railway until the 1950s. Large parts of the interior of former French West Africa are still without modern transport today. The benefits of modern transport were felt most strongly in a few territories, notably the Gold Coast, Nigeria and Senegal, whose resources were large enough for them to invest in a modern infrastructure. Once again the point emerges that the regional effects of colonial economic development were very varied. Secondly, it is a mistake to think of modern transport as creating an export economy out of nothing. Most of the leading exports were being shipped abroad *before* the introduction of railways and motor transport. Indeed, it can be said that modern transport was attracted primarily to regions which, though still full of uncertainties, had already begun to demonstrate their economic potential.[22] Thirdly, the provision of modern transport did not guarantee an automatic and dramatic expansion of exports. In Dahomey railways had relatively little impact, while in Nigeria long stretches of track were unsuccessful, either because they passed through barren land, or because freight rates on certain products were too high. Finally, it should be remembered that communications were designed mainly to evacuate exports. There were few lateral or inter-colonial links, and little attempt was made to use railways and roads as a stimulus to internal exchange.

The distributive system associated with overseas trade changed considerably during the first phase of colonial rule. Discussion of these changes has to proceed cautiously, however, for they have long been the subject of a political and economic controversy concerning the role of the expatriate firms. This debate owes much of its longevity to a lack of hard evidence, for conjecture thrives where refutation is impossible, and assertions, if repeated often enough, eventually assume the dignity and title of facts.[23] The analysis presented here has three aims: first, to outline the main changes affecting the expatriate commercial houses; second, to explain why they occurred; and third, to consider their effects on African firms.

The most striking changes involved innovations in geographical location and commercial structure. The expatriate firms, which had been situated on the coast ever since overseas trade with West Africa began, started to move inland in numbers in the 1890s. They were carried into the interior by the railway, and they travelled in the wake of the administration, having become the willing camp followers of

[21] Robert W. Fogel, *Railroads and American Economic Growth: Essays in Econometric History*, Baltimore 1964.

[22] In this respect the West African case was similar to that of Colombia, where economic growth began before the appearance of modern transport facilities. See Everett E. Hagen, *On the Theory of Social Change: How Economic Growth Begins*, Homewood 1962, p. 363.

[23] Two exceptional, pioneering studies must be mentioned, as they have both tried to disentangle fact and fiction: J. Mars, 'Extra-Territorial Enterprises' in *Mining, Commerce, and Finance in Nigeria*, ed. M. Perham, 1948, pp. 43–136, and P. T. Bauer, *West African Trade*, Cambridge 1954.

those they had roused to action. By the 1920s the leading firms had branches in the main centres of trade throughout West Africa.[24] Structural changes were of two kinds. First, the expatriate firms, from being relatively small concerns dominated by one man or by a partership, began to form limited liability companies. A few of many possible examples will suffice to illustrate this development, which began at the close of the nineteenth century: John Holt & Co. became a limited company in 1897; Cheri Peyrissac in 1908; R. & W. King, founded at the close of the seventeenth century, followed suit in 1911; and Maurel et Prom in 1919. Second, there was a move towards concentration. Many small businesses were eliminated, and the survivors amalgamated to produce a handful of very large firms. This trend was already apparent in the 1880s, and it developed still further during the first phase of colonial rule, until by 1930 there were three outstanding firms (the United Africa Company, the Compagnie Française de l'Afrique Occidentale, and the Société Commerciale de l'Ouest Africain). Between them these giants handled roughly two-thirds to three-quarters of West Africa's overseas trade, and their commercial network may be compared in size and importance with the administrative system operated by the colonial powers. Indeed, sometimes the 'District Officer' of U.A.C. had more local influence (and was certainly better paid) than the 'branch manager' of His Majesty's Government.

The most prominent of the three firms was the United Africa Company, which alone handled nearly half of West Africa's overseas trade in the 1930s. U.A.C. dominated British West Africa, and its subsidiaries bought and shipped about a quarter of the principal exports of French West Africa. U.A.C. was the weighty offspring of two sizeable parents; the Royal Niger Company, which was formed in 1886, and the African Association, which was established three years later. Although the Niger Company lost its royal charter in 1900, it continued to trade on a large scale, and in 1920 was bought by W. H. Lever, the soap magnate, for £8 million. The African Association survived until 1919, when it merged with Miller Bros and F. & A. Swanzy to form the African & Eastern Trade Corporation Ltd. In 1920 Lever just failed in a bid to buy this company too, but in 1929 the African and Eastern came to an agreement with Lever Bros., and the result was the formation of a gigantic combine known as U.A.C. The next most important firm was the Compagnie Française de l'Afrique Occidentale, which was established in 1887. C.F.A.O. also had a long West African ancestry, being descended from the Compagnie du Sénégal (1881), which was itself heir to the Marseilles house of C. A. Verminck, whose West African interests dated back to the 1840s. The third large firm, the Société Commerciale de l'Ouest Africain, was created in 1907 by a Swiss and French consortium out of another established West African concern, Ryff, Roth et Cie. S.C.O.A. had less than half the capital and far fewer branches than C.F.A.O. when it started, but overtook its rival after the Second World War. Good business histories of these three firms, which are still the leading expatriate trading concerns in West Africa today,

[24] For a contemporary guide to the expatriate firms, see A. Macmillan, *The Red Book of West Africa*, 1920.

would help to resolve the controversy which has long surrounded their activities.[25]

The chief survivors among the smaller firms were John Holt, Paterson Zochonis, Maurel et Prom, and Peyrissac. Of the few newcomers to West African trade, the most significant (apart from specialist firms like Cadbury Bros and the mining companies) were those customarily referred to as Levantines, a term which covers nationals from a large number of countries bordering the eastern Mediterranean. Levantine migrants, especially Lebanese, began settling in West Africa at the close of the nineteenth century. Most of them had originally planned to go to America, but for various reasons they failed to progress further west than the African coast. By 1929 there were just over 3,000 Levantines in French West Africa, and a slightly smaller number in the British colonies. These immigrants began trading in a small way, but because they were enterprising, low-cost operators they quickly achieved success in certain fields. They first made their mark in Guinea, where they started a boom in rubber exports in 1898. By paying in cash, they put an end to barter and forced a number of European firms out of business. Subsequently, they bought other export crops, such as groundnuts and cocoa, and sold cotton goods. In the 1920s and 1930s they spread into motor transport, and also ran hotels and restaurants. Their numbers continued to increase, and they remain important today.[26] The Levantines, though not beyond criticism, have often been treated with unjustified hostility by Europeans and Africans. Theirs is a misfortune commonly experienced by aliens who lack political influence.

It is worth noting that a high degree of concentration was also apparent in banking and shipping. Unlike the commercial firms, however, banking and shipping interests were never very numerous. The leading companies owed their positions less to successful take-overs, and more to government support, at least at the outset. The steamship companies received subsidies, and the banks were given monopolistic rights over currency issues. The result was that a few, privileged firms were able to achieve an almost unassailable ascendancy. In 1890 the British shipping companies serving the West Coast were brought fully under the control of A. L. Jones's firm, Elder, Dempster & Co. Ltd.[27] Jones's fleets increased from 35 vessels totalling 53,000 tons in 1884 to 101 vessels totalling 301,000 tons in 1909, the year of his death. French shipping became concentrated on two Marseilles companies, Chargeurs Réunis, and its smaller associate, Fabre et Fraissinet, both of which had financial and managerial links with C.F.A.O. In 1895 Elder, Dempster and the leading German

[25] A certain amount of information on U.A.C. can be found in Charles Wilson's *The History of Unilever*, 2 vols, 1954, and *Unilever, 1945–1965*, 1968. A descriptive account of the operations of the French firms is given in Jean and René Charbonneau, *Marchés et marchands d'Afrique noire*, Paris 1961.

[26] For further information, see Fuad I. Khuri, 'Kinship, Emigration, and Trade Partnership among the Lebanese of West Africa', *Africa*, 35, 1965, pp. 385–95, and William R. Stanley, 'The Lebanese in Sierra Leone: Entrepreneurs Extraordinary', *African Urban Notes*, 5, 1970, pp. 159–74.

[27] P. N. Davies, 'The African Steam Ship Company', in *Liverpool and Merseyside*, ed. J. R. Harris, 1969, pp. 212–38.

firm, Woermann Linie, reached an agreement which limited competition between them and established a joint policy towards newcomers. The French firms were not associated with this agreement because they did not compete on the same routes as the larger English and German companies. The shipping 'conference' (as such arrangements are called) enabled the two major firms to control the bulk of the West African shipping trade. Their principal weapon was the deferred rebate system, by which shippers who agreed to use only conference vessels received a refund on a proportion of their freight payments. The rebate was paid retrospectively to prevent those of wavering loyalty from switching to another line. The conference was suspended during the First World War, but it was reconstituted in 1924, and was not challenged with any measure of success until the 1930s, when U.A.C. began to run ocean-going vessels of its own.[28]

Commercial banking was dominated in the British territories by the Bank of British West Africa (1894), and in the French colonies by the Banque de l'Afrique Occidentale (1901). Not until the arrival of Barclays Bank (Dominion, Colonial & Overseas) in 1926 was there a serious threat to the position of B.B.W.A. Even so, rivalry between the two banks was limited by mutual understandings of the kind which habitually restrain members of the professions from competing too fiercely with each other.

The foregoing developments are best explained as a response to changes in the commercial environment between 1880 and 1930. Essentially, the conversion to limited liability and the emergence of a few large firms were results of the need both to conserve and to augment commercial capital. Between 1870 and 1936 nearly £50 million was invested in West Africa by private foreign interests. Most of this money was contributed by trading firms, and, understandably, virtually all of it went into commerce. The need to safeguard existing investments by eliminating competition was an important motive for amalgamation during times of unsatisfactory trade, as in the 1880s and 1920s. These periods were also characterised by temporary 'cease-fire' arrangements. The export firms, for example, would often agree to share total purchases on the basis of their past performance. Pooling agreements of this kind nearly always broke down when trading conditions improved, and when member firms decided that they could do better on their own. The need to increase capital came with the geographical advance of the expatriate firms, which was itself a product of the adverse conditions of the late nineteenth century. At a time when profit margins on traditional staples had been greatly reduced, expansion inland was necessary to secure a larger turnover, and to capture a share in any new, and more profitable, trade that might be developed. However, expansion could not be achieved without mobilising more funds than the average expatriate firm in West Africa had at its disposal. Hence the trend towards company formation and amalgamation, a trend which continued in times of prosperity, as during the years 1900–1914, as well as in periods of depression.

[28] For further details, see Charlotte Leubuscher, *The West African Shipping Trade, 1909–1959*, Leyden 1963, chs 3 and 4.

Larger firms had a number of important advantages over their smaller competitors. First, they could afford to establish branches in the interior, and to employ a greater number of skilled, but costly, expatriate staff. Second, they had the resources to finance the activities of an increased number of enterprising, but impecunious, indigenous traders, who were to play an important part in the colonial economy. Third, they had the capacity to finance stocks over a long period of time, for the scattered nature of the market in West Africa, as well as its distance from Europe, meant that turnover was habitually slow. Fourth, they could withstand sudden fluctuations in overseas trade, as occurred in 1919–1920 and 1929–1934, more easily than could small firms. Fifth, by integrating horizontally (by acquiring other trading firms) and vertically (by acquiring interests in shipping and manufacturing), the larger firms could exert a greater degree of influence over the trade as a whole. Sixth, they benefited from economies of scale: for example, by placing bulk orders they were able to buy manufactured goods more cheaply than their rivals, and they were also in a position to secure sole agencies with respect to particular brands. Finally, the large firms could count on a considerable amount of government co-operation as far as their local interests were concerned. The administration, though formally neutral in such matters, in practice showed a preference for dealing with a few, established, expatriate companies. Colonialism thus created a new 'moral community' of traders, the higher echelons of which were staffed by a small group of men who shared a common nationality, religion and social background.

Conflicting arguments concerning the role of the expatriate trading firms have long been current. On the one hand, these firms have been accused of exploitation, a charge that has rarely been closely defined, and is certainly difficult to analyse. On the other hand, the expatriate firms have complained about African traders, alleging that there were too many of them, and that their presence reduced the profits not only of the large firms themselves, but of African producers as well.

The idea of exploitation revolves around two recurrent themes: first, that the large firms made excessive profits; and second, that they eliminated an emerging generation of African merchants. At its most extreme, the view that the expatriate firms were able to make excessive profits is based on the notion that they had complete control of the market, both in Europe and in Africa. Strictly speaking, this is incorrect. Important though they were, the large commercial firms took world prices for produce as given; their profit lay in their ability to adjust their own prices (and costs) accordingly. However, the large firms did not have complete control over the African market either. Technically, it was not a monopoly which existed, but an oligopoly, that is a situation in which the market was dominated by a few competing firms. The scope for excessive profits was narrower than is sometimes assumed. African producers and consumers may well have benefited from competition among the expatriate firms, from the economies of scale which they were able to achieve, and from the regularity and continuity of service which they could offer. All the same, it is undeniable that oligopoly was closer to monopoly than it was to perfect competition, and it is also true that the large firms regarded concentration as being primarily in their own interests. John Mars, in a detailed study of the operations of expatriate enterprises in the 1930s, has shown that in certain areas and on specific commodities the large firms were occasionally able to make profits which were excessive in relation to what would have been obtained had there been greater competition.[29] On the rare occasions when competition was fully effective, as when Saul Raccah broke into the Nigerian groundnut trade in the 1930s, the farmer received a higher price for his produce.[30] Whether this example can be generalised for the trade as a whole, and over a longer period of time, is an interesting counter-factual proposition, though not one that would be easy to test.

In assessing the role of the expatriate firms it is important to distinguish between two different questions: first, what would the economic situation of West Africa have been without these companies; and second, how does their performance compare with the optimum contribution which might have been made? With regard to the first question, the chief functions of the expatriate firms were to provide and display the consumer goods which were the main incentive to export production, and to ensure that exports were marketed in the industrial countries. In carrying out these activities they incurred risks in holding stocks and promising future deliveries, and they also financed the operations of many African traders. Without the expatriate firms there would have been less investment in commerce, less expertise in international markets, and a much smaller foreign trade sector. As to the second question, it is clear that the record of the expatriate concerns fell short of what was theoretically possible. Once established, the large firms became conservative in outlook. They were concerned more to defend their existing positions than to open up new fields of enterprise. For example, down to the 1950s they showed little interest in developing local industries, partly because this was, in any case, a difficult task, and partly because they did not want to tackle unfamiliar projects.[31] The large firms also did little to encourage training in modern business management. Africans had to acquire the necessary skills on their own, and, in the event, slowly. Furthermore, it is at least an arguable probability that greater competition would have given Africans a rather better deal in terms of the prices they received for produce and paid for consumer goods. Finally, there is no doubt that a large proportion of trading profits, surplus funds and expatriate salaries were transferred abroad instead of being invested in Africa.

The position of African businessmen under colonialism was not quite as simple as it has often been made to appear. The main trends in the fortunes of indigenous import and export firms were as follows. African merchants were able to flourish during the period 1850–1880 because trading conditions at that time gave no overwhelming advantage to large firms. The restricted size of the market, the introduction of cash payments, and the advent of the steamer were circumstances which enabled small firms to achieve a considerable degree of success. From the 1880s

[29] 'Extra-Territorial Enterprises', in *Mining, Commerce, and Finance in Nigeria*, ed. M. Perham, 1948, pp. 76–87.
[30] For an outline of Raccah's career see Hancock, *Survey of British Commonwealth Affairs*, II, part 2, pp. 216–17.
[31] This question is considered in greater detail in Chapter 7.

onwards the commercial environment began to favour large firms, and many smaller concerns, European as well as African, found that they lacked the capital and skills to survive. African merchants did not give up easily, however, and by the 1920s they, too, were experimenting with company formation in an attempt to mobilise more capital. But by then the large expatriate concerns had established almost total dominance, and thereafter small firms, whatever their nationality, found the barriers to entry almost insurmountable. The two successful attempts which are often quoted were made by Levantines, not by Africans: Saul Raccah won a sizeable share of the Nigerian groundnut trade in the 1930s, and A. G. Leventis broke into the Gold Coast import and export trade during the Second World War.[32] These men found a space for themselves at the point where the economies of scale enjoyed by the large firms were outweighed by the diseconomies which resulted from the comprehensive and relatively unspecialised nature of their business. That is to say, the newcomers began by exploiting particular markets and specific lines of goods; they were in a position to make decisions on the spot instead of having to refer matters to a head office in Europe; and they were able to match pioneer aggression against an established, bureaucratic outlook. However, these exceptions, being so few in number, prove the rule, for Raccah and Leventis were particularly skilled, highly motivated and adventurous businessmen.

The conclusions which can be derived from this survey of changing business fortunes need to be stated carefully. In the first place, it is likely that African import and export firms suffered a decline in the proportion of overseas trade which they handled, at least as far as the established staples were concerned. However, the extent of this decline should not be exaggerated, for the European firms already dominated the trade of the main ports in the period 1850–1880—a fact that is not always emphasised. In terms of value, on the other hand, the external trade in African hands was probably greater in the 1920s than it had been in the mid-nineteenth century. What happened was that all groups gained from the expansion of trade during the first phase of colonial rule, but that the expatriate firms gained relatively more than the indigenous firms. Secondly, it is misleading to point to the decline of Africans in the traditional import and export trades without at the same time recognising their enterprise in other branches of commerce. Many Africans were astute enough to realise that their best course lay in developing new types of trade rather than in trying to compete with the large two-way firms. In Nigeria, for example, Africans were the first to import and operate commercial motor vehicles, to market sewing machines, to build cinemas, and to establish a bread-making industry. Thirdly, it is important to remember that externally-induced changes in the economic environment were only partly responsible for the shift in the relative positions of expatriate and indigenous firms. Internal structural weaknesses, such as the existence of inheritance laws which made it hard to keep an African business together after the death of its founder, were also very significant.

Considerable disagreement also exists over the fortunes of the African middlemen,

---

[32] On Leventis see Bauer, *West African Trade*, pp. 79–86.

the intermediaries who linked producers and consumers to the import and export firms. Some sources claim that the middlemen were swept away at the close of the nineteenth century; others give prominence to the attacks made on them by expatriate firms in the 1930s! The first claim has arisen mainly because undue attention has been paid to the downfall of a few prominent individuals, such as Ja Ja and Nana Olomu, who ran big trading monopolies in the nineteenth century, while the activities of an expanding number of smaller traders in the twentieth century have been largely ignored. Studies by Gertzel and Ikime have made it clear that, in southern Nigeria anyway, many expatriate firms were quick to realise that they could not afford to disrupt the indigenous distributive system completely.[33] The expansion of the market in the period 1900–1930 was made possible not only by the movement inland of the expatriate firms, but also by an increase in the number of African intermediaries. In 1908 the manager of Lagos Stores Ltd, which had several branches in the interior of Nigeria, estimated that less than one per cent of his firm's total trade was transacted with the final consumer.[34] The census figures for the large towns in West Africa confirm that trade was an expanding occupation, not a declining one.

The life of Omu Okwei (1872–1943), a prominent woman trader in Onitsha, provides an interesting example of indigenous enterprise during this less publicised phase of African commercial history in the period following the decline of the great middlemen of the nineteenth century.[35] Omu Okwei's trading career was greatly helped by the inland advance of the expatriate firms after 1900. She developed close commercial relations with the Niger Company, selling palm produce to the company and retailing imported goods. By 1910 her business had grown to the point where she was allowed credit of £400 a month. By the 1920s she was diversifying her interests, putting money into property, investing in lorries and canoes, and making cash advances to other traders. At her death she left a small fortune, which included twenty-four houses in Onitsha and about £5,000 in the bank. Omu Okwei's career serves as a reminder of the presence and influence of women traders in West Africa, and as a particular illustration of the proposition that colonialism, having destroyed some of the great figures of the nineteenth century, helped to create new opportunities for at least some sections of the indigenous population.

In short, the middlemen lost the political power which formerly they had used to support their market demands, and they also had to adapt to new developments, such as the coming of the railway, but as a group they survived. However, contrary to the allegations of expatriate officials and merchants, the continued presence of a multiplicity of indigenous traders was not a wasteful allocation of human resources. As Bauer has made clear, the so-called middlemen were highly competitive and

---

[33] Cherry J. Gertzel, 'Relations Between African and European Traders in the Niger Delta, 1880–1896', *Journal of African History*, 3, 1962, pp. 361–6; Obaro Ikime, *Merchant Prince of the Niger Delta*, 1968, pp. 187–8.

[34] C.O. 520/68, Egerton to Crewe, 16 December, 1908, Public Record Office.

[35] For further details see Felicia Ekejuiba, 'Omu Okwei, the Merchant Queen of Ossomari: a Biographical Sketch', *Journal of the Historical Society of Nigeria*, 3, 1967, pp. 633–46.

generally efficient channels of collection and distribution.[36] The idea of direct trade with the producers, though appealing at a time when expatriate firms were trying to cut their costs, was an economic fantasy. In a situation where producers and consumers were both numerous and scattered, abolishing the middlemen would have meant reducing the size of the market.

The last of the external influences to require examination is the colonial monetary system. As noted in Chapter 4, the decline of transitional currencies and the spread of British and French coins date from about the middle of the nineteenth century. Thus the introduction of the colonial monetary system was not a sudden event. Once again, the role of the colonial authorities was to speed a process which was already under way. The administrations encouraged the adoption of modern money in three ways: by demonetising transitional currencies; by paying its expanding labour force in European coin; and by insisting on receiving taxes in cash rather than in kind. Some of the expatriate firms were also keen to see a cash trade develop, but others clung to barter for as long as possible. The Niger Company, for example, did not conduct a cash trade until after about 1905. The most potent agents of change were Africans themselves, especially the new generation of small export producers who realised that cash transactions would enable them to strike a better bargain. By about 1910 European currencies were widespread in West Africa. In the period 1906–1910 exports of sterling silver to British West Africa averaged £666,190 per annum, which was almost as much as was issued for the United Kingdom itself. Naturally, there were some areas which continued to use transitional currencies for local transactions during the greater part of the colonial period. Perhaps the best example was eastern Nigeria, where the government's decision to ban further imports of manillas in 1902 inadvertently had the effect of stabilising their value. In 1948–1949, when manillas were finally called in, no less than 30 million were collected![37]

The increasing circulation of European currencies led to the introduction of modern banking institutions. The first successful bank in West Africa was the Banque du Sénégal, which was established at St Louis in 1854. This bank was founded primarily to assist the development of legitimate commerce, and specifically to handle compensation payments to former slave owners following the abolition of slavery in the French empire in 1848. In 1901 the Banque du Sénégal was replaced by the Banque de l'Afrique Occidentale. B.A.O., which was designed to serve the wider area that had just been brought under French rule, was the most important bank in French West Africa during the colonial period. Towards the close of the nineteenth century several attempts were made to set up banks in the British possessions, notably in Sierra Leone and the southern part of Nigeria, but none was successful until 1894, when a group of businessmen headed by A. L. Jones, the shipping magnate, founded the Bank of British West Africa. B.B.W.A. expanded

[36] Bauer, *West African Trade*, pp. 22–34. The general point remains, even though Bauer may well have over-emphasised the extent of competition among African traders.

[37] United Africa Company, 'The Manilla Problem', *Statistical and Economic Review*, 3, 1949, pp. 44–56.

rapidly. By 1910 it had established branches in most of the leading commercial centres in the British colonies, as well as in Monrovia, the capital of Liberia. The bank's paid up capital, a mere £12,000 in 1894, had grown to £200,000; the number of its employees had increased from six to 114; its depositors from a few dozen to 4,410; and its deposits from about £30,000 to just over £1 million. B.B.W.A., though joined by a second large and successful expatriate bank, Barclays (D.C. & O.), in 1926, remained the leading bank in British West Africa throughout the colonial period.

The largely unplanned infiltration of an underdeveloped region by an advanced monetary system was a global phenomenon in the nineteenth century. The expansion of international trade and the adoption of the gold standard among the industrial powers had repercussions in India, Ceylon, Australia, Indo-China, Puerto Rico, Mexico and the Philippines—to list just some of the leading examples. It was also a process that gave rise to a number of problems. In West Africa these included the provision of satisfactory controls over the supply and repatriation of currency; the equitable division of seignorage (the difference between the bullion value and the face value of the coinage) between the metropolis and the colonies; and the maintenance of adequate reserves for currencies circulating in the colonies.[38]

The French dealt with these problems by utilising an existing private institution, the Banque de l'Afrique Occidentale, and subjecting it to an increasing degree of government control.[39] In 1901 B.A.O. was granted the privilege of becoming the sole bank of issue for French West Africa. In return, it had to make some financial contribution both to the metropolis and to the colonies; it had to ensure that currency circulating in French West Africa was freely convertible with the metropolitan franc;[40] and it had to maintain a specified ratio between reserves and currency issues. These arrangements, which were evolved between 1901 and 1929, remained substantially unchanged until 1945, when the franc zone was created and a separate currency issued for the colonies. B.A.O. continued to preside over the French West African monetary system until 1955, when a new public institution with some of the powers of a central bank was set up to handle the issue of currency. Thereafter, B.A.O. confined its activities to commercial banking, and it also lost ground to newer competitors. Between 1894 and 1911 the British also used a commercial bank, the Bank of British West Africa, as the sole bank of issue. In 1911, however, the Colonial Office and the Treasury decided that the difficulties experienced by the haphazard expansion of sterling in West Africa were best solved by creating a separate colonial currency and by establishing a new, independent institution. The outcome was the foundation of the West African Currency Board in 1912. The

---

[38] These questions are discussed further in A. G. Hopkins, 'The Creation of a Colonial Monetary System: The Origins of the West African Currency Board', *African Historical Studies*, 3, 1970, pp. 101–32.

[39] There is no satisfactory study of the colonial monetary system in French West Africa. A certain amount of historical information can be found in M. Leduc, *'Les institutions monétaires africaines: pays francophones*, Paris 1965.

[40] In practice, there was no problem of convertibility until after 1945.

W.A.C.B. supervised the issue of the new colonial currency; it managed the reserves (gold and securities); it invested and distributed the profits arising out of the introduction of the colonial currency; and it acted as a large scale money-changer, converting the colonial currency into sterling and vice versa. This system survived virtually intact until the time of independence.

Although the institutional mechanisms adopted by France and Britain differed, the operation of the colonial monetary systems was essentially the same. In both cases the monetary system was effectively an extension of that of the major power. It was related closely enough to the metropolitan system to ensure that international trade would not be unsettled by changes in the rates of exchange. At the same time, the colonial monetary system had sufficient independence, by having its own reserves, to avoid involving the parent economy in any additional monetary responsibilities. The system itself was largely self-regulating. The W.A.C.B. and B.A.O. were sole channels of supply, but they had no control over the volume of currency in circulation. In practice, the latter was tied closely to the balance of payments; the currency in circulation and the necessary reserves had to be earned by the colonies, principally through the sale of exports. Thus, the supply of money expanded at a time of boom, and contracted during a slump. Deficits were settled automatically. For example, if a colony had an excess of imports over exports the balance was settled by withdrawing money from local circulation. This reduction in the local money supply lowered incomes in the colony. The result was that imports declined to the point where they were equated with exports once more, though at a lower equilibrium level. In short, money was regarded mainly as a medium of external exchange.

Judged by nineteenth-century principles of sound money, the colonial monetary system had certain points in its favour. In the first place, the operation of the system prevented the colonies from accumulating deficits. Its self-regulating qualities, combined with the colonial tradition of balancing the budget, virtually eliminated the risk of inflation and the danger of a balance of payments crisis. Secondly, because the colonial system had close connections with the metropolis, currencies circulating in the dependencies enjoyed an international reputation and a degree of stability, though the latter advantage was more pronounced in the case of sterling than in the case of the franc. Thirdly, the profits derived from seignorage and from investing the currency reserves gave the colonies some additional revenue which had not been available previously.

The system had also had its limitations.[41] The chief disadvantage was that the growth of the internal exchange economy tended to be inhibited by monetary tightness, except when there was an export surplus. This favourable situation was often short-lived, and always unpredictable. Theoretically, there was nothing in the monetary system to prevent the commercial banks from expanding the money

[41] For a full discussion see two pioneering studies: J. Mars, 'The Monetary and Banking System and the Loan Market of Nigeria', in *Mining, Commerce, and Finance in Nigeria*, ed. M. Perham, 1948, pp. 177–224; and W. T. Newlyn and D. C. Rowan, *Money and Banking in British Colonial Africa*, Oxford 1954.

supply through lending operations, but in practice banking policy was passive, and remained so, as Killick has shown with reference to the Gold Coast, down to the time of independence.[42] Three particular features of banking policy are worth noting in this connection. First, the banks usually invested their money in the metropolis, in the same way as the W.A.C.B. and B.A.O. invested the currency reserves outside the West African colonies. The underdeveloped colonies found themselves loaning money to the advanced countries, principally because of a lack of acceptable local investment opportunities. Second, bank lending policy generally followed the trade cycle by expanding credit during a boom and reducing it at a time of slump. This practice tended to magnify rather than diminish the fluctuations in trade experienced by primary export producers in the colonies. Third, bank loans were confined mainly to the large expatriate firms, thus reinforcing their dominant position in commerce. The banks were willing to accept deposits from Africans, and as early as 1910 £263,000 (about a quarter of B.B.W.A.'s total deposits) belonged to African customers. When it came to borrowing, however, Africans ran into difficulties. They found it hard to present themselves as being personally trustworthy in the eyes of expatriates, and they also faced problems of supplying the kind of security thought normal in Europe, chiefly because indigenous customs regarding the ownership of property often meant that individuals were not free to negotiate mortgages.

The foregoing discussion of government policy, transport, the distributive system, and money and banking has attempted to clarify what might be called the external contribution to the development of the open economy. The main conclusion to emerge, whatever judgements are made about the beneficial or deleterious effects of colonialism, is that the expatriate role was less dynamic and more circumscribed than is often supposed. Within the limits indicated, external influences were important and necessary, but it would be mistaken to conclude that they were sufficient to guarantee an automatic expansion of the export sector. Indeed, it is possible to conceive of circumstances in which the efforts of expatriates might have produced only meagre results. The fact that, with certain regional qualifications, the results were substantial implies that other factors, especially those relating to the responsiveness of African societies, were of critical significance. The remaining task is to assess the nature and extent of the indigenous contribution by focusing on the utilisation of land and labour resources.

2 The African contribution

There is one important preliminary issue which has to be settled, namely, why it was that agricultural production remained almost exclusively in African hands, especially since colonial rule was regarded by its advocates as an agency for modernisation, and modernisation involved a reappraisal of the means of exploiting the natural resources

[42] Tony Killick, 'The Monetary and Financial System', in *A Study of Contemporary Ghana*, 1, *The Economy of Ghana*, ed. Walter Birmingham, I. Neustadt and E. N. Omaboe, 1966, pp. 294–331.

of the region. For reasons outlined in the previous chapter, the limitations imposed on foreign firms in this sector had a profound effect on the course of West African development in the twentieth century. Yet the motives for constraining expatriate enterprise in agriculture have not received serious attention since Professor Hancock published his celebrated *Survey of British Commonwealth Affairs* thirty years ago.[43] Indeed, some recent accounts, in summarising Hancock's views, or views derived ultimately from his work, have tended to oversimplify and distort the issue. It is often suggested that colonial policy towards the alienation of land was fully defined by about 1900, and that the confirmation of African rights was a triumph for the custodians of the humanitarian conscience over powerful commercial interests— the last act of a long-running melodrama which began with the campaign for the abolition of the Atlantic slave trade. Both interpretations require revision.

At the beginning of the colonial period, official policy regarding expatriate participation in production was still very flexible. Had this not been the case, it would be impossible to explain how it was that expatriate interests *did* establish a foothold, though a restricted one, in mining and agriculture. European mining operations in West Africa began in the late 1870s and continued throughout the colonial period. Production was dominated by a few large concerns, such as Ashanti Goldfields Corporation (1897), the Sierra Leone Development Corporation (1929), the Consolidated African Selection Trust (1932)—later the Sierra Leone Selection Trust (1935)—and Amalgamated Tin Mines of Nigeria Ltd (1939). The prominence of expatriate firms in this sector is usually explained by saying that modern mining operations require considerable capital and a high degree of technical skill. Without denying the general truth of this proposition, it is important to point out that in West Africa a number of minerals can be worked on a small scale and without massive financial resources. In these cases it would seem more accurate to explain the prominence of expatriate companies in terms of the need to confer rights in order to encourage prospecting in the first place, and of the convenience of collecting royalties and taxes from a few substantial and reliable concerns. The Nigerian coal mines (near Enugu) were managed by the colonial government, and are interesting not only as an example of an unusual degree of official participation in production, but also because coal was the only local mineral to be used extensively in West Africa instead of being exported. Africans were not completely excluded from mineral production, and small scale indigenous enterprise was found in areas where minerals could be extracted by inexpensive and simple methods, as was the case to some extent with gold, diamonds and tin.

At the turn of the century there was also a reasonable chance that extensive, foreign-owned plantations would be established in West Africa. French firms received substantial concessions in the Ivory Coast in the 1890s and in Dahomey in 1901. German merchants established plantations in Togo and, on a larger scale, in the Cameroons in the 1890s. In 1913 there were 58 plantations in the Cameroons covering an area of about 75,000 square miles and employing 18,000 African workers. In British West Africa a few expatriate plantations were established on the

[43] II, part 2, 1942, pp. 175–200.

Gold Coast (near Accra) and in southern Nigeria (in the Lagos hinterland) at the turn of the century. The British Cotton Growing Association (1902) advanced plans for planting and ginning operations, and W. H. Lever, the Liverpool soap and margarine magnate, mounted a powerful campaign in favour of plantations in West Africa. This campaign, which began in 1906, came near to success after the First World War, but ended with Lever's death in 1925.

The demand for plantations arose during the trade depression of the late nineteenth century, and was revived whenever expatriate business interests felt their prosperity and security threatened by the commercial fluctuations of the early colonial period. Plantations, so it was claimed, would be highly efficient, and would produce a greater yield per tree as well as better quality produce. For a manufacturer like Lever they were also a means of regulating supplies and controlling the cost of raw materials. The campaign for plantations received a degree of official backing which made it respectable, and consequently influential, in government circles. In British West Africa, Lord Lugard and Governor Slater of Sierra Leone both showed some sympathy with Lever's petitions in the 1920s, and at least two Colonial Secretaries, Harcourt and Ormsby-Gore, were prepared to consider the case with more than formal interest. Their concern was not simply a response to Lever's pressure, but arose out of a fear that the greater technical efficiency achieved by plantation developments in other parts of the world would make it impossible for indigenous producers in West Africa to compete in international markets. Their attitude shows that British policy at least was not clearly laid down right at the start of the colonial era.

Nevertheless, the planters' frontier made little headway in West Africa. In the French territories concessions were limited shortly after the turn of the century, and some were cancelled altogether. The only plantations worth noting were those in the southern part of the Ivory Coast.[44] These expanded briefly in the 1920s, but declined rapidly after the Second World War. By 1955 little more than 200 French planters remained, and they produced only a very small proportion of total exports. In German West Africa the initial rate of expansion was not maintained, and plantation development was brought to a halt by the First World War.[45] In British West Africa the oil mills which Lever had been allowed to start in Sierra Leone proved unsuccessful, his more ambitious plans for palm oil plantations were frustrated, and he was forced to transfer his interest to the Congo, where the Belgian government adopted a more generous approach to the distribution of African land. Lever fulminated against the backwardness of indigenous methods of extracting

[44] H. Frechou, 'Les plantations européennes en Côte d'Ivoire', *Cahiers d'Outre-Mer*, 8, 1955, pp. 56–83. A small number of banana plantations were established in French Guinea in the 1930s.

[45] After the First World War the plantations were run by Britain under the mandate of the League of Nations. They reverted to Germany in the 1920s, but were taken over again by Britain after the Second World War. See S. H. Bederman, 'Plantation Agriculture in Victoria Division, West Cameroons: an Historical Introduction', *Geography*, 51, 1966, pp. 349–60, and, for a study of the operation of these plantations, E. Ardener, S. Ardener, and W. A. Warmington, *Plantation and Village in the Cameroons*, 1960.

palm oil, but these methods, though technically inferior, had overall advantages which expatriates found hard to match.[46] Ironically, the one area where expatriate plantations did become important was Liberia, the only politically independent state in West Africa. The Liberian economy had limped along from crisis to crisis since the second half of the nineteenth century, unable to find a permanently successful export, and accumulating a number of external debts. By the 1920s it was clear that a substantial injection of foreign capital was needed to retrieve the situation, and in 1926 the government leased one million acres to a large American firm, the Firestone Rubber Company, for a term of 99 years.[47] Rubber exports began to expand in the late 1930s, and by 1950 accounted for about 90 per cent of the value of all Liberia's exports.

The reasons why the colonial powers decided to limit foreign concessions in West Africa are more complex than is usually thought. To start with, it is necessary to dispose of two traditional explanations which have long camouflaged more important influences. In the first place, it is often said that plantations failed to become established in West Africa because the climate was unsuitable for white settlers. There is no force in this argument. The alleged unhealthiness of the tropics did not prevent the establishment of European plantations in the Belgian Congo, French Equatorial Africa, or Malaya, and it did not discourage serious applicants in West Africa either. Furthermore, the control of malaria and other tropical diseases was becoming more effective by the start of the twentieth century, and the so-called White Man's Grave was beginning to lose some of its unsavoury reputation.[48] Secondly, in the case of the British colonies it has been argued that the government was committed by its policy of trusteeship to maintaining the land in African hands. This is an unsatisfactory explanation because trusteeship was an eclectic concept, at least as far as means were concerned. The Dutch, for example, had a policy of trusteeship which was used to justify the introduction of plantations into Indonesia; Britain, too, was prepared to permit plantation developments in certain parts of the empire; and substantial concessions were granted in French Equatorial Africa.[49] The problem cannot be solved simply by a general reference to the notion of the dual mandate: the question that has to be answered is why trusteeship took the particular form it did in West Africa.

There were four main reasons why Europeans failed to play a dominant part in the production of West African exports. The first reason relates specifically to minerals; the remaining three concern agricultural production. In the case of mineral resources considerable weight must be given to a fortuitous geological fact,

[46] Peter Kilby, *Industrialization in an Open Economy: Nigeria 1945–1966*, Cambridge 1969, pp. 146–68.

[47] Firestone's, of course, had its own reasons for entering Liberia. For further information see the items by Brown, McLaughlin and Taylor listed in the bibliography.

[48] Raymond E. Dumett, 'The Campaign against Malaria and the Expansion of Scientific, Medical and Sanitary Services in British West Africa, 1898–1910', *African Historical Studies*, 1, 1968, pp. 153–97.

[49] S. Amin and C. Coquéry-Vidrovitch, *Histoire économique du Congo, 1880–1968*, Dakar 1970, part 1.

namely that known and commercially exploitable deposits were not distributed profusely throughout West Africa. Had the gold mining boom of 1899–1902 lasted beyond the Boer War, and had many other mineral resources been found about the same time, then the economic history of West Africa might well have taken a very different course. It is conceivable that trusteeship would have been interpreted in a way which was more favourable to expatriate interests, for it would have been hard to resist the argument that European capital and skill were needed to benefit Africans as well as Europeans. The discovery of iron and diamonds in Sierra Leone in the 1930s, and their exploitation by expatriate firms, is an exceptional case which supports this hypothesis.

Of the three reasons why expatriate plantations were of little significance in West Africa, two have been almost entirely ignored, and the third needs to be given greater emphasis than it has in the past. First, it is important to appreciate that the planters' frontier was held back partly by strong opposition from established trading interests. Many of those who pressed for agricultural concessions, men such as Verdier and Lever, were also engaged in buying, shipping and selling produce. Other expatriate traders who lacked either the capital or the inclination to enter production feared that their more adventurous rivals would be in a position to under-cut them by a considerable margin and to establish a monopoly over the supply of export crops. This anxiety explains why German traders opposed concessions in Togo, why C.F.A.O. was hostile to plantations in French West Africa, and why Manchester and Liverpool traders mounted a powerful campaign in opposition to Lever's demands between 1906 and 1920. In the latter year Lever bought up the Niger Company and with it much of the opposition to his schemes. Neverthe-less, the profound split among expatriate business interests in West Africa undoubtedly did much to weaken the case put forward by those who wished to see extensive European plantations established in that part of the continent.

The second and equally neglected reason is that the few European plantations which were established in colonial West Africa nearly all failed. They started with two serious drawbacks, a considerable ignorance of tropical conditions and a notable lack of capital, which had also characterised previous experiments during the era of legitimate commerce. These handicaps often proved fatal at the outset. Even if they were overcome, two more problems arose almost immediately. The first was a shortage of labour, which also meant that wages had to be relatively high. The second problem was that plantations, being highly specialised, were particularly susceptible to shifts in world supply. Many of the early expatriate planters in West Africa committed themselves heavily to coffee production, and were eliminated by competition from South America soon after the turn of the century. Both problems are illustrated by the history of French plantations on the Ivory Coast, which survived in the second half of the colonial period only because they received large subsidies in the form of forced labour and tariff preference. The record of expatriate plantations in the West African colonies was scarcely one to encourage either a very widespread demand for concessions, or wholehearted government support for European adventures in African agriculture.

The third reason is perhaps more obvious, but it still needs to be stressed. It is that by the time controversy over concessions was at its height, Africans had already succeeded in generating an export economy by their own efforts. Exports of palm products recovered from the difficulties of the 1880s and 1890s, and expanded after the turn of the century; the Gold Coast cocoa industry had become the largest in the world by 1910; and groundnuts, long established as the main export staple in Senegambia, and in any case not suited to plantation production, had become very important in northern Nigeria by 1914. Peasant production had proved itself; plantations had not. Furthermore, plantations were bound to interfere with traditional land rights, and to lead to disputes over labour recruitment. Both matters were guaranteed to arouse widespread protests from Africans. Their hostility could easily find political expression, and so threaten the colonial authorities and colonial rule itself. This evidence, and its implications, proved decisive. The French gave their backing to indigenous farmers in West Africa specifically to avoid the complications which expatriate enterprise had brought in Algeria and Indo-China, and the majority of British officials, led by Clifford, the influential Governor of the Gold Coast (1912–1919) and Nigeria (1919–1925), agreed to a similar course of action. In Chapter 4 it was argued that the nineteenth century saw the rise of a new generation of export producers, and that the partition of West Africa was motivated partly by the need to create an economic environment which would allow them to flourish. In restricting the planters' frontier in West Africa, and in supporting African producers, the colonial powers were carrying nineteenth-century policy to a fruitful conclusion.

The foregoing argument can be summarised in three statements. First, official policy towards concessions was not settled by 1900, but evolved gradually during the initial phase of colonial rule. Second, the controversy was not simply between enlightened, liberal civil servants on the one hand, and the 'soap boilers of the world', as Hancock called them, on the other, but between combinations of various interests with officials and businessmen represented on both sides. Third, to understand why expatriate plantations were unimportant in West Africa it is necessary to focus not on climatic or vaguely humanitarian explanations, but on the failure rate among those plantations which were established, on the ability of the indigenous society to produce the required exports, and on the relative strengths of expatriate traders and expatriate planters. The hypothesis advanced here is that expatriate plantations were more likely to become established in parts of the tropics where opposition from traders was non-existent or ineffective, and where peasant exports were slow to respond to external demands.

To these three statements may be added a final comment about the wisdom of the policy adopted by the colonial powers. Some writers have argued that by preventing the development of a free market in land the authorities deprived the community of the benefits which would have arisen from a more efficient utilisation of resources.[50] This criticism is open to question. It fails to appreciate that policy was fluid enough at

[50] For example, F. J. Pedler, *Economic Geography of West Africa*, 1955, pp. 38–9.

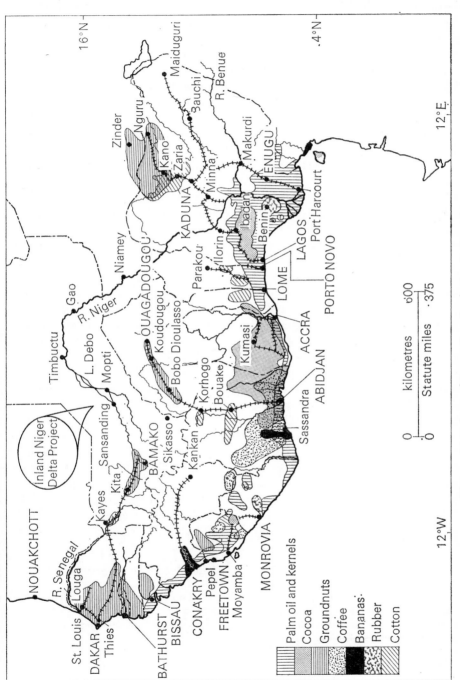

MAP 13. Main Areas of Export Crop Production in the 1960s.

the start of the colonial period to allow some plantations to be started, and that these experiments were unable to survive without official aid. Furthermore, there was no guarantee that the benefits of plantation development would have accrued mainly to the producing country. Plantations have often formed enclaves which have failed to transmit growth to the domestic economy. The oft-predicted downfall of West African palm produce exports has not occurred. Plantations of palm trees can supply better quality produce, but the achievement may involve higher production costs. Where plantations have succeeded in reducing production costs, their advantage has sometimes been cancelled by political instability, as in the cases of Indonesia and the Congo.[51] The moral is an important one: decisions on agricultural policy should also consider the wider social and political implications of changes in the means of working the land.

Ten years ago, an historical analysis of the African contribution to the development of the export economy would have had to rely heavily on a mixture of untested traditions and speculation. Today, as a result of some painstaking empirical research, reliable information is available for certain areas and products, though more work still needs to be undertaken.[52] Two contrasting regions and exports will be considered here; the Gold Coast cocoa industry, which has been examined in a series of important studies by Polly Hill,[53] and the origins of the northern Nigerian groundnut trade, which has been reconstructed, most valuably, by Jan Hogendorn.[54] Both examples will be supplemented by evidence relating to French West Africa.

In less than twenty years (1892–1911) shipments of cocoa from the Gold Coast grew from nothing to around 40,000 tons, making the colony the largest cocoa exporter in the world. This position has been maintained ever since. Today, Ghana exports around 400,000 tons of cocoa a year, the cocoa belt covers some 4 million acres, and the industry provides employment for several million people. The rapid expansion of the early days is all the more remarkable when it is remembered that the cocoa tree is not indigenous to West Africa, that it takes several years before it begins to yield, and that it does not reach maturity until it is about fifteen years old. Cocoa farming was a thoroughly capitalist enterprise from the outset: it involved taking risks with an unfamiliar product; substantial investments of time and money; the ability to plan ahead; and a willingness to defer present consumption for the sake of future returns. This major innovation used to be explained by stressing the role of government sponsorship and supervision, and by underplaying the contribution

[51] Peasant exports have also been affected by political instability in the post-colonial era, as the example of eastern Nigeria makes clear.

[52] The chief gaps are as follows: groundnuts in Senegambia; palm products in Sierra Leone and Nigeria; cocoa on the Ivory Coast and in Ashanti on the Gold Coast. These topics have been considered to some extent by geographers, anthropologists and economists, but not by economic historians. The Nigerian cocoa industry has been investigated by Dr Sara Berry and also by the present writer.

[53] See especially *The Migrant Cocoa-Farmers of Southern Ghana*, Cambridge 1963.

[54] J. S. Hogendorn, *The Origins of the Groundnut Trade in Northern Nigeria*, University of London Ph.D. thesis, 1966.

made by Africans. In particular, it was thought that cocoa was simply added piece-meal to the traditional activities of small scale, settled farmers, and so made few demands on the indigenous economic and social structure.

The reality was very different. Although the government played some part in making seeds and plants available, it is now clear that neither colonial officials nor expatriate firms had much idea of what was happening in the interior until *after* the cocoa industry was firmly established. Polly Hill's field work has revealed that the innovators were not settled 'peasants', but migrant farmers in the south-east part of the Gold Coast, who began to move in the 1890s from the Akwapim ridge to virgin land in nearby Akim Abuakwa.[55] The migrants were pulled into this adventure mainly by a desire to find a replacement for the flagging staples of legitimate com-merce, in which they were involved as producers or traders. They may also have been pushed into colonising new land by population pressure in their home areas. These farmers did not merely add cocoa to their traditional activities; they migrated specifically to grow cash crops for export, and food production had to be fitted into this primary objective. Indeed, specialisation in cocoa production by some farmers soon led others to concentrate on growing foodstuffs for sale. Finally, it is important to realise that generalisations about the scale of agricultural operations in West Africa can be very misleading. While it is apparent that the majority of cocoa far-mers operated on a small scale in comparison with the plantations (of several hundred acres) which dominated production in other parts of the world, it is equally true that the size (and shape) of farms on the Gold Coast varied greatly, and that individual farmers might own one plot or several plots. Diversity was both a sensitive adapta-tion to local geography, and an indication of the varied skills, ambitions and fortunes of export producers.

The so-called 'traditional' social structure proved to be an asset rather than a liability.[56] Established forms of co-operative enterprise were harnessed or adapted to finance the migration itself, and to purchase land in new areas. Two types of group organisation were especially prominent: first the 'company', which was an association of non-kinsmen similar to the traditional *huza* system of the Krobo people, and was common among migrants from patrilineal societies; and second, a system of pur-chasing family lands, which was adopted by groups of kinsmen from matrilineal societies, such as the Aburi and Akropong. Both arrangements gave individuals group support, yet neither inhibited them from exercising their initiative or from profiting by it. For example, migrants from matrilineal societies allowed their kins-men usufructuary rights on part of the land they had purchased, but they also retained large tracts for themselves. Furthermore, the migrants did not find themselves fettered by communal obligations when it came to running their farms. On the

---

[55] Dr Hill is careful to point out that in dispelling one myth she is anxious not to create another. The migrant farmers studied by her are only part of the story; the subsequent develop-ment of cocoa farming in the large Ashanti region in the 1920s and 1930s has yet to be examined in a work of comparable scope or depth.

[56] The brief discussion in this paragraph should be related to the extended analysis of the 'traditional' economy presented in Chapter 2.

contrary, they usually found it advantageous to employ cheap family labour, at least at the outset, and to continue to co-operate with kinsmen and friends in tasks which were beyond the reach of individuals, such as the construction of roads and bridges. Hired labour became significant only after the turn of the century, when some established farmers found that they could afford to supplement their family labour force by employing outsiders, and so could expand their farming activities. Migration was a continuous process and is still going on today. As nearby lands were taken up, and as motor transport became available in the 1920s, the migrants began to move further afield, though they never lost contact with their homelands. Thus the cocoa belt has changed its size and shape over the years as new lands have been developed through the reinvestment of past profits, and as old farms have gradually fallen into disuse.

The development of cocoa in the Ivory Coast presents some interesting parallels with the Gold Coast. There, too, migrants were first in initiating and then in expanding cocoa farming.[57] The earliest migrants were Dioula from north of the forest, who travelled south to take up land in the 1910s. Many Dioula financed their agricultural ventures with funds which they had accumulated in pre-colonial trading activities. Some were rich enough to buy land outright, and also to hire labourers from the outset. A second group of migrants, the Baoule, came from a poor farming area in the savanna, and so started with few resources. They often had to begin as *abusa* labourers, that is men who harvested the crop in return for a one third share of it. Dioula and Baoule farmers used family labour as well, especially migrants who came south to work for their relatives on a seasonal basis. The host communities were sufficiently adaptable to meet these new demands, and local farmers also took up cocoa farming successfully, as Köbben's studies of the Agni and Bete have demonstrated.[58] Strangers were welcomed not only because of the rents they paid, but because they added to the manpower, and hence to the political importance, of the local community. Indeed, in some villages immigrant farmers came to outnumber their hosts. Although land was occasionally sold, the indigenous authorities preferred to alienate the use of land rather than land itself. This arrangement preserved the interests of the local community, and at the same time allowed scope for individual enterprise. Usufructuary rights gave the immigrant farmer sufficient incentive and security, for he acquired absolute rights over property created by his own efforts, such as cocoa trees and food crops.

The main contrast between cocoa production on the Gold Coast and on the Ivory Coast is that the French colony developed later and also more slowly. The explanation of this distinction must remain tentative, at least until a full comparative analysis has been undertaken. The main reason, however, appears to lie in the nature of the external authority rather than in a sharp contrast in the geographical endowment or in the receptivity of indigenous societies in the two colonies. The effect of French policy was to retard the development of cash crops in the Ivory Coast. In

[57] Marguerite Dupire, 'Planteurs autochtones et étrangers en basse Côte d'Ivoire orientale', *Études Éburnéennes*, 8, 1960, pp. 7–237.

[58] A. J. F. Köbben, 'Le planteur noir', *Études Éburnéennes*, 5, 1956, pp. 7–185.

1908 Governor Angoulvant tried to revive the colony's flagging export trade and public revenue by making cocoa farming compulsory. The timing of this effort was scarcely propitious, for the governor, beneath whose iron exterior there beat a heart of steel, was also engaged in vigorous military operations in the forest zone in an attempt to complete the pacification of the country. Without adequate monetary incentives, the local inhabitants showed no enthusiasm for growing export crops. Later on, in the 1920s and 1930s, French officials favoured expatriate cocoa and coffee planters rather than indigenous farmers, notably by supplying the expatriates with forced labour. Not surprisingly, the local inhabitants reacted sharply against the government's measures: many Africans spent a great deal of unproductive time hiding from the administration, while the administration occupied itself, equally unproductively, in trying to find them. Forced labour was abolished in 1946, and Africans were then able to enter export production in conditions that were much closer to those which had long pertained on the Gold Coast. The results were dramatic. Within a few years the expatriate planters had almost been eliminated by African competitors; there was a massive increase in the volume of exports; and the Ivory Coast joined Senegal as France's richest West African colony.

The production of groundnuts differs from cocoa in several obvious respects. Groundnuts are found mainly in the savanna; they are an annual crop, yielding a return in the season in which they are planted; and some varieties are indigenous to West Africa, where they have long been grown as foodstuffs. Yet the rapid expansion of groundnut exports, no less than the story of cocoa farming, is worth studying because it, too, raises questions of why and how African farmers decided to commit themselves to production for an overseas market, and so illuminates the process of growth from an indigenous base.

Exports of groundnuts from northern Nigeria were negligible before the First World War, yet within a few years had become one of Nigeria's most important sources of foreign earnings. In 1913, 19,300 tons valued at £175,000 were exported, and in 1920, after some war-time fluctuations, shipments reached 45,000 tons worth £1,120,000. By the 1950s Nigeria and Senegal produced between them, and in roughly equal proportions, over three-quarters of the world's exports of groundnuts. An additional amount, equivalent to about half the volume of exports, was produced for home consumption. In the early 1960s, according to Helleiner's estimate, as many as nine million people were involved in groundnut production in northern Nigeria.[59] The initial expansion in northern Nigeria was made possible by the completion of the Lagos railway, which reached Kano in 1911. Once again, however, it is important to emphasise that changes within the agricultural sector itself owed little or nothing to external influences. Indeed, the British spent their time trying to promote cotton rather than groundnuts. These cotton growing experiments ran true to West African form: they failed. In any case, farmers near Kano had already taken up groundnut farming for export, and for the best of reasons. They found that

[59] Gerald K. Helleiner, *Peasant Agriculture, Government, and Economic Growth in Nigeria*, Homewood 1966, p. 107.

groundnuts gave a better return than cotton, which required more labour, took more out of the soil, and, in the last resort, could not be eaten.

The innovators were a readily identifiable group, not migrant farmers in this case, but Hausa traders. The Hausa had been involved in long distance trade throughout West Africa for several centuries before the advent of colonial rule.[60] They had commercial skill, organisation and capital. They also had an incentive to develop new activities, for their traditional trades were no longer as secure or as profitable as they had been; to the north, trans-Saharan commerce was in decline, and in the south the traditional kola routes were shifting to the coast. A small group of Hausa traders perceived that groundnuts offered a new, and potentially lucrative, commercial opportunity. They contacted their established agents and suppliers in the villages around Kano, persuaded farmers to grow more groundnuts, or to grow them for the first time, offered financial assistance, and gave guarantees regarding the purchase of the harvest. The fact that local farmers were prepared to trust the Hausa traders and to treat them as opinion leaders was vital to the success of the enterprise. European advisers, whose record was in any case rather poor, made far less of an impression. These Hausa buyers sold the crop to the expatriate firms, which purchased it somewhat reluctantly at first, and then rather more eagerly when it was found that shipments fetched good prices. It was the sudden rise of the groundnut trade which finally forced the Niger Company to complete the modernisation of its business—a very different story from the conventional notion of expatriate firms dragging Africans into the commercial world of the twentieth century!

The Kano area had long produced grain and cotton for the market, so agriculture was far from being stuck in a subsistence groove. Farmers were keen to develop a profitable export crop in order to pay taxes, to finance their trading activities in the dry season, and generally to expand their purchasing power. Agriculture in the Kano region was a subtle mixture of shifting and permanent cultivation, the latter being associated with manuring, water and soil conservation, and, wherever possible, irrigation. Traditional rules governing the tenure and use of land did not present an obstacle to capitalist enterprise. Household farming was organised on an individual as well as on a communal basis, and measures were taken to ensure that, as far as possible, the products of labour went to the person concerned, and that usufructuary rights could be inherited. The massive increase in groundnut production was achieved partly by reducing the amount of land under other foodstuffs and cotton, but mainly by introducing minor, though highly effective, changes in technique, which made more efficient use of existing land and labour resources. These changes involved shorter fallow periods, increased manuring, and a greater degree of interplanting. It was only in the 1920s and 1930s, with the advent of the motor car and better roads, that expansion took the form of increasing the amount of land and the number of labourers employed in the industry. Between 1911 and 1937 about one million acres around Kano were brought under groundnut cultivation, and many

[60] See above, pp. 58–66.

thousands of migrants from other parts of northern Nigeria came in to swell the numbers engaged in groundnut production. Despite the simplicity of the techniques used and the intensity with which the whole area is now farmed, yields per acre are still among the best in the world.

The case of northern Nigeria is paralleled in certain important respects by the example of Senegal.[61] The main historical difference, as noted in Chapter 4, is that groundnut exports from Senegambia date from the era of legitimate commerce. The rise of the industry again resulted from the initiative of African farmers at a time when European interests in the region were centred on other products. From the 1880s onwards groundnuts expanded on the extensive margin following the progress of the Senegal railway. By 1908, before exports from Nigeria had even begun, Senegal was already the world's leading supplier. In due course, societies such as the Wolof, the Fulani and the Serer, which had different institutions and economies, all became involved in groundnut farming. Each adapted successfully by releasing individual skills and energies, by developing co-operative organisations, and by modifying traditional agricultural practices, as the Serer, for example, substituted groundnuts for millet, while at the same time keeping their cattle economy intact. These societies made use of family labour, but they also showed a willingness to accept outsiders, and adjust to their presence. Immigrant labourers (known as *navétanes* in Senegal, and as 'strange' farmers in Gambia) were an important feature of export production right from the start of the groundnut trade. Sometimes they simply rented land and farmed it; often they agreed to work for two or three days a week on their landlord's farm in return for food, lodging, and enough time to grow groundnuts on their own account.

The new economy even found a new ideology. The Mourides, a Muslim sect founded in 1886, began to win converts in the groundnut areas of Senegal from the 1890s, notably among the Wolof. An important doctrine of this sect was the belief that hard physical work in this world was a passport to salvation in the next.[62] This tenet was turned to practical advantage through the establishment of groundnut farms managed by lay instructors and worked by initiates. When these novices had demonstrated their mastery of Mouride doctrine, and had also shown themselves to be proficient farmers, they spread out, set up farms of their own, and attracted a new set of followers. The Mourides, who now have about 700,000 adherents, became prominent groundnut producers during the colonial period, and they also acquired considerable political influence. They provide a good example of how precolonial, Islamic frontiers came into contact with influences from the Western world, were modified by them, but survived to exert a strong and constructive economic influence under colonialism.[63] A parallel may be drawn with the onward

---

[61] See the publications by Fouquet, Jarrett, Pehaut, Pélissier and Pitot listed in the bibliography.

[62] Abdoulaye Wade, 'La doctrine économique du mouridisme', *Annales Africaines*, 1967, pp. 175–206.

[63] It should be added that in many respects the Mourides have now become a conservative force. For a recent account see Donal B. Cruise O'Brien, *The Mourides of Senegal*, Oxford 1970.

march of the Christian frontier in the cocoa regions of the forest zone, where the religion of the West was also adapted to give effective support to new economic activities.[64]

The preceding survey of agricultural developments shows that societies in different parts of West Africa were willing and able to supply innovators, to reconcile and capitalise on individual and communal loyalties, to venture into new regions in order to make money, to draw upon existing skills and established sources of finance, and to pursue capitalist undertakings unimpeded by indigenous or acquired values.[65] These conclusions reinforce the argument developed in Chapter 2 that 'traditional' societies are far more flexible and far less hostile to 'modern' economic activities than is often assumed.

This account of the ways in which Africans contributed to the creation of the colonial economy will be completed by an outline of changes affecting the labour force during the early phase of colonial rule. The information presented here will enlarge on points which were either made briefly or were implicit in the preceding description of the development of export crops. The purpose of the discussion is to underline the contributions made by Africans to the expansion of the open economy by showing that unskilled labour, whether self-employed or not, responded positively to monetary incentives, and did not need to be coerced into wage employment, except when the rewards were inadequate. Shortages occurred, but these were often in the relatively small, though highly publicised, government sector, and can be attributed more to mismanagement on the demand side than to blockages in supply. One preliminary warning is necessary: West African demographic material tends to be patchy and unreliable for the twentieth century, as for earlier periods, so the few figures quoted in this discussion are to be interpreted merely as illustrative approximations.

Employers in the twentieth century faced much the same basic difficulty as had African employers in the past: that is to say, their main task was to transfer manpower from huge areas of dispersed and scanty settlement to a relatively few points of concentrated demand. However, the colonial labour 'problem', as it came to be known in official circles, had a number of distinctive features. The demand for labour was much greater than it had ever been before; it developed rapidly between 1890 and 1920; and, with a few exceptions, it was located in a number of favoured coastal areas. By far the most important demand for labour (outside subsistence farming) came from commercial agriculture. The main export-producing regions were unable to supply all the labour they needed from local sources, so extra hands had to be imported from other parts of West Africa. In the 1920s the groundnut

[64] J. B. Webster, 'Agege: Plantations and the African Church, 1901–1920', *Nigerian Institute of Social and Economic Research, Conference Proceedings*, 1962, pp. 124–30.

[65] The examples cited should be sufficient to establish these conclusions. For two further, supporting case studies see Sara S. Berry, 'Christianity and the Rise of Cocoa Growing in Ibadan and Ondo', *Journal of the Historical Society of Nigeria*, 4, 1968, pp. 439–51, and Raymond Dumett, 'The Rubber Trade of the Gold Coast and Asante in the Nineteenth Century: African Innovation and Responsiveness', *Journal of African History*, 12, 1971, pp. 79–102.

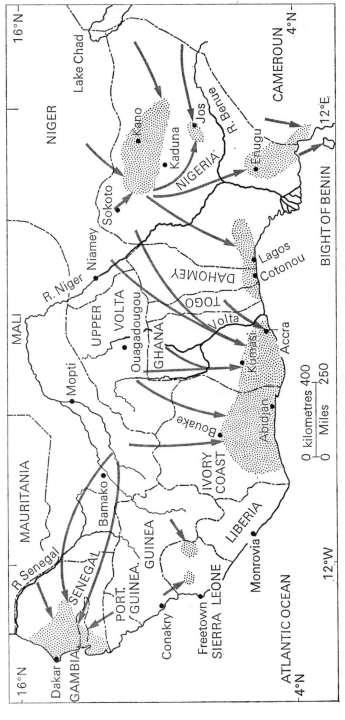

MAP 14. Migrant Labour in West Africa in the 1950s.

farms of Senegal and Gambia attracted between 60,000 and 70,000 temporary immigrants each year, and in the 1950s 150,000 to 200,000 labourers entered the Gold Coast annually to work on the cocoa farms. Mining was an additional, though less significant, source of demand. The gold mines of the Gold Coast employed an average of about 15,000 unskilled workers a year between 1905 and 1918, while in the Nigerian tin fields between 1918 and 1939 the labour force ranged from 15,000 men a year to a peak of 40,000. Finally, labour was required by the colonial governments in connection with various public works, and, to a lesser extent, by the expatriate commercial firms, principally for handling stocks. Much of this demand was urban based, but labourers also followed official enterprise outside the towns, notably to build railways and roads, and to carry equipment in the pre-lorry age.

The supply of labour can be considered under four main headings, though these by no means exhaust the subject: population growth; geographical mobility; social change; and official policy.

In 1910 West Africa's population was about 36 million. This figure is rather greater than others which are sometimes quoted, as there are grounds for thinking that early estimates were the result of substantial undercounting.[66] By 1965 the population had reached roughly 88 million. It seems safe to say that on a conservative estimate the total population has doubled in about fifty years. In general terms this rapid increase was the result of a high birth rate coupled with a falling death rate. However, it is important to note that the rate of increase was much slower during the early phase of colonial rule than it was in the period after 1945, because it was only after the Second World War that medical and sanitary services underwent major improvements, and so began to have a marked effect on the death rate. Indeed, before 1945 it is likely that the increase in the mobility of West African peoples may have assisted the spread of fatal and incapacitating diseases. The conclusion which can be drawn from this information is that while the growth of population is necessary to an understanding of the process of economic change during the colonial period as a whole, it is far less relevant to an explanation of the early expansion of, for example, cocoa farming on the Gold Coast or groundnut exports from Nigeria, for both occurred in a relatively short space of time, and long before the population 'explosion' had begun.

Much more important in the present context was the increased geographical mobility of the population. As has been stressed on several occasions already, the mobility of the labour force was a long-established feature of the West African economy; it ante-dated the Atlantic slave trade, and its importance grew during the era of legitimate commerce. In the pre-colonial period there had been a sizeable movement of manpower northwards as far as the desert oases. In the twentieth century, by contrast, it is the inhabitants of the Western Sudan who travel to the coast, and as wage-earners rather than as slaves. Greater mobility was achieved by the imposition of a common political authority over wide areas, by the introduction of modern transport, and by the emergence of a free (wage) labour force. These

---

[66] I should like to thank my colleague, Dr P. K. Mitchell, for assistance on this question.

innovations have sometimes led to the movement of whole settlements, which have abandoned defensive and often crowded hilltop sites, and ventured down into the plains.[67] They have also brought about an expansion in the number of what might be termed 'shuttle migrants', that is men who leave their homes for a short period to work in agriculture or in the mines, often travelling great distances to do so.

Migrant labour has frequently been condemned by commentators who have seen little difference between a shifting and a shiftless labour force. However, thanks largely to Elliot Berg's pioneering work, it is now realised that migrant labour, though it has drawbacks, also makes sense in West African conditions.[68] In the first place, the demand for labour in agriculture is highly seasonal, and is best met by a temporary increase in the work force. Moreover, the increase can usually be achieved without disrupting the domestic economy of the migrants.[69] For example, many of the workers on Nigerian cocoa farms come from the north, where the peak demand for labour occurs at a different time of the year. Secondly, where migrant labour persists in sectors such as mining, where there are no marked seasonal demands, it is indicative not of backwardness on the part of Africans in committing themselves fully to wage employment, but of backwardness on the part of expatriates in persisting with a low-wage policy. The reasons for this policy will be considered later on.

The improvement in geographical mobility was closely associated with an important social change in the late nineteenth and early twentieth centuries, namely the decline of internal slavery and the rise of a free (wage) labour force. This event, which is certain to become one of the central themes in the as yet unwritten labour history of Africa, deserves a great deal more attention from historians than it has received so far. In the context of the argument advanced in Chapter 4 on imperialism, the ending of slavery is to be seen as a major feature of the social revolution which originated early in the nineteenth century, when the new export economy began to offer wider opportunities to ordinary Africans, free as well as unfree. Not surprisingly, the unfree were among the last to be allowed to participate independently in activities which would enable them to assert themselves against their masters. With regard to the utilisation of labour resources under colonialism, the significance of the collapse of slavery is not that the traditional slave labour force was markedly inefficient in performing the duties allotted to it, but that many of the numerically preponderant farm slaves were employed outside the expanding export sectors, and were also highly immobile—for reasons which are obvious enough.

---

[67] This movement has been investigated with reference to Nigeria, Togo and Dahomey by M. B. Gleave in 'Hill Settlements and their Abandonment in Tropical Africa', *Transactions of the Institute of British Geographers*, 40, 1966, pp. 39–49.

[68] See especially 'The Economics of the Migrant Labour System', in *Urbanisation and Migration in West Africa*, ed. Hilda Kuper, Berkeley 1965, pp. 160–81. Mention should also be made of Walter Elkan's *Migrants and Proletarians*, 1960, a model of careful scholarship which deals principally with Uganda.

[69] For a recent survey of the literature on this question, see Marvin P. Miracle and Sara S. Berry, 'Migrant Labour and Economic Development', *Oxford Economic Papers*, 22, 1970, pp. 86–108.

French and British attitudes towards internal slavery are classic illustrations of the struggle between the normative and the pragmatic that characterised imperial policy in so many fields. The formal position was quite clear: France and Britain had made opposition to slavery part of official policy, and were committed to its abolition in all their territories. At the same time, however, both governments sought for practical reasons to control the pace of emancipation. In the first place they did not wish to risk disrupting export production by provoking sudden social upheaval. Secondly, they needed the co-operation of at least some of the indigenous rulers, and therefore could scarcely demolish one of the bases of their power. Thirdly, they faced some very real problems of defining slavery, of identifying slaves, and of enforcing anti-slavery legislation. Fourthly, the colonial powers themselves made use of forced labour in the twentieth century. Faced with a shortage of unskilled labour, they, like African rulers before them, had recourse to compulsion. Forced labour was never very widespread in West Africa as a whole, though it survived in French West Africa until 1946, and it had some local importance, as, for example, in the European plantations on the Ivory Coast and in the construction of the Dakar–Bamako railway. Despite these four qualifications, it remains true that the colonial powers regarded slavery as obstructing their long-term economic interests. Their presence in West Africa undoubtedly encouraged emancipation, though the practical difficulties which they encountered meant that slavery was not abolished overnight, but tended instead to wither away.

The main stages of emancipation in West Africa can be outlined quite briefly. A start was made early in the nineteenth century, but at that time official action was confined to a few coastal colonies, and consequently did not have any direct effect on the interior. Freed slaves were enrolled in various apprenticeship schemes, they were recruited into the armed forces, and the French even experimented with a dubious plan for 'free' emigration to North America. The Act of 1833, abolishing slavery throughout the British empire, did not have much effect on West Africa. However, when the French parliament passed a similar measure in 1848, some further steps were taken, especially at Gorée and St Louis in Senegal, where several thousand slaves were freed and their masters compensated.[70] Nevertheless, no serious attack on internal slavery was made until the 1880s, and then it came as a by-product of the partition of Africa.

When the Europeans advanced inland, they quickly realised that they had underestimated the size of the problem of slavery. According to an estimate made in 1905, there were about two million slaves in French West Africa, and it was reckoned that in the heart of the large Muslim states between a quarter and a half of the total population was in a state of enslavement. In these circumstances hasty and enforced emancipation might have had unwelcome consequences. Indeed, by the start of the twentieth century the exodus of slaves had deprived the desert oases of the cheap labour they needed to maintain their complex systems of irrigated agriculture, and

---

[70] M'baye Guèye, 'La fin de l'esclavage à Saint Louis et à Gorée en 1848', *Bulletin de l'IFAN*, B, 28, 1966, pp. 637–56, and Roger Pasquier, 'A propos de l'émancipation des esclaves au Sénégal en 1848', *Revue Française d'Histoire d'Outre-Mer*, 54, 1967, pp. 188–208.

so had accelerated the decline of the already waning trans-Saharan trade.[71] Beginning in 1887, the French attempted to stabilise the situation by establishing a series of *villages de liberté*, which had the declared aim of resettling homeless slaves and achieving gradual emancipation. The reality was rather different.[72] The *villages*, far from developing into the Freetowns and Librevilles of the interior, acted as disincentives to emancipation, for their luckless inhabitants became the *captifs du commandant*, the unfree labourers and porters of the local administration. The limitations of the *villages* were eventually acknowledged by the French government, and most of them were closed down between 1907 and 1910. The problem of rootless ex-slaves was less serious for the British than it was for the French, though after the turn of the century Lugard did establish a few settlements for freed slaves in northern Nigeria, including in Bornu one memorial to Victorian principles called Liberty Village.

Emancipation progressed more quickly after 1900. In 1905, following an incident in which a well-connected French official in Senegal was shot by an equally well-connected African who had been accused of slave trading, a decree was issued authorising stronger action against internal slavery.[73] In the period 1905–1907 about 300,000 slaves were freed in French West Africa, and substantial numbers continued to be released in the years which followed.[74] The liberators, judging all slave-holders to be bad, but regarding some as more dangerous than others, concentrated on areas where unfree labour was thought to underpin the opposition of indigenous rulers to the French presence. In 1911, to take one example, about 1,500 slaves were given their freedom after the collapse of the Fulani revolt in Guinea. The British also tightened up their legislation against slavery during this period, though without becoming involved in such extensive military activities. From the 1920s the process of liberation was greatly helped by the spread of motor vehicles, which released labour previously tied up in the costly business of moving goods by head-loading. By about 1930 emancipation was well advanced, though instances of slavery and slave trading are still occasionally reported today.

On the whole, the transition from slave to free labour was achieved without widespread economic and social dislocation. The quiescence of the change has undoubtedly contributed to the neglect of what was nevertheless an event of fundamental importance in West African history. To some extent the relative ease of transition was the product of the delaying tactics adopted by the major powers. The British, whose policy of indirect rule gave support to indigenous authorities in certain areas, were more successful in this than the French, whose military vigour led to the elimination of a number of important African rulers, and to greater

---

[71] J. Aymo, 'Notes de sociologie et de linguistique sur Ghadames', *Bulletin de Liaison Saharienne*, 10, 1959, pp. 129–57.

[72] Denise Bouche, *Les villages de liberté en Afrique noire*, Paris 1968.

[73] M'baye Guèye, 'L'Affaire Chautemps (avril 1904) et la suppression de l'esclavage de case au Sénégal', *Bulletin de l'IFAN*, B, 27, 1965, pp. 543–59.

[74] J-L. Boutillier, 'Les captifs en A.O.F. (1903–1905)', *Bulletin de l'IFAN*, B, 30, 1968, pp. 513–35.

problems of resettlement. To some extent, too, the ease of transition reflected the fact that many so-called slaves were virtually indistinguishable from free men, and were not interested in supporting sudden social revolution. Yet neither of these explanations is wholly satisfactory: colonial policy was unable fully to control events, and slavery, in the sense of well-defined economic and social deprivation, *was* a reality for numerous Africans in many areas.

The explanation advanced here is that the smoothness of the transition was largely a function of the availability of acceptable alternative opportunities.[75] In the first place, land suitable for export cultivation was at hand, and could be taken up at little cost save the labour involved in clearing it. Secondly, much of the critical period of emancipation coincided with a trading boom after the turn of the century, which made export production attractive. Thirdly, social change, in this context at least, did not involve widespread occupational mobility. That is to say, most slaves were farmers, or, if not, they knew how to farm, and they either remained in or entered the agricultural sector, the main difference being that now they worked for themselves instead of for an overlord. Problems of resettlement, it is suggested, arose chiefly in areas where these opportunities did not exist. This was especially the case in the far-flung and poor French colonies. As Verdier has pointed out, there are former slaves in Niger who still constitute a servile labour force largely because they have great difficulty in becoming anything else.[76] In short, most slaves stayed in agriculture and assisted the expansion of the colonial economy. Unlike nineteenth-century England, men were not pushed off the land to make way for a new type of agriculture, and to provide labour for a growing industrial sector. In West Africa there was no landless proletariat shifting, as it were, from parish to parish. A permanent urban labour force was slow to develop, but migrant labour was purposeful and anchored to the land. No extensive retraining was needed because traditional techniques and implements remained dominant. There were no machine breakers because there were few machines to break.

The rise of this generation of independent export producers inevitably brought about a decline in the position of former slave holders. Some owners lost their wealth overnight as a result of the escape of their slaves. A British official noted one instance in 1898, where

> a great change arose as over 400 of this chief's slaves, whose average value at that time was £10 to £12, ran away and never returned. He thus lost at least £4,000 and is in consequence a poor man now. This speaks for itself and I think explains the dread with which rich natives in the Interior view our advance into the country.[77]

[75] For a similar conclusion in a different context see Benedicte Hjejle, 'Slavery and Agricultural Bondage in South India in the Nineteenth Century', *Scandinavian Economic History Review*, 15, 1967, pp. 71–126.

[76] R. Verdier, 'Problèmes fonciers nigeriens', *Penant*, 74, 1964, pp. 587–93.

[77] Quoted in A. G. Hopkins, 'The Lagos Strike of 1897: an Exploration in Nigerian Labour History', © The Past and Present Society, Corpus Christi College, Oxford. The extract from this article is reprinted with the permission of the Society from *Past and Present, A Journal of Historical Studies*, 35, 1966, p. 141.

Nevertheless, it would be naive to conclude that all former slave owners were completely eliminated. Some managed to adapt by becoming *rentiers*, collecting dues from ex-slaves in exchange for granting rights of cultivation. Others acquired the skills needed for survival by going into trade or agriculture, or by selling their political expertise—if they had any—to the colonial rulers. As Toupet has shown with reference to Mauritania, the Littama, formerly a tribe of warriors and slave-owners, moved south and became settled cultivators, whereas the Haratin, a group of freed slaves, did not adapt so well.[78] For them, the abandonment of the nomadic way of life led to poverty, and to the forced sale of their only asset, their cattle. Assessing the rise and fall of social classes is acknowledged to be one of the most subtle of historical problems; further research will doubtless show that this is as true of Africa as it is of Europe.

Although the African labour force managed to adapt itself in the ways indicated, there was still a shortage of unskilled labour in the period 1890–1930, especially in the expatriate sectors. Some perplexed officials advocated importing 'the industrious Chinaman' to fill the gap; others preferred Indian labour; while the real enthusiasts wanted Indian elephants as well! The reasons originally given by colonial observers for the shortage of labour have led to a number of misconceptions which, regrettably, can still be found today in some textbook generalisations about development problems.

Traditional explanations stress factors such as the tenacity of pre-industrial social systems, the lack of psychological preparedness for modern employment, and the limited wants of the potential labour force. The latter notion has given rise to the concept of the target worker, that is someone who enters wage employment with a specific aim in mind—the stock example is to buy a bicycle—and then leaves for home again. However, in spite of his desire to own a bicycle, the African labourer, so it has been alleged, was characterised by inefficiency and by a high rate of absentee-ism. This interpretation of the motivation and performance of African workers has had far-reaching practical implications. For example, it was largely responsible for the persistence of a low wage rate during the early phase of colonial rule. According to conventional supply and demand analysis, employers should have responded to a shortage of labour by raising wages. But the belief that Africans were target workers was used to justify the payment of low wages in order to prevent employees from reaching their targets too quickly. High wages, it was argued, would have dimin-ished the volume of labour in employment by making targets attainable in a short time. On these assumptions, the predominance of migrant labour was held to prove that Africans had cultural and psychological blockages which prevented them from committing themselves fully to wage employment. Migrant labour was also thought to be responsible for the low productivity of wage-earners, and so contributed to the low wages which were paid. Forced labour was justified, though never too loudly, on the grounds that by helping to overcome these blockages it had an educative effect on primitive peoples.

[78] 'Quelques aspects de la sédentarisation des nomades en Mauritanie sahélienne', *Annales de Géographie*, 73, 1964, pp. 738–45.

The evidence now available makes it clear that the conventional view, though it may be relevant in certain cases, can no longer remain the central explanation of the general shortage of wage labour in West Africa during the first phase of colonial rule. The point made by Adam Smith with reference to eighteenth-century England is equally applicable to the African labour force during the colonial period: 'Some workmen indeed, when they can earn in four days what will maintain them through the week will be idle the other three. This however is by no means the case with the greater part.'[79] With regard to the so-called tenacity of traditional social systems, this book has attempted to show that to categorise pre-industrial societies in this way is to lose contact with reality, and that in any case West African peoples were reorganising to meet the new demands of the Western world in the period of legitimate commerce—before the advent of colonial rule. The related notions of psychological unpreparedness and limited wants founder on the import and export figures, which show that Africans were eager to expand their purchases of consumer goods, and that to do so they created a series of export economies in ways which have already been indicated. Wage-earners responded positively to monetary incentives; the aggregate supply curve of labour did not become regressive at an early point; and the concept of West Africans as target workers needs to be seriously modified.[80] As to the alleged inefficiency of African labour, this, too, is a subject where prejudice has long survived unquestioned. By looking at the facts of this particular matter Peter Kilby has made an unusual and most welcome contribution to African labour economics.[81] His survey in 1961 of 63 establishments in Nigeria employing some 50,000 workers revealed that the performance of the labour force was related primarily to working conditions and levels of pay, and not to culturally determined attitudes towards wage employment. Where conditions were good and wages high, the labour force was efficient, stable and regular in its attendance.

The problem was not that Africans suffered from a general reluctance to enter wage employment, but that they were particularly unwilling to take unskilled jobs with expatriate employers. There were two main reasons for this. First of all, the work tended to be hard, uncongenial and of low status. In these respects it compared unfavourably with farming, where the work was familiar, where the relationship between employer and employee was more fluid, and where the wage-earner kept his self-respect. An idea of the gruelling conditions experienced by some of these early African wage-earners is conveyed in the following quotations from the records of the Gold Coast Transport Department for the year 1908:[82]

with constant walking for a twelve month averaging 400 miles a month, the work this year having been rather harder than usual, a large number of carriers have been

[79] Quoted in Phyllis Deane, *The First Industrial Revolution*, Cambridge 1965, p. 141.
[80] Elliot J. Berg, 'Backward-Sloping Labor Supply Functions in Dual Economies—the Africa Case', *Quarterly Journal of Economics*, 75, 1961, pp. 468–92.
[81] 'African Labour Productivity Reconsidered', *Economic Journal*, 71, 1961, pp. 273–91.
[82] Quoted in D. K. Greenstreet, 'The Transport Department—the First Two Decades', *Economic Bulletin of Ghana*, 10, 1966, p. 42.

incapacitated from sore feet, the metalling of new roads making matters worse. In one gang . . . the majority had their soles almost completely worn through, to say nothing of cracks.

However, the official mind, though not quite equal to the problem, did not lack inspiration:

The experiment was then tried of tarring the carriers' feet. Coal tar is most suitable. It fills the cracks and is good antiseptic, besides affording some protection if applied thick. The results have proved quite good and many carriers are now able to keep to the road who would otherwise have to lie up.

Fortunately, the introduction of the motor car, and the spread of an even older Western product—boots—quickly consigned this experiment to the locker of discarded colonial remedies, and so forestalled the rise of a new breed of heavy-footed porters throughout the tropical colonies.

The second reason for the shortage of labour was simply that the pay offered was not high enough to tempt the labour force of an underpopulated area into taking disagreeable jobs, when there were more rewarding alternatives available, notably in agriculture. If the Chinaman was an industrious government employee, it was mainly because he had fewer options open to him. On the occasions when high wages were paid in West Africa, labour was usually forthcoming. But the notion of the target worker died hard, and there were always additional reasons for holding down wages, ranging from the almost permanent need for budgetary economies to a stubborn reluctance to admit that the African labourer was worthy of his hire. Instead of migrant labour producing low wages, as expatriates alleged, it was the low level of wages which encouraged the development of migrant labour in non-seasonal occupations, for low wages were only acceptable to Africans providing they did not have to sacrifice their main source of income, which came mostly from farming. The justification for forced labour was entirely bogus; Africans did not need educating in the ways of the modern money economy, and even assuming they did, there were better ways of setting about it. Forced labour could put a man off capitalism for life, even if the path to modernity did not always have to be trodden with tarred feet.

3 The mechanics of export growth

It is now possible to offer a more formal analysis of the process of export expansion in West Africa in terms of factor mobilisation. A large part of the explanation advanced here derives ultimately from Adam Smith's vent-for-surplus theory of international trade, which has been elaborated in recent years by Myint, applied to the Gold Coast by Szereszewski, and to Nigeria by Helleiner.[83] The theory will first be summarised, and then a number of modifications will be introduced to take account of additional points arising out of the historical evidence presented in this chapter.

The vent-for-surplus theory is based on three assumptions which are held to be generally consistent with the known facts of West African development. These are that the massive growth in the volume of exports was achieved without a comparable increase in population, without a significant reduction in the amount of land and time involved in the production of traditional goods and services, and without the adoption of any major improvements in agricultural techniques. Given these conditions, it is hard to avoid the conclusion that the rise in output resulted mainly from increased inputs of land and labour, and therefore that both factors had been to some extent underemployed previously.

The economics of labour utilisation in this situation require careful consideration. It is particularly important to distinguish between overpopulated parts of the world, where underemployment may arise because insufficient land is available to provide full employment for all members of the household, and under-populated regions, such as West Africa, where the agricultural labour force may be underemployed because of a lack of effective demand for its potential output.[84] A certain number of man-hours was spent unproductively, not through choice, and not as a result of a culturally-determined rejection of profitable opportunities, but because the only alternative was to produce goods for which there was no market. The increased demand for West African exports in the early colonial period altered the traditional relationship between goods and leisure. In terms of foregone opportunities, leisure became more expensive because Africans could now choose to improve their material incomes by earning the cash to buy imported goods. This option was taken up; existing export producers decided to work harder, and newcomers were attracted to the export sector. The allocation of labour inputs between various alternatives was determined by the relative efficiency of these alternatives in purchasing consumer goods, as witness the swing away from traditional staples in the 1880s, the rubber boom at the turn of the century, and the preference which farmers in the

---

[83] H. Myint, *The Economics of the Developing Countries*, 1964; R. Szereszewski, *Structural Changes in the Economy of Ghana, 1891–1911*, 1965; and Gerald K. Helleiner, *Peasant Agriculture, Government, and Economic Growth in Nigeria*, Homewood 1966. Myint's book, which combines brevity, lucidity and originality, must rank as one of the very best of the numerous attempts which have been made to comprehend the process of economic growth. Szereszewski's study is full of bold and stimulating ideas, though it is handicapped somewhat by a theoretical framework which is too sophisticated for the evidence. Helleiner's work has set a high standard in relating data and theory, and is indispensable for serious students of African development problems.

[84] For a useful summary of the literature on this subject see Charles H. C. Kao, Kurt R. Anschel and Carl K. Eicher, 'Disguised Unemployment in Agriculture: a Survey', in *Agriculture in Economic Development*, ed. Carl K. Eicher and Lawrence W. Witt, New York 1964, pp. 129–44.

savanna showed for groundnuts instead of for cotton. Thus West Africa had a built-in capacity to increase its production of exportable commodities, and the main function of expatriate influences was to create the conditions which gave Africans a better vent for their latent, surplus resources.

Myint has stressed the value of this theory for an understanding of the speed and relative ease of 'peasant' export development in underpopulated regions such as West Africa. Four main points emerge from his analysis. First, the expansion of output was achieved without an agricultural revolution. Productivity per man increased, but productivity per man hour or per acre remained unchanged. Second, export production was self-financing in the sense that farmers employed family labour, used traditional tools, and had access to land that was virtually costless. Third, the risks involved in entering export production were minimised because Africans did not have to reduce their output of foodstuffs at the same time. This favourable situation contrasts with certain overpopulated parts of the world, where the export sector has been slow to develop partly because farmers have had to choose between these two types of activity, and have been understandably reluctant to place their supply of essential foodstuffs at risk. Fourth, Myint has suggested that the pattern of export development in underpopulated regions falls into two stages: the first occurs when farmers take up export production in an unspecialised way as an adjunct to subsistence farming; the second arises later on, when a certain number of farmers, encouraged by their early success, decide to devote more of their resources to export production, and become dependent on others for part of their food supplies.

The vent-for-surplus theory has the advantage of being much closer to the facts than many previous development theories, which tended to assume that underdevelopment was a homogeneous, as well as a global, phenomenon. Myint's theory also takes an important step towards reality by attempting to distinguish between various kinds of underdevelopment. It divides the overpopulated from the underpopulated parts of the Third World, and it separates the foreign enclaves from the peasant economies. In dealing with peasant economies the theory has the further merit of focusing on the positive contribution made by indigenous societies. As a corollary, it places the expatriate role in what is regarded here as its proper perspective, that is as being important in specific fields, but by no means being synonymous with the whole development process. However, the vent-for-surplus theory cannot be applied to West Africa without some modification. Its basic limitation springs from the economist's highly compressed view of history. Compression sometimes has advantages in producing a degree of synthesis and clarity which the historian himself, with his nose pressed too faithfully to his documents, often fails to achieve. At the same time, as the following comments will suggest, it can lead to the omission not merely of trivia, but of significant facts.

The three main assumptions of the vent-for-surplus theory cannot stand without modification. In the first place, while it is true that the growth of total population is not vital to an explanation of the increase in labour inputs, the mobility of the population is relevant, as has been shown with reference to the development of migrant labour. Thus the expansion of population in specific areas, albeit on a temporary basis, is necessary to a full understanding of the rise in output. This qualification need not contradict the view that the migrant labour force was under-used in its home area, but it does suggest that the argument needs to be checked care-fully by case studies of the domestic economy of labour-exporting regions. Secondly, it is oversimple to assert that the rise in exports was achieved without a decline in the production of traditional goods and services. There was no wholesale liquidation of traditional crafts,[85] but there were examples of farmers committing themselves to export production at the expense of food crops, and of the decline of some pre-colonial occupations. A good illustration of the former is provided by Senegal, where groundnut production expanded to some extent at the expense of foodstuffs, with the result that large quantities of rice had to be imported from the 1930s on-wards. The collapse of indigenous military systems, and of the slavery which was associated with them, also led to a certain amount of occupational change.[86] Particularly important, and virtually ignored, in this context was the reallocation of labour between the sexes, as men gave up their military functions and became more involved in farming, an occupation which traditionally had been dominated by women in many areas.[87] Thirdly, greater output was sometimes the result of improved techniques arising out of a reorganisation of farming practices, as was the case at the start of the Nigerian groundnut industry, when relatively minor changes produced a substantial increase in productivity.

Modifying the assumptions on which the theory is based also has implications for its capacity to explain the speed and alleged ease of West African export growth. It may well be true that most Africans did not have to grapple with the problems of an agricultural revolution in the conventional sense, but the case of northern Nigeria shows that there was at least one exception to this rule, and since research into the agricultural history of West Africa is only just beginning, it would be unwise at this stage to assume that this particular example is of limited importance. It is also true that agricultural development was self-financing in the sense of not requiring *expatriate* capital, but it is inaccurate to suggest that each household was capable of entering export production without additional help from *indigenous* sources. The examples of cocoa and groundnut farming have shown that, in the initial stages, group co-operation and financial reserves accumulated from previous economic activities were essential to the success of these ventures. Next, the idea that risks were minimised because of the unspecialised nature of early exporting activities pre-supposes a greater degree of homogeneity in the structure of agricultural production than was actually the case, and it fails to do justice to the considerable entrepreneurial abilities of the innovators. Those who started the cocoa industries of the Gold Coast

---

[85] This subject is dealt with in Chapter 7, section 2.

[86] See J. Clauzel, 'Evolution de la vie économique et des structures sociales du pays nomade du Mali, de la conquête française à l'autonomie interne, 1893–1958', *Tiers-Monde*, 9–10, 1962, pp. 283–311, and D. J. Siddle, 'War Towns in Sierra Leone: a Study in Social Change', *Africa*, 38, 1968, pp. 47–55.

[87] An important general survey of this subject is the study by Ester Boserup, *Woman's Role in Economic Development*, 1970.

and Nigeria, and the groundnut industry of northern Nigeria, were heavily committed to export production right from the outset. For them, novelty and risk were two of the most prominent features of these ventures. Finally, Myint's concept of two stages of peasant export expansion, though not invalidated, is too schematic, for there were specialised and unspecialised producers in both phases of development. In the case of West Africa, it may be more realistic to think in terms of three overlapping stages: the first in which small groups of innovating entrepreneurs experimented in a fairly specialised way with a variety of export crops; the second in which their total or partial success led to widespread imitation by small scale, semi-specialised farmers; and the third in which rural differentiation encouraged the appearance of a new and much larger group of specialists.[88]

Colonial rule did not create modernity out of backwardness by suddenly disrupting a traditional state of low-level equilibrium. On the contrary, the nature and pace of economic development in the early colonial period can be understood only when it is realised that the main function of the new rulers was to give impetus to a process which was already under way. An economic structure based on 'peasant' export production and offering the prospect of a mass market had begun to emerge early in the nineteenth century. Towards the close of the century, however, it became apparent that this economy could not attain its full potential simply by relying on the working of the natural laws in which mid-nineteenth century liberals had placed such faith. Foreign intervention was needed to remove constraints which threatened to make West Africa uncompetitive in world markets, which retarded the development of expatriate commercial interests, and which inhibited the growth of indigenous capitalist enterprise. These problems led first to partition, and then to the colonial solution described in the preceding pages. By creating the conditions which gave Europeans and Africans both the means and the incentive to expand and diversify legitimate commerce, colonial rule completed the integration of West Africa into the economy of the industrial world, and marked a further stage in the growth of the market. Important though it was, the expatriate role did not extend much beyond this general function of connecting West Africa to international markets. It was Africans who grasped the new opportunities, made the key entrepreneurial decisions, and introduced fundamental changes in the vital agricultural sector. They did so by utilising established and allegedly antiquated economic and social institutions.

The export economy which had emerged by 1930 came as close to the ideal-type open economy as West Africa was to reach. Since the foregoing pages have concentrated on the role of man, especially African man, in creating this economy, it is appropriate at this point to recall that the influence of rulers and ruled alike was constrained, above all, by the resource base of the region. Factor endowments can change, but the change is rarely accomplished quickly. West Africa's comparative advantage lay in supplying the world market with tropical produce. It was this activity which offered the region the best prospect of expanding its domestic, as well

---

[88] This third stage is considered in Chapter 7, part 1.

as its overseas, market. The colonial rulers did not need to legislate against industrialisation[89] because there were already weighty reasons—such as low incomes, poor infrastructure, and lack of capital and skills—why modern manufacturing plant was not established in West Africa during the first half of the colonial era. However, the open economy was not a frozen economy, and after 1930 it underwent important modifications, as will now be shown.

[89] The claim that the *pacte colonial* operated to prevent industrialisation needs to be reconsidered in the light of Mark Karp's article, 'The Legacy of French Economic Policy in Africa', in *French-Speaking Africa*, ed. William H. Lewis, 1965, pp. 145–53.

seven

The open economy under strain

In the 1920s and 1930s the colonial economy was considered as much part of the natural order as was the House of Lords or the Third Republic. None of the respected commentators on imperial affairs envisaged or desired any radical alternative, and it was generally agreed that the colonial, export economies would continue to function in such a way as to bring about prosperity and progress for all concerned. Similarly, orthodox wisdom held that colonial rule would endure to a point so remote in time as to defy precise calculation. Independence was an event which was an arguable possibility, like the agnostic's view of the Day of Judgement, but not one to be prepared for seriously. In the second half of the colonial period these assumptions about normality were challenged with a speed and insistence that made even British empiricism seem a doctrine of inflexibility. During the 1940s and 1950s the open economies of West Africa underwent important modifications, with the result that by about 1960 few operated in their original, classical form. Moreover, between 1957 and 1965 the whole of colonial West Africa (with one exception) achieved political independence. The exception was Portuguese Guinea, a tiny possession that continues, so it is claimed, to move slowly (indeed, virtually imperceptibly) towards the realisation of the assimilationist ideals which are advertised as the chief motive for the continued presence of West Africa's first colonial power.

The purpose of this chapter is to describe and account for the modifications which were made to the open economies of West Africa during the years 1930–1960. More has been written about this phase of African history than about any preceding period of comparable length. The problem is no longer to secure enough historical information, as was the case in Chapter 2, but rather to compress, without too much distortion, the important specialised work which has been carried out in recent years, notably by economists and political scientists. There is the further complication that some of the major developments of this era were not peculiar to West Africa, or even to Africa as a whole, but had global significance. The Second World War, for example, was as important for the ending of colonialism throughout the world as were the American and French Revolutions in encouraging the rise of liberal nationalism in Europe during the nineteenth century. Consequently, any explanation of economic and political change which focuses solely on relations between Africans and their rulers is bound to be incomplete. An attempt will be made to take account of extra-African influences, though restrictions of space will prevent them from being treated on a scale appropriate to their importance. In spite of these difficulties there is still room, even within the compass of one brief chapter, for a degree of novelty both in presentation and in argument, if only for the reason that no general interpretation of this concluding phase of colonial rule has been advanced by an economic historian with respect to French and British West Africa.

In essence, it will be argued that modifications were introduced as a consequence of severe strains experienced by the open economy in the second half of the colonial era. It will be suggested that these strains were of two contrasting kinds. The first was imposed by a long period of hardship between 1930 and 1945, when export expansion was checked and the frontiers of the market economy contracted. It was at this time that Africans began to demonstrate their dissatisfaction with the open economy and with the alien rulers who presided over it. Initially, the response of the colonial powers was slow and inadequate, but by 1945 Britain and France had acknowledged the need for changes in official policy. The second strain was imposed by the expansion of the open economy after the Second World War, when there was a vigorous revival of exports and renewed growth in the domestic market. This period saw not only the implementation of changes made necessary by the pressures built up between 1930 and 1945, but also a novel development in the capacity of the open economy to generate structural change (albeit on a modest scale) through the establishment of modern manufacturing activities. African opposition to colonialism was not dissolved by this economic recovery. On the contrary, aspirations multiplied, and prosperity helped to finance the rise of political organisations which were to lead eventually to independence.

The simplest way of presenting this argument would be to proceed immediately to an examination of the two periods of strain noted above. However, two issues require investigation first of all, if this analysis of the pressures on the open economy is to be complete. To begin with, it is necessary to give further consideration to occupational roles in the export sector, and to degrees of specialisation within these roles, in order to stress the differential effects of fluctuations in the performance of the open economy. Next, it is essential to explore developments in domestic exchange activity, since the West African variant of the open economy grew out of the indigenous economy and continued to interact with it. These subjects have been neglected in the past, yet both should be central to the study of African economic and social history in the twentieth century.

1   Specialisation in the export sector

The previous chapter showed that Africans played an important part as farmers, traders and labourers in creating the colonial economy, but it did not attempt to investigate differentiation within these occupations. In the case of the farmers there came a stage, though its timing was not the same in all parts of West Africa, when groups of specialised producers began to emerge. Little is known about the elements of luck, skill and necessity which led to the development of this 'kulak' class. Nevertheless, the evidence points to the growth of inequalities among farming communities in the second half of the colonial period.

On the Gold Coast a small group of wealthy farmers, who were responsible for a disproportionately large amount of the cocoa shipped from the colony, had already appeared by 1930.[1] In Nigeria about a quarter of the farmers in Oyo province depended primarily on the production of cocoa in the 1930s, and no longer grew all the foodstuffs they needed.[2] By the 1950s about 10 per cent of cocoa farmers held 41 per cent of the land under cocoa in Nigeria, and over half the total volume of cocoa was grown by a minority of producers each of whose aggregate holdings exceeded six acres.[3] A parallel trend appeared on the Ivory Coast following the rapid expansion of cocoa farming after the Second World War, though there it was often 'strangers' who accumulated large holdings. Evidence for the regions exporting palm oil and kernels is harder to find because the economic history of these products in the twentieth century has been unjustly neglected, but there are indications, at least in eastern Nigeria, that a similar process of differentiation occurred. The groundnut producing areas have been better documented. In northern Nigeria inequalities in one rural community have been studied in depth,[4] while in Senegal it is clear that a relatively small number of wealthy Mourides managed to perpetuate the dominance they had achieved in the late nineteenth century.

Specialisation in export production did not lead to the creation of a distinct class of large landlords, which explains, perhaps, why the phenomenon of rural inequality has almost escaped attention. Typically, the holdings of substantial producers were scattered, and their employees were either members of their families, or were labourers who usually had some land of their own. Nevertheless, the appearance of groups of specialised producers had a considerable effect on the local economy. First, the expansion of their activities speeded the commercialisation of land. The twentieth century saw an increase in the amount of land in the export producing regions held virtually as freehold. This trend resulted partly from a general rise in the demand for farm land, and partly from a specific need to secure rights to a particular plot for more than one season, especially in areas where tree crops were grown. Secondly, the large farmers, though sometimes temporarily in debt themselves, stood as creditors at the head of an extensive network of financial relations, and frequently advanced money (usually on a seasonal basis) to the smaller farmers in the locality. Finally, the large farmers had the capital to introduce certain kinds of costly innovations. For example, with the mechanisation of groundnut farming in Senegal after the Second

---

[1] S. Rhodie, 'The Gold Coast Cocoa Hold-up of 1930–31', *Transactions of the Historical Society of Ghana*, 9, 1968, pp. 105–18.

[2] Daryll Forde, 'The Rural Economies', in *The Native Economies of Nigeria*, ed. Daryll Forde and R. Scott, 1946, pp. 86–7.

[3] R. Galletti, K. D. S. Baldwin and I. O. Dina, *Nigerian Cocoa Farmers*, Oxford 1956, pp. 149–52.

[4] Polly Hill, 'The Myth of the Amorphous Peasantry: a Northern Nigerian Case Study', *Nigerian Journal of Economic and Social Studies*, 10, 1968, pp. 239–60.

World War, the leading producers bought tractors, which they used themselves and also leased to the poorer farmers, thus reinforcing, by means of modern technology, their established position in the rural areas.

A similar process of differentiation occurred among African commercial firms operating in the overseas trade sector. This is not to deny, of course, that the distributive chain included many petty traders. Some, such as the 'pan' or 'basket' buyers in the cocoa regions, specialised in purchasing small quantities of produce. In 1938 it was estimated that there were no less than 37,000 of these small traders (sometimes called sub-brokers) on the Gold Coast. Other small traders retailed manufactured imports of the cheapest possible kind, such as yellow dusters—those banners of underdevelopment which are still flaunted in every urban centre. However, it is a mistake, though a common one, to interpret African commercial history in the twentieth century as being concerned entirely with the activities of these numerous, minor traders. There were substantial merchants too, men and women whose operations, though restricted in comparison with the expatriate firms, were on a scale which made them seem giants in the eyes of the average African trader.

Some of these African merchants concentrated on the export trade. On the Gold Coast in 1938, for example, there were about 1,500 cocoa brokers, that is large traders who bought from the sub-brokers and sold direct to the expatriate firms. Successful brokers sometimes became producers as well, as did Chief J. A. Obesesan of Ibadan, who started as a cocoa buyer in 1914 and subsequently invested some of his profits in farms, which were managed by paid agents. In northern Nigeria groundnut purchases were made by chains of buyers, many of which were controlled by substantial Hausa merchants. Agents (or clients) purchased groundnuts and brought them to the house of their principal (or patron), where they were bulked and re-sold to the expatriate firms. This organisation can be thought of as the commercial equivalent of indirect rule. On the import side there were a number of prominent wholesaling and retailing concerns. One of the most important was the Nigerian firm established by J. H. Doherty (1866–1928) and continued by his son, T. A. Doherty, down to the present day.[5] Doherty, the son of Christian, Egbado parents, started life as a clerk in an African firm in Lagos, and began trading on his own in 1891 with £47 capital. The expansion of colonial rule did not inhibit the growth of his business, for during the three years 1899–1901 Doherty's average net receipts from sales amounted to nearly £50,000 per annum. By 1904 Doherty had established branches in Lagos and in the interior, and by 1911 he was referred to as 'the leading native trader in Lagos in imported textiles'.[6] The firm's growth was checked in the 1920s, but at his death Doherty was still a very wealthy man. His son modernised the business by forming a limited liability company in 1930, and by introducing the structure and style of a department store after the Second World War. Some of the trading profits were reinvested in the company: the remainder

[5] I should like to thank Chief T. A. Doherty for helping me reconstruct the history of his family.
[6] C.O. 520/106, Egerton to Harcourt, 21 September 1911, Public Record Office.

went, in sizeable sums, into property, education and, inevitably, politics. When Chief Doherty's Rolls-Royce sweeps by, the yellow dusters wave in acknowledgement of an indigenous commercial success.

Developments affecting the wage labour force are also relevant to the argument advanced in this chapter. To begin with, the number of Africans in paid employment underwent a marked increase during the second half of the colonial period, and especially with the expansion of the economy and administration after 1945. Occasionally, the growth of employment opportunities occurred in an almost dramatic way, as in the case of Guinea, where the discovery and rapid exploitation of minerals in the 1950s created a paid labour force where previously almost none had existed. By 1960 the wage labour force in West Africa was estimated, conservatively, to be roughly two million strong, though this was still only about six per cent of the total labour force of 33 million.[7] In addition, a reserve army of unemployed arose in the towns during and after the 1930s, by which time the acute shortage of unskilled labour had been overcome.

Various explanations have been advanced to account for this persistent search for employment in the second half of the colonial period.[8] What might be called, loosely, an anthropological argument suggests that the expedition to secure work is a modern version of traditional initiation rites, after which the returning migrant, having overcome a series of hazards, can present himself to his elders as a fully-fledged adult. This view, though not without value, has been exaggerated in the past mainly, it seems, because for some time after it became established no one thought of an alternative. What might be termed, even more loosely, a psychological explanation holds that Africans continue to be lured to centres of employment by the promise of bright lights and excitement. Again, there may be some truth in this interpretation, but as it stands it rests on a naive assumption regarding the motivation of African migrants. A more recent view, which has achieved popularity among a number of economists, suggests that the increase in the number of Africans presenting themselves for paid employment in the towns was the result of a differential between urban wages and rural incomes. Belief in the significance of this differential has led some commentators to refer to African urban employees as an 'aristocracy' of labour. It is true that some highly qualified Africans held well paid and attractive jobs, but the majority of urban employees were unskilled men who earned relatively low wages. By the time their higher outgoings (urban rents, food and the maintenance of incoming relatives) have been taken into account, the net differential, if it existed, was scarcely sufficient to maintain seigneurial standards of consumption.

An alternative explanation of the growth in the volume of labour on offer should be based on the following considerations, which are extensions of the approach

[7] K. C. Doctor and H. Gallis, 'Size and Characteristics of Wage Employment in Africa: Some Statistical Estimates', *International Labour Review*, 93, 1966, pp. 149–73.

[8] These explanations have been put forward mainly with urban migrants in mind, though some of the reasons summarised here have also been thought to apply to agricultural migrations.

adopted in the last chapter.[9] In the first place, knowledge of employment opportunities was more widespread after 1930 than before. Secondly, with the spread of motor vehicles the means of reaching the centres of demand were more readily available and were also cheaper. Thirdly, improved conditions of work, reflected in a fall in accident and mortality rates, increased the attractions of certain kinds of employment.[10] Fourthly, family connections and ethnic organisations had been developed to assist newcomers, and these eliminated some of the problems which had faced the early, pioneer migrants.[11] Finally, the assessment which individuals made of their employment prospects was more optimistic than was warranted by a detached appraisal of the total employment situation.[12] Towns were regarded as places where advancement was possible, and African immigrants were no more deterred by the existence of widespread unemployment than was that famous English migrant, Dick Whittington, when he set out to make his fortune in London in the fourteenth century.[13] The 'aristocratic' urban employee was important as an ideal rather than as a reality.

Certain features of this enlarged wage labour force need emphasising. To begin with, an increasing proportion of wage earners took permanent jobs in the second half of the colonial period. Next, a substantial part of the wage labour force outside agriculture shared a common and readily identifiable employer, namely the colonial government, while most of the remainder worked for expatriate commercial and mining firms. Furthermore, employees in the 'modern' sector tended to be located in concentrated settlements. Indeed, immigration was largely responsible for a remarkable expansion in the size of West African towns in the second half of the colonial era. Increases of between three and ten times over a period of twenty to forty years were common, as the following examples show: the population of Dakar rose from 94,000 in 1939 to nearly 400,000 in 1960; that of Abidjan from 18,000 to 180,000 during the same period; Freetown grew from 44,000 in 1921 to 128,000 in 1963; and Lagos from 99,000 in 1936 to 675,000 by 1962. Finally, institutions were introduced to help employees cope with their new environmental and work situations. Africans adapted indigenous associations to deal with these urban problems, just as they did in agriculture and trade, so there was no sudden destruction of that once popular textbook figure—tribal man. As some of the migrants became proletarians, they also adopted modern organisations, notably trade unions. Modern trade unions existed in West Africa even before the First World War, but were confined to a very small minority of skilled workers, such as civil servants. During and after the Second World War, however, came the growth of 'new unionism', which began to embrace the unskilled wage earners. These unions were urban based; they relied heavily

[9] See above, pp. 222–31.

[10] Marvin P. Miracle and Bruce Fetter, 'Backward-Sloping Labour Supply Functions and African Economic Behaviour', *Economic Development and Cultural Change*, 18, 1970, pp. 240–51.

[11] K. Little, *West African Urbanization*, Cambridge 1965.

[12] This point emerges clearly from Guy Pfeffermann's study, *Industrial Labour in the Republic of Senegal*, New York 1968.

[13] The fact that much of Dick Whittington's story is myth merely underlines the point!

on permanent wage earners for their membership; and they were particularly strong in the public sector. The part they played during the periods of strain experienced by the open economy will be considered later in this chapter.

The foregoing survey of three major occupations is intended in general to contribute to the writing of indigenous history, and in particular to correct the conventional portrayal of the role of Africans in the export sector. The analysis has questioned the belief that Africans (or Chinese for that matter) can be referred to in aggregate, as if their daily lives approximated closely to a notional idea of unremarkable and uniform simplicity. In this instance the economist's formal assumption that each factor of production is homogeneous is seriously at variance with reality. A more complex view, it is suggested, is more accurate, and is of greater value in understanding the final phase of colonial rule. There has been a tendency, for example, to exaggerate the so-called 'buffer capacity' of African producers. It is often said that Africans can absorb the effects of a slump in the export sector because the typical cocoa or groundnut farmer grows his own foodstuffs as well, the typical trader is also a farmer, and the typical labourer is a migrant who can easily return to the land. This argument ignores the existence of specialised groups in each category, men who could revert to self-sufficiency only by restructuring their economic activities and by taking a substantial cut in their living standards. The large farmers, the leading traders and the permanent wage earners stood to gain most from the expansion of the open economy, but were also most at risk when it entered a stagnant phase. These men, though numerically a small proportion of the total population, were highly significant in economic and political terms. Knowledge of the composition of the independence movements, it is suggested, helps to explain the nature of their demands, their relations with the colonial powers, and the character of the new governments which were established in West Africa after 1957.

2   The domestic economy

The discussion can now move on to consider the domestic economy. This topic is important in relation to the main theme of this book, namely the development of a market economy, and to the specific interpretation advanced in this chapter. With regard to the first aspect, it was argued in Chapter 4 that the early nineteenth century saw the emergence of an export economy which was recognisably modern, in the sense that its structure resembled that which exists today. The growth of the new economy has been examined already with reference to changes within the export sector itself, but it remains to be shown (though it has been asserted) that this pattern of development established close links with the domestic market. As to the second aspect, a study of the domestic economy is necessary for an appreciation of the full extent of the strain experienced in West Africa during the period 1930–1945, and also for an understanding of the capacity of the open economy to generate a market which was large enough to sustain modern manufacturing industries in the period after 1945.

The domestic economy was largely ignored by the colonial administration because it was not, on the whole, an important source of public revenue, and it was also neglected by the expatriate commercial firms, which chose to concentrate on the staples of the import and export trade. Oddly enough, the very success of the African distributive system, which transferred goods and services with unobtrusive efficiency, seems to have confirmed the low priority accorded by expatriates to internal trade. Had indigenous channels proved inadequate, serious shortages would have occurred; the administration would have had to intervene; reports would have been written; and scholars would probably have become interested in the subject at an earlier date. In fact, it was not until the 1950s that economists discovered the existence of internal trade,[14] and it is only in the last few years that they, together with geographers and anthropologists, have begun to examine this topic in detail.[15] As yet, no one has attempted to write an economic history of the domestic trade of West Africa during the period of colonial rule. However, lack of comprehensive descriptive information and statistical data has not prevented a number of assertions from gaining currency. Perhaps the most widespread of these is the generalisation that many items of traditional trade declined in the twentieth century as a result of competition from foreign imports. It will be argued here that the evidence available at present shows not only that internal trade survived, but that it underwent considerable expansion. This interpretation is not intended as a defence of colonialism, but rather as a tribute to the skill and adaptability of Africans at a time when unprecedented demands were being placed on indigenous production and marketing arrangements. It is hoped that the remarks which follow will encourage other historians to investigate this important subject in greater depth.

Expanding demand for domestic goods and services in the twentieth century was brought about by a reduction in internal transport costs, by rising per capita incomes, particularly in the towns and in wealthy, export-producing, rural areas, by increased specialisation, and by population growth. Indigenous marketing channels were called on to supply new geographical regions, to adapt to modern transport facilities, to adjust to the colonial monetary system, and to fight foreign competition. The response of African entrepreneurs to this situation will be illustrated in the following ways: by taking foodstuffs as an example of what, traditionally, was a local trade, by using kola and livestock as case studies of long distance trade, and by looking at the position of domestic manufactures, which were traded locally and over long distances.

Figures showing the expansion of food production are hard to come by, and, when found, are subject to a wide margin of error. Nevertheless, specialised studies clearly indicate that there was a substantial increase in the volume of foodstuffs placed on the market, particularly in the period following the Second World War.

[14] A. R. Prest and I. G. Stewart, *The National Income of Nigeria, 1950–51*, 1953, and P. T. Bauer, *West African Trade*, Cambridge 1954, ch. 27.

[15] See, for example, Bernard Vinay, *L'Afrique commerce avec l'Afrique*, Paris 1968; Alan M. Hay and Robert H. T. Smith, *Interregional Trade and Money Flows in Nigeria*, Ibadan 1970; and Paul Bohannan and George Dalton, eds., *Markets in Africa*, Evanston 1962.

In the case of French West Africa, for instance, Capet has estimated that production of the main foodstuffs grew by an average of about 50 per cent between 1947 and 1954.[16] Rising demand was met by the development of specialised food-producing regions in West Africa. These served the main towns, and, less obviously, the food deficient rural areas, typically where farmers had concentrated on export production, but occasionally where population density was too great for self-sufficiency to be possible, as in the case of the area around Onitsha and Owerri in eastern Nigeria. Reliance by rural areas on external supplies was on the whole unusual, and of two kinds. The first was found in places where the pattern of export production placed an exceptional strain on the domestic economy. The best example is the huge groundnut-producing region of Senegal, which began to import sizeable quantities of rice, mostly from Indo-China, in the 1930s. Dependence on foreign imports derived from the fact that groundnuts compete with foodstuffs for land and labour to a much greater extent than do cocoa, coffee and palm products. The Gambia also needed additional foodstuffs, but met the demand from within West Africa, chiefly by purchasing rice from Sierra Leone. Northern Nigeria, the other large groundnut-producing region in West Africa, has not experienced the same problem. Its economy is more varied than that of Senegambia, and it has received a degree of natural protection from imports by being located so far from the sea. The second type of local deficiency was in certain quality foods, such as sugar, wheat and wheat flour, imports of which increased during the 1950s. This was a special case, brought about partly by the presence of expatriates, and partly by the diversification of tastes among wealthier Africans, and did not reflect a failure in indigenous production of basic foods.

Two novel features of the trade in foodstuffs during the twentieth century are worth noting for purposes of comparison with the pre-colonial period. First, improved crop storage facilities have tended to reduce seasonal variations in the market availability of food. This innovation has been influential not only in enlarging the business of food traders, but also in making possible the maintenance of a permanent labour force outside agriculture. Second, transport developments, especially the introduction of motor vehicles, have blurred the distinction drawn in Chapter 2 between local and long distance trade. For the first time it has become profitable to trade staple food crops outside the area of production, as the case of Accra illustrates.[17] In 1957–1958 Accra imported 144,000 tons of foodstuffs (mainly plantains, processed manioc and root manioc) from the interior. A proportion of this total was supplied by local market gardens, but 55 per cent was brought from between fifty and one hundred miles away, and no less than 30 per cent came from distances of more than a hundred miles, stretching as far as the Northern Territories. Moreover, since the food trade is highly competitive, each region in the hinterland

---

[16] Marcel Capet, *Traité d'économie tropicale*, Paris 1958, pp. 276–7. This neglected work contains a great deal of useful information about French West Africa during the period 1945–54.

[17] H. P. White, 'Internal Exchange of Staple Foods in the Gold Coast', *Economic Geography*, 32, 1956, pp. 115–25, and Thomas T. Poleman, 'The Food Economies of Urban Middle Africa: the Case of Ghana', *Food Research Institute Studies*, 2, 1961, pp. 121–74.

has been encouraged to specialise in the production of a particular type of food for the Accra market. A similar extension of the food trade can be seen in other parts of West Africa: in the Ivory Coast, for instance, where the cocoa and coffee farmers in the south imported about 12,000 tons of rice a year from northern parts of the country in the 1950s; and in Nigeria, where rice, cowpeas and guinea corn are sent several hundred miles to southern destinations, and palm oil travels from the forest to the savanna.

The main items of long distance trade also survived colonial rule, and at least some grew in volume. As was shown in the last chapter, the movement of labour increased in the twentieth century following the decline of slavery and the rise of wage employment opportunities. It is highly probable that the traditional fish trade also expanded. The specialised communities which paid their taxes in fish on the middle Niger during the sixteenth century now supply urban centres hundreds of miles away: in 1954, for example, Mopti and Segou sent 10–12,000 tons of dried fish to the Ivory Coast alone.[18] Similarly, local salt from Bilma in Niger continues to have a wide sale in northern Nigeria, where it is exchanged against grain.[19] Certain other minerals, notably gold and iron, are still produced by traditional means and traded over long distances, though information about quantities is insufficient to permit comparisons with the pre-colonial period. There is enough evidence, however, to demonstrate the impressive development of two of the greatest traditional trades— kola and livestock.

The western part of the savanna continues to receive its supplies of kola nuts from the Ivory Coast and, to a lesser extent, from Sierra Leone, as in the pre-colonial period.[20] Exports by land and sea from the Ivory Coast grew from two or three thousand tons a year at the beginning of the present century to 28–30,000 tons in 1954, by which time kola had become the colony's most valuable export after coffee and cocoa. About a third of this total was destined for consumption in Senegal, where the expansion of groundnut exports had raised domestic purchasing power. This increased trade, however, no longer passes along the ancient caravan routes. Most exports now move north by lorry to Bamako, the capital of Mali, and are then taken by rail to Senegal, while the remainder are sent by steamer to Dakar. The eastern part of the savanna is supplied by Ghana (formerly the Gold Coast) and by Nigeria.[21] Northern Nigeria, long established as the major market, became even more important during the colonial period as a result of the development of the

[18] Jean Tricart, 'Les échanges entre la zone forestière de Côte d'Ivoire et les savanes soudaniennes', *Cahiers d'Outre-Mer*, 9, 1956, p. 219.

[19] Capitaine Grandin, 'Notes sur l'industrie et le commerce du sel au Kawar et en Agram', *Bulletin de l'IFAN*, B, 13, 1951, pp. 488–533; Maurice Fievet, 'Salt Caravan', *Nigeria Magazine*, 41, 1953, pp. 4–20.

[20] Jean-Loup Amselle, 'Les réseaux marchands Kooroko', *African Urban Notes*, 5, 1970, pp. 143–58.

[21] A. G. Hopkins, *An Economic History of Lagos, 1880–1914*, University of London Ph.D. thesis, 1964, pp. 407–13, and Paul E. Lovejoy, 'The Wholesale Kola Trade of Kano', *African Urban Notes*, 5, 1970, pp. 129–42.

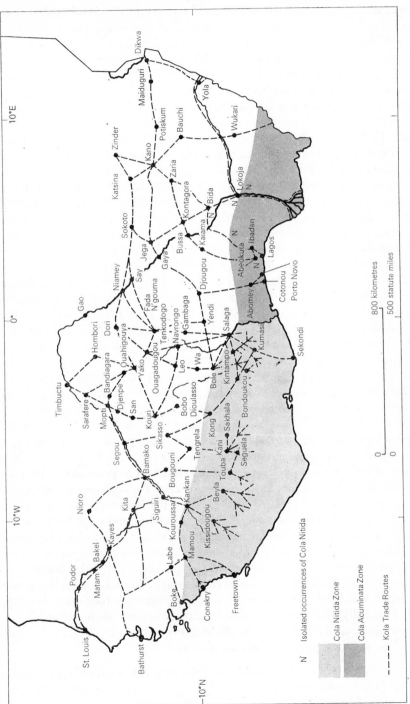

MAP 15. Distribution of Kola and Kola Trade Routes about 1910.

N   Isolated occurrences of Cola Nitida

Cola Nitida Zone

Cola Acuminata Zone

- - - - Kola Trade Routes

groundnut trade. Traditionally, the main channel of distribution for this region was an overland route from the Gold Coast, which delivered about 500 tons of kola nuts a year in the late nineteenth century. Two innovations have brought about a fundamental reorientation of this pre-colonial marketing arrangement. First, in the 1880s a group of Hausa merchants began to use the regular steamship service to transport kola to Lagos from Accra and Cape Coast. The modernisation of the kola trade was completed in 1911, when the railway reached Kano; from then on it was no longer necessary to use porters and pack animals to carry the nuts north from Lagos. The trade expanded, and in 1924 almost 10,000 tons of kola were imported into Nigeria by way of the new sea route. Second, during the 1920s kola trees of the type found in the Gold Coast began to be grown in Nigeria itself, with the result that domestic production eventually supplanted imports. In 1964 no less than 54,000 tons of kola were sent to northern Nigeria from the south. However, this Nigerian initiative did not lead to the demise of the Gold Coast kola industry. Traders in that colony reacted, in characteristic fashion, by seeking out new markets, and with the aid of the motor lorry they succeeded in establishing themselves elsewhere, notably in Upper Volta and parts of Mali and Niger.

Although the history of commerce in livestock has still to be written, there is no doubt that this trade also expanded in the twentieth century.[22] Today, the production of cattle and sheep is especially important in the territories of former French West Africa, particularly Mali, Upper Volta and Niger. The sale of livestock provides these countries with one of their few close connections with the leading export-producing regions, and helps them to buy imported consumer goods and local products, such as kola nuts. In 1936 Niger and Soudan exported at least 65,000 head of cattle to other parts of West Africa; twenty years later, this trade had reached the 200,000 mark. The chief recipients were Senegal, the Ivory Coast, the Gold Coast and Nigeria. The largest single market is still southern Nigeria, which is supplied by the northern part of the country as well as by Niger and Chad. In 1906 about 8,000 cattle, sheep and goats were recorded passing into southern Nigeria from the north. In the 1930s the figure rose to just over 200,000, and by 1964 no less than 300,000 head of cattle alone were imported into the south together with 118,000 sheep, rams, goats and pigs. As in the case of the kola trade, the railways have captured a great deal of this traffic, though substantial numbers of livestock are still brought to market on the hoof. Contrary to a common assumption, the growth of the trade was not the result of colonial tutelage overcoming an ingrained preference for hoarding cattle, for commerce in livestock is as old as the earliest written records relating to West Africa.[23] Nor should the negative stimulus of cattle taxes, such as the *jangali*, which was first imposed in northern Nigeria in 1905–1906, be exaggerated. Essentially, the trade expanded because it became more profitable, and it became more profitable because the effective demand for meat increased as Africans earned money through the sale of export crops.

[22] For an account of one branch of this trade see Polly Hill, *Studies in Rural Capitalism in West Africa*, Cambridge 1970, pp. 80–140.

[23] See Chapter 2, part 2.

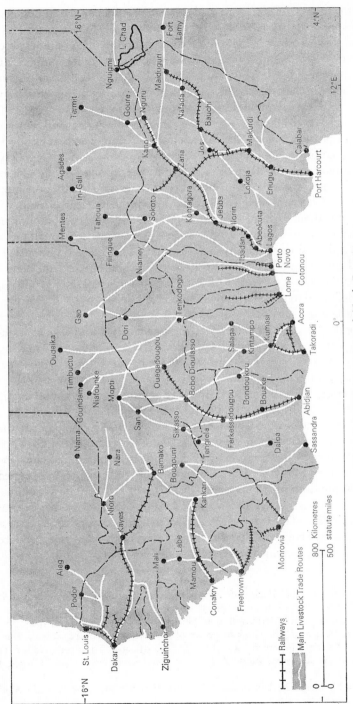

MAP 16. Present Day Livestock Trade Routes.

Railways

Main Livestock Trade Routes

800 Kilometres
500 statute miles

From the number of assertions made about the elimination of traditional crafts, it might be supposed that the subject had been thoroughly investigated. This is not the case. In practice these assertions rest on the assumption that domestic products *must* have declined because they were in competition with cheaper imports. The argument is appealing, but it is also misleading. While it is likely that certain types of craft products in particular areas suffered from European competition, what little work has been carried out indicates that there was no wholesale liquidation of local manufactures, even though expatriate officials and merchants emphasised the advantages of discarding traditional crafts in favour of export production. It is interesting to note that one of the few detailed studies made of this question reaches a broadly similar conclusion with reference to the fortunes of the Chinese textile industry.[24] The *proportion* of manufactured goods supplied by domestic industry undoubtedly fell sharply from the second half of the nineteenth century onwards: by 1962 only about eight per cent of textiles intended for consumption in Nigeria were produced by traditional hand-weavers. However, a substantial proportionate decline is still consistent with an *absolute* rise in the volume of traditional production because the market underwent a massive expansion during the same period. Indeed, the evidence suggests that some African crafts, having resisted the initial impact of imports delivered to the interior by rail, received a new lease of life during the latter half of the colonial era.

It is quite clear, for example, that the manufacture and sale of leather goods increased with the growth of the livestock trade. It is equally certain that the production of clay pots also survived. One local study has shown that the pottery industry of the Shai people in the southern part of the Gold Coast expanded during the colonial period, and now has an output of about half a million pots a year.[25] Thus part of the demand for palm wine and water containers is still met by domestic products, even though the Gold Coast has long been one of the greatest importers of European manufactures in West Africa! Another specialised piece of research has drawn attention to the continuing dynamism of the traditional cloth industry at Iseyin in western Nigeria.[26] It is known, too, that the production of expensive and weighty Kente cloth still flourishes in Ghana, for in 1962 output was estimated to be about two million square yards, or almost 900 tons.[27] These two cases are not isolated exceptions. Even as late as 1964, when modern textile factories had been established in West Africa, traditional hand-weavers using hand-spun yarn produced about 9,000 tons of textiles, which was roughly a third of total domestic output. The main

[24] Albert Feuerwerker, 'Handicraft and Manufactured Cotton Textiles in China, 1871–1910', *Journal of Economic History*, 30, 1970, pp. 338–78.

[25] A. K. Quarcoo and Marion Johnson, 'Shai Pots', *Baessler-Archiv*, 16, 1968, pp. 47–88.

[26] Jennifer M. Bray, 'The Craft Structure of a Traditional Yoruba Town', *Transactions of the Institute of British Geographers*, 46, 1969, pp. 179–93, and 'The Economics of Traditional Cloth Production in Iseyin, Nigeria', *Economic Development and Cultural Change*, 17, 1969, pp. 540–51.

[27] United Nations, 'The Textile Industry in the West African Sub-region', *Economic Bulletin for Africa*, 7, 1968, pp. 103–25.

areas of production in that year were Nigeria, Mali, Upper Volta, Ghana, the Ivory Coast and Senegal. Again, it is striking that the regions where traditional manufactures continue to thrive include countries which are also the largest importers of consumer goods. Finally, it is worth noting that the growth and diversification of the open economy has encouraged the rise of new types of 'cottage' industry, such as bicycle repairing, which have helped to offset losses suffered by those crafts that were affected by European competition.

There are four main reasons for the survival of traditional manufactures in the twentieth century. First, certain products are protected by proximity to the market and by low overheads at the manufacturing stage. This is particularly true of hollow-ware, such as pots, which are costly to transport over long distances, and which are produced in West Africa mainly by cheap family labour. Second, some products continue to sell, even though they compete directly with cheaper European imports, because they are highly regarded by consumers. Local salt remains in demand because its taste is preferred and because it is thought to enhance virility. Similarly, local iron-ware is held to be stronger and more durable than imported substitutes. It is easy to deride these beliefs as examples of the 'primitive' nature of consumer behaviour in the underdeveloped world. However, it is as well to remember that the agents of what is, technically, the modern world also sell their products—from beer to cars—by appealing to human ambitions and weaknesses. It would be fairer to say that modern advertising has failed to dissolve established brand loyalties. Third, traditional crafts survived because they were able to secure a niche as special lines in a differentiated product market. Consumers bought imported *and* domestic textiles because there were hundreds of varieties of cloth, and not all served the same purpose or suited the same tastes. Indeed, as the colonial period advanced, traditional textiles became increasingly fashionable as an index of status and as a symbol of identification with African culture and with the nationalist movement.[28] Fourth, some crafts survived by employing new techniques. Thus the use of sewing machines enabled tailors to cut their production costs and increase their output.

By far the greater part of domestic trade remained in the hands of Africans themselves. The success of local traders in expanding and redirecting internal trade in the twentieth century is a feat which has not been fully acknowledged, yet one which merits comparison with the more publicised achievements of Africans in export production. Just as indigenous, and allegedly antiquated, institutions proved their dynamism in agriculture, so, too, the pre-colonial distributive system fostered the growth of trade in the twentieth century. All the main features of commercial organisation discussed in Chapter 2, such as rotating markets, landlords, brokers, credit and the family firm, survived. It was the attributes of the family firm, particularly its flexible size, low overheads, familiarity with local conditions, reserves of skill, goodwill and capital, and wide geographical coverage, that made expansion

---

[28] In England the traditional crafts of sadlers and thatchers have experienced a revival since the Second World War as a result of the increasing affluence and changing aspirations of new social classes.

possible. On the whole, the economic unity of areas which had been linked by market transactions in the pre-colonial period was not severed by European rule. Under the French and British, as in the time of Mansa Musa, long distance trade continued to span political divisions. Ironically, it was the achievement of political independence which led to the erection of barriers to the internal flow of goods and services, the claims of territorial sovereignty proving in this instance more than a match for the ideals of pan-Africanism.

Continuity with the past is exemplified by the way in which the Hausa and Dioula, the great long distance traders of the pre-colonial period, managed to perpetuate their dominance in the twentieth century. Admittedly, their success has been helped by the continued presence of long-established barriers to entry. Capital, for example, remains scarce, and credit tends to be issued by a relatively few substantial traders, with the result that small groups control the main items of long distance trade. The oligopoly which Bauer identified in external trade is paralleled in certain branches of internal trade as well: each has its own commercial Establishment. Nevertheless, supremacy was not maintained automatically, and traditional groups have been involved in a sustained struggle with new competitors and with changing economic opportunities. As to the first, Abner Cohen has analysed how the Hausa community of Ibadan manipulated traditional religious and political means of maintaining group solidarity in order to protect its control over the kola trade.[29] With regard to the second, Peter Garlick has shown how the Kwahu, a Gold Coast people with a long tradition of commercial specialisation, adapted from trading to the north in slaves early in the nineteenth century, to sending rubber to the south in the period 1874–1914, then to selling imported goods in the expanding cocoa-farming areas, and finally to becoming settled shopkeepers in Accra from the 1930s onwards.[30]

The success of the indigenous distributive system owed a great deal to its capacity to innovate as well as to its ability simply to perpetuate, and occasionally modify, essentially unchanged virtues. Three innovations in particular seem to have been significant, though doubtless the number will be extended by future research. In the first place, there were important changes in personnel. As traditional ties of dependence, notably slavery, were loosened, a large new group of independent traders began to make its mark. Ja Ja represented such a change in the export trade, and Omu Okwei, though not a slave, may stand as an example of a similar departure in internal trade.[31] Women traders have always been important in West Africa, but the growth of the economy in the twentieth century, and especially since the Second World War, has enabled some of them to expand their activities and to invest in other enterprises, as the ubiquitous 'Mammy wagons' testify. A rather different illustration of increased social mobility in commerce is provided by the Saharan salt trade. Today, the trade from Bilma is conducted in independent family units by those who

---

[29] Abner Cohen, *Custom and Politics in Urban Africa*, 1969.

[30] Peter C. Garlick, 'The Development of Kwahu Business Enterprise in Ghana since 1874—an Essay in Recent Oral Tradition', *Journal of African History*, 8, 1967, pp. 463–80.

[31] See above, pp. 146 and 205.

were slaves and vassals of the Tuareg, while their former masters, reluctantly breaking with tradition, now have to work for a living. Second, the pre-colonial distributive system has had to adjust to the advent of modern technology. Traders who used to patrol the frontiers of the exchange economy on foot have reorganised to take advantage of the steamship, the railway engine and the motor lorry. Production for internal exchange has also been affected by Western technology. The traditional fishermen on the middle Niger have been joined by migrants who employ more modern techniques,[32] while on the coast fishing is becoming mechanised.[33] Third, just as wage-earners established trade unions, so, too, the indigenous distributive system spawned new commercial organisations, where these were needed. The traditional communal network, for example, is not well suited to the motor transport business, which demands a particularly individualistic pattern of labour organisation. This problem has been solved by the development of novel institutions, such as the Ivory Coast Transporters' Association, which grew up in the 1950s.[34]

The foregoing examination of domestic exchange is related to the analysis of the strain exerted on the open economy in two ways. To begin with, it is important to appreciate that growth in the domestic economy was determined primarily by the performance of the export sector: that is to say, the amount of money spent on local goods and services fluctuated with the level of receipts from exports, given that the proportion of earnings exchanged for imports remained more or less constant for the greater part of the colonial period. Thus the poor terms of trade in the period 1930–1945 had a serious effect on the internal market. In general it can be said that when the export trade was depressed fewer cattle were sent south, fewer kola nuts were imported into the savanna, fewer craft products were sold, fewer labourers were employed and so fewer foodstuffs were produced for exchange. In short, a depression in world trade affected not only the export-producing regions themselves, but a complex network of multilateral connections in the domestic economy.[35] This conclusion, though it has rarely been emphasised, is essential to a full understanding of the stresses experienced in West Africa after 1930. Next, though all traders in the domestic economy suffered to some extent from this long period of depression, they did not suffer equally. In internal trade, as in the export-producing regions, it was the specialised personnel who were hit hardest. An appreciation of the differential effects of commercial fluctuations should lead to a more accurate view of what is usually referred to simply as 'African' opposition to colonialism.

[32] S. Jacquemond, 'Les pêcheurs de la boucle du Niger', *Bulletin du Comité de Travaux Historiques et Scientifiques: Section de Géographie*, 71, 1958, pp. 103–35.

[33] Rowena Lawson, 'The Transition of Ghana's Fishing from a Primitive to a Mechanized Industry', *Transactions of the Historical Society of Ghana*, 9, 1968, pp. 90–104.

[34] Barbara Lewis, 'Ethnicity, Occupational Specialization, and Interest Groups: the Transporters' Association of the Ivory Coast', *African Urban Notes*, 5, 1970, pp. 95–115.

[35] E. K. Hawkins, 'The Growth of a Money Economy in Nigeria and Ghana', *Oxford Economic Papers*, 10, 1958, pp. 339–54.

3 Strains on the open economy, 1930–45

From 1930 until the end of the Second World War, West Africa experienced a period of severe and increasing hardship as the barter and income terms of trade of export producers underwent a serious deterioration. After 1930 a given 'basket' of exports purchased a progressively smaller 'basket' of imports, and Africans had to step up the volume, and hence raise the value, of cash crop production merely to maintain existing levels of import consumption. This course of action led to increased production costs, in spite of the advent of the motor lorry, because at that time there was no way of expanding exports without purchasing additional inputs of land and labour. Even with a larger export volume, producers were still unable to halt the slide in their total import-purchasing power, and the result was that their real incomes fell. The reactions of African farmers, traders and wage-earners to this situation clearly show that they were, or at least considered themselves to be, worse off than they had been before. As far as the historian is concerned, it is the subjective evaluation of participants which is of chief interest, for it was this which caused them to try and influence the course of events.

The principal tactic adopted by farmers in defence of their living standards was to make adjustments to the supply of produce. The volume of exports expanded considerably in the 1930s, and shipments of groundnuts and cocoa reached record levels. This 'perverse' response of primary producers (so-called because the orthodox, capitalist reaction to declining profits is to cut back production) is not hard to understand. In the case of annual crops, such as groundnuts, investment in production was short-term, and in theory could be varied from season to season. In practice, however, exports continued to rise because farmers were committed to a standard of living which was derived from export earnings, and no alternative means of buying imports could be devised. Faced with a similar situation in the 1880s and 1890s, farmers had begun to develop new export crops, but in the 1930s no further diversification was possible, or at least was achieved. During the Second World War it became very difficult to obtain imported goods, especially in French West Africa, and at that point farmers did reduce production. In 1943 groundnut exports from Senegal fell to 35,000 tons, a figure which was lower than at any time since the 1880s. The frontiers of the exchange economy contracted, and there was a retreat into subsistence as farmers began to plant millet instead of groundnuts. Clearly, the process of market growth in the colonial period, as in preceding centuries, was fitful and far from irreversible. In the case of tree crops, such as cocoa and coffee, farmers were stuck with an investment which could not be reallocated easily. This lack of flexibility in the production structure meant that Africans had little choice but to harvest as much of their existing tree-crops as possible in an attempt to compensate for falling produce prices. At the same time, however, they planted fewer *new* trees, a decision which demonstrates that in the long run their response to declining profits was entirely orthodox.[36] Thus the impressive expansion of exports during the 1930s

[36] On this lagged response see Robert M. Stern, 'The Determinants of Cocoa Supply in West Africa', in *African Primary Products and International Trade*, ed. I. G. Stewart and H. W. Ord, Edinburgh 1965, pp. 65–82.

was not an indication of prosperity (a response to high produce prices) but was squeezed out of the economy by an adverse movement in the terms of trade.

At particularly critical times farmers demonstrated their dissatisfaction with the state of the economy in more militant ways, principally by withholding supplies in the hope of forcing buyers to offer increased prices. This was a well established technique, and one which had given expression to African resentment, frustration and despair during periods of unsatisfactory trade in the nineteenth century. A number of protests of this kind took place in the years between the two World Wars, the best known being the three principal cocoa hold-ups on the Gold Coast. The first was in 1921, when the post-war boom in cocoa prices suddenly came to an end;[37] the second occurred in 1930–1931 following the onset of the world slump;[38] and the third, which also involved Nigeria, took place in 1937 and was a reaction to a further downturn in the terms of trade and to a market-sharing agreement made by the European buying firms.[39] These rural 'strikes' were led by substantial, specialised farmers, men whose 'buffer capacity' was limited and who strove to persuade the small farmers (who had less to lose) to present a united front against the buying firms. The hold-ups failed, but, in failing, worsened Afro-European relations, and in particular increased the hostility of the larger farmers towards the expatriate firms and towards the expatriate government, which was regarded as supporting the existing marketing system.

The decline in the producers' terms of trade also affected traders. Business became less profitable, but few traders were able to introduce compensating reductions in operating costs because their overheads were already very low. They, too, expressed their opposition by demonstrations against measures which weighed on them particularly heavily, such as increased taxation and the issue of trading licences during the Second World War. Usually, however, their protests were small scale, spontaneous, and of short duration. With the possible exception of the women's riots in eastern Nigeria in 1929, in which commercial interests played a prominent part, none of the traders' demonstrations had the impact of the hold-ups organised by the farmers. Nevertheless, a group of merchants in Nigeria and the Gold Coast did initiate one important and constructive move, and this is worth mentioning as evidence of the reactions of 'Westernised' African businessmen to the problems of the inter-war period.

At the beginning of the twentieth century the common assumption among the educated, and the predominantly Christian, merchants in the large coastal entrepôts was that the implementation of colonial notions of partnership and assimilation would present them with more opportunities for advancement than they had enjoyed previously. The reality was rather different. By about the time of the post-war slump of 1921, it was clear that African import and export merchants had

[37] David Kimble, *A Political History of Ghana, 1850–1928*, Oxford 1963, pp. 49–51.

[38] S. Rhodie, 'The Gold Coast Cocoa Hold-up of 1930–31', *Transactions of the Historical Society of Ghana*, 9, 1968, pp. 105–18.

[39] Josephine Milburn, 'The 1938 Gold Coast Cocoa Crisis: British Business and the Colonial Office', *African Historical Studies*, 3, 1970, pp. 57–74.

9*

suffered a serious decline relative to their European rivals. Some Africans dropped out of the direct import and export business. Those who remained recognised that it was necessary to adopt Western business institutions if they were to remain in what they termed 'the commercial race'. In the 1920s and 1930s African merchants tried to establish limited liability companies and modern banking institutions of their own in an attempt to find ways of competing with the massive expatriate combines, which were themselves products of the new and more competitive commercial environment of the twentieth century. Perhaps the best examples of the commercial ambitions of the time were the spectacular ventures mounted by the Gold Coast businessman, Tete-Ansa, who became known, momentarily, as the 'Napoleon' of West African commerce.[40] Between 1925 and 1935 Tete-Ansa founded producers' co-operatives in Nigeria and the Gold Coast in an attempt to strengthen the bargaining position of farmers and lower their costs; he formed the Industrial and Commercial Bank in Nigeria, which was intended to finance African participation in external trade; and he set up an agency in New York to sell produce and to buy imports for shipment to West Africa. The scheme was a radical one, but the aims behind it were moderate enough. Tete-Ansa and his backers were seeking a better place for Africans (especially educated Africans) within the colonial system, but they were not asking for total African control of the economy, still less for political independence. Tete-Ansa's plans were unsuccessful: but the Waterloo of this Napoleon had its significance. The liquidation of Tete-Ansa's companies and his own self-imposed exile in Canada symbolised the failure of his brand of moderate leadership and reformist proposals. By the late 1930s Africans were beginning to undertake a more fundamental re-appraisal of their predicament.

As members of the coastal elite, African merchants suffered social humiliation as well as economic defeat. Educated, Christian Africans found themselves treated with less consideration after the expansion of colonial rule than they had been in the nineteenth century. Since their aspirations and life-styles were linked more closely to those of the European community than was the case with the majority of African colonial subjects, they were especially sensitive to social rebuffs stemming from racial prejudice. They were excluded from a number of commercial organisations and social clubs, some of which had begun on a multiracial basis. Even cricket, that most imperial of games, failed to act as an integrative force. As early as 1898 one British governor on the West Coast ordered two cricket pitches to be laid, 'one for the Europeans the other for the natives'.[41] Matches played between the two teams became tests of the capacity of the races, a practical application of Carlyle's bizarre theories, though when the African side hit a winning streak the series was discontinued! The French, lacking cricket, but possessing an alternative and more explicit instrument in their policy of assimilation, were equally unsuccessful. In practice very few Africans became 'Frenchmen'. Fewer still wished to do so after

---

[40] A. G. Hopkins, 'Economic Aspects of Political Movements in Nigeria and in the Gold Coast, 1918–1939', *Journal of African History*, 7, 1966, pp. 133–52.

[41] C.O. 147/116, McCallum to Chamberlain, 31 August 1897, Public Record Office.

1940, when the attractions of becoming citizens of a defeated nation and a declining imperial power were scarcely compelling. On the other hand, a number of Frenchmen 'went native', took African wives, and settled in Africa. This was assimilation in reverse, and it was severely frowned on because it was regarded as diluting the physical and moral strength of the 'superior' race. Thus the period 1930–1945 saw the further alienation of an elite of articulate and influential Africans, men who had hoped for a partnership under colonial rule, but who discovered that there was no way of 'playing the white man' and winning.

Evidence concerning the fortunes of African wage-earners relates mainly to employees in the so-called modern sector, and even that is incomplete at present. Nevertheless, it seems certain that urban employees suffered a serious fall in their living standards during the period 1930–1945.[42] Some wage-earners were thrown out of work as expatriate firms and government departments reduced the size of their labour forces. Others experienced a cut in their rates of pay: the average weekly wage of unskilled workers in the Nigerian tin mines, for example, fell from between 6s and 7s a week in 1928 to 3s 6d in 1937. However, most wage-earners remained in employment, and were affected not by a downward pressure on money wages but by an upward movement of costs as imported goods, urban rents and some foodstuffs became more expensive, especially during the Second World War. The money wages of the majority of urban employees remained stationary for a period of about fifty years: from the 1890s down to about 1940 the ruling rate for unskilled workers in the main urban centres of British West Africa was between 9d and 1s a day. During the Second World War this stability was broken, and some wage increases were granted. However, the increments tended to lag behind the rise in prices, and in any case were inadequate to compensate for them. Consequently, real incomes fell.

Africans reacted forcefully to this erosion of their living standards. Urban protests, ranging from organised strikes to spontaneous demonstrations and riots, became increasingly frequent. Public employees, especially railway workers, were the pace-setters in forming unions and promoting militant action. The history of strike action in West Africa goes back to the nineteenth century, but widespread labour protests in the region as a whole date from the First World War. Thereafter strikes became a fairly common way of expressing grievances, and reached a peak (in terms of frequency and lost working days) during the Second World War. The following are among the most prominent examples of urban protests between 1918 and 1945, though only a few of these have been studied in detail. In French West Africa there was a strike of dock workers at Conakry in 1919; serious riots in Porto Novo in 1923;[43] a strike of railway workers on the Dakar–Niger line in 1925; disturbances at Lome in 1933; another railway workers' strike (at Thiès) in 1938, resulting in military intervention, six deaths and a further thirty men wounded; and a series of

---

[42] Elliot J. Berg, 'Real Income Trends in West Africa, 1939–1960', in *Economic Transition in Africa*, ed. Melville J. Herskovits and Mitchell Harwitz, 1964, pp. 199–238.
[43] John A. Ballard, 'The Porto Novo Incidents of 1923: Politics in the Colonial Era', *Odu*, 2, 1965, pp. 52–75.

protests against the use and abuse of compulsory labour in Senegal and the Ivory Coast during the Second World War. In British West Africa there were serious strikes and demonstrations in all four colonies. In the Gambia there were strikes in 1921 and 1929.[44] In Sierra Leone the railway workers came out in 1919, 1920 and 1926; the miners struck in 1935 and 1937; a wide range of employees in the public and private sectors stopped work in 1938–1939; and a peak of thirteen serious stoppages was recorded in 1942.[45] The Gold Coast experienced a strike of public employees in 1919 and 1921; strikes in the gold mines in 1924 and 1930; a series of stoppages among railway workers, miners and Public Works Department employees in the late 1930s, of which the most important was the railwaymen's strike of 1939; and ten major strikes in 1942. Nigeria had a strike of railway workers in 1920; disturbances in Benin in 1937–1939;[46] mass protests by the railway workers, led by Michael Imoudu, in 1941–1942; and a successful general strike in 1945, which involved seventeen unions representing about 30,000 employees, and lasted for thirty-seven days.

It is appropriate at this point to consider expatriate economic policy during the period 1930–1945. This subject will be related to the argument advanced in the present chapter in the following ways: in the first place, it will be contended that the nature of the problems demanding attention and the limitations on the range of possible solutions were determined by the adverse economic circumstances of the period rather than by any grand, independent conception of the imperial mission in the tropics; secondly, it will be shown that the policies adopted by private enterprise and by the public authorities not only failed to make any impression on the economic problems facing West Africa, but also heightened the tension existing between colonial subjects and their rulers.

The main aim of the expatriate firms during this period was self-preservation. Mining and trading companies in Africa did not achieve immunity from the world slump or from the conflict of 1939–1945 merely because they happened to be foreign. The white man's business magic (double-entry book-keeping and the limited liability company) proved insufficient to ward off the effects of these two great crises, and many firms went into liquidation. Mars calculated that 197 expatriate commercial companies existed in Nigeria at one time or another between 1921 and 1936, but that only fourteen of these enjoyed an unbroken existence as independent firms.[47] The majority of the remainder either went out of business or were taken over by more substantial rivals, thus completing a process of amalgamation

[44] Christopher Allen, 'African Trade Unionism in Microcosm: the Gambia Labour Movement, 1939–67', in *African Perspectives*, ed. C. H. Allen and R. S. Johnson, Cambridge 1970, pp. 393–426.

[45] H. E. Conway, 'Labour Protest Activity in Sierra Leone During the Early Part of the Twentieth Century', *Labour History*, 15, 1968, pp. 49–63.

[46] Philip A. Igbafe, 'The Benin Water Rate Agitation, 1937–39: an Example of Social Conflict', *Journal of the Historical Society of Nigeria*, 4, 1968, pp. 355–75.

[47] J. Mars, 'Extra-Territorial Enterprises', in *Mining, Commerce and Finance in Nigeria*, ed. Margery Perham, 1948, p. 52.

begun in similar circumstances at the close of the nineteenth century. The most spectacular failure occurred in 1931, with the collapse of Lord Kylsant's shipping empire, which included the main British steamship companies serving West Africa.[48] Almost as serious were the insolvencies of the Banque Commerciale Africaine and the Banque Française de l'Afrique in the same year. The former concern was rescued by the Banque de l'Afrique Occidentale, but the latter went into liquidation. Clearly, it was not only African banks and mercantile firms that ran into difficulties at this time.

The surviving firms adopted two main defensive tactics. To begin with, they decided to close many of their retail outlets and up-country branches in order to economise on overheads. In 1929, for example, the newly-formed United Africa Company possessed about 80 out-stations in the Kano area alone; by the close of the 1930s the number had been reduced to twenty-five. A similar policy of retrenchment was pursued by Peyrissac in Senegal and by the Société Commerciale de l'Ouest Africain throughout French West Africa. Next, the large firms divided the import and export trade on an agreed basis with the aim of restraining competition and limiting risks. During the First World War a few substantial, mainly British, companies formed the Association of West African Merchants (AWAM), which was designed to represent their interests in official quarters and to co-ordinate policy in the private sector. The import trade was divided among the leading companies by the Staple Lines Agreement (1934), and by a more comprehensive Merchandise Agreement which replaced it in 1937 and survived until shortly after the end of the Second World War. Market-sharing arrangements were made in the produce trade, too, through the formation of 'pools', in which member firms aggregated their individual purchases and then divided them according to previously agreed proportions. Some mining interests operated much the same system on an international scale: Nigerian tin output, for instance, was controlled by the terms of the International Tin Agreement between 1931 and 1946. Measures to restrain competition reached their high point during the Second World War, when the large expatriate firms became the main agents of the official Marketing Boards, and also received preferential treatment in the issue of import licences.

The policy of 'safety first' enabled most of the leading expatriate firms to keep afloat. However, survival was bought at a price. In pursuing what they regarded as their legitimate business interests the expatriate companies helped to foster African discontent. By failing to diversify, and by reducing their existing commitments, the main agents of capitalist enterprise in the colonies acknowledged their inability to initiate a move from slump to boom conditions. Disinvestment, though understandable, simply depressed the economy further, and was regarded by Africans as an indictment of foreign private enterprise in the empire. Moreover, the widespread and hostile publicity which appeared whenever 'secret' trade agreements were concluded ensured that African dissatisfaction was directed firmly towards the

---

[48] P. N. Davies, 'The African Steam Ship Company', in *Liverpool and Merseyside*, ed. J. R. Harris, 1969, pp. 231–4.

expatriate firms concerned. The standing of the authorities also suffered: it was hard to see how the doctrine of trusteeship was being applied impartially when governments gave protection to those most fitted to stand on their own feet, while allowing African businessmen, such as Tete-Ansa, to remain exposed to the full rigour of market forces.

A study of government policy between 1900 and 1945 reveals that the colonial authorities, far from imposing themselves on events, as the *Annual Reports* contrived to suggest, were engaged in the less majestic task of coping with developments which they had not initiated, which they understood imperfectly, and which threatened to undermine their position in Africa. The colonial powers made some attempt to influence the performance of the open economy, but on the whole their efforts were unsuccessful. The official record during this period can be considered under four headings: capital investment and economic planning; agriculture; manufacturing; and overseas trade.

The depressed state of trade affected the colonial governments directly because of the close connection between public revenue and customs receipts. In French West Africa the Federation's income from customs duties dropped by 47 per cent between 1930 and 1931. Elsewhere the fall, though not so dramatic, was still serious. The case of Sierra Leone, where customs receipts declined by about a third between 1928 and 1934, was typical of the British colonies.[49] At the same time, fixed outgoings (chiefly salaries, pensions and repayments on loans) were very much greater than they had been earlier in the century. Consequently, the colonies entered a phase of budgetary crisis. The authorities reacted to this unwelcome situation in three ways. First, they increased customs duties in a bid to maintain total revenue at its customary level. This tactic was unsuccessful, and its main result was to increase the prices Africans paid for imported goods. Second, they pursued a policy of retrenchment, the orthodox response of the time, and one which was also adopted in Europe. Retrenchment involved drastic reductions in expenditure on public works together with staffing economies, such as early retirement in the case of European officials and loss of work in the case of unskilled African labourers. Expenditure on new public works in both French and British colonies did not regain the levels of the 1920s until the close of the 1930s, by which time military considerations were beginning to influence the direction as well as the size of additional investment. Third, public money in the form of grants and loans was made available by the metropolitan governments to help the colonies through their financial difficulties. This policy marked a further departure, albeit an enforced one, from the prevailing doctrine of colonial self-sufficiency; it implied acceptance of a more active government role in the economy; and, more specifically, it represented an advance from the endeavours of Chamberlain, Guggisberg and Sarraut in the direction of economic planning. Yet these were tentative beginnings. There was no sharp break with the past; loans remained more

[49] One of the few detailed studies of public finance during this period is to be found in N. A. Cox-George, *Finance and Development in West Africa: the Sierra Leone Experience*, 1961, ch. 13.

important than grants; the sums advanced were relatively modest; and the results were far from dramatic, as the examples which follow show.

In France the Great Colonial Loan was authorised in 1931, and its expenditure tied initially to the Maginot Plan, which was promulgated in the same year. The greatness of this loan owed more to the interest rates charged than to the generosity of the sums advanced, for by 1939 only about £7 million (less than half the amount authorised) had been spent in French West Africa. This sum, which was roughly the same as was expended in public works from the Federation's own resources in the 1920s, was invested mainly in transport improvements and in the ill-fated Niger agricultural scheme. The Maginot Plan itself was as ineffective in developing the empire as was that unfortunate minister's more notorious Line in repelling German troops in 1940. A further economic plan for the colonies, drawn up by the Popular Front government in 1936, was buried as speedily as was its sponsor. Britain's approach to the financial problems of the colonies was symbolised by the Colonial Development Act of 1929. The Act was designed as much to reduce unemployment in the United Kingdom (by stimulating exports) as to help the colonies.[50] About £6,500,000 was advanced under the terms of the Act down to 1939. A substantial proportion of this total was in the form of grants to assist insolvent colonies balance their budgets; the remainder took the form of loans, on which interest was payable. A great deal of the expenditure went on projects such as the provision of mining equipment, which mainly benefited industrialists in the United Kingdom, at least in the initial stages. British West Africa's share of funds amounted to only £500,000, and the largest single sum (about £250,000) went to support the activities of the Sierra Leone Development Company (DELCO), an expatriate firm formed in 1930 to exploit the iron ore resources of the colony. The investment proved successful, and from the 1930s Sierra Leone's economy of 'legitimate' commerce, inherited from the nineteenth century, at last began to change. The shortcomings of the 1929 Act were recognised in the Colonial Development and Welfare Act of 1940, which aimed at giving the colonies more comprehensive and more generous assistance. However, this Act achieved few practical results because war-time needs caused a diversion of funds and led to a shortage of skilled administrators.

The limited influence of the colonial governments is further illustrated by their endeavours in the huge agricultural sector. This is not to deny that a measure of success was attained by a number of dedicated officials, men who really did 'serve' in the empire. One of the most notable achievements was the elimination of rinderpest, which spread into Africa in the 1890s, and decimated herds in many parts of the continent before being brought under control in the 1920s and 1930s. On the whole, however, the efforts of officials were seriously hampered by shortage of money, lack of knowledge of tropical agriculture, and by the long-term nature of research in this field, which meant that many of the experiments undertaken in the 1930s did not

[50] George C. Abbott, 'A Re-examination of the 1929 Colonial Development Act', *Economic History Review*, 24, 1971, pp. 68–81.

begin to yield results until after the Second World War.[51] At a time when Africans were looking for cost-reducing innovations and alternative exports, government policy was memorable chiefly for its failures, some of which were spectacular.

Between 1930 and 1934 the French established Sociétés Indigènes de Prévoyance (S.I.P.) throughout their West African colonies. These organisations, which originated in Senegal in 1909, were supposed to improve agricultural methods, organise the storage of food crops and provide credit for farmers. In practice the S.I.P. became officially-sponsored tax gathering agencies, and were also used as a means of political control. Compulsory co-operatives were a contradiction, and it is not surprising that they won little local support.[52] The next failure was the attempt to create, in Governor Carde's phrase, 'an island of prosperity' in the interior of French West Africa. The original plan, put forward in 1919 and backed by French textile manufacturers, was to use the Niger to irrigate land for the production of cotton in Soudan. Preliminary work started in 1924, and in 1931 the scheme was incorporated in the Maginot Plan, which made provision for the cultivation of rice as well as of cotton. The Office du Niger was created in the following year to carry out the project. The officials of this new institution certainly did not lack imagination. Their aim was to irrigate nearly 2 million acres and to settle 1½ million African colonists in the area. Unfortunately, the technical expertise of the administrators did not match their breadth of vision. By 1937 the Niger scheme had cost over £1 million; by 1940 there were about 12,000 settlers on three sites which were more like refugee camps than model villages; and by 1953 only about 62,000 acres had been irrigated. In 1929 the British administration also began to introduce co-operatives. These were planned on a more modest scale than in French West Africa, but the results were equally disappointing.[53] The failure to invest sufficient money in agricultural research was exposed in a dramatic way by the outbreak of a disease known as swollen shoot, which began to attack cocoa trees on the Gold Coast in the late 1930s. The only remedy that could be devised was the drastic one of cutting down infected trees. This solution, however necessary, was scarcely calculated to improve relations between farmers and officials, especially at a time when the export trade was seriously depressed.

The subject of industrialisation is introduced at this point solely with reference to the present argument, and will be accorded more general treatment in the next section of this chapter.[54] The history of modern manufacturing in West Africa dates

---

[51] W. K. Hancock, *Survey of British Commonwealth Affairs, 1918–1939*, II, part 2, 1942, pp. 326–69; R. H. Green and S. H. Hymer, 'Cocoa in the Gold Coast: A Study in the Relations Between African Farmers and Agricultural Experts', *Journal of Economic History*, 26, 1966, pp. 299–319; A. Pitot, 'L'homme et les sols dans les steppes et savannes de l'A.O.F.', *Cahiers d'Outre-Mer*, 5, 1952, pp. 215–40.

[52] J. Suret-Canale, *Afrique noire occidentale et centrale: L'ère coloniale 1900–1945*, Paris 1964, pp. 299–310.

[53] J. C. de Graft-Johnson, *African Experiment: Co-operative Agriculture and Banking in British West Africa*, 1958, chs 4–7.

[54] It is hoped that the comments in this and the following paragraph will stimulate further research into the early phase of industrialisation in West Africa.

from the First World War, though down to 1945 progress was very slow and was confined to a few centres and to a narrow range of products. Constraints on industrial development were not determined simply by colonial policy, as is sometimes suggested. Nevertheless, the conservatism of the expatriate firms, combined with the indifference of the colonial authorities, meant that opportunities which did exist were not exploited fully. It seems fair to suggest that before 1945 industrial enterprise in West Africa sprang neither from official plans to develop the colonies, nor from market growth in the region itself, but from a need to support the Allied cause during two World Wars.

During these periods of emergency the colonial powers were concerned to secure tropical raw materials while at the same time economising on scarce shipping space. Hence the main form of industrial activity, and one which usually involved government participation or encouragement, was export processing. Perhaps the best example is the groundnut crushing industry of Senegal.[55] This industry began during the First World War, but afterwards experienced some difficulty in making progress, and in the 1920s most of its output was consumed locally. However, in 1933 vegetable oils from the French colonies were given preference in the metropolitan market, and in 1936 groundnut oil began to be shipped from Senegal. Small though the industry was, it ran into opposition from processing firms in Marseilles, and a limit was placed on the volume of refined oil shipped to France from West Africa. With the outbreak of the Second World War the needs of France became more pressing than those of Marseilles; additional mills were set up in Soudan, Upper Volta and Niger in 1941–1942, and exports of groundnut oil increased from less than 6,000 tons a year to a peak of 31,000 tons in 1945. Other export-processing industries which expanded in West Africa as a result of war-time needs were saw-milling, palm-oil bulking, cotton ginning, and fish canning. The conditions of siege which prevailed during the two World Wars also stimulated the development of import-substituting industries. These were attempts to achieve self-sufficiency in essential items, such as cement and other building materials, and to maintain the flow of exports by supplying scarce consumer manufactures, such as household goods, cigarettes and processed foodstuffs, notably sugar. When these local industries proved unable to compensate for war-time deficiencies, the Allies made use of forced labour in export production. The establishment of modern industries failed to mitigate the hardship suffered by indigenous interest groups between 1930 and 1945, but it did demonstrate that manufacturing plant could operate in tropical Africa. This was a lesson which African leaders were to use against their mentors after 1945.

Discussions of government intervention in overseas trade between 1930 and 1945 usually concentrate on the Marketing Boards established in British West Africa during the Second World War. There are grounds for thinking that this bias has led to the neglect of issues which are relevant not only to an appreciation of the historical

[55] J. Suret-Canale, 'L'industrie des oléagineux en A.O.F.', *Cahiers d'Outre-Mer*, 3, 1950, pp. 280–8.

context in which the Boards were conceived and established, but also to an understanding of changes in the role of government in the economy during this period. It will be suggested here that the Marketing Boards were just one feature of a search for security which was the prime concern of the two major colonial powers in the years between the onset of the world slump and the end of the Second World War. It will be shown that the Boards were part of a package of measures, including tariff changes, which were designed to influence the performance of the economy after 1930; that plans for Marketing Boards ante-date the Nowell Commission, whose report in 1938 is customarily regarded as inspiring their foundation; and that the French experimented with broadly similar arrangements at an earlier date than did the British, a point which is not mentioned in the standard works on Marketing Boards in the British territories. French commercial strategy will be considered first in the hope that the analysis, though necessarily brief, will by its prominence encourage historians and economists to treat the comparative aspects of official policy more seriously than they have done in the past.

French commitment to free trade had long been half-hearted. As early as 1892 a limited range of measures aimed at protecting French exporters had been applied to certain West African colonies, and would probably have been extended had not Britain succeeded in 1898 in negotiating an agreement which guaranteed equal treatment for her traders and goods in the Ivory Coast and Dahomey. Disappointment with the results of this modified system of free trade, combined with a desire to ensure that the colonies assisted the reconstruction of France after the First World War, led to renewed clamour for the introduction of protectionist measures. In 1928 the Federation (with the exception of the Ivory Coast and Dahomey) was brought under the preferential tariff regime already operated by France with respect to various other parts of her empire.[56] Steps were taken to reinforce this legislation as a result of the world slump. Durand has estimated that no fewer than fifty measures regulating the overseas trade of French West Africa were introduced between 1931 and 1941.[57] The most important of these were the imposition in 1934 of quotas on foreign goods imported into parts of the Federation not covered by the Anglo-French convention of 1898, and the ending of the convention itself in 1936, with the result that the Ivory Coast and Dahomey were included in the tariff arrangements introduced in the rest of French West Africa eight years earlier.

The system of imperial preference was supported by two new institutions. As far as exports from West Africa were concerned, *caisses de compensation* were formed for rubber and coffee (1931), bananas (1932) and vegetable products (1933–1934). These compensation funds were built up by levying a surcharge on foreign imports of these products at the ports of entry in France, and were then paid out to support producer prices in the colonies at times when these fell below a certain minimum level. The aim, price stabilisation, was clearly an anticipation of measures which were adopted by Britain and France during the Second World War, though at this

---

[56] Poquin, *Les relations économiques* . . . , pp. 145–57.
[57] Durand, *Essai sur la conjoncture* . . . , p. 52.

stage there was no attempt to establish a government monopoly of exports. On the import side, *comités de surveillance* were created in 1936 to keep a check on the prices of goods shipped to the colonies. A price freeze was imposed in 1937 and again in 1939, though it is hard to see how practical effect could have been given to this intention. Between 1939 and 1941 the metropolitan government took over the functions of the various funds and boards, and assumed complete control of overseas trade, though still employing the expatriate firms to act as its agents.

In Britain, as in France, the First World War helped revive interest in tariff reform, though in the event only slight changes were made to existing customs regulations. In 1919 duties were imposed on palm kernels and tin leaving West Africa, and a rebate allowed on imports of these commodities entering the United Kingdom. The rebate on palm kernels failed to divert trade to Britain and was withdrawn in 1922, but the duty on tin remained until 1938. The world slump caused a more widespread conversion to protectionism, and the Ottawa Conference of 1932 had an important effect on the tariff regime of the West African colonies. Sierra Leone and the Gambia were brought into the new system of imperial preference immediately. Nigeria and the Gold Coast could not be assimilated fully because of treaty obligations to other powers. Nevertheless, from 1932 the exports of all four colonies were allowed free entry into the United Kingdom, whereas those from outside the Empire had to pay duties, and from 1934 quotas were applied to goods sent to British West Africa from countries such as Japan, which had no formal rights guaranteeing equal treatment. The days when Britain's commercial policy was based on maintaining an open door in all parts of the world had ended.[58]

The slump (and the cocoa hold-up of 1930–1931) also led to a number of proposals in favour of official intervention in the export market. The most prominent of the schemes put forward in the early 1930s was the Bartholomew Plan of 1931, which was designed to use government power to influence the world cocoa market and to stabilise prices on the Gold Coast.[59] This plan was rejected by the Gold Coast government, which argued against official intervention in 1931 on much the same grounds as Professor Bauer was to use in 1954 in his more comprehensive attack on the marketing monopolies which the authorities did eventually establish![60] The persistence of the depression in overseas trade, together with the hold-up of 1937, caused the government to modify its position to the extent of appointing a commission to investigate the arrangements for marketing cocoa. The Nowell Commission's Report, which appeared in 1938, recommended the creation of collective marketing agencies, but no action had been taken by the time of the outbreak of war, and in the event it was the emergency caused by hostilities which led to official control of overseas trade. The Ministry of Food took over the purchase of the cocoa crop in 1939; the West African Cocoa Control Board was set up in 1940; and the

[58] The open economies of British West Africa still remained open, of course, with respect to Britain.

[59] *West Africa*, 19 September 1931, pp. 1146–7.

[60] *West Africa*, 17 October 1931, p. 1262, and a further comment by Bartholomew in *ibid*, 25 February 1933, p. 177.

West African Produce Control Board, which handled all the main export crops, was established in 1942. Under the new arrangements, private firms still purchased exports in Africa, but they sold to one buyer, the official Board, which also fixed the prices to be paid.

Official intervention in overseas trade failed to solve West Africa's problems, and was of little help to France and Britain either. In the case of the French colonies, imperial preference strengthened bilateral trading links and gave both parties a measure of certainty with respect to markets for their products. However, French West Africa had to pay for this security by becoming integrated in a high-cost, high-price trading system, which, among other disadvantages, meant that the colonies had to buy relatively expensive French consumer goods. Imperial preference was worth even less to British West Africa. Britain's attempt to shelter tropical exports was unsuccessful, first because she consumed only a small proportion of the empire's total output of the main staples, and second because the new tariff system did nothing to diminish competition among producers *within* the Empire. At the same time, the colonies failed to derive any advantages from the privileges accorded to imports from Britain. The imposition of quotas, for example, prevented Africans from buying cheaper Japanese textiles and footwear. African producers also failed to benefit from the various Funds and Boards which were set up to stabilise prices and incomes. Indeed, the low buying prices fixed by the Marketing Boards in British West Africa amounted, in effect, to a forced loan in aid of the war effort. The main beneficiaries of the statutory monopolies were the large expatriate firms. Official patronage confirmed and extended the private 'pooling' arrangements which they had operated previously. These firms not only supported state intervention; they even helped to plan it.[61]

The stress experienced by the open economy between 1930 and 1945 had a profound influence on the course of West African history. The favourable terms of trade, the swelling public revenues and the optimism of the early twentieth century had first made possible, and then sustained, a policy of co-operation between colonial rulers and key interest groups among their African subjects. The unfavourable terms of trade, the declining revenues and the pessimism of the period 1930–1945 were reflected in the discontent expressed by African farmers, traders and wage-earners, and led to mounting criticism of the colonial regime.

Expatriate reactions failed either to improve the performance of the open economy or to dissolve African hostility. Officials and firms retrenched and waited for a boom that did not come until the end of the Second World War. After 1930 there was some pretence, but little reality, about developing the estates of the Empire. Many of the poorer parts of West Africa, though they still found a place in the speeches of politicians and on the maps of Empire, were in effect abandoned by the colonial rulers. To the extent that the colonial governments and commercial firms did take effective action, it was in support of expatriate rather than African interests. It was

---

[61] P. T. Bauer, 'Origins of the Statutory Export Monopolies of British West Africa', *Business History Review*, 28, 1954, pp. 204–7.

possible to discern the beginnings of a change in government attitudes early in the 1930s, and more explicit recognition of the need for reform was made during the Second World War, but there was no New Deal for the colonies before 1945. This was a time when the white man's burden consisted of the politicians of Europe rather than the subject peoples of Africa.

The depressed state of trade and the bankruptcy of colonial policy had a fundamental influence on the nature and organisation of African opposition to foreign rule. By the close of the 1930s the gradualist approach of moderate Africans, such as Macaulay, Diagne and Tete-Ansa, had been discredited, and new, more radical leaders, such as Azikiwe, Danquah, Wallace-Johnson and Lamine Gueye, had begun to emerge. Instead of calling for a reinterpretation of the dual mandate within the imperial context, some of these men, in their different ways, pressed for political independence and for a re-structuring of the colonial economy. 'It is not enough,' proclaimed Danquah, 'to live in the old agricultural economy. We must manufacture and buy our own goods. We must industrialise our country.'[62] Whereas the following of the moderate leadership had been confined to the elite of a few large urban centres, the new leaders began to mobilise mass support by incorporating farmers, traders and wage-earners into modern political organisations. Thus the period 1930–1945 is to be treated as an integral part of an explanation of the rise of nationalism in West Africa, and not merely as a 'background' to the more publicised events of the years which followed the end of the Second World War.

4 Strains on the open economy, 1945–60

The period from 1945 to 1960 was one of economic expansion and returning prosperity. The barter terms of trade recovered from the depths plumbed during the Second World War and remained highly favourable to primary exporters until the close of the 1950s. Furthermore, between 1945 and 1955 the volume of exports quadrupled, and there was a six-fold increase in West Africa's total importing capacity. The boom in the export sector was transmitted to the domestic economy: as receipts from overseas sales rose, Africans not only bought more consumer imports, they also spent more money on local goods and services. Indeed, there is some evidence, admittedly sketchy, to show that the domestic market may have grown even faster than the export sector in the post-war era.[63]

Important modifications were made to the open economies of West Africa in the years between 1945 and 1960. Undoubtedly the most fundamental change was the discarding of the doctrine of colonial self-sufficiency. Substantial infusions of metropolitan capital made it possible to remove, for the first time, the constraint by which

---

[62] J. B. Danquah, *Self-Help and Expansion*, Accra 1943, p. 15.

[63] E. K. Hawkins, 'The Growth of a Money Economy in Nigeria and Ghana', *Oxford Economic Papers*, 10, 1958, p. 353.

the level of demand in West Africa had been determined almost entirely by the size of export proceeds. Other developments associated with this innovation were an expansion in the economic role of government, seen chiefly in the growth of the public sector and in the beginnings of development planning; a move towards structural economic change, following the introduction of modern manufacturing activities; and increased Africanisation in public and private sectors, a process which culminated in the achievement of political independence.

These modifications, it is suggested, were the result of four interacting causes. First, the improved performance of the open economy helped to foster structural change, and also influenced the climate of Afro-European relations. Second, international pressures arising out of the new power relationships which had grown up as a result of the Second World War altered the attitudes of both Africans and Europeans towards colonial rule. Third, African agitation for economic and political reforms, though generated before 1945, increased greatly after the war. Fourth, modifications were brought about partly through the self-interest of the colonial powers. Ideally, these four themes should be treated simultaneously in order to emphasise the interaction among them; unfortunately, the medium of the printed word does not allow this freedom. The compromise adopted here is to deal in turn with the history of African pressures and European policy, and to relate the remaining themes (the performance of the open economy and the changing climate of international relations) to them.

Although economic expansion began in 1945, prosperity did not return to West Africa immediately the war ended. The barter and income terms of trade started to recover, but it was not until the close of the 1940s that the losses suffered during the war years were made good, and it was only in the 1950s that living standards rose clearly above the levels of the 1930s. There were two main reasons for this delay: on the import side consumer goods were in short supply during the immediate post-war years, and so were expensive—in Europe as well as in Africa; and on the export side part of the earnings of producers continued to be withheld by official marketing agencies, which fixed prices at levels lower than those ruling in world markets. Farmers and traders were not worse off than they had been during the war, but their living standards did not improve as fast as they had expected. The same was true of employees in the public sector, whose wage rates, though beginning to move upwards, still lagged behind increases in the cost of living. In understanding African reactions to this situation it is important to appreciate that what mattered was not so much the relationship between the standard of living and an objectively-defined poverty line, as the failure of slowly rising living standards to catch up with rapidly rising expectations. In attempting to retain the loyalty of their subjects during the war years, the colonial powers had not only used the stick of compulsory labour, but had dangled some carrots as well. Statements on colonial policy held out the promise of a 'New Deal' once the struggle to safeguard democracy and freedom had been won. Around the corner were better times and homes fit, as it were, for African heroes to live in. When, inevitably, reforms took longer to implement than had been anticipated, African disappointment was the more acute.

The outcome of this set of circumstances was predictable: some of the most widely-supported demonstrations of discontent in the whole colonial period occurred between 1945 and 1950, and governments in Africa were subjected to greater pressures than they had ever experienced. African discontent continued to find expression in ways which had become familiar during the period 1930–1945. The best known examples of these protests are the Nigerian national strike of 1945 (noted in the previous section of this chapter), the strike on the Dakar railway in 1947–1948,[64] the riots on the Gold Coast in 1948, involving a boycott of European firms and mass demonstrations by African ex-servicemen,[65] and the highly publicised shooting incident at the Enugu coal mines in 1949, in which twenty-one miners lost their lives.[66] One, admittedly imperfect, index of militancy among wage-earners is provided by the record of man–days lost through strike action. A recent study of Nigerian labour history during the period 1940–1960 has shown that the greatest number of withdrawals occurred between 1945 and 1950, when over 100,000 man–days were lost every year.[67]

African protest movements acquired one additional, highly distinctive feature in the post-war era: they assumed a more organised and a more overt political form. This development began, as has been shown, in the 1930s, but during the Second World War political expression in the colonies was restricted for security reasons. After 1945, however, continuing discontent in Africa supplied the incentive to mobilise and co-ordinate sectional interests, and to provide them with a political forum. The years between 1945 and 1950 saw an upsurge of militant, anti-colonial activities in the West African territories—in the Press, in mass demonstrations and in confrontations between African leaders and colonial officials. At the same time, it was becoming hard for the victors of a war fought to preserve free speech to justify restraining political expression among their colonial subjects. The creation of the United Nations in 1945 provided an international platform for the declamation of anti-colonial sentiments, while at the national level the rise to power of the Labour Party in Britain and the prominence of the Communist Party in France brought about a more sympathetic attitude towards colonial grievances. Consequently, colonial officials were inhibited from adopting extreme punitive measures. In West Africa political leaders were 'agitators'; they were never forced to become 'terrorists'.

It is not the purpose of this book to provide a detailed account of the political parties which arose after the Second World War.[68] Nevertheless, some of the more

---

[64] A semi-fictional, and most readable, account of this strike has been given by Sembene Ousmane, *Les bouts de bois de Dieu*, Paris 1960.

[65] Colonial Office, *Report of the Commission of Enquiry into Disturbances in the Gold Coast*, 1948.

[66] Agwu Akpala, 'The Background of the Enugu Colliery Shooting Incident in 1949', *Journal of the Historical Society of Nigeria*, 3, 1965, pp. 335–64.

[67] Robin Cohen, *The Role of Organised Labour in the Nigerian Political Process*, University of Birmingham Ph.D. thesis, 1971, p. 248.

[68] See Thomas Hodgkin, *African Political Parties*, Harmondsworth 1961. Only a few of the many studies of West African politics can be mentioned here. Three valuable books which

prominent organisations need to be mentioned in order to illustrate the evolution of political parties in West Africa, and to support the contention that specialised interest groups of farmers, traders and wage-earners were an important source of their strength. At the same time, it should be recognised that the leading parties also drew support from other quarters, particularly from the professions and from ethnic associations in which occupational role was a secondary consideration, and that there were some parties which did not represent the interests specified here, and which evolved partly to counterbalance them. A good example of this type of conservative party is provided by the Northern People's Congress, which was formed in 1949 partly to champion the cause of the traditional elite of northern Nigeria.

In French West Africa the most influential of the parties claiming to represent the region as a whole was the Rassemblement Démocratique Africain (R.D.A.), which was founded in 1946. The R.D.A. had close links with the Communist Party in France, and was supported in Africa by trade unions, export-crop producers and traders. The Dioula, who were specialists in long-distance trade, played a considerable part in building up the R.D.A., which they saw as a means of safeguarding their cosmopolitan commercial interests. The R.D.A. also had a number of sections based on the constituent territories of French West Africa. Two of the most important of these sections were the Parti Démocratique de la Côte d'Ivoire (P.D.C.I.) and the Parti Démocratique de Guinée (P.D.G.). The P.D.C.I. was founded in 1945 by Felix Houphouet-Boigny, a wealthy planter, and drew much of its support from local coffee and cocoa farmers. The P.D.G. was established in 1947, but did not achieve prominence until the 1950s, with the emergence of a wage labour force and a strong union organisation following the discovery of mineral resources in the territory. The Bloc Démocratique Sénégalais (B.D.S.) was linked to another inter-territorial grouping, the Indépendants d'Outre-Mer. The B.D.S. was founded in 1948 by Léopold Senghor and derived most of its strength from the groundnut farmers in the provinces, though it also established connections with wage-earners in the industrial complex around Dakar.

In British West Africa political development after the war took place mainly on a territorial basis. The National Council of Nigeria and the Cameroons (N.C.N.C.), launched by Nnamdi Azikiwe in 1944, was based initially on urban immigrants and trade unions, but later became identified with Ibo economic interests. In 1951 there

---

deal with the region as a whole are Thomas Hodgkin, *Nationalism in Colonial Africa*, 1956, Ken Post, *The New States of West Africa*, Harmondsworth 1964, and Aristide R. Zolberg, *Creating Political Order*, Chicago 1966. Important studies of specific territorial units are Dennis Austin, *Politics in Ghana, 1946–60*, Oxford 1964; James S. Coleman, *Nigeria: Background to Nationalism*, Berkeley and Los Angeles 1958; Richard L. Sklar, *Nigerian Political Parties*, Princeton 1963; Martin L. Kilson, 'Nationalism and Social Classes in British West Africa', *Journal of Politics*, 20, 1958, pp. 368–87; and the same author's *Political Change in a West African State: a Study of the Modernization Process in Sierra Leone*, Cambridge, Mass., 1966; John R. Cartwright, *Politics in Sierra Leone, 1947–1967*, Toronto 1970; Ruth Schachter Morgenthau, *Political Parties in French-Speaking West Africa*, Oxford 1964; and Aristide R. Zolberg, *One-Party Government in the Ivory Coast*, Princeton 1964.

arose another party, the Action Group, which stood for the cocoa farmers and wealthy traders of the country's Western Region. On the Gold Coast the first important party was the United Gold Coast Convention (U.G.C.C.), which was founded by J. B. Danquah and others in 1947. Two years later the U.G.C.C. was joined, and soon eclipsed, by the Convention People's Party (C.P.P.), led by Kwame Nkrumah. Both parties drew on support from cocoa farmers, traders and trade unions, but the C.P.P. was especially successful in appealing to the younger and poorer rural and urban migrants. The Sierra Leone People's Party (S.L.P.P.), formed in 1951, derived much of its initial inspiration and funds from provincial Mende commercial interests.

It is hard to discern any detailed, constructive economic proposals in the programmes of these political organisations, though economic grievances, and generalised solutions to them, clearly occupied a prominent place.[69] The main emphasis, understandably enough, was on attacking colonialism, and there was a tendency to assume that the end of colonial rule would itself be sufficient to solve basic economic problems. Once African leaders controlled the 'commanding heights' of the economy, sizeable gains, so it was said, would accrue to their supporters. A reorganisation of the Marketing Boards, combined with controls on the exporting firms, would give farmers a better price for their produce; restrictions on the activities of the expatriate commercial firms would provide more opportunities for African traders; and industrialisation would lead to improved living standards for wage-earners, and would also benefit the economy as a whole. Indeed, there was a tendency to regard industrialisation as a cure-all: Durand has commented on the mystique which surrounded the concept in the French territories,[70] and the same phenomenon was found in British West Africa. The Commission of Enquiry appointed to investigate the riots on the Gold Coast in 1948 reported that 'at every turn we were pressed with the cry of industrialisation. We doubt very much if the authors of this cry really understood more than their vague desire for something that promised wealth and higher standards of life.'[71] It was a sign of the times that the Commission (which itself knew little about industrialisation) went on to recommend the introduction of certain types of secondary industry.

The character of African opposition to colonialism underwent a change after 1950, as the bitterness and militancy which had characterised the immediate postwar years were replaced by a more conciliatory and co-operative mood. There were two main reasons for this change. In the first place, West Africans were beginning to receive some of the benefits of economic expansion, and secondly the colonial powers had started to make substantial concessions to African demands by promoting a greater degree of self-government, and (as will be shown later) by introducing a number of economic reforms. Two events symbolised this transition: in 1950

[69] There is an interesting study to be made of the origins and evolution of African economic thought between 1930 and 1960.

[70] Durand, *Essai sur la conjoncture . . . .* , p. 144.

[71] Colonial Office, *Report of the Commission of Enquiry into the Disturbances in the Gold Coast*, 1948, p. 54.

Houphouet-Boigny agreed to sever his links with the French Communist Party in return for the introduction of a more progressive regime on the Ivory Coast; and in 1951 Nkrumah was released from prison and appointed Leader of Government Business on the Gold Coast. In political terms the 1950s are best regarded as a period of dyarchy, in which power was increasingly shared between the colonial rulers and the wealthier, more articulate and more influential of their subjects. Neither prosperity nor access to political power served to retard the movement towards independence. On the contrary, once Africans perceived that their aspirations were attainable, progress was made at an even faster pace. As de Tocqueville remarked about an earlier revolutionary process, 'evils which are patiently endured when they seem inevitable become intolerable when once the idea of escape from them is suggested.'[72]

The new spirit of co-operation is illustrated by the improvement in the fortunes of the three groups of specialists which supported the principal political parties. The marked recovery in the barter terms of trade in the 1950s presented producers with incentives and opportunities which had not arisen since the end of the First World War, and then only briefly. Farmers found it profitable to increase the volume of foodstuffs to meet the growing needs of the domestic market, and to expand export production, which reached record levels in the 1950s, in spite of the fact that in the British territories the Marketing Boards still retained a large slice of export proceeds.

The growth of agricultural output was achieved mainly by traditional means, that is by applying underused labour to underused land. This further development on the extensive margin was made possible by the expansion of motor transport and by the increased use of bicycles, which helped farmers commute between plots. However, there were also signs, which were important for the future of West African agriculture, of a rise in productivity (an increase in output per man and per acre) through the application of chemical fertilisers, higher yielding seeds and pest controls. These innovations affected both established export staples and products destined for domestic consumption. In the case of exports, the addition of potassium fertilisers increased the yield from oil palms, pesticides eliminated some of the diseases afflicting the cocoa tree, and new varieties of groundnut helped conserve nutrients in the soil. With regard to the domestic economy, improved types of grass provided better pasture, livestock selection and breeding schemes raised the quality of cattle, and plans to expand the output of swamp rice, vegetables, poultry and dairy produce were implemented.[73]

The motives underlying agricultural improvements were of two kinds. Originally, the colonial rulers wanted to ensure that West Africa was self-sufficient during the war years, and could also produce the quantity of exports needed to aid the war effort and to speed Europe's recovery after 1945. Then, from the 1950s, concern was expressed about the future of West African agriculture, which, it was feared, would run into the problem of diminishing returns if, in the absence of scientific and managerial improvements, labour continued to be applied in increasing quantities to

---

[72] Aléxis de Tocqueville, *The Old Regime and the French Revolution*, New York 1856, p. 214.
[73] For further details see W. B. Morgan and J. C. Pugh, *West Africa*, 1969, ch. 10.

a fixed amount of land. Fortunately, West Africa still has time to avert this danger. Although population is growing rapidly, farming land is still available in most parts of the region.

Indigenous businessmen were equally quick to take advantage of the openings presented in the 1950s by the growth and diversification of the economy, and by the shift in political power—which put public funds into African hands. Besides expanding domestic commerce in ways outlined earlier in this chapter, Africans also increased their share of the direct import and export trade, which had long been dominated by expatriate firms. Their success was especially marked in the wealthier colonies, where the exchange economy was expanding rapidly. In Nigeria, for example, the African share of the import trade rose from five per cent in 1949 to twenty per cent in 1963. Furthermore, as will be shown shortly, aspiring business-men gained substantially from the policy of Africanisation introduced by the large expatriate firms during the 1950s. More significantly, Africans were among the first to perceive and exploit entirely new opportunities: the growth of towns meant the development of a construction industry;[74] rising urban incomes led to a demand for better quality foodstuffs; increasing literacy created a market for books and Western entertainment; and the spread of motor vehicles brought about a need for ancillary services, such as garages. Some of the most prominent Nigerian entrepreneurs of the post-war era have made their fortunes by providing for these needs: Ayo Otaru as the manufacturer of 'Lion' bread in Ibadan; Chief T. A. Odutola as a supplier of tyres and spare parts for motor vehicles; Sir Mobolaji Bank-Anthony in construc-tion, road haulage, cinemas and bookshops; and Alhaji S. L. Edu as a government food contractor. Many other, less well known, figures have engaged in similar activities on a smaller scale.[75] One of the most important consequences of the diversification of the open economy is that Africans have begun to acquire the tech-nical skills which they have lacked in the past.

Wage-earners benefited from the recovery which took place during the 1950s in two ways. First, the expansion of the economy in general, and the growth of the public sector in particular, brought new opportunities for wage employment. Second, the decade saw a rise in real wages, though the exact extent of the gains varied, being rather greater in the French territories than in British West Africa.[76] The improvement should not be exaggerated. The rise in real wages was from a low level, and it was not continuous, there being a check, for example, at the close of the 1950s. The broad, upward trend, while it did not retard the growth of trade unions

[74] Practically every book on West Africa provides some information about the growth of towns in the twentieth century; as yet little attention has been paid to the interesting question of how they were built.

[75] See, for example, the local study by R. A. Akinola, 'The Industrial Structure of Ibadan', *Nigerian Geographical Journal*, 7, 1964, pp. 116–20.

[76] Elliot J. Berg, 'Real Income Trends in West Africa, 1939–1960', in *Economic Transition in Africa*, ed. Melville J. Herskovits and Mitchell Harwitz, 1964, pp. 199–238, and John F. Weeks, 'Further Comment on the Kilby/Weeks Debate: an Empirical Rejoinder', *Journal of Developing Areas*, 5, 1971, p. 171.

or eliminate strike action,[77] did remove much of the violence from labour protest in the colonies. The emphasis of the organised labour movement was on negotiation rather than on revolution, though strong words were often spoken on the way to the conference room.

The causes of this rise in real wages are a matter of controversy, stemming on the one hand from the economist's concern with the problem of the relationship between wage rates and the development prospects of African countries, and on the other from the historian's interest, imported from Europe, in the role of trade unions as a force for economic and political change. Berg and Butler, supported by Weeks, have taken the view that African trade unions had relatively little power.[78] They have pointed out that wage-employment affected only a small proportion of the total labour force, and that many wage-earners, being migrants, had no interest in union activities. Consequently, trade unions had few members; they lacked solidarity; their financial resources were limited; and their leadership tended to be of poor calibre. The conclusion derived from this analysis is that the decision to raise money-wages in the 1940s and 1950s was made by employers, not as a result of union pressure, but in recognition of the increased cost of living and of the need to maintain a stable labour force. Against this view it has been argued by Warren and Kilby, with support from Cohen, that unions had strengths as well as weaknesses.[79] They were located in strategically sensitive places, such as capital cities; their members were well represented in key jobs, notably in public service; their activities attracted publicity, both in Africa and in sympathetic newspapers in England and France; and at times when discontent was widespread they were able to mobilise non-union support, especially from the urban unemployed, and to mount demonstrations which were impressive in size and threatening in appearance. The conclusion drawn from this evidence is that unions *were* influential in extracting concessions from employers during the 1940s and 1950s, even though results fell some way short of expectations.

[77] There were major strikes in the Gold Coast, Nigeria and Sierra Leone in 1955-6.

[78] Elliot J. Berg and Jeffrey Butler, 'Trade Unions', in *Political Parties and National Integration in Tropical Africa*, ed. James S. Coleman and Carl G. Rosberg, Berkeley 1964, pp. 340-81; John F. Weeks, 'A Comment on Peter Kilby: Industrial Relations and Wage Determination', *Journal of Developing Areas*, 3, 1968, pp. 7-17; Elliot J. Berg, 'Urban Real Wages and the Nigerian Trade Union Movement, 1939-60: a Comment', *Economic Development and Cultural Change*, 17, 1969, pp. 604-17; and John F. Weeks, 'Further Comment on the Kilby/Weeks Debate: an Empirical Rejoinder', *Journal of Developing Areas*, 5, 1971, pp. 165-74.

[79] W. M. Warren, 'Urban Real Wages and the Nigerian Trade Union Movement, 1939-60', *Economic Development and Cultural Change*, 15, 1966, pp. 21-36; Peter Kilby, 'Industrial Relations and Wage Determination: Failure of the Anglo-Saxon Model', *Journal of Developing Areas*, 1, 1967, pp. 489-520; the same author's 'A Reply to John F. Weeks' Comment', *Journal of Developing Areas*, 3, 1968, pp. 19-26; W. M. Warren, 'Urban Real Wages and the Nigerian Trade Union Movement, 1939-60: Rejoinder', *Economic Development and Cultural Change*, 17, 1969, pp. 618-33; Robin Cohen, 'Further Comment on the Kilby/Weeks Debate', *Journal of Developing Areas*, 5, 1971, pp. 155-64; and Kilby's 'Final Observations', *ibid*, 5, 1971, pp. 175-6.

The friction generated by this debate arises not merely because both sides believe themselves to be correct, but because they probably are. Berg and Butler are right to draw attention to weaknesses in African trade unions. It would be a mistake to regard the unions as a compelling, or even as a dominant, force in the economic and political history of West Africa between 1945 and 1960. This is one reason why the analysis presented in this chapter has concentrated on *three* major African interest groups, and why the third group, the labour force, has not been treated as if its history were synonymous with that of trade unions. At the same time, it is equally clear that the authorities could not afford to ignore the presence of organised labour. Unions were much stronger after 1945 than they had been beforehand, and they had a special significance in certain colonies, such as Guinea. Governments *may* have been prepared to grant wage increases simply in response to a rise in the cost of living, and in the absence of any organised pressure to do so, but the fact that pressure existed is likely to have influenced both the timing and the nature of the settlement. Generalisations, if stretched too far, lose their explanatory power. The question of the effectiveness of unions in raising wages is one which needs to be decided with reference to particular colonies and to particular points in time.

The foregoing survey completes the analysis of the evolution of African interests between 1945 and 1960. It remains to view this same period from the standpoint of the colonial powers.

A ruling power (or class) can meet demands for radical reform in one or more of three ways. It can do nothing at all, in the hope that the problem will solve itself; it can adopt a policy of repression; and it can try conciliation. West Africa has experienced all three approaches. A policy of 'wait and see' prevailed during the period 1930–1945, and, as has been shown, proved unsuccessful. A policy of repression was used occasionally during the Second World War and in the immediate post-war years. Until about 1950 Britain and France were still unsure of the strength of African opposition, and they had not appreciated the extent to which their own power had declined. Consequently, coercion was used at times in an attempt to control the growth of anti-colonial organisations. In 1949–1950 large numbers of Africans were killed, wounded or imprisoned in an aggressive campaign against the P.D.C.I. and Houphouet-Boigny, while on the Gold Coast strong action was taken against the C.P.P. and Nkrumah, who was jailed in 1950. These measures were partly a reflection of the belief, popular among defenders of the 'free' world at the time of the 'cold' war, that foreign nationalists were really communists in disguise.[80] The Colonial Office, though well stocked with historians, seems momentarily to have forgotten the recommendations made by that expert observer, Benjamin Franklin, on how to lose an empire without intending to. One of his rules for achieving unpremeditated decolonisation was for the imperial government to insist, despite the evidence, that the complaints of subject peoples were 'invented and prompted by a

---

[80] Colonial Office, *Report of the Commission of Enquiry into Disturbances in the Gold Coast*, 1948, p. 91, where the governor's views on 'communist' methods are recorded.

few factious demagogues, whom if you could catch and hang, all would be quiet.'[81]

On the whole, however, the period 1945–1960 was marked by the adoption of a conciliatory policy, and coercion was the exception rather than the rule. Indeed, concessions were already being made before the end of the Second World War. In 1944 substantial reforms were promised at a conference at Brazzaville presided over by General de Gaulle. One important result of this meeting was the abolition in 1946 of forced labour, long a deep grievance in French West Africa. In 1945 Britain revived the Colonial Development and Welfare Act (1940) and presented it in a more generous form. In the 1950s the policy of co-operation was developed even more fully in French and British West Africa. The reasons behind this policy, noted at the beginning of this section, will now be considered in greater detail, and its consequences explored with reference to the modification of the open economy. To complement the organisation of the previous section of this chapter, the expatriate firms will be dealt with first, followed by an examination of government policy.

Insufficient attention has been paid to changes in the role and structure of the expatriate firms. Historians tend to assume that the functions of these companies were defined at an early point in the colonial period, and remained essentially unchanged down to the time of independence. It will be contended here that this view is mistaken, and that after 1945 the expatriate firms implemented the most fundamental reorganisation of their activities since the close of the nineteenth century, when they began to move inland for the first time. It will be shown that notable innovations were made not only by adapting traditional mercantile functions, but also by introducing modern manufacturing activities, and it will be argued that these changes were prompted by two considerations; the growth of the market and the rise of African nationalism. Of course, innovations were more pronounced in some countries than in others. It is entirely consistent with the interpretation advanced here that smaller colonies with less developed markets tended to lag behind,[82] and that the pace-setters were the relatively wealthy regions, such as Nigeria, the Gold Coast, Senegal and the Ivory Coast, which offered new and more profitable opportunities.[83]

[81] Benjamin Franklin, 'Rules for Reducing a Great Empire to a Small One', *Works*, 3, 1806, p. 343.

[82] Sierra Leone is a case in point. See Ralph Gerald Saylor, *The Economic System of Sierra Leone*, Durham N.C., 1967, pp. 95, 147–57.

[83] Much of the foregoing interpretation, and virtually the whole of the exposition which follows, is derived from the work of four scholars, all of whom arrived, quite independently, at complementary conclusions. Elements of the basic argument were first advanced by Marcel Capet in his neglected study of the period 1945–54 entitled *Traité d'économie tropicale: les économies d'A.O.F.*, Paris 1958, pp. 123–32, 163–72. Ten years later two studies of changes in the mercantile functions of the expatriate firms appeared: Atsé-Léon Bonnefonds, 'La transformation du commerce de traite en Côte d'Ivoire depuis la dernière guerre mondiale et l'indépendance', *Cahiers d'Outre-Mer*, 21, 1968, pp. 395–413, and Charles Wilson, *Unilever, 1945–1965*, 1968, pp. 213–26. Then, in the following year, came Peter Kilby's comprehensive and indispensable volume, *Industrialization in an Open Economy: Nigeria, 1945–60*, Cambridge 1969.

Expansion and diversification made West African trade attractive to newcomers, and presented the expatriate firms with a degree of competition which they had not experienced since the brief boom that followed the First World War. They faced serious rivalry from low-cost operators, especially Indian, Levantine and African traders, and from overseas industrial concerns, such as Imperial Chemical Industries, which set up their own local outlets. The established, horizontally-integrated structure of U.A.C., C.F.A.O. and S.C.O.A. was ill-suited to do battle with specialised competitors. Engaging in trade in products such as motor vehicles and machinery put pressure on capital resources; selling and servicing new imports, such as electrical goods, required an expertise which the traditional firms did not possess; and stocking an increasingly diverse range of commodities led to a rise in handling costs.

By about 1950 the established firms had realised that the market was too large and competition too fierce for them to continue to dominate virtually all branches of the import and export trade, as they had done previously. Consequently, they, too, began to transform themselves into specialists, thus reducing capital requirements, focusing skills on a limited range of goods, and cutting handling costs. The leading commercial firms completely reorganised their retail outlets, and concentrated mainly on wholesaling activities. Direct retailing became centred on a few, large department stores and supermarkets, such as Kingsway, Monoprix and Printania, and most of the established retail outlets were handed over to Africans. In 1956, for example, the Avion chain, making use of former S.C.O.A. shops and staffed by Africans, was started on the Ivory Coast. In addition, subsidiaries with African directors were set up to import and distribute particular items, such as motor vehicles, and finance companies were formed to enable independent African traders to develop their own businesses. The results were dramatic: whereas in 1949 the three leading commercial firms in Nigeria accounted for 49 per cent of all imports, by 1963 this figure had fallen to 16 per cent. One of the best examples of the process of 'Africanisation' is provided by U.A.C. In 1939 Africans accounted for only seven per cent of the company's total management staff in West Africa: by 1957 the proportion had risen to twenty-one per cent; and by the end of 1964 it had reached forty-three per cent.[84] A similar policy of training African technical and managerial staff was launched by the mining companies.[85] Africanisation made sound commercial sense. Africans were much cheaper to employ than Europeans; they knew the country and its languages better; their local connections were frequently helpful in opening up

---

[84] United Africa Company, *Statistical and Economic Review*, 20, 1957, pp. 39–45; 30, 1965, p. 57. It is planned to increase the proportion to eighty per cent by 1980. Critics of the expatriate commercial firms have argued, with some justification, that these changes amounted to little more than 'window dressing'. This criticism does not invalidate the point made here that there was a gain in status and pay for a small, but important, indigenous interest group.

[85] At least one firm was also affected by a type of unplanned Africanisation. The monopoly of the Sierra Leone Selection Trust, granted in 1935, was undermined after the Second World War by the illicit activities of African diggers and Levantine traders. This development received formal recognition in 1956, when African miners were granted licences. Saylor, *The Economic System of Sierra Leone*, ch. 4, provides a summary view. For a comprehensive account of the industry as a whole see H. L. van der Laan, *The Sierra Leone Diamonds*, 1965.

new markets and holding on to established ones; and they were often outstandingly successful businessmen. The decision to make room for aspiring Africans was also an astute political move. By the close of the 1940s it was apparent that the long term interests of the expatriate firms lay in securing a stake for themselves in an Africa ruled by Africans rather than by Europeans. By providing more opportunities for indigenous traders, the expatriate firms advanced their own interests and also improved their image in the eyes of their most vociferous critics.

The second, and more radical, innovation was the introduction of modern industry. It is widely, but incorrectly, assumed that the expatriate companies were firmly opposed to industrialisation in Africa throughout the colonial period. That they showed little or no interest in modern manufacturing before 1945 is undoubtedly true. Their skills were those of general merchants, and, as merchants, they presided comfortably over commercial empires in which market-sharing agreements had blunted aggressive entrepreneurial drives. Moreover, industrialisation meant complications and risks. The establishment of local industries might have offended metropolitan manufacturers and aroused the displeasure of the shipping companies which dominated the West African carrying trade. Above all, there was no clear indication that the local market was large enough to justify experiments of this kind, especially in the depressed economic climate which existed between 1930 and 1945.

After the Second World War, a departure from traditional attitudes became less risky and more compelling. By the 1950s the effective demand for manufactures had reached the point in some parts of West Africa where it could sustain at least a few firms of the size needed to produce the goods most commonly required, and for those firms to operate at sufficient capacity to keep their costs down and the prices of their products competitive with imports from Europe.[86] Furthermore, the expansion of the market, by introducing a greater degree of competition, had reduced profit margins on many staple imports. The traditional firms not only countered this challenge by specialising, as has been shown, but also by becoming manufacturers, in the hope that they could achieve sufficient savings in production and transport costs to undersell their new rivals. It was no coincidence that the leading manufacturers in West Africa during the 1950s were established commercial firms, such as U.A.C., C.F.A.O., S.C.O.A., John Holt and Maurel et Prom, all of which had to undertake considerable internal reorganisation and acquire staff with the necessary technical skills. By starting modern industries, as by specialising in trade, these firms also helped to further Afro-European co-operation during the final phase of colonial rule.

The production of goods for domestic consumption, such as processed food, drink, clothing and construction materials, accounted for the largest share of modern manufacturing output in West Africa during the 1950s and 1960s. This emphasis is

---

[86] These remarks barely hint at a complex problem. For a discussion of the importance of economies of scale in different types of import-substituting industries, and of variations in factor proportions among firms within particular industries see Kilby, *Industrialization in an Open Economy*, ch. 11.

understandable, given the relatively low level of purchasing power, the need to manufacture for a mass market, and the motives of the first industrialists. However, it was not feasible to produce a complete range of these items locally. The advantage lay with industries which could achieve the greatest saving in costs by being located near their final market. Factories using a high proportion of local materials, especially items which were expensive to transport, such as timber, lime, clay and water, were particularly favoured, as were industries in which freight charges on finished articles were higher than on the constituent raw materials, as was the case with hollow-ware.[87] Typical import-substituting industries established in the 1950s were those producing cigarettes, beer, cement, footwear, textiles, furniture and utensils, and the principal concentrations of modern manufacturing were in the four wealthiest colonies, the leading centres being Lagos and Dakar. Export processing also underwent further development in the 1950s, chiefly as a result of the introduction of power-driven machinery. Once again, the main economy was the saving made in freight charges by processing heavy raw materials, such as timber and minerals, at source. Finally, it should be noted that the expatriate firms invested in service industries, especially those requiring technical skills. This involvement became necessary to meet demands derived from the satisfaction of prior wants: the spread of motor vehicles, for example, made it essential to set up service stations.

Changes in the economic role of colonial governments after 1945 were as striking as those affecting the expatriate firms, and have certainly attracted more scholarly attention. Innovations in the public sector were partly the result of African pressures, and were partly conceived in self-interest, but they were also influenced by shifts in the global balance of power after the Second World War. Britain and France emerged from the war as victors, but with their economies run down and their international position irretrievably weakened. Large parts of their empires had been overrun by enemy forces, and France herself had been occupied by German troops. After 1945 both powers began to lose their grip on political developments in their overseas territories. By the time nationalist movements were gathering momentum in West Africa, important concessions had already been made elsewhere. After much heart-searching, Britain granted independence to India in 1947, and France was forced to relinquish her possessions in Indo-China between 1950 and 1955. Other commitments remained, and both countries found themselves engaged in some painful rearguard actions, particularly in areas where the issue of self-government was complicated by the presence of white settlers, as in the cases of Algeria and Kenya. Nevertheless, even colonial powers learn lessons in the end, and by the early 1950s, if not before, it was clear that Britain and France had decided not to try and retain West Africa by force.

Alterations to government policy after 1945 centred on one outstanding development—the expansion of the public sector. This innovation involved changes in the level of public investment, the introduction of economic planning, and the exercise

[87] As pointed out in Chapter 2, these principles also influenced the location of manufacturing activity in the pre-colonial period.

of controls over the marketing of export crops. These three features of official policy will be considered in turn.

Assessing the volume of capital flows to underdeveloped countries is not an easy task, partly because of the empirical difficulty of locating all the sources of supply, and partly because of the conceptual problem of deciding what constitutes investment. However, in the case of West Africa the main trend is not in dispute: there was a marked increase in foreign investment after the Second World War. Between 1947 and the end of 1956 French public investment in her West African territories amounted to 106 billion 1956 C.F.A. francs, compared to 46 billion 1956 C.F.A. francs for the period 1903–1946. Thus the volume of investment was more than twice as great in the ten years between 1947 and 1956 as in the whole of the previous forty-three years.[88] Overseas public investment in British West Africa, though running at less than half the level of French aid, was also greater between 1946 and 1960 than in the period between 1900 and 1945.[89] These figures do not tell the entire story. A substantial percentage of public investment after 1945 took the form of grants rather than loans, which meant that the recipients carried proportionately lighter burdens of repayment than in the pre-war era. Furthermore, fragmentary though the available statistics are, it is clear that private investment also rose following the revival of the export market after the Second World War. Finally, it should not be forgotten that the colonies had access to funds derived from local sources, especially customs duties and (in the case of British West Africa) revenues supplied by the Marketing Boards. A study of these sources reveals an important contrast. In the case of French West Africa domestic funds accounted for twenty-five to thirty per cent of official development expenditure between 1946 and 1958, whereas in the four British territories the proportion was almost reversed: only about twenty-five per cent of the total came from overseas public agencies in the period 1945–1959.[90]

The increase in the resources at the disposal of public authorities made it possible to undertake measures to expand exports and to assist new projects outside the export sector. The rise in the volume of overseas aid, together with the funds accumulated by the marketing boards, weakened the relationship between overseas earnings and domestic demand, and enabled the economy to grow to some extent independently of the performance of the export sector. After 1945 imports into

[88] Elliot J. Berg, 'The Economic Basis of Political Choice in French West Africa', *American Political Science Review*, 54, 1960, pp. 394–5. Capet's estimate (*Traité d'économie tropicale*, p. 293) suggests an even greater contrast between pre-war and post-war levels of investment. As there is no obvious means of choosing between the two sources, I have used Berg's more conservative figures.

[89] There is no work on British Africa to compare with Teresa Hayter's *French Aid*, 1966. For a general survey see Leonard Rist, 'Capital and Capital Supply in Relation to the Development of Africa', in *Economic Development for Africa South of the Sahara*, ed. E. A. G. Robinson 1964, pp. 444–74.

[90] Ona B. Forrest 'The Financing of the Present Development Plans of West Africa', in *International Finance and Development Planning in West Africa*, ed. Sune Carlson and O. Olakanpo, Lund 1964, pp. 55–6.

French West Africa began to expand faster than exports. Ten years later the same trend appeared in the British territories. The economy remained open, but it no longer operated in its pure form. Two, more specific, comments should be added to this general observation. In the first place, modifications to the open economy were most pronounced in Nigeria, the Gold Coast, Senegal and the Ivory Coast, for it was these richer colonies which attracted most of the foreign capital (public and private) invested in West Africa, and which were in a position to tap substantial domestic funds as well. Consequently, post-war economic development further accentuated already established regional inequalities. Secondly, though the sources of foreign capital proliferated after the Second World War, Britain and France remained the chief suppliers.[91] Of the two, French investment was greater in absolute terms, and it formed a higher proportion of total public funds available in the colonies. Bilateral aid played a part in modifying the open economy, but it also helped to maintain, and in the case of France to strengthen, ties between the metropolis and the dependencies.

The considerable rise in public investment brought into being a new service industry of economists and administrators. Indeed, the period after 1945 has some claims to being termed the Age of the Planners. On this occasion there was no bonfire of controls, as there had been at the end of the First World War.[92] The victors began to talk of 'winning' the peace, of a 'strategy' for growth, and of a 'big push' towards development. The rise to power of left wing parties in Britain and France ensured that these ideas were translated into plans and given high priority. Just as the Marshall Plan (1948) was designed to aid the reconstruction of Europe, so the colonial powers initiated programmes for speeding economic recovery in their empires.

This was the time, again following a precedent set during the war, when a whole new language, a kind of Esperanto for planners, was created from initials. As far as French West Africa was concerned, the main agency was F.I.D.E.S. (Fonds d'Investissement pour le Développement Économique et Social), which was established in 1946. F.I.D.E.S., which had both general and local sections and a wide range of specialised subsidiaries, was responsible for the P.M.E. (Plan de Modernisation et d'Équipement). This was a ten-year plan, which was produced in 1946 and had the distinction of not being revised until 1953. F.I.D.E.S. itself survived until 1959, when it was replaced by F.A.C. (Fonds d'Aide et Co-opération). In the case of British West Africa external public investment came mainly from successive C.D.W. (Colonial Development and Welfare) Acts, and was tied to plans which were drawn up for each colony in the immediate post-war years. This source was supplemented by the C.D.C. (Colonial Development Corporation), which was formed in 1948. The C.D.C., besides having borrowing powers of its own, also participated actively in specific projects aimed at developing agricultural and mineral resources.

The first plans had fairly modest aims, and consisted mainly of 'shopping lists' of

[91] America was the leading foreign investor in Liberia.
[92] R. H. Tawney, 'The Abolition of Economic Controls, 1918–1921', *Economic History Review*, 13, 1943, pp. 1–30.

desirable items, very much on the lines of the plans devised by Sarraut and Guggis-berg in the 1920s.[93] It was not until the close of the 1950s that more sophisticated plans dealing with the economy as a whole, co-ordinating development between sectors, and prescribing growth rates, were introduced. In the 1960s 'the plan' became the talisman of politicians anxious for quick results. However, in practice the plans introduced around the time of independence proved not to have magical powers: they were frequently over-ambitious; they were based on questionable statistical data; and they were often overtaken by political events.[94] The early plans had obvious theoretical limitations, and they sponsored a number of ill-judged projects, but they were probably at least as effective as those produced in later years.

The plans of the British and French colonies allocated investment in broadly similar ways.[95] Substantial sums were set aside for the social services, especially health and education. In the economic sectors priority was given to transport, which accounted for roughly forty per cent of the money spent by F.I.D.E.S. between 1946 and 1958, and for about thirty per cent of public investment in the four British territories during the same period. Agriculture was next on the list, receiving about twenty to twenty-five per cent of the total, and industry (mainly power and other utilities) came third.

The greater part of public investment in transport was spent on road improve-ments. The only important railway developments were the construction of short lines to serve mines in Mauritania, Guinea, Sierra Leone and Liberia, and extentions from Jos to Maiduguri (in Nigeria) and from Bobo Dioulasso to Ouagadougou (in Upper Volta). Measuring the expansion of road transport in terms of the number of miles of road built is an exercise which may well be a cure for insomina, but as an index of economic change it can easily be misleading. Apart from the fact that many West African roads disappear during the rainy season, there is also the basic problem, which is sometimes ignored, of deciding what constitutes a road in an under-developed economy. There seems little point in providing detailed lists of 'relevant' figures, though this could be done without difficulty. All that will be said here is that on a conservative estimate the number of miles of *tarred* roads increased about ten times (admittedly from a very low base) between 1945 and 1960. In the case of Nigeria, which has been studied in some detail, there were about 8,000 miles of tarred roads in 1963, compared with just over 500 miles in 1945. A more certain indication of road improvements is provided by the number of motor vehicles, which also grew about ten-fold in the period 1945–1960. In 1959 there were just over

[93] D. K. Greenstreet, 'Public Administration: Development and Welfare in the British Territories of West Africa During the Forties', *Economic Bulletin of Ghana*, 1, 1971, pp. 3–23.

[94] For an interesting comparative study of recent planning experiences see R. H. Green, 'Four African Development Plans: Ghana, Kenya, Nigeria, and Tanzania', *Journal of Modern African Studies*, 3, 1965, pp. 249–79.

[95] I have refrained from quoting detailed figures because I have been unable to reconcile many of the statistics cited in the secondary sources. A thorough, comparative study is needed to overcome this difficulty.

180,000 motor vehicles in West Africa, of which total 94,000 were in the British territories and 86,000 in the French colonies.

The rapid expansion of the road transport industry galvanised activity on several fronts. It assisted the expansion of export crops; it stimulated internal trade; and it helped manufacturers, both by reducing the cost of delivering raw materials to the factory and by distributing finished products to a wider market. Although motor vehicles were first envisaged as feeding the railway, they managed to capture a substantial share of the import and export traffic after the Second World War. Road transport benefited from cost-reducing innovations, such as the diesel engine, but it was no cheaper than the railway, except on certain short-haul journeys. Its competitive advantage stemmed from its geographical mobility, its speed, and its organisational flexibility, which meant that it could vary rates quickly, adjust schedules to deal with particularly profitable (or unprofitable) items, and provide a door to door service.

The 1950s saw the beginnings of consistent and widespread success in applying scientific knowledge to tropical agriculture. The best results, as noted earlier, were achieved by introducing new types of plants, seeds, fertilisers and pesticides to existing agricultural systems. The failures, which received much more publicity, were all in the established West African tradition of undertaking grandiose projects that departed radically from long-standing practices. An extraordinary plan for producing eggs in the Gambia, started in 1948 under the direction, appropriately enough, of Dr Fowler, was wound up in 1951 at a cost of about £1 million,[96] and an ambitious scheme to mechanise agriculture in Nigeria, launched in 1949, sank, weighed down by its own rusty tractors, in 1953.[97] A more cautious approach has prevailed since the early 1960s.[98] Mechanisation is no longer regarded as a way of producing an instant agricultural revolution in the tropics, and officials have ceased to assume that large farms can be equated automatically with high productivity. A salutory side-effect of scientific research has been to give Western experts more respect for the methods employed by African farmers.

Official enterprise has been important throughout West Africa in encouraging industrial development since the 1950s. Government involvement of an indirect kind has been most evident in measures to assist private manufacturers establish import-substituting and export-processing industries. These measures included protective import duties and quotas, grants and cheap loans, guaranteed purchases of certain products, and tax relief for infant industries.[99] In French West Africa part of what was termed 'industrial' investment was also spent developing mineral resources, particularly bauxite deposits in Guinea and iron ore in Mauritania. Direct public enterprise has concentrated mainly on expanding public utilities, notably electricity.

[96] Harry A. Gailey, *A History of the Gambia*, 1964, pp. 151–8.
[97] K. D. S. Baldwin, *The Niger Agricultural Project*, Cambridge, Mass., 1957.
[98] Although Ghana and Nigeria can provide some exceptions to this generalisation.
[99] For two case studies see Helleiner, *Peasant Agriculture, Government, and Economic Growth in Nigeria*, pp. 310–20, and Saylor, *The Economic System of Sierra Leone*, pp. 147–57.

The most striking plan of this kind was the Volta River Project, which was a comprehensive and costly scheme for generating hydro-electric power, producing aluminium from local bauxite and irrigating farms in the south-east part of the Gold Coast.[100] Since electricity is virtually the only form in which power for modern industry is stored in West Africa (and production can be measured accurately), it provides a useful indication of the level of industrial development in the region. In 1962 total electricity production for the whole of West Africa was 1745 kilowatt-hours. By international standards this total was very low, being less than one fifth of production in the United Kingdom, which had additional sources of power and a much smaller population. The unevenness of development within West Africa is demonstrated by the fact that four countries accounted for eighty-six per cent of total production, and Nigeria alone for forty-five per cent.[101]

No satisfactory comparison of French and British policy towards the overseas trade of their West African possessions has been undertaken. Most research has centred on the operation of the Marketing Boards in British West Africa; neither the French marketing system nor tariff policy has been studied in depth. Much of the discussion which follows must be regarded, inevitably, as tentative.[102] It will be suggested that the policies of the two principal colonial powers were broadly a continuation of those formulated in the period 1930–1945; that these policies were adapted to take account of two new requirements—the need to assist Europe's post-war recovery and the desirability of making concessions to African pressures; and that while there were, as is commonly accepted, important contrasts in the means adopted by France and Britain, there were also some interesting similarities which have gone largely unremarked.

Britain and France faced serious balance of payments difficulties after the Second World War, and were particularly short of dollars, which were needed to settle debts with the United States. In these circumstances empire trade assumed a vital role because it could be conducted without touching scarce reserves of foreign exchange, and it was a means of earning money to pay off debts elsewhere. The policy of imperial preference, which was begun in the 1930s, was continued and elaborated after 1945. Additional quotas were imposed on goods imported into the colonies from outside the empire, and exchange controls were employed to conserve stocks of gold and dollars. These controls were part of wider developments, namely the growth of the sterling area and of the franc zone. The evolution of the sterling area did not alter the existing monetary system in British West Africa. The creation of the franc zone, however, was followed in 1945 by the introduction of the C.F.A. (Colonies Françaises d'Afrique) franc and by the formation of a currency board, the

[100] Plans for this project were drawn up during the 1950s, but not implemented until the following decade.

[101] The leading producers in 1962 were Nigeria (786 million kilowatt-hours), Ghana (431), Senegal (172) and the Ivory Coast (120).

[102] And is partly designed to stimulate further research into the neglected aspects of these subjects. Anyone who undertakes a full study of the marketing systems operating in French West Africa after 1945 will be making a useful contribution to the recent economic history of the region.

Caisse Centrale de la France d'Outre-Mer.[103] In this way French West Africa acquired a separate currency and a formal machinery which paralleled the arrangements made for the British territories in 1912.[104]

There was some relaxation of preferential policies in the 1950s. By then the dollar problem had ceased to be acute; tropical raw materials were no longer in short supply; manufacturers in Britain and France were making headway in markets outside their empires; and African demands for wider trading opportunities could not be ignored. In practice, however, liberalisation proceeded faster in British than in French West Africa. By 1960 Britain's share of the overseas trade of her West African colonies was about twenty-five per cent less than it had been in 1945. In the case of France the decline was only about five per cent, and it was not until the development of the European Economic Community in the 1960s that bilateral links weakened noticeably. It was in the 1950s, too, that tariffs were used for the first time to protect infant industries in West Africa, instead of being regarded solely as instruments for raising revenue and controlling the direction of trade.

Imperial preference, though purporting to offer advantages to the colonies, was inspired primarily by a desire to safeguard the interests of the colonial powers. Marketing policy, as reshaped after the Second World War, was advertised as being in the interests of Africans, and can be regarded as an attempt to modify the operation of the open economy by eliminating fluctuations in produce prices and in producer incomes.

In the immediate post-war years French governments were uncertain both about the need for stabilisation, given the high prices ruling in the world and within the preferential system, and about the means by which it might be achieved. However, support funds (*caisses de soutien*) guaranteeing minimum produce prices were formed for most export crops between 1946 and 1949. In the Ivory Coast, for example, funds for coffee and cocoa were established by means of export levies imposed at the ports of exit.[105] This arrangement proved unpopular with the farmers who were supposed to benefit from it, and in 1950 a proposal to raise the levies was met by a number of protests in the true Gallic tradition of direct peasant action. The farmers objected because a proportion of the levy went to the Federation and was used to support groundnut prices in Senegal, and because the *caisse* had ceased to act as a stabilising body and had become simply a tax-gathering agency. In the period 1949–1950 the powers of the various *caisses* were reduced and the marketing system became, in the words of Ramboz, 'incoherent and ineffectual'. Between 1954 and 1956 a series of new stabilisation funds (*caisses de stabilisation*) were created for the principal French West African exports. This development was prompted by

---

[103] In 1955 an Institut d'Émission was set up for French West Africa, and in 1959 this body became the Banque Centrale des États de l'Afrique de l'Ouest.

[104] The principal difference was that the C.F.A. franc did not follow the several devaluations of the metropolitan franc after the war, and therefore had a higher value, whereas currencies in the sterling area continued to exchange at par.

[105] A rare and neglected case study of the French marketing system is Yvonne-Claude Ramboz, 'La politique caféière de Côte d'Ivoire et la réforme de la caisse de stabilisation des prix du café et du cacao', *Revue Juridique et Politique*, 19, 1965, pp. 194–218.

two events: the initiation of a more liberal tariff regime, which threatened, ulti-mately, to expose French Africa to the lower prices which prevailed outside the preferential system; and the fall in world produce prices at the end of the Korean war. The stabilisation funds aimed at fixing producer prices and guaranteeing mini-mum incomes, and were financed by levies on exporters, by export duties, and by a central fund in Paris (Fonds National de Régularisation des Cours des Produits d'Outre-Mer). With some modifications, the reformed *caisses* survived down to, and in many cases after, independence.

An accurate assessment of the effectiveness of the French marketing system cannot be made until the necessary research has been completed. On present evidence it is highly unlikely that any notable achievements were recorded before 1954. After the reforms of 1954–1956 there seems to have been a considerable degree of success in fixing producer prices, but there is little information about the more crucial issue of the stabilisation of incomes. Producer prices were set well above world prices, but consumer imports were, on average, equally highly priced. However, it is worth mentioning that the *caisses*, unlike the marketing boards in British West Africa, made serious efforts to influence incomes by trying to control the volume of produce placed on the market, and they also used their reserves to support prices when the market weakened, as it did in the second half of the 1950s.

The British government had few doubts about the desirability of stabilising the prices paid to producers, mainly because exports from the British colonies were more exposed to the world market than was the case with French West Africa. Officials were also confident that the marketing system established during the war was capable of achieving this aim. Some institutional reorganisation was carried out between 1947 and 1949, when the West African Produce Control Board was replaced by separate commodity boards in each of the four colonies. Subsequently, the only alteration of importance took place in 1954, when the Nigerian Marketing Boards were reconstituted to operate on a regional basis. The Marketing Boards, while still employing the expatriate firms as buying agents, used their monopoly powers to fix the prices paid to producers. Their declared policy was to set this price below the world price during times of prosperity, and to use the difference to form a reserve, which would then be paid out to support producer prices when the world market became depressed. In practice the policy pursued by the Boards took a rather different course. In the decade after the war, when world prices were buoyant, substantial reserves were accumulated, as was intended. However, when the demand for tropical raw materials slackened, as it did from the mid-1950s, the boards still fixed prices slightly below the levels ruling in international markets, and so con-tinued to acquire funds, albeit on a much reduced scale. It has been calculated that export producers in the Gold Coast lost as much as forty-one per cent of their potential gross incomes as a result of deductions made by the Marketing Boards between 1947 and 1961, and that Nigerian farmers lost an average of twenty-seven per cent.[106] The reserves were certainly spent in the late 1950s and early 1960s, but

[106] The figure for Nigeria is an unweighted average of the losses from cocoa, groundnuts and palm produce.

they were used, in the main, to finance government development projects, and not, as originally planned, to compensate export-producers.

The initial policy of stabilisation, and the subsequent deviation from it, have provoked a major controversy among economists concerned with African development. The claim that the Boards had stabilised prices was first attacked by Professor Bauer in a now famous study of the marketing system in British West Africa.[107] Bauer pointed out that the imperial government never defined what it meant by stabilisation. He showed that to stabilise producer prices was not necessarily to stabilise incomes because the farmers' total receipts depended on the volume of sales as well as on their unit price. Volume could be neither controlled nor, of greater practical relevance, predicted. Bauer's analysis of the historical record led him to conclude that while the Boards had virtually eliminated intra-seasonal price fluctuations, they had achieved little success in stabilising prices from season to season, and had totally failed to stabilise incomes. Indeed, Bauer contended that incomes were more unstable under the Marketing Board system than they would have been in its absence. He went on to suggest that the Boards had had a generally depressive effect on the economy by damping down demand and possibly by blunting the incentive to invest in productive enterprises within and outside agriculture. Bauer's critique did not pass unchallenged at the time, but later research has substantiated his main arguments.

Bauer's study was published in 1954, at a time when the Marketing Boards were still accumulating funds and pursuing their stated aim of price stabilisation. Helleiner, writing in 1966, was in a position to assess their subsequent performance.[108] His analysis confirmed that the Boards had failed to stabilise incomes, and also showed that they had virtually abandoned any attempt to do so. Helleiner then went on to argue that the role of the Boards had changed in the second half of the 1950s, and that they were to be judged primarily as agencies promoting economic development. His detailed survey of Nigerian experience led him to conclude that while some of the reserves had been mis-spent, most of the funds accumulated by the Boards had been invested usefully in various government-sponsored projects, notably agricultural research, road construction and local industries. Helleiner contended that the Boards had proved to be effective in mobilising savings for investment which otherwise would not have been made: if the reserves had been paid out direct to the farmers, the greater part of the additional income would have been spent on imported consumer goods, thus perpetuating the open economy rather than assisting diversification. The strength of Helleiner's case lies in his ability to point to factual achievements. To suggest that the reserves would have been spent more wisely if they had been returned to the farmers is to pose a question about an event that did not take place. Nevertheless, the evidence presented in this chapter makes it possible to add one, possibly interesting, speculation. Since diversification

---

[107] P. T. Bauer, *West African Trade*, Cambridge 1954.
[108] Gerald K. Helleiner, *Peasant Agriculture, Government, and Economic Growth in Nigeria*, Homewood, Illinois, 1966.

10*

was taking place in the 1950s as a result of market growth, and not solely through government initiative, there would seem to be a case for supposing that had the funds accumulated by the Boards been left in the hands of the farmers, the market would have grown faster and expenditure on consumer goods would have given further impetus to import-substituting industries.[109] Merely to raise the possibility is to draw attention to the fact that the controversy over the Marketing Boards is also a debate about wider issues, which are not always stated explicitly: about private versus public enterprise; about the emphasis to be given to consumption as opposed to investment; and about the meaning of 'desirable' expenditure in an era in which 'development' is sometimes a euphemism for redistribution.

5 The open economy modified

A study of the recent economic history of West Africa provides a new perspective on events which have been the preserve of economists and political scientists. The evidence presented in this chapter makes it possible to re-interpret two central and controversial problems—the nature of colonial economic development and the rise of African nationalism.

According to one popular belief, structural economic change in West Africa was not possible until after the achievement of independence. To accept this view is to misunderstand the timing of economic change and the character of the governments which came to power in the 1960s. Between 1945 and 1960 the open economy underwent substantial modifications, the chief of which centred on the expansion of the public sector, the transfer of commercial and political power to Africans, and the beginning of modern industry. Just as the colonial period witnessed the continuation of trends which were already apparent in the mid-nineteenth century, so, too, most of the new African governments pursued policies in the 1960s which, in the main, were already being implemented, or had been agreed on, in the 1950s.

Three observations about the nature of economic change before 1960 should be set down at this stage. To begin with, it is important to realise that the innovations of the period 1945–1960 were not solely the result of government initiative, as is often thought, but stemmed partly from the internal dynamics of the open economy itself. Export growth after 1945 enabled the domestic market to expand to the point where it could support at least some kinds of modern manufacturing industries. This novel opportunity was perceived and exploited by private enterprise, European and African. It has not been widely appreciated that West Africa took this particular path towards structural change, though the route is by no means unique. A similar pattern of development occurred during the twentieth century in parts of the Far

---

[109] An argument on these lines is developed further by Cyril Ehrlich, 'Marketing Boards in Retrospect—Myth and Reality', in *African Public Sector Economics*, Centre of African Studies, Edinburgh 1970, pp. 121–45.

East, such as Japan, Hong Kong and Taiwan,[110] and also in some Latin American countries, notably Argentina and Brazil.[111]

Next, it should now be clear that officials were instruments as well as originators of change. Governments, whether European or African, have a common concern with publicising their achievements and minimising their failures. Critics and defenders of colonialism both share the assumption that the local administration exercised greater control over events than it actually did. Governors were umpires rather than dictators. Their task was to mediate between competing local and metropolitan interests. Of necessity, their leadership was more like that of the Duke of York than that of the Duke of Wellington. Innovations in policy were largely reactions, though often delayed, to variations in the performance of the open economy, to African demands, and to the less vociferous (but equally pressing) claims of the expatriate firms. In this connection it is worth noting that insufficient recognition has been given to the extent to which changes introduced after the Second World War had their origins in pressures built up and remedies canvassed during the period 1930–1945. By about 1950 the major colonial powers were clearly moving with the new tide, trying on the one hand to placate their African subjects, and on the other to safeguard the future of the expatriate business interests which had played such an important part in installing them in the continent in the first place. Judged by these criteria, decolonisation in West Africa was one of colonialism's greatest triumphs.

Finally, an examination of the role of the government in modifying the open economy reveals a marked contrast between French and British West Africa. The French colonies were on the whole poorer, and they relied heavily on French capital, markets and personnel.[112] The British colonies, besides being wealthier, were also less dependent on imperial aid and markets. The modifications made to the economies of French West Africa after 1945 had the effect of integrating the Federation more closely with the metropolis, whereas in British West Africa economic innovation sprang mainly from the expansion of the open economy itself, and so was self-financing to a much greater extent. This distinction had far-reaching political implications: it helps to explain why the Gold Coast and Nigeria took the lead in demanding and achieving independence, and why the French colonies, when offered independence in 1958, chose, with the exception of Guinea, to remain temporarily within the French Community.[113]

This chapter has offered an economic interpretation of the rise of African nationalism that also runs counter to some well known, if simplistic, beliefs. In the first place,

---

[110] Wontack Hong, 'Industrialisation and Trade in Manufactures: the East Asian Experience', in *The Open Economy*, ed. Peter B. Kenen and Roger Lawrence, New York 1968, pp. 213–39.

[111] Celso Furtado, *Economic Development of Latin America*, Cambridge 1970, pp. 75–81.

[112] This distinction has been drawn out by Elliot J. Berg in a typically incisive article, 'The Economic Basis of Political Choice in French West Africa', *American Political Science Review*, 54, 1960, pp. 391–405.

[113] The timing of independence was as follows: the Gold Coast (Ghana), 1957; Guinea, 1958; Nigeria, 1960; the constituent states of the Federation of French West Africa (apart from Guinea), 1960; Togo, 1960; Sierra Leone, 1961; and Gambia, 1965.

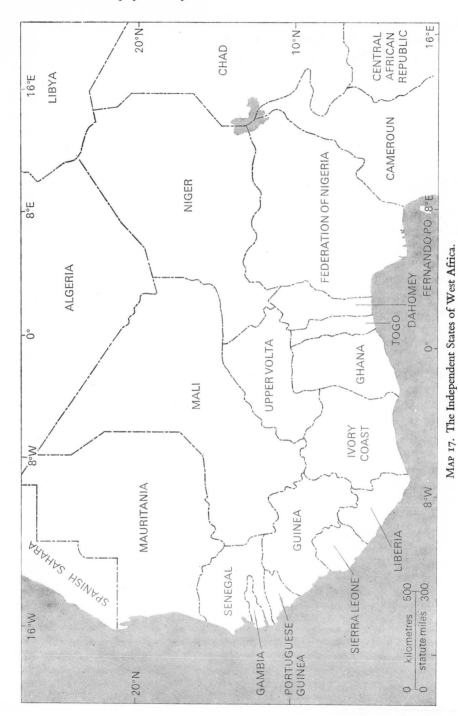

Map 17. The Independent States of West Africa.

it should be clear that independence was not a result of the enlightened policy of rulers who managed to steer their subject peoples towards self-government in accordance with a grand plan laid down at the outset of the colonial period. Only hindsight suggests that the granting of independence was anything other than a belated recognition of the unforeseen. Secondly, it is equally certain that African nationalism was not simply a spontaneous, mass movement of the downtrodden, directed against sun-helmeted, exploiting masters and led by men whose readiness for self-sacrifice was matched only by their determination to survive long enough to improve the living standards of their fellow countrymen.

Opposition to colonialism was based on an imperfect alliance of three major interest groups of farmers, traders and wage-earners, all of whom shared a degree of commitment to the exchange economy which distinguished them from the bulk of the population. Political leaders were drawn from the higher, more affluent echelons of these groups and from representatives of privileged, minority occupations, such as teaching, journalism and the law. Discontent among the leaders and the upper ranks of their supporters sprang not from their proximity to an objectively-defined poverty line (from which, indeed, they were far removed), but from their sense of relative deprivation, which in turn derived from the fact that they aimed at European standards of consumption. The leadership had to frame a programme which would hold this alliance together and also appeal to those whose interests were by no means the same as their own. Consequently, nationalist organisations began to extend the political arena after the Second World War, in order to bolster their claims to be representative and so exert greater pressure on the colonial powers.[114]

By taking a disaggregated view of what is often regarded simply as 'African' opposition to colonialism, it becomes possible to relate the evolution of nationalism to the performance of the open economy. The argument advanced here has combined elements of the Marxist approach, with its stress on declining living standards producing a revolutionary situation, and of de Tocqueville's theory that revolutionary change is likely to occur only after a period of social and economic progress.[115] It has been shown that nationalism, in its modern forms, had its origins in the period 1930–1945, when a serious downturn in real and anticipated living standards occurred, following a phase of sustained, if modest, advance. Between 1945 and 1950 real incomes, though improving, did not rise fast enough to satisfy the expectations of the three groups most heavily involved in the colonial economy. After a brief trial of strength in the later 1940s the colonial rulers began to recognise, in Coser's terminology, the 'clues' which have to be followed before conflict can be resolved with a measure of satisfaction to both sides.[116] During the 1950s the nationalist movement was reinforced and subtly changed by the return of prosperity

---

[114] This task was helped (and made necessary) by extensions to the franchise and by the introduction of local elections after 1945.

[115] James C. Davies, 'Toward a Theory of Revolution', *American Sociological Review*, 27, 1962, pp. 5–19.

[116] Lewis A. Coser, 'The Termination of Conflict', *Journal of Conflict Resolution*, 11, 1958, pp. 170–83.

and by the new spirit of co-operation which grew up between African leaders and colonial officials. The leaders and their principal followers began to attain the goals they had set themselves, they started to quarrel over the spoils of a victory that was no longer in dispute,[117] and they also acquired a more realistic appreciation of the difficulties involved in achieving a fundamental reconstruction of the economy. This explains why nationalism lacked a revolutionary edge, and why the period immediately after independence saw a continuation of existing policies, rather than a sharp break with the past.

[117] French West Africa was split up at independence largely because the wealthy colonies, especially the Ivory Coast, did not want to continue subsidising the poorer parts of the Federation.

eight

The economy in retrospect

The strategy adopted in this book has been to state the argument at the outset, and then to develop it, step by step, in successive chapters. Consequently, no revelations have been saved for these final pages, which will recall, briefly, the main points of interpretation.

The central theme of this study has been the interaction of the various internal and external factors which have determined the structure and performance of the market economy. Older views of the development of the West African economy stressed the importance of external influences, principally colonial rule, and focused on a comparatively short and recent time span. The colonial rulers were thought to have started with a static, subsistence economy, and to have brought about a transformation which was almost as impressive as that once achieved with the loaves and fishes. The present work has noted the inaccuracies of the myth of Primitive Africa, has emphasised the role of the indigenous population, and has covered a long period of time. However, this study has also shown that what has become known as 'the African point of view' is to some extent a misnomer, which stems from the myth of Merrie Africa and from an exaggerated belief in the communal solidarity of pre-industrial societies. In reality, there are various African points of view, each of which needs to be analysed before a satisfactory account of indigenous economic history can be constructed.

The interpretation put forward here has explained stability and change in the market economy by making use of concepts which will also be familiar to historians and economists specialising in other parts of the underdeveloped world. The analysis presented in Chapter 2 was principally a commentary on the stereotype of the 'traditional' society. It was argued that this concept is of questionable value because it greatly exaggerates differences between the aims of pre-industrial and of industrial societies, and because the institutional characteristics it describes have little foundation in fact. Ideal-types are not designed to represent reality, but they are supposed to illuminate it. When they fail to do this, they serve only to direct research along false trails. Like Platonic Ideas, they need keeping in their heavenly place. The pre-colonial economy was complex, efficient and adaptable, and it had reached a relatively advanced stage of commercial capitalism long before the impact of the Western world was felt in Africa. It was not the will to achieve that was lacking,[1] but

[1] David C. McClelland's stimulating theory, presented in *The Achieving Society*, Princeton 1961, has little relevance for West Africa.

the means of achieving which were limited. The expansion of the domestic market was retarded not by institutional rigidities determined by anti-capitalist values, but by identifiable economic obstacles, especially by a deficiency of effective demand, which was related, in turn, to the land–labour ratio and to high distribution costs. This conclusion, it is suggested, is important for an understanding of the West African past (and present), and is also in agreement with recent research on other parts of the underdeveloped world.[2]

Chapter 3 considered the possibility that these internal obstacles might have been overcome by means of international trade. The concept of dualism was used to explain why the external commercial relations which existed before the nineteenth century failed to establish strong, beneficial linkages with the domestic economy. This approach involved a consideration of the economics of slave-producing, as well as, more conventionally, of the role of Africans in slave-trading. It was concluded that Saharan and Atlantic commerce were privately profitable, but that their social benefits were at best limited and in some cases were non-existent.

Chapter 4 argued that the early nineteenth century saw the start of the modern economic history of West Africa, in the sense that the economic structure which began to take shape at that time was essentially that which existed at the close of the colonial era. The history of the nineteenth century was analysed in terms of staple theory,[3] which was used to show how the growth in exports of vegetable oils mobilised factors within the domestic economy, and led to the integration, for the first time, of internal and external exchange sectors. This development created tensions within Africa by shifting economic power from a few, large exporters to numerous, small-scale farmers, and it also involved producers in the cyclical fluctuations generated by industrial Europe. It was contended that the initial structural changes and the subsequent performance of the new, 'legitimate' exports were central to an understanding of the motives for, and the timing of, the scramble for West Africa in the late nineteenth century.

A formal model of this developing, export economy was outlined in Chapter 5 and applied to the period of colonial rule. The model made use of the concepts of 'open' and 'closed' economies, and refined them to fit West African circumstances and to suit the purposes of history rather than of economic policy. The performance of the West African economies during the colonial era was charted by means of the terms of trade, which were used to identify periods of market contraction and growth. It was suggested that the multiplier effects of staple exports were weaker in open economies based on indigenous, 'peasant' producers than in countries of recent settlement, such as Canada and Australia, where there were considerable

---

[2] See Morris D. Morris, 'Towards a Reinterpretation of Nineteenth-Century Indian Economic History', *Journal of Economic History*, 23, 1963, pp. 606–18; T. Scarlett Epstein, *Capitalism, Primitive and Modern: Some Aspects of Tolai Economic Growth*, Canberra 1968; and David Pitt, *Tradition and Economic Progress in Samoa*, Oxford 1970.

[3] For a discussion of the historical role of foreign trade in promoting development see K. Berrill, 'International Trade and the Rate of Economic Growth', *Economic History Review*, 12, 1960, pp. 351–9.

advantages of capital and skills, and where economic policy enjoyed a greater degree of independence. At the same time, it was contended that open economies which relied on 'peasant' exports established stronger linkages than those associated with mining and plantation enclaves, where there was little connection between 'modern' and domestic sectors, and where the tendency for foreign trade earnings to be leaked abroad was more pronounced.

Chapter 6 focused on export growth during the first half of the colonial period (1900–1930), and evaluated expatriate and indigenous contributions to the completion of the open economy. The expatriate role, though necessary to the expansion which was achieved, was seen as encouraging a process which was under way *before* the partition of Africa. Innovations in the key agricultural sector were made by African farmers themselves. Indigenous producers of all ethnic groups, whether in the forest or savanna, whether growing annuals or perennials, whether Muslim or Christian (or neither), proved that they were responsive to monetary incentives, that they were prepared to travel to distant places, that they were willing to experiment with new crops and with novel techniques of farm management, and that they were ready, on occasion, to provide their own social overhead capital (in the shape of roads and bridges) in advance of government action. The so-called 'traditional' society was not eliminated: export expansion involved a certain amount of social change, as the example of the decline of slavery made clear, but in general pre-colonial economic and social institutions survived and proved functional to the development of the open economy. The mobilisation of domestic factors of production was considered in terms of the vent-for-surplus theory of international trade, which was modified to take account of historical evidence relating to the role of African producers.

Chapter 7 identified the disfunctional elements which caused the open economy to be modified during the second half of the colonial period (1930–1960). To begin with, attention was paid to differentiation within the export sector and to developments in the domestic economy in order to stress the importance of the quantitative size of the market, its geographical extent, and the social composition of those involved in exchange activities.[4] This analysis was then related to changes in the barter and income terms of trade in an attempt to explain why the open economy experienced severe strains after 1930. This period of stress, it was argued, was causally linked to the rise of the nationalist movement and to the beginnings of industrialisation. After 1945 governments started to intervene in the 'natural' working of the open economy. At the same time, growth within the existing export sectors began to lead, at least in some countries, to development, that is to structural change involving the introduction of modern manufacturing industries. The appearance of these novel features at the close of the colonial period makes the achievement of independence a suitable terminal point for this study.

[4] In West Africa the 'traditional' sector survived and expanded *because* of export growth. In some other parts of the world it survived because it remained isolated from the foreign trade sector. See Chi-Ming Hou, 'Economic Dualism: the Case of China, 1840–1937', *Journal of Economic History*, 23, 1963, pp. 277–97.

There is a moralist in every historian. The moral of this book is mainly didactic, though it has prescriptive implications. The history presented here has sought to direct attention away from the adventures and triumphs of great leaders, past and present, and towards the activities of the overwhelming majority of Africans, those who have never ranked among the élite. This shift of emphasis may have beneficial academic consequences if it encourages researchers to leave the air-conditioned corridors of power and venture into the farms and markets. It may also have some practical use if it reminds those who formulate policy and exercise authority that the skills and energies of ordinary Africans are probably the continent's greatest assets. This is one lesson which the present can, and should, learn from the past.

Bibliography

Bibliographies are the basis of all academic study, and they are particularly important in enabling new subjects to be pursued independently and outside a small group of specialists. The principles underlying the compilation and organisation of the present bibliography are as follows:

1 The entries consist of books and articles published since 1945, though a few, earlier works of outstanding importance have been included.

2 The bibliography contains most of the secondary works which can be defined as economic history, but it includes only a small selection of the contributions of political historians, geographers, economists and anthropologists, which are also relevant to the study of economic history.

3 The entries have been arranged under the chapter headings of this book. The allocation reflects, though none too precisely, the use made of the various items here, but it does not mean that the works concerned have no value in other contexts. A few studies appear under more than one chapter heading. No entries have been made for Chapters 1 and 8 because these chapters contain only brief introductory and concluding comments.

4 Books are referred to by listing author, title, place of publication (if other than London), and date of publication. Articles are referred to by listing author, title, name of the journal, volume number (where available), year of publication, and page numbers. Where authors have published the same piece on more than one occasion, only the most recent reference has been included.

Chapter 2   The domestic economy: structure and function

Agboola, S. A., 'The Introduction and Spread of Cassava in Western Nigeria', *Nigerian Journal of Economic and Social Studies*, 3, 1968, pp. 369–86.

Ames, David W., 'The Economic Basis of Wolof Polygyny', *Southwestern Journal of Anthropology*, 11, 1955, pp. 391–403.

——, 'The Use of a Transitional Cloth-money Token among the Wolof', *American Anthropologist*, 57, 1955, pp. 1016–23.

Anyane, S. La, *Ghana Agriculture*, 1963.

Arhin, K., 'Status Differentiation in Ashanti in the Nineteenth Century: a Preliminary Study', *Research Review*, Institute of African Studies, University of Ghana, 4, 1968, pp. 34–52.

——, 'Aspects of Ashanti Northern Trade in the Nineteenth Century', *Africa*, 40, 1970, pp. 363–73.

Arnold, Rosemary, 'Separation of Trade and Market: Great Market of Whydah', in *Trade and Market in the Early Empires*, ed. Karl Polanyi *et. al.*, Glencoe 1957, pp. 177–87.

Aymo, G., 'Notes de sociologie et de linguistique sur Ghadamès', *Bulletin de Liaison Saharienne*, 10, 1959, pp. 129–57.

Baker, H. G., 'Comments on the Thesis that there was a Major Centre of Plant Domestication Near the Headwaters of the River Niger', *Journal of African History*, 3, 1962, pp. 229-33.

Barbour, K. M., and Prothero, R. M., eds, *Essays on African Population*, 1961.

Bascom, William R., 'The Esusu: a Credit Institution of the Yoruba', *Journal of the Royal Anthropological Institute*, 82, 1952, pp. 63-9.

——, 'Urbanization among the Yoruba', *American Journal of Sociology*, 60, 1955, pp. 46-54.

——, 'Les premiers fondemonts historiques de l'urbanisme Yoruba', *Présence Africaine*, 23, 1958-9, pp. 22-40.

——, 'Urbanism as a Traditional African Pattern', *Sociological Review*, 7, 1959, pp. 29-43.

Biebuyck, Daniel, ed., *African Agrarian Systems*, 1963.

Bohannan, Paul, 'Some Principles of Exchange and Investment among the Tiv', *American Anthropologist*, 57, 1955, pp. 60-70.

——, and Bohannan, Laura, *Tiv Economy*, 1968.

——, and Dalton, George, eds, *Markets in Africa*, Evanston 1962.

Bray, Jennifer M., 'The Organization of Traditional Weaving in Iseyin, Nigeria', *Africa*, 38, 1968, pp. 270-80.

Buchanan, K. M., and Pugh, J. C., *Land and People in Nigeria*, 1955.

Callaway, Archibald, 'From Traditional Crafts to Modern Industries', *Odu*, 2, 1965, pp. 28-51.

Capot-Rey, R., and Damade, W., 'Irrigation et structure agraire à Tamentit', *Travaux de l'Institut de Recherches Sahariennes*, 21, 1962, pp. 99-119.

Carter, G. F., 'Archaeological Maize in West Africa: a Discussion of Stanton and Willett', *Man*, 64, 1964, pp. 85-6.

Cauneille, J., and Dubief, J., 'Les Reguibat Legouacem: chronologie et nomadisme', *Bulletin de l'IFAN*, B, 17, 1955, pp. 528-50.

Centre of African Studies, *Markets and Marketing in West Africa*, Edinburgh 1966 (mimeo.).

Chilver, E. M., 'Nineteenth-Century Trade in the Bamenda Grassfields, Southern Cameroons', *Afrika und Übersee*, 45, 1961, pp. 233-58.

Cissoko, Sèkéné-Mody, 'Famines et épidémies à Tombouctou et dans la boucle du Niger du XVIe au XVIIIe siècle', *Bulletin de l'IFAN*, B, 30, 1968, pp. 806-21.

Clarke, J. Desmond, 'The Spread of Food Production in Sub-Saharan Africa', *Journal of African History*, 3, 1962, pp. 211-28.

——, *The Prehistory of Africa*, 1970.

Cohen, Abner, 'The Social Organization of Credit in a West African Cattle Market', *Africa*, 35, 1965, pp. 8-20.

Cohen, Ronald, 'Some Aspects of Institutionalized Exchange: a Kanuri Example', *Cahiers d'Études Africaines*, 5, 1965, pp. 353-69.

——, 'The Dynamics of Feudalism in Bornu', *Boston University Papers on Africa*, 2, 1966, pp. 87-105.

Coquery-Vidrovitch, Catherine, 'Anthropologie politique et historique de l'Afrique noire', *Annales*, 24, 1969, pp. 142-63.

——, 'Recherches sur un mode de production africain', *Pensée*, 144, 1969, pp. 3-20.

Daget, G., and Ligers, Z., 'Une ancienne industrie malienne: les pipes en terre', *Bulletin de l'IFAN*, B, 24, 1962, pp. 12-53.

Davies, Oliver, 'The Origins of Agriculture in West Africa', *Current Anthropology*, 9, 1968, pp. 479–82.

Deme, Kalidou, 'Les classes sociales dans le Sénégal précoloniale', *Pensée*, 130, 1966, pp. 11–33.

Diarra, S., 'La pêche fluviale au Niger', *Revue de Géographie de l'Afrique Occidentale*, 3, 1966, pp. 61–81.

Dickson, K. B., 'The Agricultural Landscape of Southern Ghana and Ashante-Brong Ahafo: 1800–1850', *Bulletin of the Ghana Geographical Association*, 9, 1964, pp. 25–35.

——, 'Trade Patterns in Ghana at the Beginning of the Eighteenth Century', *Geographical Review*, 56, 1966, pp. 417–31.

Dorjahn, V. R., and Tholley, A. S., 'A Provisional History of the Limba, with Special Reference to Tonko Limba Chiefdom', *Sierra Leone Studies*, 12, 1959, pp. 273–83.

Doutressoule, G., *L'elevage en Afrique occidentale française*, Paris 1947.

Dumanowski, Boleslaw, 'The Influence of Geographical Environments on the Distribution and Density of Population in Africa', *Africana Bulletin*, 9, 1968, pp. 9–33.

Dupire, Marguerite, 'Organisation sociale du travail dans la palmeraie Adioukrou (basse Côte d'Ivoire)', *Revue de l'Institut de Sociologie Solvay*, 2, 1956, pp. 371–92.

——, *Peuls nomades*, Paris 1962.

Edokpayi, S. I., 'The Niger and the Benue in Nigeria's Economy: Past, Present and Future', *Nigerian Journal of Economic and Social Studies*, 3, 1961, pp. 68–79.

Fage, John D., 'Some Remarks on Beads and Trade in Lower Guinea in the Sixteenth and Seventeenth Centuries', *Journal of African History*, 3, 1962, pp. 343–7.

——, 'Some Thoughts on Migration and Urban Settlement', in *Urbanization and Migration in West Africa*, ed. Hilda Kuper, Berkeley 1965, pp. 39–49.

——, and Oliver, R. A., eds, *Papers in African Prehistory*, Cambridge 1970.

Fagg, B. E. B., 'The Nok Culture in Pre-History', *Journal of the Historical Society of Nigeria*, 1, 1959, pp. 288–93.

Fallers, Lloyd, 'Are African Cultivators to be Called "Peasants"?', *Current Anthropology*, 2, 1961, pp. 108–10.

Fisher, Allan G. B., and Fisher, Humphrey J., *Slavery and Muslim Society in Africa*, 1970.

Forde, C. Daryll, 'The Cultural Map of West Africa: Successive Adaptations to Tropical Forest and Grasslands', in *Cultures and Societies of Africa*, ed. Simon and Phoebe Ottenberg, New York 1960, pp. 116–38.

Gallais, J., 'La signification du village en Afrique soudanienne de l'Ouest', *Cahiers de Sociologie Économique*, 2, 1960, pp. 128–62.

Gery, R., 'Une industrie autochtone nigérienne: les sauniers du Manga', *Bulletin de l'IFAN*, B, 14, 1952, pp. 309–20.

Glanville, R. R., 'Salt and the Salt Industry of the Northern Province', *Sierra Leone Studies*, 16, 1930, pp. 52–6.

Goody, Jack, *Technology, Tradition, and the State in Africa*, 1971.

——, and Mustapha, T. M., 'The Caravan Route from Kano to Salaga', *Journal of the Historical Society of Nigeria*, 3, 1967, pp. 611–16.

Grandin, Capitaine, 'Notes sur l'industrie et le commerce du sel au Kawar et en Agram', *Bulletin de l'IFAN*, B, 13, 1951, pp. 488–533.

Green, M. M., *Igbo Village Affairs*, 1947.

Guèye, Youssouf, 'Essai sur les causes et les conséquences de la micropropriété au Fouta-Toro', *Bulletin de l'IFAN*, B, 19, 1957, pp. 28–42.

Halpern, Jan, 'Traditional Economy in West Africa', *Africana Bulletin*, 7, 1967, pp. 91–112.

Harris, Jack S., 'Some Aspects of Slavery in South-Eastern Nigeria', *Journal of Negro History*, 27, 1942, pp. 37–54.

Harris, Rosemary, 'The Influence of Ecological Factors and External Relations on the Mbembe Tribes of South-East Nigeria', *Africa*, 32, 1962, pp. 38–52.

Havinden, M. A., 'The History of Crop Cultivation in West Africa: a Bibliographical Guide', *Economic History Review*, 23, 1970, pp. 532–55.

Helleiner, Gerald K., 'Typology in Development Theory: The Land Surplus Economy (Nigeria)', *Food Research Institute Studies*, 6, 1966, pp. 181–94.

Hill, Polly, 'Some Characteristics of Indigenous West African Economic Enterprise', *Economic Bulletin of Ghana*, 6, 1962, pp. 3–14.

——, 'Notes on Traditional Market Authority and Market Periodicity in West Africa', *Journal of African History*, 7, 1966, pp. 295–311.

——, 'Landlords and Brokers: a West African Trading System', *Cahiers d'Études Africaines*, 6, 1966, pp. 349–66.

——, *Studies in Rural Capitalism in West Africa*, Cambridge 1970.

Hiskett, E. M., 'City of History: the Story of Kano', *West African Review*, 28, 1957, pp. 849–56.

——, 'Materials Relating to the Cowry Currency of the Western Sudan', *Bulletin of the School of Oriental and African Studies*, 29, 1966, pp. 122–42 and 339–66.

Hodder, B. W., 'Some Comments on the Origins of Traditional Markets in Africa South of the Sahara', *Transactions of the Institute of British Geographers*, 36, 1965, pp. 97–105.

——, 'Some Comments on Markets and Market Periodicity', in *Markets and Marketing in West Africa*, Centre of African Studies, University of Edinburgh 1966 (mimeo.), pp. 97–106.

——, and Ukwu, U. I., *Markets in West Africa*, Ibadan 1969.

Holas, B., 'Les peuplements de la Côte d'Ivoire', *Cahiers Charles de Foucauld*, 35, 1954, pp. 49–69.

——, 'Les poids à peser l'or', *Notes Africaines*, 104, 1964, pp. 113–16.

Hopen, Edward C., *The Pastoral Fulbe Family in Gwandu*, 1958.

Hopkins, A. G., 'Underdevelopment in the Empires of the Western Sudan', *Past & Present*, 37, 1967, pp. 149–56, and the 'Rejoinder' by Professor Malowist, *ibid.*, pp. 157–62.

Horton, Robin, 'The Ohu System of Slavery in a Northern Ibo Village-Group', *Africa*, 24, 1954, pp. 311–36.

——, 'African Traditional Thought and Western Science', *Africa*, 37, 1967, pp. 50–71 and 155–87.

Huard, Paul, 'Contribution à l'étude du cheval, du fer et du chameau au Sahara oriental', *Bulletin de l'IFAN*, B, 22, 1960, pp. 134–78.

Hunter, J. M., 'Seasonal Hunger in a Part of the West African Savanna: a Survey of Body-weights in Nangodi, N.E. Ghana', *Transactions of the Institute of British Geographers*, 41, 1967, pp. 167–86.

Hurault, J., 'Antagonisme de l'agriculture et de l'élevage sur les hauts plateaux de l'Adamawa', *Études Rurales*, 15, 1964, pp. 22–71.

Hymer, Stephen H., 'Economic Forms in Pre-Colonial Ghana', *Journal of Economic History*, 31, 1970, pp. 33–50.

Jacquemond, S., 'Les pêcheurs de la boucle du Niger', *Bulletin du Comité de Travaux Historiques et Scientifiques, Section de Géographie*, 71, 1958, pp. 103–55.

Jeffreys, M. D. W., 'Some Negro Currencies in Nigeria', *South African Museums' Association Bulletin*, 5, 1954, pp. 405–16.

——, 'How Ancient is West African Maize?', *Africa*, 33, 1963, pp. 115–31.

Johansson, Sven-Olaf, *Nigerian Currencies*, Norrköping 1967.

Johnston, Bruce F., *The Staple Food Economies of Western Tropical Africa*, Stanford 1958.

Johnson, Marion, 'The Nineteenth-Century Gold "Mithqal" in West and North Africa', *Journal of African History*, 9, 1968, pp. 547–69.

——, 'The Cowrie Currencies of West Africa', *Journal of African History*, 11, 1970, pp. 17–49 and 331–53.

Jones, William O., *Manioc in Africa*, Stanford 1959.

——, 'The Food and Agricultural Economies of Tropical Africa: a Summary View', *Food Research Institute Studies*, 2, 1961, pp. 3–20.

Kabore, Gomkoudougou V., 'Caractère "féodale" du système politique mossi', *Cahiers d'Études Africaines*, 2, 1962, pp. 609–63.

Karpinski, Rafal, 'Considérations sur les échanges de caractère local et extérieur de la Sénégambie dans la deuxième moitié du XVe et au début du XVIe siècle', *Africana Bulletin*, 8, 1968, pp. 65–84.

Kirk-Greene, A. H. M., 'The Major Currencies in Nigerian History', *Journal of the Historical Society of Nigeria*, 2, 1960, pp. 132–50.

Krapf-Askari, Eva, *Yoruba Towns and Cities*, Oxford 1969.

Krieger, Kurt, 'Kola-Karawanen. Ein Beitrag zur Geschichte des Hausahandels', *Mitteilungen des Instituts für Orientforschung*, 2, 1954, pp. 289–324.

——, 'Notizen zur Eisengewinnung der Hausa', *Zeitschrift für Ethnologie*, 88, 1963, pp. 318–31.

Kup, A. P., 'An Account of the Tribal Distribution of Sierra Leone', *Man*, 60, 1960, pp.116–19.

Latham, A. J. H., 'Currency, Credit and Capitalism on the Cross River in the Pre-Colonial Era', *Journal of African History*, 12, 1971, pp. 599–605.

Lawson, Rowena M., 'The Traditional Utilisation of Labour in Agriculture in the Lower Volta, Ghana', *Economic Bulletin of Ghana*, 12, 1968, pp. 54–61.

Levtzion, N., *Muslims and Chiefs in West Africa*, 1968.

Lewicki, Tadeusz, 'Animal Husbandry among Medieval Agricultural People of Western and Middle Sudan', *Acta Ethnographica*, 14, 1965, pp. 165–78.

Lhote, Henri, 'Le cheval et le chameau dans les peintures et les gravures rupestres du Sahara', *Bulletin de l'IFAN, B*, 15, 1953, pp. 1138–1228.

——, 'L'extraordinaire aventure des Peuls', *Présence Africaine*, 22, 1958, pp. 48–57.

Lloyd, P. C., 'Craft Organisation in Yoruba Towns', *Africa*, 23, 1953, pp. 30–44.

——, *Yoruba Land Law*, 1962.

Lo, Capitaine, 'Les *foggaras* du Tidikelt', *Travaux de l'Institut des Recherches Sahariennes*, 10, 1953, pp. 139–79; 11, 1954, pp. 49–77.

Lombard, Jacques, 'Aperçu sur la technologie et l'artisanat Bariba', *Études Dahoméennes*, 18, 1957, pp. 5–60.

——, *Structures de type 'féodal' en Afrique noire*, Paris 1965.

Lovejoy, Paul E., 'Long-Distance Trade and Islam: the Case of the Nineteenth-Century Hausa Kola Trade', *Journal of the Historical Society of Nigeria*, 5, 1971, pp. 537–47.

Mabogunje, Akin L., 'Some Comments on Land Tenure in Egba Division, Western Nigeria', *Africa*, 31, 1961, pp. 258–69.

McLoughlin, Peter F. M., ed., *African Food Production Systems*, Baltimore 1970.

Malowist, M., 'The Social and Economic Stability of the Western Sudan in the Middle Ages', *Past & Present*, 33, 1966, pp. 3–15.

Maquet, Jacques J., 'A Research Definition of African Feudality', *Journal of African History*, 3, 1962, pp. 307–10.

Mauny, Raymond, 'Essai sur l'histoire des métaux en Afrique occidentale', *Bulletin de l'IFAN*, B, 14, 1952, pp. 543–95.

——, 'La monnaie marginelloide de l'ouest africain', *Bulletin de l'IFAN*, B, 19, 1957, pp. 659–69.

——, 'Anciens ateliers monétaires ouest-africains', *Notes Africaines*, 78, 1958, pp. 34–5.

——, *Tableau géographique de l'ouest africain au moyen âge*, Dakar 1961.

Meillassoux, Claude, 'Essai d'interprétation du phénomène économique dans les sociétés traditionnelles d'autosubsistence', *Cahiers d'Études Africaines*, 4, 1960, pp. 38–67.

——, 'L'économie des échanges précoloniaux en pays Gouro', *Cahiers d'Études Africaines*, 3, 1963, pp. 551–76.

——, *Anthropologie économique des Gouro de Côte d'Ivoire*, Paris 1964.

——, ed., *The Development of Indigenous Trade and Markets in West Africa*, 1971.

Menzel, Brigitte, *Goldweights from Ghana*, Berlin, 1968.

Mercier, Paul, 'Travail et service public dans l'ancien Dahomey', *Présence Africaine*, 13, 1952, pp. 84–91.

Miège, J., 'Les cultures vivrières en Afrique occidentale', *Cahiers d'Outre-Mer*, 7, 1954, pp. 25–50.

Miner, Horace M., *The Primitive City of Timbuctoo*, Princeton 1953.

Miracle, Marvin P., 'Interpretation of Evidence on the Introduction of Maize into West Africa', *Africa*, 33, 1963, pp. 132–5.

——, 'The Introduction and Spread of Maize in Africa', *Journal of African History*, 6, 1965, pp. 39–55.

Morgan, W. B., 'The "Grassland Towns" of the Eastern Region of Nigeria', *Transactions of the Institute of British Geographers*, 23, 1957, pp. 213–24.

——, 'Agriculture in Southern Nigeria (Excluding the Cameroons)', *Economic Geography*, 35, 1959, pp. 138–50.

——, 'Peasant Agriculture in Tropical Africa', in *Environment and Land Use in Africa*, ed. M. F. Thomas and G. W. Whittington, 1969, pp. 241–71.

——, and Pugh, J. C., *West Africa*, 1969.

Murdock, George Peter, *Africa: its Peoples and their Culture History*, New York 1959. Also the review by J. D. Fage, *Journal of African History*, 2, 1961, pp. 299–309.

Nadel, S. F., *A Black Byzantium*, Oxford 1942.

Netting, Robert McC., 'Household Organisation and Intensive Agriculture: the Kofyar Case', *Africa*, 35, 1965, pp. 422–8.

——, 'A Trial Model of Cultural Ecology', *Anthropological Quarterly*, 38, 1965, pp. 81–96.

——, *Hill Farmers of Nigeria*, Seattle 1968.

Niane, D. J., 'Recherches sur l'empire du Mali au moyen âge', *Recherches Africaines*, 1959, pp. 35–46; 1960, pp. 17–36; 1961, pp. 31–51.

——, 'Mise en place des populations de la Haut-Guinée', *Recherches Africaines*, 1960, pp. 40–53.

Niangoran-Bouah, Georges, 'Poids à peser l'or', *Présence Africaine*, 46, 1963, pp. 202–20.

Nicolaisen, Johannes, 'Ecological and Historical Factors: a Case Study from the Ahaggar Tuareg', *Folk*, 6, 1964, pp. 75–81.

Nicolas, François-J., 'Le bouracan ou bougran, tissu soudanais du moyen âge', *Anthropos*, 53, 1958, pp. 265–8.

Nicolas, G., 'Circulation des biens et échanges monétaires au nord Niger', *Cahiers de l'Institut de Science Économique Appliquée*, Supplement 129, 5, 1962, pp. 49–62.

Oroge, E. A., *The Institution of Slavery in Yorubaland with Particular Reference to the Nineteenth Century*, University of Birmingham Ph.D. thesis, 1971.

Ott, A., 'Historical Significance of Akan Gold Weights', *Transactions of the Historical Society of Ghana*, 9, 1968, 17–42.

Pageard, R., 'Note sur le peuplement de l'est du pays du Ségou', *Journal de la Société des Africanistes*, 31, 1961, pp. 83–90.

Palausi, G., 'Un projet d'hydraulique fluviale soudanaise au XVᵉ siècle: le canal de Soni-Ali', *Notes Africaines*, 78, 1958, pp. 47–9.

Perie, J., and Sellier, M., 'Histoire des populations du cercle de Dosso', *Bulletin de l'IFAN*, B, 12, 1950, pp. 1015–74.

Portères, Roland, 'Vieilles agricultures de l'Afrique intertropicale', *Agronomie Tropicale*, 5, 1950, pp. 489–507.

——, 'L'introduction du maïs en Afrique', *Journal d'Agriculture Tropicale et de Botanique Appliquée*, 2, 1955, pp. 221–31.

——, 'La monnaie de fer dans l'ouest-africain au XXᵉ siècle', *Recherches Africaines*, 1960, pp. 3–13.

——, 'Berceaux agricoles primaires sur le continent africain', *Journal of African History*, 3, 1962, pp. 195–210.

Reyburn, William D., 'Polygamy, Economy and Christianity in the Eastern Cameroun', *Practical Anthropology*, 6, 1959, pp. 1–19.

Riad, Mohammed, 'The Jukun: an Example of African Migrations in the Sixteenth Century', *Bulletin de l'IFAN*, B, 22, 1960, pp. 476–85.

Richard-Molard, J., 'Les densités de population au Fouta-Djallon', *Présence Africaine*, 15, 1952, pp. 95–106.

Rougerie, Gabriel, 'Lagunaires et terriens de la Côte d'Ivoire', *Cahiers d'Outre-Mer*, 3, 1950, pp. 370–7.

Schneider, Harold K., 'A Model of African Indigenous Economy and Society', *Comparative Studies in Society and History*, 7, 1964, pp. 37–55.

Sellnow, Irmgard, 'Die Stelling der Sklaven in der Hausa-Gesellschaft', *Mitteilungen des Instituts für Orientforschung*, 10, 1964, pp. 85–102.

Skinner, Elliott P., *The Mossi of the Upper Volta*, Stanford 1964.

——, 'West African Economic Systems', in *Economic Transition in Africa*, ed. Melville J. Herskovits and Mitchell Harwitz, 1964, pp. 77–97.

Smith, Michael G., 'A Study of Hausa Domestic Economy in Northern Zaria', *Africa*, 22, 1952, pp. 333–47.

Smith, Robert, 'The Canoe in West African History', *Journal of African History*, 11, 1970, pp. 515–33.

Stanton, W. R., 'The Analysis of the Present Distribution of Varietal Variation in Maize, Sorghum and Cowpea in Nigeria as an Aid to the Study of Tribal Movement', *Journal of African History*, 3, 1962, pp. 251–62.

——, and Willett, Frank, 'Archaeological Evidence for Changes in Maize Type in West Africa', *Man*, 63, 1963, pp. 117–23.

Stenning, Derrick, J., 'Transhumance, Migratory Drift, Migration: Patterns of Pastoral Fulani Nomadism', *Journal of the Royal Anthropological Institute*, 87, 1957, pp. 57–73.

——, *Savannah Nomads*, 1959.

Sundström, Lars, *The Trade of Guinea*, Lund 1965.

Suret-Canale, Jean, 'Les sociétés traditionnelles en Afrique tropicale et le concept de mode de production asiatique', *Pensée*, 117, 1964, pp. 21–42.

Toupet, C., 'La vallée de la Tamourt en Naaj: problèmes d'aménagement', *Bulletin de l'IFAN*, B, 20, 1958, pp. 68–110.

Tymowski, Michal, 'Le Niger, voie de communication des grands états du Soudan occidentale jusqu'à la fin du XVIᵉ siècle', *Africana Bulletin*, 6, 1967, pp. 73–95.

——, 'La pêche à l'époque du moyen âge dans la boucle du Niger', *Africana Bulletin*, 12, 1970, pp. 7–26.

Ukwu, U. I., 'The Development of Trade and Marketing in Iboland', *Journal of the Historical Society of Nigeria*, 3, 1967, pp. 647–62.

Verdier, Raymond, 'Féodalités et collectivismes africains', *Présence Africaine*, 39, 1961, pp. 79–101.

Wilks, Ivor, 'A Medieval Trade-Route from the Niger to the Gulf of Guinea', *Journal of African History*, 3, 1962, pp. 337–41.

——, *The Northern Factor in Ashanti History*, Legon 1962.

Willett, Frank, 'The Introduction of Maize into West Africa: An Assessment of Recent Evidence', *Africa*, 32, 1962, pp. 1–13.

Wills, J. B., ed., *Agriculture and Land Use in Ghana*, Oxford 1962.

Wrigley, Christopher, 'Speculations on the Economic Pre-history of Africa', *Journal of African History*, 1, 1960, pp. 189–203.

Chapter 3   External trade: the Sahara and the Atlantic

Aguirre-Beltran, G., 'Tribal Origins of Slaves in Mexico', *Journal of Negro History*, 31, 1946, pp. 269–352.

Akinjogbin, I. A., *Dahomey and its Neighbours, 1708–1818*, 1967.

Alagoa, E. J., 'Long-distance Trade and States in the Niger Delta', *Journal of African History*, 11, 1970, pp. 319–29.

——, 'The Development of Institutions in the States of the Eastern Niger Delta', *ibid.*, 12, 1971, pp. 269–78.

Anstey, Roger T., 'Capitalism and Slavery: a Critique', *Economic History Review*, 21, 1968, pp. 307–20.

Ardener, Edwin, 'Documentary and Linguistic Evidence for the Rise of the Trading Polities between Rio del Rey and Cameroons, 1500–1650', in *History and Social Anthropology*, ed. I. M. Lewis, 1968, pp. 81–126.

Arhin, K., 'The Financing of Ashanti Expansion, 1700–1820', *Africa*, 37, 1967, pp. 283–91.

Arnold, Rosemary, 'A Port of Trade: Whydah on the Guinea Coast', in *Trade and Market in the Early Empires*, ed. K. Polanyi, C. M. Arensberg and Harry Pearson, Glencoe 1957, pp. 154–76.

——, 'Separation of Trade and Market: Great Market of Whydah', *ibid.*, pp. 177–87.

Bénard, J. Cl., 'L'armement honfleurais et le commerce des esclaves à la fin du XVIIIᵉ siècle', *Annales de Normandie*, 10, 1960, pp. 249–64.

Bennett, Norman Robert, 'Christian and Negro Slavery in Eighteenth-Century North Africa', *Journal of African History*, 1, 1960, pp. 65–82.

Berbain, Simone, *Le comptoir français de Juda (Ouidah) au XVIIIᵉ siècle*, Paris 1942.

Bethel, Leslie, 'The Mixed Commissions for the Suppression of the Transatlantic Slave Trade in the Nineteenth Century', *Journal of African History*, 7, 1966, pp. 79–93.

Blake, J. W., *European Beginnings in West Africa, 1454–1578*, 1937.

Boahen, A. Adu, *Britain, the Sahara, and the Western Sudan, 1788–1861*, Oxford 1964.

Bolt, Christine, *The Anti-Slavery Movement and Reconstruction*, Oxford 1969.

Booth, Alan R., 'The United States African Squadron, 1843–1861', *Boston University Papers in African History*, 1, 1964, pp. 79–117.

Bovill, E. W., *The Golden Trade of the Moors*, 2nd edn 1968.

Brown, George W., 'The Origins of Abolition in Santo Domingo', *Journal of Negro History*, 7, 1922, pp. 365–76.

Brunschwig, Henri, 'La troque et la traite', *Cahiers d'Études Africaines*, 2, 1962, pp. 339–46.

Centre of African Studies, *The Transatlantic Slave Trade from West Africa*, Edinburgh 1965 (mimeo.).

Checkland, S. G., 'American Versus West Indian Traders in Liverpool, 1793–1815', *Journal of Economic History*, 18, 1958, pp. 141–60.

——, 'Finance for the West Indies, 1780–1815', *Economic History Review*, 10, 1958, pp. 461–9.

Chiché, Marie-Claire, *Hygiène et santé à bord des navires négriers au XVIIIᵉ siècle*, Paris 1957.

Chilver, E. M., and Kaberry, P. M., 'Sources of the Nineteenth-Century Slave Trade: Two Comments', *Journal of African History*, 6, 1965, pp. 117–20.

Curtin, Philip D., *Africa Remembered: Narratives by West Africans from the Era of the Slave Trade*, Madison 1967.

——, 'Epidemiology and the Slave Trade', *Political Science Quarterly*, 83, 1968, pp. 190–216.

——, *The Atlantic Slave Trade: a Census*, Madison 1969.

——, and Vansina, Jan, 'Sources of the Nineteenth-Century Atlantic Slave Trade', *Journal of African History*, 5, 1964, pp. 185–208.

Daaku, K. Y., *Trade and Politics on the Gold Coast, 1600–1720*, Oxford 1970.

Daget, Serge, 'L'abolition de la traite des noirs en France de 1814 à 1831', *Cahiers d'Études Africaines*, 11, 1971, pp. 14–58.

Davidson, Basil, *Black Mother: the Years of the African Slave Trade*, 1961.

Davies, K. G., *The Royal African Company*, 1957.

Davis, David B., 'James Cropper and the British Anti-Slavery Movement, 1821–1823', *Journal of Negro History*, 45, 1960, pp. 241–58.

——, 'James Cropper and the British Anti-Slavery Movement, 1823–1833', *ibid.*, 46, 1961, pp. 154–73.

Debbasch, Y., 'Poésie et traite; l'opinion française sur le commerce négrier au début du XIXᵉ siècle', *Revue Française d'Histoire d'Outre-Mer*, 48, 1961, pp. 311–52.

Debien, G., 'Les origines des esclaves des Antilles', *Bulletin de l'IFAN*, B, 23, 1961, pp. 363–87; 25, 1963, pp. 215–66; 26, 1964, pp. 166–211, 601–75; 27, 1965, pp. 319–71, 755–99; 29, 1967, pp. 536–58.

Delcourt, André, 'La finance parisienne et le commerce négrier au milieu du XVIIIᵉ siècle', *Bulletin de la Société d'Études Historiques, Géographiques et Scientifiques de la Région Parisienne*, 22, 1948, pp. 21–8.

——, *La France et les établissements français au Sénégal entre 1713 et 1763*, Dakar 1952.

De Souza, N. F., 'Contribution à l'histoire de la famille Souza', *Études Dahoméenes*, 13, 1955, pp. 17–21.

Donnan, Elizabeth, *Documents Illustrative of the History of the Slave Trade to America*, 4 vols., Washington 1930–5.

Dorjahn, V. R., and Fyfe, Christopher, 'Landlord and Stranger: Change in Tenancy Relations in Sierra Leone', *Journal of African History*, 3, 1962, pp. 391–7.

Duignan, Peter, and Clendenen, Clarence, *The United States and the African Slave Trade, 1619–1862*, Stanford 1963.

Dumbell, Stanley, 'The Profits of the Guinea Trade', *Economic History*, 2, 1931, pp. 254–7.

Everaert, J., 'Les fluctuations du trafic négrier nantais (1763–1792)', *Cahiers de Tunisie*, 11, 1963, pp. 37–62.

Fage, J. D., 'Slavery and the Slave Trade in the Context of West African History', *Journal of African History*, 10, 1969, pp. 393–404.

Farnie, D. A., 'The Commercial Empire of the Atlantic, 1607–1783', *Economic History Review*, 15, 1962, pp. 205–18.

Forde, C. Daryll, ed., *Efik Traders of Old Calabar*, 1956.

Fourneau, J., and Kravetz, L., 'Le pagne sur la côte de Guinée et au Congo du XVᵉ siècle à nos jours', *Bulletin de l'Institut d'Études Centrafricaines*, 7–8, 1954, pp. 5–21.

Gleave, M. B., and Prothero, R. M., 'Population Density and "Slave Raiding"—a Comment', *Journal of African History*, 12, 1971, pp. 319–24, and Mason's 'Reply', *ibid.*, pp. 324–7.

Graham, James D., 'The Slave Trade, Depopulation and Human Sacrifice in Benin History', *Cahiers d'Études Africaines*, 5, 1965, pp. 317–34.

Grey, R. F. A., 'Manillas', *Nigerian Field*, 16, 1951, pp. 52–66.

Hargreaves, John, D., 'The Slave Traffic', in *Silver Renaissance*, ed. A. Natan, 1961, pp. 81–101.

——, 'European Relations with Africa, 1763–1793', *New Cambridge Modern History*, 8, 1965, pp. 236–51.

Harrop, Sylvia, 'The Economy of the West African Coast in the Sixteenth Century', *Economic Bulletin of Ghana*, 8, 3, 1964, pp. 15–33; 8, 4, 1964, pp. 19–36.

Heers, J., 'Le Sahara et le commerce méditerranéen à la fin du moyen âge', *Annales de l'Institut d'Études Orientales*, 16, 1958, pp. 247–55.

Hennessy, James Pope, *Sins of the Fathers*, 1967.

High, James, 'The African Gentleman: a Chapter in the Slave Trade', *Journal of Negro History*, 44, 1959, pp. 285–307.

Hill, Adelaide, C., 'Revolution in Haiti, 1791 to 1820', *Présence Africaine*, 20, 1958, pp. 5–24.

Hirschberg, H. Z., 'The Problem of the Judaized Berbers', *Journal of African History*, 4, 1963, pp. 313–39.

Hunwick, J. O., 'Ahmad Baba and the Moroccan Invasion of the Sudan', *Journal of the Historical Society of Nigeria*, 2, 1962, pp. 311–28.

Hyde, F. E., Parkinson B. B., and Marriner, S., 'The Nature and Profitability of the Liverpool Slave Trade', *Economic History Review*, 5, 1953, pp. 368–77.

Johnson, Marion, 'The Ounce in Eighteenth-Century West African Trade', *Journal of African History*, 7, 1966, pp. 197–214.

Johnson, Vera M., 'Sidelights on the Liverpool Slave Trade, 1789–1807', *Mariner's Mirror*, 38, 1952, pp. 276–93.

Jones, G. I., 'Native and Trade Currencies in Southern Nigeria during the Eighteenth and Nineteenth Centuries', *Africa*, 28, 1958, pp. 43–54.

Jore, Léonce, 'Les établissements français sur la côte occidentale d'Afrique de 1758 à 1803', *Revue Française d'Histoire d'Outre-Mer*, 51, 1964, pp. 7–477.

Karpinski, R., 'Considérations sur les échanges de caractère local et extérieure de la Sénégambie dans la deuxième moitié du XVe et au début du XVIe siècle', *Africana Bulletin*, 8, 1968, pp. 65–83.

Kleist, Alice M., 'The English African Trade under the Tudors', *Transactions of the Historical Society of Ghana*, 3, 1957, pp. 137–50.

Klingberg, Frank J., *The Anti-Slavery Movement in England*, New Haven 1926.

Kup, A. P., 'Early Portuguese Trade in the Sierra Leone and Great Scarcies Rivers', *Boletim Cultural da Guiné Portuguesa*, 18, 1963, pp. 107–24.

Lacroix, Louis, *Les derniers négriers*, Paris, 1952.

Latham, A. J. H., *Old Calabar, 1600–1891: the Economic Impact of the West upon a Traditional Society*, University of Birmingham Ph.D. thesis, 1970.

Laufry, J., 'Chronique de Ghadames', *Ibla*, 32, 1945, pp. 367–85; 33, 1946, pp. 343–71.

Law, R. C. C., 'The Garamantes and Trans-Saharan Enterprise in Classical Times', *Journal of African History*, 8, 1967, pp. 181–200.

Levy, Claude, 'Slavery and the Emancipation Movement in Barbados, 1650–1833', *Journal of Negro History*, 55, 1970, pp. 1–14.

Lewicki, Tadeusz, 'L'état nord-africain de Tahert et ses relations avec le Soudan occidentale à la fin de VIIIe et au IXe siècle', *Cahiers d'Études Africaines*, 2, 1962, pp. 513–35.

——, 'Traits d'histoire du commerce trans-saharien', *Etnograia Polska*, 3, 1964, pp. 291–311.

——, 'Arab Trade in Negro Slaves up to the End of the XVIth Century', *Africana Bulletin*, 6, 1967, pp. 109–11.

Lhote, H., 'Note sur l'origine des lames d'épées des Touaregs', *Notes Africaines de l'Institut Français d'Afrique Noire*, 61, 1954, pp. 9–12.

Lloyd, Christopher, *The Navy and the Slave Trade*, 1949.

Ly, Abdoulaye, *La compagnie du Sénégal*, Paris 1958.

Malowist, Marian, 'Le commerce d'or et d'esclaves au Soudan occidentale', *Africana Bulletin*, 4, 1966, pp. 49–72.

——, 'Les fondemonts de l'expansion européenne en Afrique au XVe siècle; Europe, Maghreb et Soudan occidentale', *Acta Poloniae Historica*, 18, 1968, pp. 156–79.

Malowist, Marion, 'Les débuts du système de plantations dans la période des Grandes Découvertes', *Africana Bulletin*, 10, 1969, pp. 9–30.

Manning, Patrick, 'Slaves, Palm Oil and Political Power on the West African Coast', *African Historical Studies*, 2, 1969, pp. 279–88.

Mannix, Daniel P., and Cowley, Malcolm, *Black Cargoes*, 1962.

Marshall, Peter, *The Anti-Slave Trade Movement in Bristol*, Bristol 1968.

Martin, Gaston, *Nantes au XVIIIᵉ siècle: l'ère des négriers (1714–44)*, Paris 1931.

——, *Histoire de l'esclavage dans les colonies françaises*, Paris 1948.

Mason, Michael, 'Population Density and "Slave Raiding"—the Case of the Middle Belt of Nigeria', *Journal of African History*, 10, 1969, pp. 551–64.

Mathieson, W. L., *Great Britain and the Slave Trade, 1839–1865*, 1929.

Maugat, M. E., 'La traite clandestine à Nantes au XIXᵉ siècle', *Bulletin de la Société Archéologique et Historique de Nantes et de la Loire-Inférieure*, 93, 1954, pp. 162–9.

Mauny, Raymond, *Les navigations médiévales sur les côtes sahariennes antérieures à la découverte portugaise (1434)*, Lisbon 1960.

——, *Tableau géographique de l'ouest africain au moyen âge*, Dakar 1961.

Merritt, J. E., *The Liverpool Slave Trade from 1789 to 1791*, University of Nottingham M.A. thesis, 1959.

——, 'The Triangular Trade', *Business History*, 3, 1960, pp. 1–7.

Meyer, J., 'Le commerce négrier nantais (1774–1792)', *Annales*, 15, 1960, pp. 120–9.

——, 'Du nouveau sur le commerce négrier nantais du XVIIIᵉ siècle', *Annales de Bretagne*, 2, 1966, pp. 229–39.

Minchinton, W. E., 'The Voyage of the Snow *Africa*', *Mariner's Mirror*, 37, 1951, pp. 187–96.

Monod, T., 'Le Rev. John Newton: matelot, négrier et pasteur', *Notes Africaines*, 89, 1961, pp. 18–23.

Morton-Williams, Peter, 'The Oyo Yoruba and the Atlantic Trade, 1690–1830', *Journal of the Historical Society of Nigeria*, 3, 1964, pp. 25–45.

——, 'The Influence of Habitat and Trade on the Politics of Oyo and Ashanti', in *Man in Africa*, ed. Mary Douglas and Phyllis M. Kaberry, 1969, pp. 79–98.

usnier, J., ed., *Journal de la traite des noirs*, Paris 1957.

Pearsall, A. W. H., 'Sierra Leone and the Suppression of the Slave Trade', *Sierra Leone Studies*, 12, 1959, pp. 211–29.

Polanyi, Karl, 'Sortings and "Ounce Trade" in the West African Slave Trade', *Journal of African History*, 5, 1964, pp. 381–93.

——, *Dahomey and the Slave Trade*, Seattle and London 1966.

Porter, Dale H., *The Abolition of the Slave Trade in England, 1784–1807*, Hampden Connecticut, 1970.

Porter, R., 'The Crispe Family and the African Trade in the Seventeenth Century', *Journal of African History*, 9, 1968, pp. 57–77.

——, 'English Chief Factors in the Gold Coast, 1632–1753', *African Historical Studies*, 1, 1968, pp. 199–209.

Priestley, Margaret, *West African Trade and Coast Society*, Oxford 1969.

Richardson, P. D., *The Bristol Slave Trade in the Eighteenth Century*, University of Manchester M.A. thesis, 1969.

Rinchon, Père D., 'Les armements négriers au XVIIIᵉ siècle', *Academie Royale des Sciences Coloniales Memoires*, 7, 1956, pp. 1–178.
——, *Pierre-Ignace-Liévin van Alstein, capitaine négrier*, Dakar 1964.
Rodney, Walter, 'Portuguese Attempts at Monopoly on the Upper Guinea Coast, 1580–1650', *Journal of African History*, 6, 1965, pp. 307–22.
——, 'African Slavery and Other Forms of Social Oppression on the Upper Guinea Coast, in the Context of the Atlantic Slave Trade', *Journal of African History*, 7, 1966, pp. 431–43.
——, *West Africa and the Atlantic Slave Trade*, Historical Association of Tanzania, 1967.
——, 'Gold and Slaves on the Gold Coast', *Transactions of the Historical Society of Ghana*, 10, 1969, pp. 13–28.
——, 'Upper Guinea and the Significance of the Origins of Africans Enslaved in the New World', *Journal of Negro History*, 54, 1969, pp. 327–45.
——, *A History of the Upper Guinea Coast, 1545–1800*, Oxford 1970.
Ronen, Dov, 'On the African Role in the Trans-Atlantic Slave Trade in Dahomey', *Cahiers d'Études Africaines*, 11, 1971, pp. 5–13.
Ryder, A. F. C., 'The Re-establishment of Portuguese Factories on the Costa da Mina to the Mid-Eighteenth Century', *Journal of the Historical Society of Nigeria*, 1, 1958, pp. 157–81.
——, 'An Early Portuguese Trading Voyage to the Forcados River', *Journal of the Historical Society of Nigeria*, 1, 1959, pp. 294–321.
——, 'Dutch Trade on the Nigerian Coast during the Seventeenth Century', *Journal of the Historical Society of Nigeria*, 3, 1965, pp. 195–210.
——, *Benin and the Europeans, 1485–1897*, 1969.

Seeber, Edward D., *Anti-Slavery Opinion in France during the Second Half of the Eighteenth Century*, Baltimore 1937.
Sheridan, R. B., 'The Commercial and Financial Organization of the British Slave Trade, 1750–1807', *Economic History Review*, 11, 1958, pp. 249–63.
——, 'The Plantation Revolution and the Industrial Revolution, 1625–1775', *Caribbean Studies*, 9, 1969, pp. 5–25.
Suret-Canale, Jean, 'Contente et conséquences sociales de la traite africaine', *Présence Africaine*, 50, 1964, pp. 127–50.

Thornton, A. P., 'The Organization of the Slave Trade in the English West Indies, 1660–1685', *William and Mary Quarterly*, 12, 1955, pp. 399–409.
Trepp, Jean, 'The Liverpool Movement for the Abolition of the English Slave Trade', *Journal of Negro History*, 13, 1928, pp. 265–85.

Valensi, L., 'Esclaves chrétiens et esclaves noirs à Tunis au XVIIIᵉ siècle', *Annales*, 22, 1967, pp. 1267–88.
Verger, Pierre, *Bahia and the West Coast Trade (1549–1851)*, Ibadan 1964.
——, 'Rôle joué par le tabac de Bahia dans la traite des esclaves au Golfe de Bénin', *Cahiers d'Études Africaines*, 4, 1964, pp. 349–69.
——, 'Mouvements de navires entre Bahia et le golfe de Bénin (XVIIIᵉ–XIXᵉ siècles)', *Revue Française d'Histoire d'Outre-Mer*, 55, 1968, pp. 5–36.
——, *Flux et reflux de la traite des nègres entre le golfe de Bénin et Bahia de Todos os Santos du 17ᵉ et au 19ᵉ siècle*, Paris and the Hague 1968.
Vidalenc, Jean, 'La traite des nègres en France au début de la Révolution (1789–1793)', *Annales Historiques de la Révolution Française*, 29, 1957, pp. 56–69.

Ward, W. E. F., *The Royal Navy and the Slavers*, New York 1969.

Williams, Eric, *Capitalism and Slavery*, 2nd edn, 1964.

Wrigley, C. C., 'Historicism in Africa: Slavery and State Formation', *African Affairs*, 70, 1971, pp. 115–23.

Wurie, A., 'The Bundukas of Sierra Leone', *Sierra Leone Studies*, 1, 1953, pp. 14–25.

Wyndham, H. A., *The Atlantic and Slavery*, 1935.

——, *The Atlantic and Emancipation*, 1937.

Zerbo, G. K., 'L'économie de traite en Afrique noire ou le pillage organisé (XVᵉ–XXᵉ siècles)', *Présence Africaine*, 11, 1956–57, pp. 7–31.

Chapter 4 The economic basis of imperialism

Aderibigbe, A. B., 'Trade and British Expansion in the Lagos Area in the Second Half of the Nineteenth Century', *Nigerian Journal of Economic and Social Studies*, 4, 1962, pp. 188–95.

Ajayi, J. F. A., 'The British Occupation of Lagos, 1851–61: a Critical Review', *Nigeria Magazine*, 69, 1961, pp. 96–105.

Akintoye, S. A., 'The Economic Background of the Ekitiparapo, 1878–1893', *Odu*, 4, 1968, pp. 30–52.

Arhin, K., 'The Structure of Greater Ashanti', *Journal of African History*, 8, 1967, pp. 65–85.

Amenumery, D. E. K., 'The Extension of British Rule to Anlo (South-East Ghana), 1850–1890', *Journal of African History*, 9, 1968, pp. 99–117.

——, 'Gerado de Lima: a Reappraisal', *Transactions of the Historical Society of Ghana*, 9, 1968, pp. 65–78.

Andrew, C. M., and Kanya-Forstner, A. S., 'The French "Colonial Party": Its Composition, Aims and Influence, 1885–1914', *The Historical Journal*, 14, 1971, pp. 99–128.

Anjorin, A. O., 'European Attempts to Develop Cotton Cultivation in West Africa, 1850–1910', *Odu*, 3, 1966, pp. 3–15.

Atger, Paul, *La France en Côte d'Ivoire de 1843 à 1893*, Dakar 1962.

Austen, Ralph A., 'The Abolition of the Overseas Slave Trade: A Distorted Theme in West African History', *Journal of the Historical Society of Nigeria*, 5, 1970, pp. 257–74.

Awe, B., 'The Ajele System: a Study of Ibadan Imperialism in the 19th Century', *Journal of the Historical Society of Nigeria*, 3, 1964, pp. 43–60.

Baillet, Emile, 'La rôle de la marine de commerce dans l'implantation de la France en A.O.F.', *Revue Maritime*, 135, 1957, pp. 832–40.

Bennett, Norman R., and Brooks, George E., eds, *New England Merchants in Africa: a History through Documents, 1802 to 1865*, Boston 1965.

Bevin, H. J., 'The Gold Coast Economy about 1880', *Transactions of the Gold Coast and Togoland Historical Society*, 2, 1956, pp. 73–86.

——, 'M. J. Bonnat: Trader and Mining Promoter', *Economic Bulletin of Ghana*, 4, 1960, pp. 1–12.

Brooks, George E., 'American Trade as a Factor in West African History in the Early Nineteenth Century: Senegal and the Gambia, 1815–1835', in *Western African History*, ed. Daniel F. McCall, Norman R. Bennett and Jeffrey Butler, New York 1969, pp. 132–52.

——, *Yankee Traders, Old Coasters and African Middlemen: a History of American Legitimate Trade with West Africa in the Nineteenth Century*, Boston 1970.

Brunschwig, Henri, *French Colonialism, 1871–1914: Myths and Realities*, 1966.

Centre of African Studies, *The Theory of Imperialism and the European Partition of Africa*, Edinburgh 1967 (mimeo.).

Chamberlain, M. E., 'Lord Aberdare and the Royal Niger Company', *Welsh History Review*, 3, 1966, pp. 45–62.

Charpy, Jacques, *La fondation de Dakar*, Paris 1958.

Clinton, J. V., 'King Eyo Honesty II of Creek Town', *Nigeria Magazine*, 69, 1961, pp. 182–8.

Coquery-Vidrovitch, Catherine, 'Le blocus de Whydah (1876–1877) et la rivalité franco-anglaise au Dahomey', *Cahiers d'Études Africaines*, 2, 1962, pp. 373–419.

Davies, P. N., 'The African Steam Ship Company', in *Liverpool and Merseyside*, ed. J. R. Harris, 1969, pp. 212–38.

Désiré-Vuillemin, Geneviève, 'Un commerce qui meurt: la traite de la gomme dans les escales du Sénégal', *Cahiers d'Outre-Mer*, 5, 1952, pp. 90–4.

Dessertine, A., 'Naissance d'un port: Kaolack, des origines à 1900', *Annales Africaines*, 1960, pp. 225–59.

Dickson, K. B., 'Evolution of Seaports in Ghana: 1800–1928', *Annals of the Association of American Geographers*, 55, 1965, pp. 98–111.

Dike, K. O., *Trade and Politics in the Niger Delta, 1830–1885*, Oxford 1956.

Dumett, R. A., *British Official Attitudes to Economic Development on the Gold Coast, 1874–1905*, University of London Ph.D. thesis, 1966.

Flint, J. E., *Sir George Goldie and the Making of Nigeria*, 1960.

Foster, C. J., 'The Colonization of Free Negroes in Liberia, 1816–35', *Journal of Negro History*, 38, 1953, pp. 41–67.

Fyfe, Christopher H., 'The Life and Times of John Ezzidio', *Sierra Leone Studies*, 4, 1955, pp. 213–23.

——, 'Four Sierra Leone Recaptives', *Journal of African History*, 2, 1961, pp. 77–85.

——, *A History of Sierra Leone*, Oxford 1962.

Ganier, G., 'Lat Dyor et le chemin de fer de l'arachide (1876–1886)', *Bulletin de l'IFAN*, B, 27, 1965, pp. 223–81.

Gertzel, Cherry J., *John Holt: A British Merchant in West Africa in the Era of Imperialism*, University of Oxford D.Phil. thesis, 1959.

——, 'Relations Between African and European Traders in the Niger Delta, 1880–1896', *Journal of African History*, 3, 1962, pp. 361–6.

——, 'Commercial Organisation on the Niger Coast, 1852–1891', in *Historians in Tropical Africa*, Salisbury, Rhodesia, 1962, pp. 289–304.

Gifford, Prosser, and Louis, William R., *Britain and Germany in Africa: Imperial Rivalry and Colonial Rule*, New Haven 1967.

Hargreaves, J. D., 'Towards a History of the Partition of Africa', *Journal of African History*, 1, 1960, pp. 97–109.

——, *Prelude to the Partition of West Africa*, 1963.

——, 'African Colonization in the Nineteenth Century: Liberia and Sierra Leone', *Boston University Papers in African History*, 1964, pp. 57–76.

——, 'West African States and the European Conquest', in *Colonialism in Africa, 1870–1960*, ed. L. H. Gann and Peter Duignan, 1, *The History and Politics of Colonialism, 1870–1914*, Cambridge 1969, pp. 199–219.

Hieke, E., *G. L. Gaiser: Hamburg—Westfrika*, Hamburg 1949.

Hopkins, A. G., 'Richard Beale Blaize, 1854–1904: Merchant Prince of West Africa', *Tarikh*, 1, 1966, pp. 70–9.

——, 'The Currency Revolution in South-West Nigeria in the Late Nineteenth Century', *Journal of the Historical Society of Nigeria*, 3, 1966, pp. 471–83.

——, 'Economic Imperialism in West Africa: Lagos, 1880–92', *Economic History Review*, 21, 1968, pp. 580–606.

Horton, Robin, 'From Fishing Village to City State: A Social History of New Calabar', in *Man in Africa*, ed. Mary Douglas and Phyllis M. Kaberry, 1969, pp. 37–58.

Howard, Allen, 'The Role of Freetown in the Commercial Life of Sierra Leone', in *Freetown: a Symposium*, ed. Christopher Fyfe and Eldred Jones, Freetown 1968, pp. 38–64.

Hoyt, Joseph B., 'Salem's West Africa Trade, 1835–1863, and Captain Victor Francis Debaker', *Essex Institute Historical Collections*, 102, 1966, pp. 37–73.

Igbafe, Philip A., 'The Fall of Benin: a Reassessment', *Journal of African History*, 11, 1970, pp. 385–400.

Ijagbemi, E. A., 'The Freetown Colony and the Development of "Legitimate" Commerce in the Adjoining Territories', *Journal of the Historical Society of Nigeria*, 5, 1970, pp. 243–56.

Ikime, Obaro, *Merchant Prince of the Niger Delta*, 1968.

Johnson, Marion, 'Migrants' Progress', *Bulletin of the Ghana Geographical Association*, 9, 1964, pp. 4–27 and 10, 1965, pp. 13–40.

——, 'The Cowrie Currencies of West Africa', *Journal of African History*, 11, 1970, pp. 331–53.

Jones, G. I., *The Trading States of the Oil Rivers*, Oxford 1963.

Kanya-Forstner, A. S., *The Conquest of the Western Sudan: A Study in French Military Imperialism*, Cambridge 1969.

Klein, Martin A., *Islam and Imperialism in Senegal*, Edinburgh 1968.

——, 'Slavery, the Slave Trade, and Legitimate Commerce in Late Nineteenth-Century Africa', *Études d'Histoire Africaine*, 2, 1971, pp. 5–28.

Kopytoff, Jean Herskovits, *A Preface to Modern Nigeria: the Sierra Leoneans in Yoruba, 1830–1890*, Madison 1965.

Laffey, John F., 'The Roots of French Imperialism in the Nineteenth Century: the Case of Lyon', *French Historical Studies*, 6, 1969, pp. 78–92.

Latham, A. J. H., *Old Calabar, 1600–1891: the Economic Impact of the West Upon a Traditional Society*, University of Birmingham Ph.D. thesis, 1970.

Limberg, L., 'The Economy of the Fanti Confederation', *Transactions of the Historical Society of Ghana*, 11, 1970, pp. 83–103.

Lloyd, P. C., 'The Isekiri in the Nineteenth Century: An Outline Social History', *Journal of African History*, 4, 1963, pp. 207–31.

McIntyre, W. D., *The Imperial Frontier in the Tropics, 1865–75*, 1967.

McPhee, Allan, *The Economic Revolution in British West Africa*, 1926.

Mabogunje, Akin L., 'Some Comments on Land Tenure in Egba Division, Western Nigeria', *Africa*, 31, 1961, pp. 258–69.

Mahoney, F., 'Notes on Mulattoes of the Gambia Before the Mid 19th Century', *Transactions of the Historical Society of Ghana*, 8, 1965, pp. 120–9.

Manning, Patrick, 'Some Export Statistics for Nigeria, 1880–1905', *Nigerian Journal of Economic and Social Studies*, 9, 1967, pp. 229–34.

——, *An Economic History of Southern Dahomey, 1880–1914*, University of Wisconsin Ph.D. thesis, 1969.

Mitchell, P. K., 'Trade Routes of the Early Sierra Leone Protectorate', *Sierra Leone Studies*, 16, 1962, pp. 204–17.

Newbury, C. W., 'The Development of French Policy on the Lower and Upper Niger, 1880–98', *Journal of Modern History*, 31, 1959, pp. 16–26.

——, *The Western Slave Coast and its Rulers*, Oxford 1961.

——, 'North African and Western Sudan Trade in the Nineteenth Century: a Re-evaluation', *Journal of African History*, 7, 1966, pp. 233–46.

——, 'The Protectionist Revival in French Colonial Trade: the Case of Senegal', *Economic History Review*, 21, 1968, pp. 337–48.

——, 'Trade and Authority in West Africa from 1850 to 1880', in *Colonialism in Africa, 1870–1960*, ed. L. H. Gann and Peter Duignan, 1, *The History and Politics of Colonialism, 1870–1914*, Cambridge 1969, pp. 66–99.

——, 'The Tariff Factor in Anglo-French West African Partition', in *France and Britain in Africa: Imperial Rivalry and Colonial Rule*, ed. Prosser Gifford and William R. Louis, New Haven 1971, pp. 221–59.

——, 'Credit in Early Nineteenth-Century West African Trade', *Journal of African History*, 13, 1972, pp. 81–95.

——, and Kanya-Forstner, A. S., 'French Policy and the Origins of the Scramble for West Africa', *Journal of African History*, 10, 1969, pp. 253–76.

Pasquier, Roger, 'En marge de la guerre de sécession: les essais de culture du coton au Sénégal', *Annales Africaines*, 1955, pp. 185–202.

——, 'En marge du centenaire de Dakar; Bordeaux et les débuts de la navigation à vapeur vers le Brésil', *Revue Historique de Bordeaux et du Département de la Gironde*, 1957, pp. 219–37.

——, 'Villes du Sénégal au XIXe siècle', *Revue Française d'Histoire d'Outre-Mer*, 47, 1960, pp. 387–426.

——, 'A propos de l'emancipation des esclaves au Sénégal en 1848', *Revue Française d'Histoire d'Outre-Mer*, 54, 1967, pp. 188–208.

Pearson, Scott R., 'The Economic Imperialism of the Royal Niger Company', *Food Research Institute Studies*, 10, 1971, pp. 69–88.

Person, Yves, 'Samori et la Sierra Leone', *Cahiers d'Études Africaines*, 7, 1967, pp. 5–26.

Porter, Arthur T., *Creoledom*, Oxford 1963.

Robinson, Ronald, and Gallagher, John, with Denny, Alice, *Africa and the Victorians*, 1961.

Ross, David A., 'The Career of Domingo Martinez in the Bight of Benin, 1833–64', *Journal of African History*, 6, 1965, pp. 79–90.

Schnapper, Bernard, 'La fin du régime de l'exclusif, le commerce étranger dans les possessions françaises d'Afrique tropicale (1817–1870)', *Annales Africaines*, 1959, pp. 149–200.

——, *La politique et le commerce français dans le Golfe de Guinée de 1838 à 1871*, Paris 1961.

Stilliard, N. H., *The Rise and Development of Legitimate Trade in Palm Oil with West Africa*, University of Birmingham M.A. thesis, 1938.

von Strandmann, Hartmut Pogge, 'Germany's Colonial Expansion under Bismarck', *Past & Present*, 42, 1969, pp. 140–59.

Swanzy, Henry, 'A Trading Family in the Nineteenth-Century Gold Coast', *Transactions of the Gold Coast and Togoland Historical Society*, 2, 1956, pp. 87–120.

Thompson, William, *Glasgow and Africa: Connexions and Attitudes, 1870–1900*, University of Strathclyde Ph.D. thesis, 1970.

Vignes, K., 'Étude sur la rivalité d'influence entre les puissances européennes en Afrique équatoriale et occidentale depuis l'acte général de Berlin jusqu'au seuil du XXᵉ siècle', *Revue Française d'Histoire d'Outre-Mer*, 48, 1961, pp. 5–95.

Webster, J. B., 'The Bible and the Plough', *Journal of the Historical Society of Nigeria*, 2, 1963, pp. 418–34.

Wehler, Hans-Ulrich, 'Bismarck's Imperialism, 1862–1890', *Past & Present*, 48, 1970, pp. 131–9.

Wilks, Ivor, 'Ashanti Government', in *West African Kingdoms in the Nineteenth Century*, ed. Daryll Forde and P. M. Kaberry, 1967, pp. 206–38.

——, 'Asante Policy Towards Hausa Trade in the Nineteenth Century', in *The Development of Indigenous Trade and Markets in West Africa*, ed. Claude Meillassoux, 1971, pp. 124–41.

Wolfson, Freda, 'A Price Agreement on the Gold Coast—the Krobo Oil Boycott, 1858–1866', *Economic History Review*, 6, 1953, pp. 68–77.

Wright, E. J., 'Remarks on the Early Monetary Position in Sierra Leone, with a Description of the Coinage Adopted', *Sierra Leone Studies*, 3, 1954, pp. 136–46.

Wurie, A., 'The Bundukas of Sierra Leone', *Sierra Leone Studies*, 1, 1953, pp. 14–25.

Wylie, Kenneth, C., 'Innovation and Change in Mende Chieftaincy, 1880–96', *Journal of African History*, 10, 1969, pp. 295–307.

Zucarelli, François, 'L'entrepôt fictif de Gorée entre 1822 et 1852', *Annales Africaines*, 1959, pp. 261–82.

——, 'Le recrutement des travailleurs sénégalais par l'état indépendant du Congo (1888–1896)', *Revue Française d'Histoire d'Outre-Mer*, 47, 1960, pp. 475–81.

Chapter 5   An economic model of colonialism

Baldwin, R. E., 'Patterns of Development in Newly Settled Regions', *Manchester School of Economic and Social Studies*, 24, 1956, pp. 161–79.

Bateman, M. J., 'Aggregate and Regional Supply Functions for Ghanaian Cocoa, 1946–62', *Journal of Farm Economics*, 47, 1965, pp. 384–401.

Beckford, G. L. F., 'Secular Fluctuations in the Growth of Tropical Agricultural Trade', *Economic Development and Cultural Change*, 13, 1964, pp. 80–94.

Berg, Elliot, J., 'Real Income Trends in West Africa, 1939–1960', in *Economic Transition in Africa*, ed. Melville J. Herskovits and Mitchell Harwitz, 1964, pp. 199–238.

Bertrand, Raymond, 'Construction et emploi d'un indice du rapport d'échange pour l'Afrique occidentale française', *Revue Économique*, 7, 1956, pp. 280–307.

Board of Trade, *Statistical Abstract for the British Empire*, 1889–1913, 1924–38.
——, *Statistical Abstract for the British Commonwealth*, 1936–47.
——, *Statistical Abstract for the Commonwealth and the Sterling Area*, 1947–60.

Cox-George, N. A., *Finance and Development in West Africa*, 1961.
Crowder, Michael, 'West Africa and the 1914–18 War', *Bulletin de l'IFAN*, B, 30, 1968, pp. 227–45.

Dalton, George, 'History, Politics and Economic Development in Liberia', *Journal of Economic History*, 25, 1965, pp. 569–91.
Durand, H., *Essai sur la conjoncture de l'Afrique noire*, Paris, 1957.

Helleiner, Gerald, K., *Peasant Agriculture, Government, and Economic Growth in Nigeria*, Homewood, Illinois, 1966.
Higgins, B. H., 'The Dualistic Theory of Underdeveloped Areas', *Economic Development and Cultural Change*, 4, 1955, pp. 99–115.
Hymer, Stephen H., 'The Political Economy of the Gold Coast and Ghana', in *Government and Economic Development*, ed. G. Ranis, New Haven 1971, pp. 129–80.

Jones, William O., and Merat, Christian, 'Consumption of Exotic Consumer Goods as an Indicator of Economic Achievement in Ten Countries of Tropical Africa,' *Food Research Institute Studies*, 3, 1962, pp. 35–60.

Lawson, Rowena, M., 'Engel's Law and its Application to Ghana', *Economic Bulletin of Ghana*, 5, 1962, pp. 34–46.
League of Nations, *International Statistical Yearbook*, 1926–27, 1929.
——*Statistical Yearbook of the League of Nations*, 1930–44.
——, *International Trade Statistics*, 1931–38.

MacBean, Alasdair, *Export Instability and Economic Development*, 1966.
Morgan, W. B., 'Food Imports of West Africa', *Economic Geography*, 39, 1963, pp. 351–62.
Myint, H., *The Economics of the Developing Countries*, 1964.
——, *Economic Theory and the Underdeveloped Countries*, 1971.

Naval Intelligence Division, *French West Africa*, I, *The Federation*, 1943.
Neumark, S. Daniel, *Foreign Trade and Economic Development in Africa*, Stanford 1964.

Poquin, Jean-Jacques, *Les relations économiques extérieures des pays d'Afrique noire de l'union française (1925–1955)*, Paris 1957.

Rimmer, Douglas, 'The Crisis in the Ghana Economy', *Journal of Modern African Studies*, 4, 1966, pp. 17–32.

Seers, Dudley, 'The Stages of Economic Development of a Primary Producer in the Middle of the Twentieth Century', *Economic Bulletin of Ghana*, 7, 1963, pp. 57–69.
Singer, H. W., 'The Distribution of Gains Between Investing and Borrowing Countries', *American Economic Review*, 40, 1950, pp. 473–85.
Stewart, G. G., and Ord, H. W., eds, *African Primary Products and International Trade*, Edinburgh 1965.

315

United Nations, *Statistical Yearbook*, 1948–60.
——, *Yearbook of International Trade Statistics*, 1950–60.

Watkins, Melville, H., 'A Staple Theory of Economic Growth', *Canadian Journal of Economics and Political Science*, 29, 1963, pp. 141–58.

Chapter 6 Completing the open economy

Adomakoh, Albert, 'The History of Currency and Banking in Some West African Countries', *Economic Bulletin of Ghana*, 7, 1963, pp. 3–17.
Akinola, R. A., 'The Growth and Development of Ibadan—the Largest Yoruba Town', *Bulletin of the Ghana Geographical Association*, 2, 1966, pp. 48–63.
Ayorinde, J. A., 'Historical Notes on the Introduction and Development of the Cocoa Industry in Nigeria', *Nigerian Agricultural Journal*, 3, 1966, pp. 18–23.

Bauer, P. T., *West African Trade*, Cambridge 1954.
Bederman, S. H., 'Plantation Agriculture in Victoria Division, West Cameroons: an Historical Introduction', *Geography*, 51, 1966, pp. 349–60.
Berg, Elliot J., 'Backward-Sloping Labor Supply Functions in Dual Economies—the Africa Case', *Quarterly Journal of Economics*, 75, 1961, pp. 468–92.
——, 'The Development of a Labour Force in Sub-Saharan Africa', *Economic Development and Cultural Change*, 13, 1965, pp. 394–412.
——, 'The Economics of the Migrant Labour System', in *Urbanisation and Migration in West Africa*, ed. Hilda Kuper, Berkeley 1965, pp. 160–81.
Berry, S. S., 'Christianity and the Rise of Cocoa Growing in Ibadan and Ondo', *Journal of the Historical Society of Nigeria*, 4, 1968, pp. 439–51.
Bevin, H. J., 'Some Notes on Gold Coast Exports, 1886–1913', *Economic Bulletin of Ghana*, 4, 1960, pp. 13–20.
Birmingham, Walter, Neustadt, I., and Omaboe, E. N., eds, *A Study of Contemporary Ghana*, 1, *The Economy of Ghana*, Evanston 1966.
Boateng, E. A., 'The Tarkwa Gold Mining Industry—a Retrospect', *Bulletin of the Ghana Geographical Association*, 2, 1957, pp. 5–9.
Bohannan, Paul, 'The Impact of Money on an African Subsistence Economy', *Journal of Economic History*, 19, 1959, pp. 491–503.
Bouche, Denise, *Les villages de liberté en Afrique noire française, 1887–1910*, Paris 1968.
Boutillier, J-L., 'Les captifs en A.O.F. (1903–1905)', *Bulletin de l'IFAN*, B, 30, 1968, pp. 513–35.
Brasseur-Marion, Paule, 'Cotonou porte du Dahomey', *Cahiers d'Outre-Mer*, 6, 1953, pp. 364–78.
Brown, George W., *The Economic History of Liberia*, Washington D.C., 1941.
Burke, L. J., 'A Short Account of the Discovery of the Major Diamond Deposits', *Sierra Leone Studies*, 12, 1959, pp. 316–28.
Byl, A., 'History of the Labour Market in French-Speaking West Africa', *Cahiers Économiques et Sociaux*, 5, 1966, pp. 167–88.

Capot-Rey, R., 'Problems of Nomadism in the Sahara', *International Labour Review*, 90, 1964, pp. 472–81.

Charbonneau, Jean and René, *Marchés et marchands d'Afrique noire*, Paris 1961.

Charle, E. G., 'An Appraisal of British Imperial Policy with Respect to the Extraction of Mineral Resources in Nigeria', *Nigerian Journal of Economic and Social Studies*, 6, 1964, pp. 37–42.

Church, R. J. H., *The Railways of West Africa: a Geographical and Historical Analysis*, University of London, Ph.D. thesis, 1943.

Clauzel, J., 'Transports, automobiles et caravanes dans le Sahara soudanais', *Travaux de l'Institut des Recherches Sahariennes*, 19, 1960, pp. 161–8.

——, 'Évolution de la vie économique et des structures sociales du pays nomade du Mali, de la conquête française à l'autonomie interne, 1893–1958', *Tiers-Monde*, 9–10, 1962, pp. 283–311.

Coquery-Vidrovitch, Catherine, 'French Colonization in Africa to 1920: Administration and Economic Development', in *Colonialism in Africa, 1870–1960*, ed. L. H. Gann and Peter Duignan, 1, *The History and Politics of Colonialism, 1870–1914*, Cambridge 1969, pp. 165–98.

Cox-George, N. A., *Finance and Development in West Africa: the Sierra Leone Experience*, 1961.

Darkoh, Michael, 'The Economic Life of Buem, 1884–1914', *Bulletin of the Ghana Geographical Association*, 9, 1964, pp. 40–54.

——, 'Togoland Under the Germans: Thirty Years of Economic Growth, 1884–1914', *Nigerian Geographical Journal*, 11, 1968, pp. 153–68.

Davidson, R. B., *Migrant Labour in the Gold Coast*, Achimota 1954 (mimeo.).

Dickson, K. B., 'The Development of Road Transport in Southern Ghana and Ashanti since 1850', *Transactions of the Historical Society of Ghana*, 5, 1961, pp. 33–42.

——, *A Historical Geography of Ghana*, Cambridge 1969.

Dumett, Raymond, 'The Rubber Trade of the Gold Coast and Asante in the Nineteenth Century: African Innovation and Market Responsiveness', *Journal of African History*, 12, 1971, pp. 79–102.

Dupire, Marguerite, 'Planteurs autochtones et étrangers en basse Côte d'Ivoire orientale', *Études Éburnéennes*, 8, 1960, pp. 7–237.

——, and Boutillier, Jean-Louis, 'Le pays Adioukrou et sa palmeraie, basse Côte d'Ivoire', *L'Homme d'Outre-Mer*, 4, 1958, pp. 1–100.

Ekejuiba, Felicia, 'Omu Okwei, The Merchant Queen of Ossomari: a Biographical Sketch', *Journal of the Historical Society of Nigeria*, 3, 1967, pp. 633–46.

Elliott, C. M., 'Agriculture and Economic Development in Africa: Theory and Experience', in *Agrarian Change and Economic Development*, ed. E. L. Jones and S. G. Woolf, 1969, pp. 123–50.

Fouquet, Joseph, 'La traite des arachides dans le pays de Kaolack', *Études Sénégalaises*, 8, 1958, pp. 1–262.

Frankel, S. H., *Capital Investment in Africa*, Oxford 1938.

Fréchou, H., 'Les plantations européennes en Côte d'Ivoire', *Cahiers d'Outre-Mer*, 8, 1955, pp. 56–83.

——, 'Le régime foncier chez les Soussous du moyen—Konkouré', *Cahiers de l'Institut de Science Économique Appliquée*, Supplement 129, 1962, pp. 109–98.

Gamble, David P., 'History of the Groundnut Trade, 1829–1939', in *Contributions to a Socio-Economic Survey of the Gambia*, 1949, pp. 55–69.

Girard, Jean, 'De la communauté traditionnelle à la collectivité moderne en Casamance', *Annales Africaines*, 1963, pp. 135–65.

Gleave, Michael B., 'Hill Settlements and their Abandonment in Western Yorubaland', *Africa*, 33, 1963, pp. 343–52.

——, 'The Changing Frontiers of Settlement in the Uplands of Northern Nigeria', *Nigerian Geographical Journal*, 8, 1965, pp. 127–41.

——, 'Hill Settlements and their Abandonment in Tropical Africa', *Transactions of the Institute of British Geographers*, 40, 1966, pp. 39–49.

Gould, Peter R., *The Development of the Transportation Pattern in Ghana*, Evanston 1960.

Greenstreet, D. K., 'The Guggisberg Ten-Year Development Plan', *Economic Bulletin of Ghana*, 8, 1964, pp. 18–26.

——, 'The Transport Department—The First Two Decades (1901–20)', *Economic Bulletin of Ghana*, 10, 1966, pp. 33–44.

Guèye, M'baye, 'L'Affaire Chautemps (avril 1904) et la suppression de l'esclavage de case au Sénégal', *Bulletin de l'IFAN*, B, 27, 1965, pp. 543–59.

——, 'La fin de l'esclavage à Saint-Louis et à Gorée en 1848', *Bulletin de l'IFAN*, B, 28, 1966, pp. 637–56.

Hancock, W. K., *Survey of British Commonwealth Affairs, 1918–1939*, II, parts 1 and 2, 1942.

Haswell, Margaret R., *Economics of Agriculture in a Savannah Village*, 1953.

Hawkins, E. K., *Road Transport in Nigeria*, 1958.

Hay, Alan M., 'The Development of Road Transport in Nigeria, 1900–1940', *Journal of Transport History*, n.s., 1, 1971, pp. 95–107.

Helleiner, Gerald K., *Peasant Agriculture, Government, and Economic Growth in Nigeria*, Homewood, Illinois, 1966.

Hill, Polly, *The Gold Coast Cocoa Farmer: A Preliminary Survey*, 1956.

——, 'The History of the Migration of Ghana Cocoa Farmers', *Transactions of the Historical Society of Ghana*, 4, 1959, pp. 14–28.

——, 'The Migration of Southern Ghanaian Cocoa Farmers', *Bulletin de l'IFAN*, B, 22, 1960, pp. 419–25.

——, 'The Migrant Cocoa Farmers of Southern Ghana', *Africa*, 31, 1961, pp. 209–30.

——, *The Migrant Cocoa-Farmers of Southern Ghana*, Cambridge 1963.

Hodder, B. W., 'The Growth of Trade at Lagos (Nigeria)', *Tijdschrift voor Economische en Sociale Geografie*, 50, 1959, pp. 197–202.

Hogendorn, J. S., *The Origins of the Groundnut Trade in Northern Nigeria*, University of London Ph.D. thesis, 1966.

Holas, B., 'Le paysannat africain devant le problème des cultures industrielles: l'exemple des Oubi (Côte d'Ivoire)', *Revue de l'Institut de Sociologie Solvay*, 2, 1957, pp. 219–33.

Hopkins, A. G., 'The Lagos Strike of 1897: an Exploration in Nigerian Labour History', *Past & Present*, 35, 1966, pp. 133–55.

——, 'The Creation of a Colonial Monetary System: the Origins of the West African Currency Board', *African Historical Studies*, 3, 1970, pp. 101–32.

Hoyle, B. S., and Hilling, D., eds, *Seaports and Development in Tropical Africa*, 1970.

Jarrett, H. R., 'The Strange Farmers of the Gambia', *Geographical Review*, 39, 1949, pp. 649–57.

Kemian, Bakari, 'Une ville de la République du Soudan: San', *Cahiers d'Outre-Mer*, 12, 1959, pp. 225–50.

Khuri, Fuad I., 'Kinship, Emigration, and Trade Partnership among the Lebanese of West Africa', *Africa*, 35, 1965, pp. 385–95.

Kilby, Peter, 'African Labour Productivity Reconsidered', *Economic Journal*, 71, 1961, pp. 273–91.

Köbben, A. J. F., 'Le planteur noir', *Études Éburnéennes*, 5, 1956, pp. 7–185.

——, 'The Development of an Under-Developed Territory', *Sociologus*, 8, 1958, pp. 29–40.

Labouret, Henri, *Paysans d'Afrique occidentale*, Paris 1946.

Leduc, M., *Les institutions monétaires africaines: pays francophones*, Paris 1965.

Leubuscher, Charlotte, *The West African Shipping Trade, 1909–1959*, Leyden 1963.

Lombard, J., 'Cotonou, ville africaine', *Bulletin de l'IFAN*, B, 16, 1954, pp. 341–77.

——, 'Le problème des migrations "locales", leur rôle dans les changements d'une société en transition', *Bulletin de l'IFAN*, B, 22, 1960, pp. 455–66.

Loynes, J. B., *The West African Currency Board, 1912–1962*, 1962.

Mabogunje, Akin L., *The Changing Pattern of Rural Settlement and Rural Economy in Egba Division, South-Western Nigeria*, University of London M.A. thesis, 1958.

——, *Urbanisation in Nigeria*, 1968.

——, and Gleave, Michael B., 'Changing Agricultural Landscape in Southern Nigeria: the Example of Egba Division 1850–1950', *Nigerian Geographical Journal*, 7, 1964, pp. 1–15.

McLaughlin, R. U., *Foreign Investment and Development in Liberia*, New York 1966.

McPhee, Allan, *The Economic Revolution in British West Africa*, 1926.

Mangolte, Jacques, 'Le chemin de fer de Konakry au Niger (1890–1914)', *Revue Française d'Histoire d'Outre-Mer*, 55, 1968, pp. 37–105.

Martin, Anne, *The Oil Palm Economy of the Ibibio Farmer*, Ibadan 1956.

Meillassoux, Claude, 'The Social Structure of Modern Bamako', *Africa*, 35, 1965, pp. 125–42.

Morgan, W. B., and Pugh, J. C., *West Africa*, 1969.

Newbury, C. W., 'An Early Enquiry into Slavery and Captivity in Dahomey', *Zaïre*, 14, 1960, pp. 53–67.

——, 'The Government General and Political Change in French West Africa', *St Antony's Papers*, 10, 1961, pp. 41–59.

Newlyn, W. T., and Rowan, D. C., *Money and Banking in British Colonial Africa*, Oxford 1954.

Olusanya, G. O., 'The Freed Slaves' Homes: an Unknown Aspect of Northern Nigerian Social History', *Journal of the Historical Society of Nigeria*, 3, 1966, pp. 523–38.

Omaboe, E. M., 'Ghana's National Income in 1930', *Economic Bulletin of Ghana*, 4, 1960, pp. 6–11 and pp. 22–3.

Osoba, S. O., 'The Phenomenon of Labour Migration in the Era of British Colonial Rule: a Neglected Aspect of Nigeria's Social History', *Journal of the Historical Society of Nigeria*, 4, 1969, pp. 515–38.

Oyemakinde, J. O., *A History of Indigenous Labour on the Nigerian Railway, 1895–1945*, University of Ibadan Ph.D. thesis, 1970.

Pehaut, Y., 'L'arachide au Sénégal', *Études Sénégalaises*, 2, 1952, pp. 5–25.

Pélissier, Paul, 'Les paysans serères: essai sur la formation d'un terroir du Sénégal', *Cahiers d'Outre-Mer*, 6, 1953, pp. 105–27.

——, *Les paysans du Sénégal: les civilisations agraires du Cayor à la Casamance*, Saint-Yrieix, 1966.

Perham, Margery, ed., *The Native Economies of Nigeria*, 1946.

——, ed., *Mining, Commerce, and Finance in Nigeria*, 1948.

Pim, A., *The Financial and Economic History of the African Tropical Territories*, Oxford 1940.

Pitot, Albert, 'L'homme et les sols dans les steppes et savannes de l'A.O.F.', *Cahiers d'Outre-Mer*, 5, 1952, pp. 215–40.

Portères, R., *Aménagement de l'economie, agricole et rurale du Sénégal*, Dakar 1952.

Prothero, R. Mansell, 'Migratory Labour from North-Western Nigeria', *Africa*, 27, 1957, pp. 251–61.

Roberts, Stephen H., *The History of French Colonial Policy, 1870–1925*, 1929.

Roper, J. I., *Labour Problems in West Africa*, Harmondsworth 1958.

Rouch, J., 'Migrations au Ghana', *Journal de la Société des Africanistes*, 26, 1956, pp. 33–196.

——, 'Problèmes relatifs à l'étude des migrations traditionnelles et des migrations actuelles en Afrique occidentale', *Bulletin de l'IFAN*, B, 22, 1960, pp. 369–78.

Rudin, Harry R., *Germans in the Cameroons, 1884–1914*, New Haven 1938.

Savonnet, Georges, 'Une ville neuve du Sénégal: Thiès', *Cahiers d'Outre-Mer*, 9, 1956, pp. 70–93.

——, 'La colonisation du pays Koulango (haute Côte d'Ivoire) par les Lobi de haute-Volta', *Cahiers d'Outre-Mer*, 15, 1962, pp. 25–46.

Siddle, D. J., 'War Towns in Sierra Leone: a Study in Social Change', *Africa*, 38, 1968, pp. 47–55.

Smith, M. G., 'Slavery and Emancipation in Two Societies', *Social and Economic Studies*, 2, 1954, pp. 239–90.

Stanley, William R., 'The Lebanese in Sierra Leone: Entrepreneurs Extraordinary', *African Urban Notes*, 5, 1970, pp. 159–74.

Suret-Canale, Jean, 'La Guinée dans le système colonial', *Présence Africaine*, 1959–60, pp. 9–44.

——, *Afrique noire occidentale et centrale: l'ère coloniale (1900–1945)*, Paris 1964. Translated as *French Colonialism in Tropical Africa, 1900–1945*, 1971.

Swindell, Kenneth, 'Diamond Mining in Sierra Leone', *Tÿdschrift voor Economische en Sociale Geografie*, 57, 1966, pp. 36–104.

Szereszewski, R., *Structural Changes in the Economy of Ghana, 1891–1911*, 1965.

Tamuno, Takena N., 'Emancipation in Nigeria', *Nigeria Magazine*, 82, 1964, pp. 218–27.

——, 'Genesis of the Nigerian Railway', *Nigeria Magazine*, 83, 1964, pp. 279–92.

Tardits, Claude, 'Développement du régime d'appropriation privée des terres de la palmeraie du Sud-Dahomey', in *African Agrarian Systems*, ed. Daniel Biebuyck, 1963, pp. 297–314.

Taylor, Wayne C., *The Firestone Operations in Liberia*, Washington 1956.

Thomas, Benjamin, E., 'Trade Routes of Algeria and the Sahara', *University of California Publications in Geography*, 8, 1957, pp. 165–288.

——, *Transportation and Physical Geography in West Africa*, Los Angeles, 1960.

Thomas, L. V., 'L'organisation foncière des Diola', *Annales Africaines*, 1960, pp. 199–223.

Toupet, C., 'Quelques aspects de la sédentarisation des nomades en Mauritanie sahélienne', *Annales de Géographie*, 73, 1964, pp. 738–45.

Tricart, Jean, 'Deux types de production agricole aux environs d'Odienne (haute Côte-d'Ivoire)', *Bulletin de l'IFAN*, B, 19, 1957, pp. 284–94.

——, 'Le café en Côte d'Ivoire', *Cahiers d'Outre-Mer*, 10, 1957, pp. 209–33.

Udo, R. K., 'Disintegration of Nucleated Settlement in Eastern Nigeria', *Geographical Review*, 55, 1965, pp. 53–67.

——, 'British Policy and the Development of Export Crops in Nigeria', *Nigerian Journal of Economic and Social Studies*, 9, 1967, pp. 299–314.

United Africa Company, 'The Production of Palm Oil and Palm Kernels in Nigeria', *Statistical and Economic Review*, 1, 1948, pp. 15–31.

——, 'Produce Goes to Market. Nigeria: Palm Produce, Groundnuts', *Statistical and Economic Review*, 3, 1949, pp. 1–37; 4, 1949, pp. 1–45.

——, 'The Manilla Problem', *Statistical and Economic Review*, 3, 1949, pp. 44–56; 4, 1949, pp. 59–60.

——, 'Merchandise Trading in British West Africa', *Statistical and Economic Review*, 5, 1950, pp. 1–36; 6, 1950, pp. 1–40.

——, 'Produce Goes to Market: the Hides and Skins Trade of Nigeria', *Statistical and Economic Review*, 8, 1951, pp. 27–48.

——, 'Trading on the Gambia', *Statistical and Economic Review*, 11, 1953, pp. 1–40.

Verdier, R., 'Problèmes fonciers ivoiriens', *Penant*, 73, 1963, pp. 404–11.

——, 'Problèmes fonciers nigeriens', *Penant*, 74, 1964, pp. 587–93.

Villien-Rossi, Marie-Louise, 'Bamako, capitale du Mali', *Cahiers d'Outre-Mer*, 16, 1963, pp. 379–93.

Walker, G. J., *Traffic and Transport in Nigeria*, 1957.

Webster, J. B., 'Agege: Plantations and the African Church, 1901–1920', *Nigerian Institute of Social and Economic Research, Conference Proceedings*, 1962, pp. 124–30.

Wilson, Charles, *The History of Unilever*, 2 vols, 1954.

Winder, R. Bayly, 'The Lebanese in West Africa', *Comparative Studies in Society and History*, 4, 1962, pp. 296–336 and the 'Comment' by L. A. Fallers, *ibid.*, pp. 334–6.

Wondji, Christophe, 'La Côte d'Ivoire occidentale: période de pénétration pacifique (1890–1908)', *Revue Française d'Histoire d'Outre-Mer*, 50, 1953, pp. 346–81.

Wrigley, C. C., 'Economic and Social Developments', in *A Thousand Years of West African History*, ed. J. F. A. Ajayi and Ian Espie, 1965, pp. 423–39.

Zuccarelli, François, 'Le régime des engagés à temps au Sénégal (1817–1848)', *Cahiers d'Études Africaines*, 2, 1962, pp. 420–61.

Chapter 7　The open economy under strain

Abbott, George C., 'A Re-examination of the 1929 Colonial Development Act', *Economic History Review*, 24, 1971, pp. 68–81.

Abbott, John C., 'Agricultural Marketing Boards in the Developing Countries', *Journal of Farm Economics*, 49, 1967, pp. 705–22.

Adeyoju, S. K., 'The Benin Timber Industry Before 1939', *Nigerian Geographical Journal*, 12, 1969, pp. 99–111.

Akpala, Agwu, 'The Background of the Enugu Colliery Shooting Incident in 1949', *Journal of the Historical Society of Nigeria*, 3, 1965, pp. 335–64.

Allen, Christopher, 'African Trade Unionism in Microcosm: the Gambia Labour Movement, 1939–67', in *African Perspectives*, ed. C. H. Allen and R. S. Johnson, Cambridge 1970, pp. 393–426.

Amselle, Jean-Loup, 'Les réseaux marchands Kooroko', *African Urban Notes*, 5, 1970, pp. 143–58.

Amin, S., *Trois expériences africaines de développement: le Mali, la Guinée et le Ghana*, Paris 1965.

Baldwin, K. D. S., *The Niger Agricultural Project*, Cambridge, Mass., 1957.

——, 'Land Tenure Problems in Relation to Agricultural Development in the Northern Region of Nigeria', in *African Agrarian Systems*, ed. Daniel Biebuyck, 1963, pp. 65–82.

Ballard, John A., 'The Porto Novo Incidents of 1923: Politics in the Colonial Era', *Odu*, 2, 1965, pp. 52–75.

Bauer, P. T., 'Origins of the Statutory Export Monopolies of British West Africa', *Business History Review*, 28, 1954, pp. 197–213.

——, *West African Trade*, Cambridge 1954.

Beckett, W. H., *Akokoaso*, 1944.

Berg, Elliot J., 'The Economic Basis of Political Choice in French West Africa', *American Political Science Review*, 54, 1960, pp. 391–405.

——, and Butler, Jeffrey, 'Trade Unions', in *Political Parties and National Integration in Tropical Africa*, ed. James S. Coleman and Carl G. Rosberg, Berkeley 1964, pp. 340–81.

Binet, Jacques, 'Marchés en pays Soussou', *Cahiers d'Études Africaines*, 3, 1963, pp. 104–14.

Birmingham, Walter, 'An Index of Real Wages of the Unskilled Labourer in Accra, 1939–1959', *Economic Bulletin of Ghana*, 4, 1960, pp. 2–6.

Blanckenburg, Peter von, ed., 'The Transformation of African Peasant Farming to a Modern Agricultural Economy', *Journal of Foreign Agriculture*, Special Publication 3, 1965.

Bohannan, Paul, and Dalton, George, eds, *Markets in Africa*, Evanston 1962.

Bonnefonds, Atsé-Léon, 'La transformation du commerce de traite en Côte d'Ivoire depuis la dernière guerre mondiale et l'indépendance', *Cahiers d'Outre-Mer*, 21, 1968, pp. 395–413.

Booker, H. S., 'Debt in Africa', *African Affairs*, 48, 1949, pp. 141–9.

Bray, Jennifer M., 'The Economics of Traditional Cloth Production in Iseyin, Nigeria', *Economic Development and Cultural Change*, 17, 1969, pp. 540–51.

——, 'The Craft Structure of a Traditional Yoruba Town', *Transactions of the Institute of British Geographers*, 46, 1969, pp. 179–93.

Buell, Raymond L., *The Native Problem in Africa*, 1 and 2, Harvard 1928.

Capet, Marcel, *Traité d'économie tropicale: les économies d'A.O.F.*, Paris 1958.

Carney, David E., *Government and Economy in British West Africa*, New York 1961.

Charle, E. G., 'English Colonial Policy and the Economy of Nigeria', *American Journal of Economics and Sociology*, 26, 1967, pp. 79–92.

Cohen, Abner, 'Politics of the Kola Trade', *Africa*, 36, 1966, pp. 18–36.

——, *Custom and Politics in Urban Africa: a Study of Hausa Migrants in Yoruba Towns*, 1969.

Coleman, James S., *Nigeria: Background to Nationalism*, Berkeley and Los Angeles 1958.

Conway, H. E., 'Labour Protest Activity in Sierra Leone During the Early Part of the Twentieth Century', *Labour History*, 15, 1968, pp. 49–63.

Cox-George, N. A., 'Studies in Finance and Development: the Gold Coast (Ghana) Experience, 1914–1918', *Public Finance*, 13, 1958, pp. 146–77.

Davies, J. H., 'Manufacturing Industry in Sierra Leone', *Nigerian Institute of Social and Economic Research Conference Proceedings*, 1962, pp. 142–51.

de Graft-Johnson, J. C., *African Experiment: Co-operative Agriculture and Banking in British West Africa*, 1958.

Despois, J., 'Problèmes techniques, économiques, et sociaux des oasis sahariennes, *Revue Tunisienne de Sciences Sociales*, 2, 1965, pp. 51–7.

Doctor, K. C., and Gallis, H., 'Size and Characteristics of Wage Employment in Africa: Some Statistical Estimates', *International Labour Review*, 93, 1966, pp. 149–73.

Dresch, Jean, 'Les investissements en Afrique noire', *Présence Africaine*, 13, 1952, pp. 232–41.

Egboh, Edmund O., 'Central Trade Unionism in Nigeria (1941–1966)', *Genève-Afrique*, 6, 1967, pp. 193–215.

——, 'The Early Years of Trade Unionism in Nigeria', *Africa Quarterly*, 8, 1968, pp. 59–69.

——, 'Trade Unions in Nigeria', *African Studies*, 27, 1968, pp. 35–40.

Ehrlich, Cyril, 'Marketing Boards in Retrospect—Myth and Reality', in *African Public Sector Economics*, Centre of African Studies, Edinburgh 1970, pp. 121–45.

Eicher, Carl K., and Liedholm, Carl, eds, *Growth and Development of the Nigerian Economy*, Michigan 1970.

Fievet, Maurice, 'Salt Caravan', *Nigeria Magazine*, 41, 1953, pp. 4–20.

Foltz, William G., *From French West Africa to the Mali Federation*, New Haven 1965.

Galletti, R., Baldwin, K. D. S., and Dina, I. O., *Nigerian Cocoa Farmers: an Economic Survey of Yoruba Cocoa-Farming Families*, Oxford 1956.

Garlick, Peter C., 'African-owned Private Enterprise Company Formation in Ghana', *Economic Bulletin of Ghana*, 4, 1960, pp. 1–10.

——, 'The Development of Kwahu Business Enterprise in Ghana since 1874—an Essay in Recent Oral Tradition', *Journal of African History*, 8, 1967, pp. 463–80.

——, *African Traders and Economic Development in Ghana*, Oxford 1971.

Grandin, Capitaine, 'Notes sur l'industrie et le commerce du sel au Kawar et Agram', *Bulletin de l'IFAN*, B, 13, 1951, pp. 488–533.

Green, R. H., 'Four African Development Plans: Ghana, Kenya, Nigeria, and Tanzania', *Journal of Modern African Studies*, 3, 1965, pp. 249–79.

——, and Hymer, S. H., 'Cocoa in the Gold Coast: a Study in the Relations between African Farmers and Agricultural Experts', *Journal of Economic History*, 26, 1966, pp. 299–319.

Greenstreet, D. K., 'Public Administration: Development and Welfare in the British Territories of West Africa During the Forties', *Economic Bulletin of Ghana*, 1, 1971, pp. 3–23.

Hauser, A., 'Les industries de transformation de la région de Dakar', *Études Sénégalaises*, 5, 1954, pp. 68–83.

——, 'Quelques relations des travailleurs de l'industrie à leur travail en A.O.F.', *Bulletin de l'IFAN*, B, 17, 1955, pp. 129–41.

Hawkins, E. K., 'The Growth of a Money Economy in Nigeria and Ghana', *Oxford Economic Papers*, 10, 1958, pp. 339–54.

Hay, Alan M., and Smith, Robert H. T., *Interregional Trade and Money Flows in Nigeria*, Ibadan 1970.

Hayter, Teresa, *French Aid*, 1966.

Helleiner, Gerald K., *Peasant Agriculture, Government, and Economic Growth in Nigeria*, Homewood, Illinois, 1966.

Hill, Polly, 'Three Types of Southern Ghanaian Cocoa Farmer', in *African Agrarian Systems*, ed. Daniel Biebuyck, 1963, pp. 203–23.

——, 'The Myth of the Amorphous Peasantry: a Northern Nigerian Case Study', *Nigerian Journal of Economic and Social Studies*, 10, 1968, pp. 239–60.

——, *Studies in Rural Capitalism in West Africa*, Cambridge 1970.

Hilton, T. E., 'Industrialisation in the Ivory Coast', *Bulletin of the Ghana Geographical Association*, 10, 1965, pp. 16–28.

Hodder, B. W., 'Distribution of Markets in Yorubaland', *Scottish Geographical Magazine*, 81, 1965, pp. 48–58.

Hodgkin, Thomas, *Nationalism in Colonial Africa*, 1956.

Hopkins, A. G., 'The Lagos Chamber of Commerce, 1888–1903', *Journal of the Historical Society of Nigeria*, 3, 1965, pp. 241–8.

——, 'Economic Aspects of Political Movements in Nigeria and in the Gold Coast, 1918–1939', *Journal of African History*, 7, 1966, pp. 133–52.

Igbafe, Philip A., 'The Benin Water Rate Agitation, 1937–39: An Example of Social Conflict', *Journal of the Historical Society of Nigeria*, 4, 1968, pp. 355–75.

Ikime, Obaro, 'The Anti-tax Riots in Warri Province, 1927–28', *Journal of the Historical Society of Nigeria*, 3, 1966, pp. 559–73.

James, Rudolph W., 'The Changing Role of Land in Southern Nigeria', *Odu*, 1, 1965, pp. 3–23.

Karp, Mark, 'The Legacy of French Economic Policy in Africa', in *French-Speaking Africa*, ed. William H. Lewis, 1965, pp. 145–53.

Kilby, Peter, *African Enterprise: the Nigerian Bread Industry*, Stanford 1965.

——, *Industrialization in an Open Economy: Nigeria, 1945–60*, Cambridge 1969.

Kilson, Martin, 'Nationalism and Social Classes in British West Africa', *Journal of Politics*, 20, 1958, pp. 368–87.

——, 'The Emergent Elites of Black Africa, 1900 to 1960', in *Colonialism in Africa 1870–1960*, ed. L. H. Gann and Peter Duignan, 2, *The History and Politics of Colonialism 1914–1960*, Cambridge 1970, pp. 351–98.

Kimble, David, *A Political History of Ghana 1850–1928*, Oxford 1963.

Laan, H. L. Van der, *The Sierra Leone Diamonds*, Oxford 1965.

Lawson, Rowena M., 'The Transition of Ghana's Fishing from a Primitive to a Mechanized Industry', *Transactions of the Historical Society of Ghana*, 9, 1968, pp. 90–104.

——, *The Changing Economy of the Lower Volta, 1954–67*, 1971.

Lelong, M-H., 'La route du kola', *Revue de Géographie Humaine et d'Ethnologie*, 1, 1948, pp. 35–44.

Lewis, Barbara, 'Ethnicity, Occupational Specialization, and Interest Groups: the Transporters' Association of the Ivory Coast', *African Urban Notes*, 5, 1970, pp. 95–115.

Lewis, W. A., *Report on Industrialisation and the Gold Coast*, Accra 1953.

Little, K., *West African Urbanization*, Cambridge 1965.

Lloyd, P. C., *Africa in Social Change*, Harmondsworth 1967.

Lovejoy, Paul E., 'The Wholesale Kola Trade of Kano', *African Urban Notes*, 5, 1970, pp. 129–42.

Mabogunje, Akin L., 'The Evolution and Analysis of the Retail Structure of Lagos, Nigeria', *Economic Geography*, 40, 1964, pp. 304–23.

McLoughlin, Peter F. M., ed., *African Food Production Systems*, Baltimore 1970.

May, Ranald S., 'Direct Overseas Investment in Nigeria 1953–63', *Scottish Journal of Political Economy*, 12, 1965, pp. 243–66.

Melamid, Alexander, 'The Geography of the Nigerian Petroleum Industry', *Economic Geography*, 44, 1, 1968, pp. 37–56.

Mersadier, Yves, 'La crise de l'arachide sénégalaise au début des années trente', *Bulletin de l'IFAN*, B, 28, 1966, pp. 826–77.

Milburn, Josephine F., 'The 1938 Gold Coast Cocoa Crisis: British Business and the Colonial Office', *African Historical Studies*, 3, 1970, pp. 57–74.

Miracle, Marvin P., and Fetter, Bruce, 'Backward-Sloping Labour Supply Functions and African Economic Behaviour', *Economic Development and Cultural Change*, 18, 1970, pp. 240–51.

Morgenthau, Ruth S., *Political Parties in French-Speaking West Africa*, Oxford 1964.

November, András, '*L'évolution du mouvement syndical en Afrique occidentale*, Paris 1965.

Ojo, G. J. O., 'The Changing Patterns of Traditional Group Farming in Ekiti, North-Eastern Yoruba Country', *Nigerian Geographical Journal*, 6, 1963, pp. 31–8.

——, 'Trends Towards Mechanised Agriculture in Yorubaland', *Nigerian Geographical Journal*, 6, 1963, pp. 116–29.

Oluwasanmi, H. A., *Agriculture and Nigerian Economic Development*, 1966.

Papy, L., 'La vallée du Sénégal: agriculture traditionnelle et riziculture mechanisée', *Cahiers d'Outre-Mer*, 4, 1951, pp. 277–324.

Pélissier, P., 'L'arachide au Sénégal: rationalisation et modernisation de sa culture', *Cahiers d'Outre-Mer*, 4, 1951, 204–36.

Pfeffermann, Guy, 'Trade Unions and Politics in French West Africa During the Fourth Republic', *African Affairs*, 66, 1967, pp. 213–30.

——, *Industrial Labour in the Republic of Senegal*, New York 1968.

Poleman, T. T., 'The Food Economies of Urban Middle Africa: the Case of Ghana', *Food Research Institute Studies*, 2, 1961, pp. 121–74.

Quarcoo, A. K., and Johnson, Marion, 'Shai Pots: the Pottery Industry of the Shai People of Southern Ghana', *Baessler-Archiv*, 16, 1968, pp. 47–88.

Ramboz, Y-C., 'La politique caféière de Côte d'Ivoire et la réforme de la caisse de stabilisation des prix du café et du cacao', *Revue Juridique et Politique*, 19, 1965, pp. 194–218.

Rhodie, Sam, 'The Gold Coast Cocoa Hold-up of 1930–31', *Transactions of the Historical Society of Ghana*, 9, 1968, pp. 105–18.
Robson, P., and Lury, D. A., eds, *The Economies of Africa*, 1969.
Richard-Molard, J., 'A propos des plans d'équipement en Afrique noire', *Afrique et Asie*, 16, 1951, pp. 9–38.

Saylor, Ralph G., *The Economic System of Sierra Leone*, Durham, N. C., 1967.
Sokolski, A., *The Establishment of Manufacturing in Nigeria*, New York 1965.
Suret-Canale, Jean, 'L'industrie des oléagineux en A.O.F.', *Cahiers d'Outre-Mer*, 3, 1950, pp. 280–8.
——, *Afrique noire occidentale et centrale: l'ère coloniale (1900–1945)*, Paris 1964. Translated as *French Colonialism in Tropical Africa, 1900–1945*, 1971.

Thompson, Virginia, and Adloff, Richard, *French West Africa*, 1958.
Tricart, Jean, 'Les échanges entre la zone forestière de Côte d'Ivoire et les savanes soudaniennes', *Cahiers d'Outre-Mer*, 9, 1956, pp. 209–38.

Udo, R. K., 'Sixty Years of Plantation Agriculture in Southern Nigeria: 1902–1962', *Economic Geography*, 41, 1965, pp. 356–68.
United Nations, 'The Textile Industry in the West African Sub-region', *Economic Bulletin for Africa*, 7, 1968, pp. 103–25.

Vinay, Bernard, *L'Afrique commerce avec l'Afrique*, Paris 1968.

Wade, Aboulaye, *Économie de l'ouest africain*, Paris 1964.
Wallerstein, Immanuel, 'The Colonial Era in Africa: Changes in the Social Structure', in *Colonialism in Africa, 1870–1960*, ed. L. H. Gann and Peter Duignan, 2, *The History and Politics of Colonialism, 1914–1960*, Cambridge 1970, pp. 399–421.
Warren, W. M., 'Urban Wage Rates and the Nigerian Trade Union Movement, 1939–60', *Economic Development and Cultural Change*, 15, 1966, pp. 21–36.
Wells, F. A., and Warmington, W. A., *Studies in Industrialization: Nigeria and the Cameroons*, 1962.
Whetham, Edith H., 'Diminishing Returns and Agriculture in Northern Nigeria', *Journal of Agricultural Economics*, 17, 1966, pp. 151–8.
White, H. P., 'Internal Exchange of Staple Foods in the Gold Coast', *Economic Geography*, 32, 1956, pp. 115–25.
Wilson, Charles, *Unilever 1945–1965*, 1968.

Yesufu, T. M., *An Introduction to Industrial Relations in Nigeria*, Oxford 1962.

Zahan, Dominique, 'Problèmes sociaux posés par la transplantation des Mossi sur les terres irriguées de l'Office du Niger', in *African Agrarian Systems*, ed. Daniel Biebuyck, 1963, pp. 392–403.

Index

Major states, e.g. Senegal, Nigeria, are not indexed, and authors are indexed only if they are mentioned in the text.

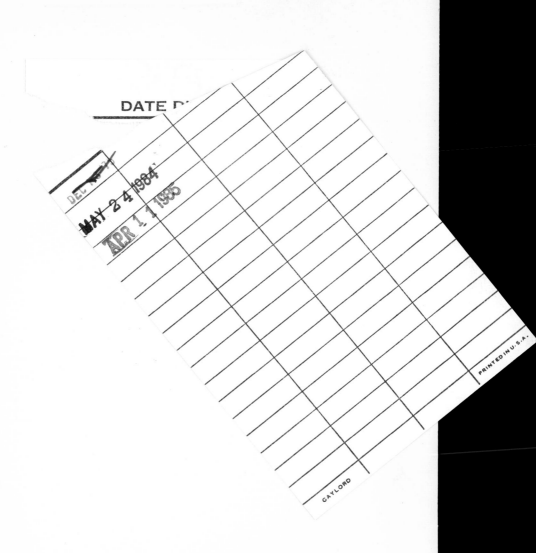

DATE D

DEC

MAY 2 4 1984

APR 1 1 1985

PRINTED IN U.S.A.

GAYLORD